De Bello Gal

by Gaius Julius Caesar

(parallel English/Latin)

translated by W.A. McDevitte and W.S. Bohn

1869

Gallic Wars Book 1 (58 B.C.E.)

1:1 All Gaul is divided into three parts, one of which the Belgae inhabit, the Aquitani another, those who in their own language are called Celts, in our Gauls, the third. All these differ from each other in language, customs and laws. The river Garonne separates the Gauls from the Aquitani; the Marne and the Seine separate them from the Belgae. Of all these, the Belgae are the bravest, because they are furthest from the civilization and refinement of [our] Province, and merchants least frequently resort to them, and import those things which tend to effeminate the mind; and they are the nearest to the Germans, who dwell beyond the Rhine, with whom they are continually waging war; for which reason the Helvetii also surpass the rest of the Gauls in valor, as they contend with the Germans in almost daily battles, when they either repel them from their own territories, or themselves wage war on their frontiers. One part of these, which it has been said that the Gauls occupy, takes its beginning at the river Rhone; it is bounded by the river Garonne, the ocean, and the territories of the Belgae; it borders, too, on the side of the Sequani and the Helvetii, upon the river Rhine, and stretches toward the north. The Belgae rises from the extreme frontier of Gaul, extend to the lower part of the river Rhine; and look toward the north and the rising sun. Aquitania extends from the river Garonne to the Pyrenaean mountains and to that part of the ocean which is near Spain: it looks between the setting of the sun, and the north star.

1:2 Among the Helvetii, Orgetorix was by far the most distinguished and wealthy. He, when Marcus Messala and Marcus Piso were consuls, incited by lust of sovereignty, formed a conspiracy among the nobility, and persuaded the people to go forth from their territories with all their possessions, [saying] that it would be very easy, since they excelled all in valor, to acquire the supremacy of the whole of Gaul. To this he the more easily persuaded them, because the Helvetii, are confined on every side by the nature of their situation; on one side by the Rhine, a very broad and deep river, which separates the Helvetian territory from the Germans; on a second side by the Jura, a very high mountain, which is [situated] between the Sequani and the Helvetii; on a third by the Lake of Geneva, and by the river Rhone, which separates our Province from the Helvetii. From these circumstances it resulted, that they could range less widely, and could less easily make war upon their neighbors; for which reason men

Gallia est omnis divisa in partes tres, quarum unam incolunt Belgae, aliam Aquitani, tertiam qui ipsorum lingua Celtae, nostra Galli appellantur. Hi omnes lingua, institutis, legibus inter se differunt. Gallos ab Aquitanis Garumna flumen, a Belgis Matrona et Sequana dividit. Horum omnium fortissimi sunt Belgae, propterea quod a cultu atque humanitate provinciae longissime absunt, minimeque ad eos mercatores saepe commeant atque ea quae ad effeminandos animos pertinent important, proximique sunt Germanis, qui trans Rhenum incolunt, quibuscum continenter bellum gerunt. Qua de causa Helvetii quoque reliquos Gallos virtute praecedunt, quod fere cotidianis proeliis cum Germanis contendunt, cum aut suis finibus eos prohibent aut ipsi in eorum finibus bellum gerunt. Eorum una, pars, quam Gallos obtinere dictum est, initium capit a flumine Rhodano, continetur Garumna flumine, Oceano, finibus Belgarum, attingit etiam ab Sequanis et Helvetiis flumen Rhenum, vergit ad septentriones. Belgae ab extremis Galliae finibus oriuntur, pertinent ad inferiorem partem fluminis Rheni, spectant in septentrionem et orientem solem. Aquitania a Garumna flumine ad Pyrenaeos montes et eam partem Oceani quae est ad Hispaniam pertinet; spectat inter occasum solis et septentriones.

Apud Helvetios longe nobilissimus fuit et ditissimus Orgetorix. Is M. Messala, [et P.] M. Pisone consulibus regni cupiditate inductus coniurationem nobilitatis fecit et civitati persuasit ut de finibus suis cum omnibus copiis exirent: perfacile esse, cum virtute omnibus praestarent, totius Galliae imperio potiri. Id hoc facilius iis persuasit, quod undique loci natura Helvetii continentur: una ex parte flumine Rheno latissimo atque altissimo, qui agrum Helvetium a Germanis dividit; altera ex parte monte Iura altissimo, qui est inter Sequanos et Helvetios; tertia lacu Lemanno et flumine Rhodano, qui provinciam nostram ab Helvetiis dividit. His rebus fiebat ut et minus late vagarentur et minus facile finitimis bellum inferre possent; qua ex parte homines bellandi cupidi magno dolore adficiebantur. Pro multitudine autem hominum et pro gloria belli atque fortitudinis angustos se fines habere

fond of war [as they were] were affected with great regret. They thought, that considering the extent of their population, and their renown for warfare and bravery, they had but narrow limits, although they extended in length 240, and in breadth 180 [Roman] miles.

1:3 Induced by these considerations, and influenced by the authority of Orgetorix, they determined to provide such things as were necessary for their expedition-to buy up as great a number as possible of beasts of burden and wagons-to make their sowings as large as possible, so that on their march plenty of corn might be in store-and to establish peace and friendship with the neighboring states. They reckoned that a term of two years would be sufficient for them to execute their designs; they fix by decree their departure for the third year. Orgetorix is chosen to complete these arrangements. He took upon himself the office of embassador to the states: on this journey he persuades Casticus, the son of Catamantaledes (one of the Sequani, whose father had possessed the sovereignty among the people for many years, and had been styled "friend" by the senate of the Roman people), to seize upon the sovereignty in his own state, which his father had held before him, and he likewise persuades Dumnorix, an Aeduan, the brother of Divitiacus, who at that time possessed the chief authority in the state, and was exceedingly beloved by the people, to attempt the same, and gives him his daughter in marriage. He proves to them that to accomplish their attempts was a thing very easy to be done, because he himself would obtain the government of his own state; that there was no doubt that the Helvetii were the most powerful of the whole of Gaul; he assures them that he will, with his own forces and his own army, acquire the sovereignty for them. Incited by this speech, they give a pledge and oath to one another, and hope that, when they have seized the sovereignty, they will, by means of the three most powerful and valiant nations, be enabled to obtain possession of the whole of Gaul.

1:4 When this scheme was disclosed to the Helvetii by informers, they, according to their custom, compelled Orgetorix to plead his cause in chains; it was the law that the penalty of being burned by fire should await him if condemned. On the day appointed for the pleading of his cause, Orgetorix drew together from all quarters to the court, all his vassals to the number of ten thousand persons; and led together to the same place all his dependents and debtor-bondsmen, of whom he had a great number; by means of those he rescued himself from [the necessity of] pleading his cause. While the state, incensed at this act, was endeavoring to assert its right by arms, and the magistrates were mustering a large body of men

arbitrabantur, qui in longitudinem milia passuum CCXL, in latitudinem CLXXX patebant.

His rebus adducti et auctoritate Orgetorigis permoti constituerunt ea quae ad proficiscendum pertinerent comparare, iumentorum et carrorum quam maximum numerum coemere, sementes quam maximas facere, ut in itinere copia frumenti suppeteret, cum proximis civitatibus pacem et amicitiam confirmare. Ad eas res conficiendas biennium sibi satis esse duxerunt; in tertium annum profectionem lege confirmant. Ad eas res conficiendas Orgetorix deligitur. Is sibi legationem ad civitates suscipit. In eo itinere persuadet Castico, Catamantaloedis filio, Sequano, cuius pater regnum in Sequanis multos annos obtinuerat et a senatu populi Romani amicus appellatus erat, ut regnum in civitate sua occuparet, quod pater ante habuerit; itemque Dumnorigi Haeduo, fratri Diviciaci, qui eo tempore principatum in civitate obtinebat ac maxime plebi acceptus erat, ut idem conaretur persuadet eique filiam suam in matrimonium dat. Perfacile factu esse illis probat conata perficere, propterea quod ipse suae civitatis imperium obtenturus esset: non esse dubium quin totius Galliae plurimum Helvetii possent; se suis copiis suoque exercitu illis regna conciliaturum confirmat. Hac oratione adducti inter se fidem et ius iurandum dant et regno occupato per tres potentissimos ac firmissimos populos totius Galliae sese potiri posse sperant.

Ea res est Helvetiis per indicium enuntiata. Moribus suis Orgetoricem ex vinculis causam dicere coegerunt; damnatum poenam sequi oportebat, ut igni cremaretur. Die constituta causae dictionis Orgetorix ad iudicium omnem suam familiam, ad hominum milia decem, undique coegit, et omnes clientes obaeratosque suos, quorum magnum numerum habebat, eodem conduxit; per eos ne causam diceret se eripuit. Cum civitas ob eam rem incitata armis ius suum exequi conaretur multitudinemque hominum ex agris magistratus cogerent, Orgetorix mortuus est; neque abest

from the country, Orgetorix died; and there is not wanting a suspicion, as the Helvetii think, of his having committed suicide.

1:5 After his death, the Helvetii nevertheless attempt to do that which they had resolved on, namely, to go forth from their territories. When they thought that they were at length prepared for this undertaking, they set fire to all their towns, in number about twelve-to their villages about four hundred-and to the private dwellings that remained; they burn up all the corn, except what they intend to carry with them; that after destroying the hope of a return home, they might be the more ready for undergoing all dangers. They order every one to carry forth from home for himself provisions for three months, ready ground. They persuade the Rauraci, and the Tulingi, and the Latobrigi, their neighbors, to adopt the same plan, and after burning down their towns and villages, to set out with them: and they admit to their party and unite to themselves as confederates the Boii, who had dwelt on the other side of the Rhine, and had crossed over into the Norican territory, and assaulted Noreia.

1:6 There were in all two routes, by which they could go forth from their country one through the Sequani narrow and difficult, between Mount Jura and the river Rhone (by which scarcely one wagon at a time could be led; there was, moreover, a very high mountain overhanging, so that a very few might easily intercept them; the other, through our Province, much easier and freer from obstacles, because the Rhone flows between the boundaries of the Helvetii and those of the Allobroges, who had lately been subdued, and is in some places crossed by a ford. The furthest town of the Allobroges, and the nearest to the territories of the Helvetii, is Geneva. From this town a bridge extends to the Helvetii. They thought that they should either persuade the Allobroges, because they did not seem as yet well-affected toward the Roman people, or compel them by force to allow them to pass through their territories. Having provided every thing for the expedition, they appoint a day, on which they should all meet on the bank of the Rhone. This day was the fifth before the kalends of April [i.e. the 28th of March], in the consulship of Lucius Piso and Aulus Gabinius [B.C. 58.]

1:7 When it was reported to Caesar that they were attempting to make their route through our Province he hastens to set out from the city, and, by as great marches as he can, proceeds to Further Gaul, and arrives at Geneva. He orders the whole Province [to furnish] as great a number of soldiers as possible, as there was in all only one legion in Further Gaul: he orders the bridge at Geneva to be broken down. When the Helvetii are apprized of his arrival they send to him, as embassadors, the

suspicio, ut Helvetii arbitrantur, quin ipse sibi mortem consciverit.

Post eius mortem nihilo minus Helvetii id quod constituerant facere conantur, ut e finibus suis exeant. Ubi iam se ad eam rem paratos esse arbitrati sunt, oppida sua omnia, numero ad duodecim, vicos ad quadringentos, reliqua privata aedificia incendunt; frumentum omne, praeter quod secum portaturi erant, comburunt, ut domum reditionis spe sublata paratiores ad omnia pericula subeunda essent; trium mensum molita cibaria sibi quemque domo efferre iubent. Persuadent Rauracis et Tulingis et Latobrigis finitimis, uti eodem usi consilio oppidis suis vicisque exustis una cum iis proficiscantur, Boiosque, qui trans Rhenum incoluerant et in agrum Noricum transierant Noreiamque oppugnabant, receptos ad se socios sibi adsciscunt.

Erant omnino itinera duo, quibus itineribus domo exire possent: unum per Sequanos, angustum et difficile, inter montem Iuram et flumen Rhodanum, vix qua singuli carri ducerentur, mons autem altissimus impendebat, ut facile perpauci prohibere possent; alterum per provinciam nostram, multo facilius atque expeditius, propterea quod inter fines Helvetiorum et Allobrogum, qui nuper pacati erant, Rhodanus fluit isque non nullis locis vado transitur. Extremum oppidum Allobrogum est proximumque Helvetiorum finibus Genava. Ex eo oppido pons ad Helvetios pertinet. Allobrogibus sese vel persuasuros, quod nondum bono animo in populum Romanum viderentur, existimabant vel vi coacturos ut per suos fines eos ire paterentur. Omnibus rebus ad profectionem comparatis diem dicunt, qua die ad ripam Rhodani omnes conveniant. Is dies erat a. d. V. Kal. Apr. L. Pisone, A. Gabinio consulibus.

Caesari cum id nuntiatum esset, eos per provinciam nostram iter facere conari, maturat ab urbe proficisci et quam maximis potest itineribus in Galliam ulteriorem contendit et ad Genavam pervenit. Provinciae toti quam maximum potest militum numerum imperat (erat omnino in Gallia ulteriore legio una), pontem, qui erat ad Genavam, iubet rescindi. Ubi de eius adventu Helvetii certiores facti sunt,

English	Latin
most illustrious men of their state (in which embassy Numeius and Verudoctius held the chief place), to say "that it was their intention to march through the Province without doing any harm, because they had" [according to their own representations,] "no other route: that they requested, they might be allowed to do so with his consent." Caesar, inasmuch as he kept in remembrance that Lucius Cassius, the consul, had been slain, and his army routed and made to pass under the yoke by the Helvetii, did not think that [their request] ought to be granted: nor was he of opinion that men of hostile disposition, if an opportunity of marching through the Province were given them, would abstain from outrage and mischief. Yet, in order that a period might intervene, until the soldiers whom he had ordered [to be furnished] should assemble, he replied to the ambassadors, that he would take time to deliberate; if they wanted any thing, they might return on the day before the ides of April [on April 12th].	legatos ad eum mittunt nobilissimos civitatis, cuius legationis Nammeius et Verucloetius principem locum obtinebant, qui dicerent sibi esse in animo sine ullo maleficio iter per provinciam facere, propterea quod aliud iter haberent nullum: rogare ut eius voluntate id sibi facere liceat. Caesar, quod memoria tenebat L. Cassium consulem occisum exercitumque eius ab Helvetiis pulsum et sub iugum missum, concedendum non putabat; neque homines inimico animo, data facultate per provinciam itineris faciundi, temperaturos ab iniuria et maleficio existimabat. Tamen, ut spatium intercedere posset dum milites quos imperaverat convenirent, legatis respondit diem se ad deliberandum sumpturum: si quid vellent, ad Id. April. reverterentur.
1:8 Meanwhile, with the legion which he had with him and the soldiers which had assembled from the Province, he carries along for nineteen [Roman, not quite eighteen English] miles a wall, to the height of sixteen feet, and a trench, from the Lake of Geneva, which flows into the river Rhone, to Mount Jura, which separates the territories of the Sequani from those of the Helvetii. When that work was finished, he distributes garrisons, and closely fortifies redoubts, in order that he may the more easily intercept them, if they should attempt to cross over against his will. When the day which he had appointed with the embassadors came, and they returned to him; he says, that he can not, consistently with the custom and precedent of the Roman people, grant any one a passage through the Province; and he gives them to understand, that, if they should attempt to use violence he would oppose them. The Helvetii, disappointed in this hope, tried if they could force a passage (some by means of a bridge of boats and numerous rafts constructed for the purpose; others, by the fords of the Rhone, where the depth of the river was least, sometimes by day, but more frequently by night), but being kept at bay by the strength of our works, and by the concourse of the soldiers, and by the missiles, they desisted from this attempt.	Interea ea legione quam secum habebat militibusque, qui ex provincia convenerant, a lacu Lemanno, qui in flumen Rhodanum influit, ad montem Iuram, qui fines Sequanorum ab Helvetiis dividit, milia passuum XVIIII murum in altitudinem pedum sedecim fossamque perducit. Eo opere perfecto praesidia disponit, castella communit, quo facilius, si se invito transire conentur, prohibere possit. Ubi ea dies quam constituerat cum legatis venit et legati ad eum reverterunt, negat se more et exemplo populi Romani posse iter ulli per provinciam dare et, si vim facere conentur, prohibiturum ostendit. Helvetii ea spe deiecti navibus iunctis ratibusque compluribus factis, alii vadis Rhodani, qua minima altitudo fluminis erat, non numquam interdiu, saepius noctu si perrumpere possent conati, operis munitione et militum concursu et telis repulsi, hoc conatu destiterunt.
1:9 There was left one way, [namely] through the Sequani, by which, on account of its narrowness, they could not pass without the consent of the Sequani. As they could not of themselves prevail on them, they send embassadors to Dumnorix the Aeduan, that through his intercession, they might obtain their request from the Sequani. Dumnorix, by his popularity and liberality, had great influence among the Sequani, and was friendly to the Helvetii, because out of that	Relinquebatur una per Sequanos via, qua Sequanis invitis propter angustias ire non poterant. His cum sua sponte persuadere non possent, legatos ad Dumnorigem Haeduum mittunt, ut eo deprecatore a Sequanis impetrarent. Dumnorix gratia et largitione apud Sequanos plurimum poterat et Helvetiis erat amicus, quod ex ea civitate Orgetorigis filiam in matrimonium duxerat, et cupiditate regni adductus

state he had married the daughter of Orgetorix; and, incited by lust of sovereignty, was anxious for a revolution, and wished to have as many states as possible attached to him by his kindness toward them. He, therefore, undertakes the affair, and prevails upon the Sequani to allow the Helvetii to march through their territories, and arranges that they should give hostages to each other-the Sequani not to obstruct the Helvetii in their march-the Helvetii, to pass without mischief and outrage.

1:10 It is again told Caesar, that the Helvetii intended to march through the country of the Sequani and the Aedui into the territories of the Santones, which are not far distant from those boundaries of the Tolosates, which [viz. Tolosa, Toulouse] is a state in the Province. If this took place, he saw that it would be attended with great danger to the Province to have warlike men, enemies of the Roman people, bordering upon an open and very fertile tract of country. For these reasons he appointed Titus Labienus, his lieutenant, to the command of the fortification which he had made. He himself proceeds to Italy by forced marches, and there levies two legions, and leads out from winter-quarters three which were wintering around Aquileia, and with these five legions marches rapidly by the nearest route across the Alps into Further Gaul. Here the Centrones and the Graioceli and the Caturiges, having taken possession of the higher parts, attempt to obstruct the army in their march. After having routed these in several battles, he arrives in the territories of the Vocontii in the Further Province on the seventh day from Ocelum, which is the most remote town of the Hither Province; thence he leads his army into the country of the Allobroges, and from the Allobroges to the Segusiani. These people are the first beyond the Province on the opposite side of the Rhone.

1:11 The Helvetii had by this time led their forces over through the narrow defile and the territories of the Sequani, and had arrived at the territories of the Aedui, and were ravaging their lands. The Aedui, as they could not defend themselves and their possessions against them, send embassadors to Caesar to ask assistance, [pleading] that they had at all times so well deserved of the Roman people, that their fields ought not to have been laid waste-their children carried off into slavery-their towns stormed, almost within sight of our army. At the same time the Ambarri, the friends and kinsmen of the Aedui, apprize Caesar, that it was not easy for them, now that their fields had been devastated, to ward off the violence of the enemy from their towns: the Allobroges likewise, who had villages and possessions on the other side of the Rhone, betake themselves in flight to Caesar, and assure him that they had nothing

novis rebus studebat et quam plurimas civitates suo beneficio habere obstrictas volebat. Itaque rem suscipit et a Sequanis impetrat ut per fines suos Helvetios ire patiantur, obsidesque uti inter sese dent perficit: Sequani, ne itinere Helvetios prohibeant, Helvetii, ut sine maleficio et iniuria transeant.

Caesari renuntiatur Helvetiis esse in animo per agrum Sequanorum et Haeduorum iter in Santonum fines facere, qui non longe a Tolosatium finibus absunt, quae civitas est in provincia. Id si fieret, intellegebat magno cum periculo provinciae futurum ut homines bellicosos, populi Romani inimicos, locis patentibus maximeque frumentariis finitimos haberet. Ob eas causas ei munitioni quam fecerat T. Labienum legatum praeficit; ipse in Italiam magnis itineribus contendit duasque ibi legiones conscribit et tres, quae circum Aquileiam hiemabant, ex hibernis educit et, qua proximum iter in ulteriorem Galliam per Alpes erat, cum his quinque legionibus ire contendit. Ibi Ceutrones et Graioceli et Caturiges locis superioribus occupatis itinere exercitum prohibere conantur. Compluribus his proeliis pulsis ab Ocelo, quod est oppidum citerioris provinciae extremum, in fines Vocontiorum ulterioris provinciae die septimo pervenit; inde in Allobrogum fines, ab Allobrogibus in Segusiavos exercitum ducit. Hi sunt extra provinciam trans Rhodanum primi.

Helvetii iam per angustias et fines Sequanorum suas copias traduxerant et in Haeduorum fines pervenerant eorumque agros populabantur. Haedui, cum se suaque ab iis defendere non possent, legatos ad Caesarem mittunt rogatum auxilium: ita se omni tempore de populo Romano meritos esse ut paene in conspectu exercitus nostri agri vastari, liberi [eorum] in servitutem abduci, oppida expugnari non debuerint. Eodem tempore quo Haedui Ambarri, necessarii et consanguinei Haeduorum, Caesarem certiorem faciunt sese depopulatis agris non facile ab oppidis vim hostium prohibere. Item Allobroges, qui trans Rhodanum vicos possessionesque habebant, fuga se ad Caesarem recipiunt et demonstrant sibi praeter agri solum nihil esse reliqui. Quibus rebus adductus

remaining, except the soil of their land. Caesar, induced by these circumstances, decides, that he ought not to wait until the Helvetii, after destroying all the property of his allies, should arrive among the Santones.

1:12 There is a river [called] the Saone, which flows through the territories of the Aedui and Sequani into the Rhone with such incredible slowness, that it can not be determined by the eye in which direction it flows. This the Helvetii were crossing by rafts and boats joined together. When Caesar was informed by spies that the Helvetii had already conveyed three parts of their forces across that river, but that the fourth part was left behind on this side of the Saone, he set out from the camp with three legions during the third watch, and came up with that division which had not yet crossed the river. Attacking them encumbered with baggage, and not expecting him, he cut to pieces a great part of them; the rest betook themselves to flight, and concealed themselves in the nearest woods. That canton [which was cut down] was called the Tigurine; for the whole Helvetian state is divided into four cantons. This single canton having left their country, within the recollection of our fathers, had slain Lucius Cassius the consul, and had made his army pass under the yoke. Thus, whether by chance, or by the design of the immortal gods, that part of the Helvetian state which had brought a signal calamity upon the Roman people, was the first to pay the penalty. In this Caesar avenged not only the public but also his own personal wrongs, because the Tigurini had slain Lucius Piso the lieutenant [of Cassius], the grandfather of Lucius Calpurnius Piso, his [Caesar's] father-in-law, in the same battle as Cassius himself.

1:13 This battle ended, that he might be able to come up with the remaining forces of the Helvetii, he procures a bridge to be made across the Saone, and thus leads his army over. The Helvetii, confused by his sudden arrival, when they found that he had effected in one day, what they, themselves had with the utmost difficulty accomplished in twenty namely, the crossing of the river, send embassadors to him; at the head of which embassy was Divico, who had been commander of the Helvetii, in the war against Cassius. He thus treats with Caesar:--that, "if the Roman people would make peace with the Helvetii they would go to that part and there remain, where Caesar might appoint and desire them to be; but if he should persist in persecuting them with war that he ought to remember both the ancient disgrace of the Roman people and the characteristic valor of the Helvetii. As to his having attacked one canton by surprise, [at a time] when those who had crossed the river could not bring assistance to their friends, that he ought not on that account to ascribe very much to his own valor, or despise

Caesar non expectandum sibi statuit dum, omnibus, fortunis sociorum consumptis, in Santonos Helvetii pervenirent.

Flumen est Arar, quod per fines Haeduorum et Sequanorum in Rhodanum influit, incredibili lenitate, ita ut oculis in utram partem fluat iudicari non possit. Id Helvetii ratibus ac lintribus iunctis transibant. Ubi per exploratores Caesar certior factus est tres iam partes copiarum Helvetios id flumen traduxisse, quartam vero partem citra flumen Ararim reliquam esse, de tertia vigilia cum legionibus tribus e castris profectus ad eam partem pervenit quae nondum flumen transierat. Eos impeditos et inopinantes adgressus magnam partem eorum concidit; reliqui sese fugae mandarunt atque in proximas silvas abdiderunt. Is pagus appellabatur Tigurinus; nam omnis civitas Helvetia in quattuor pagos divisa est. Hic pagus unus, cum domo exisset, patrum nostrorum memoria L. Cassium consulem interfecerat et eius exercitum sub iugum miserat. Ita sive casu sive consilio deorum immortalium quae pars civitatis Helvetiae insignem calamitatem populo Romano intulerat, ea princeps poenam persolvit. Qua in re Caesar non solum publicas, sed etiam privatas iniurias ultus est, quod eius soceri L. Pisonis avum, L. Pisonem legatum, Tigurini eodem proelio quo Cassium interfecerant.

Hoc proelio facto, reliquas copias Helvetiorum ut consequi posset, pontem in Arari faciendum curat atque ita exercitum traducit. Helvetii repentino eius adventu commoti cum id quod ipsi diebus XX aegerrime confecerant, ut flumen transirent, illum uno die fecisse intellegerent, legatos ad eum mittunt; cuius legationis Divico princeps fuit, qui bello Cassiano dux Helvetiorum fuerat. Is ita cum Caesare egit: si pacem populus Romanus cum Helvetiis faceret, in eam partem ituros atque ibi futuros Helvetios ubi eos Caesar constituisset atque esse voluisset; sin bello persequi perseveraret, reminisceretur et veteris incommodi populi Romani et pristinae virtutis Helvetiorum. Quod improviso unum pagum adortus esset, cum ii qui flumen transissent suis auxilium ferre non possent, ne ob eam rem aut suae magnopere virtuti tribueret aut ipsos despiceret. Se ita a patribus maioribusque suis didicisse, ut

them; that they had so learned from their sires and ancestors, as to rely more on valor than on artifice and stratagem. Wherefore let him not bring it to pass that the place, where they were standing, should acquire a name, from the disaster of the Roman people and the destruction of their army or transmit the remembrance [of such an event to posterity]."

1:14 To these words Caesar thus replied:--that "on that very account he felt less hesitation, because he kept in remembrance those circumstances which the Helvetian embassadors had mentioned, and that he felt the more indignant at them, in proportion as they had happened undeservedly to the Roman people: for if they had been conscious of having done any wrong, it would not have been difficult to be on their guard, but for that very reason had they been deceived, because neither were they aware that any offense had been given by them, on account of which they should be afraid, nor did they think that they ought to be afraid without cause. But even if he were willing to forget their former outrage, could he also lay aside the remembrance of the late wrongs, in that they had against his will attempted a route through the Province by force, in that they had molested the Aedui, the Ambarri, and the Allobroges? That as to their so insolently boasting of their victory, and as to their being astonished that they had so long committed their outrages with impunity, [both these things] tended to the same point; for the immortal gods are wont to allow those persons whom they wish to punish for their guilt sometimes a greater prosperity and longer impunity, in order that they may suffer the more severely from a reverse of circumstances. Although these things are so, yet, if hostages were to be given him by them in order that he may be assured these will do what they promise, and provided they will give satisfaction to the Aedui for the outrages which they had committed against them and their allies, and likewise to the Allobroges, he [Caesar] will make peace with them." Divico replied, that "the Helvetii had been so trained by their ancestors, that they were accustomed to receive, not to give hostages; of that fact the Roman people were witness." Having given this reply, he withdrew.

1:15 On the following day they move their camp from that place; Caesar does the same, and sends forward all his cavalry, to the number of four thousand (which he had drawn together from all parts of the Province and from the Aedui and their allies), to observe toward what parts the enemy are directing their march. These, having too eagerly pursued the enemy's rear, come to a battle with the cavalry of the Helvetii in a disadvantageous place, and a few of our men fall. The Helvetii, elated with this battle, because they had with five

magis virtute contenderent quam dolo aut insidiis niterentur. Quare ne committeret ut is locus ubi constitissent ex calamitate populi Romani et internecione exercitus nomen caperet aut memoriam proderet.

His Caesar ita respondit: eo sibi minus dubitationis dari, quod eas res quas legati Helvetii commemorassent memoria teneret, atque eo gravius ferre quo minus merito populi Romani accidissent; qui si alicuius iniuriae sibi conscius fuisset, non fuisse difficile cavere; sed eo deceptum, quod neque commissum a se intellegeret quare timeret neque sine causa timendum putaret. Quod si veteris contumeliae oblivisci vellet, num etiam recentium iniuriarum, quod eo invito iter per provinciam per vim temptassent, quod Haeduos, quod Ambarros, quod Allobrogas vexassent, memoriam deponere posse? Quod sua victoria tam insolenter gloriarentur quodque tam diu se impune iniurias tulisse admirarentur, eodem pertinere. Consuesse enim deos immortales, quo gravius homines ex commutatione rerum doleant, quos pro scelere eorum ulcisci velint, his secundiores interdum res et diuturniorem impunitatem concedere. Cum ea ita sint, tamen, si obsides ab iis sibi dentur, uti ea quae polliceantur facturos intellegat, et si Haeduis de iniuriis quas ipsis sociisque eorum intulerint, item si Allobrogibus satis faciunt, sese cum iis pacem esse facturum. Divico respondit: ita Helvetios a maioribus suis institutos esse uti obsides accipere, non dare, consuerint; eius rem populum Romanum esse testem. Hoc responso dato discessit.

Postero die castra ex eo loco movent. Idem facit Caesar equitatumque omnem, ad numerum quattuor milium, quem ex omni provincia et Haeduis atque eorum sociis coactum habebat, praemittit, qui videant quas in partes hostes iter faciant. Qui cupidius novissimum agmen insecuti alieno loco cum equitatu Helvetiorum proelium committunt; et pauci de nostris cadunt. Quo proelio sublati Helvetii, quod quingentis equitibus tantam multitudinem equitum propulerant,

hundred horse repulsed so large a body of horse, began to face us more boldly, sometimes too from their rear to provoke our men by an attack. Caesar [however] restrained his men from battle, deeming it sufficient for the present to prevent the enemy from rapine, forage, and depredation. They marched for about fifteen days in such a manner that there was not more than five or six miles between the enemy's rear and our van.

1:16 Meanwhile, Caesar kept daily importuning the Aedui for the corn which they had promised in the name of their state; for, in consequence of the coldness (Gaul, being as before said, situated toward the north), not only was the corn in the fields not ripe, but there was not in store a sufficiently large quantity even of fodder: besides he was unable to use the corn which he had conveyed in ships up the river Saone, because the Helvetii, from whom he was unwilling to retire had diverted their march from the Saone. The Aedui kept deferring from day to day, and saying that it was being collected-brought in-on the road." When he saw that he was put off too long, and that the day was close at hand on which he ought to serve out the corn to his soldiers;-having called together their chiefs, of whom he had a great number in his camp, among them Divitiacus and Liscus who was invested with the chief magistracy (whom the Aedui style the Vergobretus, and who is elected annually and has power of life or death over his countrymen), he severely reprimands them, because he is not assisted by them on so urgent an occasion, when the enemy were so close at hand, and when [corn] could neither be bought nor taken from the fields, particularly as, in a great measure urged by their prayers, he had undertaken the war; much more bitterly, therefore does he complain of his being forsaken.

1:17 Then at length Liscus, moved by Caesar's speech, discloses what he had hitherto kept secret:--that there are some whose influences with the people is very great, who, though private men, have more power than the magistrates themselves: that these by seditions and violent language are deterring the populace from contributing the corn which they ought to supply; [by telling them] that, if they can not any longer retain the supremacy of Gaul, it were better to submit to the government of Gauls than of Romans, nor ought they to doubt that, if the Romans should overpower the Helvetii, they would wrest their freedom from the Aedui together with the remainder of Gaul. By these very men, [said he], are our plans and whatever is done in the camp, disclosed to the enemy; that they could not be restrained by him: nay more, he was well aware, that though compelled by necessity, he had disclosed the matter to Caesar, at how great a risk he had done it; and for

audacius subsistere non numquam et novissimo agmine proelio nostros lacessere coeperunt. Caesar suos a proelio continebat, ac satis habebat in praesentia hostem rapinis, pabulationibus populationibusque prohibere. Ita dies circiter XV iter fecerunt uti inter novissimum hostium agmen et nostrum primum non amplius quinis aut senis milibus passuum interesset.

Interim cotidie Caesar Haeduos frumentum, quod essent publice polliciti, flagitare. Nam propter frigora [quod Gallia sub septentrionibus, ut ante dictum est, posita est,] non modo frumenta in agris matura non erant, sed ne pabuli quidem satis magna copia suppetebat; eo autem frumento quod flumine Arari navibus subvexerat propterea uti minus poterat quod iter ab Arari Helvetii averterant, a quibus discedere nolebat. Diem ex die ducere Haedui: conferri, comportari, adesse dicere. Ubi se diutius duci intellexit et diem instare quo die frumentum militibus metiri oporteret, convocatis eorum principibus, quorum magnam copiam in castris habebat, in his Diviciaco et Lisco, qui summo magistratui praeerat, quem 'vergobretum' appellant Haedui, qui creatur annuus et vitae necisque in suos habet potestatem, graviter eos accusat, quod, cum neque emi neque ex agris sumi possit, tam necessario tempore, tam propinquis hostibus ab iis non sublevetur, praesertim cum magna ex parte eorum precibus adductus bellum susceperit; multo etiam gravius quod sit destitutus queritur.

Tum demum Liscus oratione Caesaris adductus quod antea tacuerat proponit: esse non nullos, quorum auctoritas apud plebem plurimum valeat, qui privatim plus possint quam ipsi magistratus. Hos seditiosa atque improba oratione multitudinem deterrere, ne frumentum conferant quod debeant: praestare, si iam principatum Galliae obtinere non possint, Gallorum quam Romanorum imperia perferre, neque dubitare [debeant] quin, si Helvetios superaverint Romani, una cum reliqua Gallia Haeduis libertatem sint erepturi. Ab isdem nostra consilia quaeque in castris gerantur hostibus enuntiari; hos a se coerceri non posse. Quin etiam, quod necessariam rem coactus Caesari enuntiarit, intellegere sese quanto id cum periculo fecerit, et ob eam causam quam diu potuerit tacuisse.

that reason, he had been silent as long as he could."

1:18 Caesar perceived that by this speech of Liscus, Dumnorix, the brother of Divitiacus, was indicated; but, as he was unwilling that these matters should be discussed while so many were present, he speedily dismisses: the council, but detains Liscus: he inquires from him when alone, about those things which he had said in the meeting. He [Liscus] speaks more unreservedly and boldly. He [Caesar] makes inquiries on the same points privately of others, and discovered that it is all true; that "Dumnorix is the person, a man of the highest daring, in great favor with the people on account of his liberality, a man eager for a revolution: that for a great many years he has been in the habit of contracting for the customs and all the other taxes of the Aedui at a small cost, because when he bids, no one dares to bid against him. By these means he has both increased his own private property, and amassed great means for giving largesses; that he maintains constantly at his own expense and keeps about his own person a great number of cavalry, and that not only at home, but even among the neighboring states, he has great influence, and for the sake of strengthening this influence has given his mother in marriage among the Bituriges to a man the most noble and most influential there; that he has himself taken a wife from among the Helvetii, and has given his sister by the mother's side and his female relations in marriage into other states; that he favors and wishes well to the Helvetii on account of this connection; and that he hates Caesar and the Romans, on his own account, because by their arrival his power was weakened, and his brother, Divitiacus, restored to his former position of influence and dignity: that, if any thing should happen to the Romans, he entertains the highest hope of gaining the sovereignty by means of the Helvetii, but that under the government of the Roman people he despairs not only of royalty, but even of that influence which he already has." Caesar discovered too, on inquiring into the unsuccessful cavalry engagement which had taken place a few days before, that the commencement of that flight had been made by Dumnorix and his cavalry (for Dumnorix was in command of the cavalry which the Aedui had sent for aid to Caesar); that by their flight the rest of the cavalry were dismayed.

1:19 After learning these circumstances, since to these suspicions the most unequivocal facts were added, viz., that he had led the Helvetii through the territories of the Sequani; that he had provided that hostages should be mutually given; that he had done all these things, not only without any orders of his [Caesar's] and of his own state's, but even without their [the Aedui] knowing any thing of it themselves; that he [Dumnorix] was reprimanded: by the [chief] magistrate of the Aedui; he

Caesar hac oratione Lisci Dumnorigem, Diviciaci fratrem, designari sentiebat, sed, quod pluribus praesentibus eas res iactari nolebat, celeriter concilium dimittit, Liscum retinet. Quaerit ex solo ea quae in conventu dixerat. Dicit liberius atque audacius. Eadem secreto ab aliis quaerit; reperit esse vera: ipsum esse Dumnorigem, summa audacia, magna apud plebem propter liberalitatem gratia, cupidum rerum novarum. Complures annos portoria reliquaque omnia Haeduorum vectigalia parvo pretio redempta habere, propterea quod illo licente contra liceri audeat nemo. His rebus et suam rem familiarem auxisse et facultates ad largiendum magnas comparasse; magnum numerum equitatus suo sumptu semper alere et circum se habere, neque solum domi, sed etiam apud finitimas civitates largiter posse, atque huius potentiae causa matrem in Biturigibus homini illic nobilissimo ac potentissimo conlocasse; ipsum ex Helvetiis uxorem habere, sororum ex matre et propinquas suas nuptum in alias civitates conlocasse. Favere et cupere Helvetiis propter eam adfinitatem, odisse etiam suo nomine Caesarem et Romanos, quod eorum adventu potentia eius deminuta et Diviciacus frater in antiquum locum gratiae atque honoris sit restitutus. Si quid accidat Romanis, summam in spem per Helvetios regni obtinendi venire; imperio populi Romani non modo de regno, sed etiam de ea quam habeat gratia desperare. Reperiebat etiam in quaerendo Caesar, quod proelium equestre adversum paucis ante diebus esset factum, initium eius fugae factum a Dumnorige atque eius equitibus (nam equitatui, quem auxilio Caesari Haedui miserant, Dumnorix praeerat): eorum fuga reliquum esse equitatum perterritum.

Quibus rebus cognitis, cum ad has suspiciones certissimae res accederent, quod per fines Sequanorum Helvetios traduxisset, quod obsides inter eos dandos curasset, quod ea omnia non modo iniussu suo et civitatis sed etiam inscientibus ipsis fecisset, quod a magistratu Haeduorum accusaretur, satis esse causae arbitrabatur quare in eum aut ipse animadverteret aut civitatem animadvertere iuberet.

[Caesar] considered that there was sufficient reason, why he should either punish him himself, or order the state to do so. One thing [however] stood in the way of all this-that he had learned by experience his brother Divitiacus's very high regard for the Roman people, his great affection toward him, his distinguished faithfulness, justice, and moderation; for he was afraid lest by the punishment of this man, he should hurt the feelings of Divitiacus. Therefore, before he attempted any thing, he orders Divitiacus to be summoned to him, and, when the ordinary interpreters had been withdrawn, converses with him through Caius Valerius Procillus, chief of the province of Gaul, an intimate friend of his, in whom he reposed the highest confidence in every thing; at the same time he reminds him of what was said about Dumnorix in the council of the Gauls, when he himself was present, and shows what each had said of him privately in his [Caesar's] own presence; he begs and exhorts him, that, without offense to his feelings, he may either himself pass judgment on him [Dumnorix] after trying the case, or else order the [Aeduan] state to do so.

1:20 Divitiacus, embracing Caesar, begins to implore him, with many tears, that "he would not pass any very severe sentence upon his brother; saying, that he knows that those charges are true, and that nobody suffered more pain on that account than he himself did; for when he himself could effect a very great deal by his influence at home and in the rest of Gaul, and he [Dumnorix] very little on account of his youth, the latter had become powerful through his means, which power and strength he used not only to the lessening of his [Divitiacus] popularity, but almost to his ruin; that he, however, was influenced both by fraternal affection and by public opinion. But if any thing very severe from Caesar should befall him [Dumnorix], no one would think that it had been done without his consent, since he himself held such a place in Caesar's friendship: from which circumstance it would arise, that the affections of the whole of Gaul would be estranged from him." As he was with tears begging these things of Caesar in many words, Caesar takes his right hand, and, comforting him, begs him to make an end of entreating, and assures him that his regard for him is so great, that he forgives both the injuries of the republic and his private wrongs, at his desire and prayers. He summons Dumnorix to him; he brings in his brother; he points out what he censures in him; he lays before him what he of himself perceives, and what the state complains of; he warns him for the future to avoid all grounds of suspicion; he says that he pardons the past, for the sake of his brother, Divitiacus. He sets spies over Dumnorix that he may be able to know what he does, and with whom he communicates.

His omnibus rebus unum repugnabat, quod Diviciaci fratris summum in populum Romanum studium, summum in se voluntatem, egregiam fidem, iustitiam, temperantiam cognoverat; nam ne eius supplicio Diviciaci animum offenderet verebatur. Itaque prius quam quicquam conaretur, Diviciacum ad se vocari iubet et, cotidianis interpretibus remotis, per C. Valerium Troucillum, principem Galliae provinciae, familiarem suum, cui summam omnium rerum fidem habebat, cum eo conloquitur; simul commonefacit quae ipso praesente in concilio [Gallorum] de Dumnorige sint dicta, et ostendit quae separatim quisque de eo apud se dixerit. Petit atque hortatur ut sine eius offensione animi vel ipse de eo causa cognita statuat vel civitatem statuere iubeat.

Diviciacus multis cum lacrimis Caesarem complexus obsecrare coepit ne quid gravius in fratrem statueret: scire se illa esse vera, nec quemquam ex eo plus quam se doloris capere, propterea quod, cum ipse gratia plurimum domi atque in reliqua Gallia, ille minimum propter adulescentiam posset, per se crevisset; quibus opibus ac nervis non solum ad minuendam gratiam, sed paene ad perniciem suam uteretur. Sese tamen et amore fraterno et existimatione vulgi commoveri. Quod si quid ei a Caesare gravius accidisset, cum ipse eum locum amicitiae apud eum teneret, neminem existimaturum non sua voluntate factum; qua ex re futurum uti totius Galliae animi a se averterentur. Haec cum pluribus verbis flens a Caesare peteret, Caesar eius dextram prendit; consolatus rogat finem orandi faciat; tanti eius apud se gratiam esse ostendit uti et rei publicae iniuriam et suum dolorem eius voluntati ac precibus condonet. Dumnorigem ad se vocat, fratrem adhibet; quae in eo reprehendat ostendit; quae ipse intellegat, quae civitas queratur proponit; monet ut in reliquum tempus omnes suspiciones vitet; praeterita se Diviciaco fratri condonare dicit. Dumnorigi custodes ponit, ut quae agat, quibuscum loquatur scire possit.

1:21 Being on the same day informed by his scouts, that the enemy had encamped at the foot of a mountain eight miles from his own camp; he sent persons to ascertain what the nature of the mountain was, and of what kind the ascent on every side. Word was brought back, that it was easy. During the third watch he orders Titus Labienus, his lieutenant with praetorian powers, to ascend to the highest ridge of the mountain with two legions, and with those as guides who had examined the road; he explains what his plan is. He himself during the fourth watch, hastens to them by the same route by which the enemy had gone, and sends on all the cavalry before him. Publius Considius, who was reputed to be very experienced in military affairs, and had been in the army of Lucius Sulla, and afterward in that of Marcus Crassus, is sent forward with the scouts.

1:22 At day-break, when the summit of the mountain was in the possession of Titus Labienus, and he himself was not further off than a mile and half from the enemy's camp, nor, as he afterward ascertained from the captives, had either his arrival or that of Labienus been discovered; Considius, with his horse at full gallop, comes up to him says that the mountain which he [Caesar] wished should be seized by Labienus, is in possession of the enemy; that he has discovered this by the Gallic arms and ensigns. Caesar leads off his forces to the next hill: [and] draws them up in battle-order. Labienus, as he had been ordered by Caesar not to come to an engagement unless [Caesar's] own forces were seen near the enemy's camp, that the attack upon the enemy might be made on every side at the same time, was, after having taken possession of the mountain, waiting for our men, and refraining from battle. When, at length, the day was far advanced, Caesar learned through spies, that the mountain was in possession of his own men, and that the Helvetii had moved their camp, and that Considius, struck with fear, had reported to him, as seen, that which he had not seen. On that day he follows the enemy at his usual distance, and pitches his camp three miles from theirs.

1:23 The next day (as there remained in all only two day's space [to the time] when he must serve out the corn to his army, and as he was not more than eighteen miles from Bibracte, by far the largest and best-stored town of the Aedui), he thought that he ought to provide for a supply of corn; and diverted his march from the Helvetii, and advanced rapidly to Bibracte. This circumstance is reported to the enemy by some deserters from Lucius Aemilius, a captain, of the Gallic horse. The Helvetii, either because they thought that the Romans, struck with terror, were retreating from them, the more so, as the day before, though they had seized on the higher grounds,

Eodem die ab exploratoribus certior factus hostes sub monte consedisse milia passuum ab ipsius castris octo, qualis esset natura montis et qualis in circuitu ascensus qui cognoscerent misit. Renuntiatum est facilem esse. De tertia vigilia T. Labienum, legatum pro praetore, cum duabus legionibus et iis ducibus qui iter cognoverant summum iugum montis ascendere iubet; quid sui consilii sit ostendit. Ipse de quarta vigilia eodem itinere quo hostes ierant ad eos contendit equitatumque omnem ante se mittit. P. Considius, qui rei militaris peritissimus habebatur et in exercitu L. Sullae et postea in M. Crassi fuerat, cum exploratoribus praemittitur.

Prima luce, cum summus mons a [Lucio] Labieno teneretur, ipse ab hostium castris non longius mille et quingentis passibus abesset neque, ut postea ex captivis comperit, aut ipsius adventus aut Labieni cognitus esset, Considius equo admisso ad eum accurrit, dicit montem, quem a Labieno occupari voluerit, ab hostibus teneri: id se a Gallicis armis atque insignibus cognovisse. Caesar suas copias in proximum collem subducit, aciem instruit. Labienus, ut erat ei praeceptum a Caesare ne proelium committeret, nisi ipsius copiae prope hostium castra visae essent, ut undique uno tempore in hostes impetus fieret, monte occupato nostros expectabat proelioque abstinebat. Multo denique die per exploratores Caesar cognovit et montem a suis teneri et Helvetios castra, movisse et Considium timore perterritum quod non vidisset pro viso sibi renuntiavisse. Eo die quo consuerat intervallo hostes sequitur et milia passuum tria ab eorum castris castra ponit.

Postridie eius diei, quod omnino biduum supererat, cum exercitui frumentum metiri oporteret, et quod a Bibracte, oppido Haeduorum longe maximo et copiosissimo, non amplius milibus passuum XVIII aberat, rei frumentariae prospiciendum existimavit; itaque iter ab Helvetiis avertit ac Bibracte ire contendit. Ea res per fugitivos L. Aemilii, decurionis equitum Gallorum, hostibus nuntiatur. Helvetii, seu quod timore perterritos Romanos discedere a se existimarent, eo magis quod pridie superioribus locis occupatis proelium non commisissent, sive eo quod

they had not joined battle or because they flattered themselves that they might be cut of from the provisions, altering their plan and changing their route, began to pursue, and to annoy our men in the rear.

1:24 Caesar, when he observes this, draws off his forces to the next hill, and sent the cavalry to sustain the attack of the enemy. He himself, meanwhile, drew up on the middle of the hill a triple line of his four veteran legions in such a manner, that he placed above him on the very summit the two legions, which he had lately levied in Hither Gaul, and all the auxiliaries; and he ordered that the whole mountain should be covered with men, and that meanwhile the baggage should be brought together into one place, and the position be protected by those who were posted in the upper line. The Helvetii having followed with all their wagons, collected their baggage into one place: they themselves, after having repulsed our cavalry and formed a phalanx, advanced up to our front line in very close order.

1:25 Caesar, having removed out of sight first his own horse, then those of all, that he might make the danger of a11 equal, and do away with the hope of flight, after encouraging his men, joined battle. His soldiers hurling their javelins from the higher ground, easily broke the enemy's phalanx. That being dispersed, they made a charge on them with drawn swords. It was a great hinderance to the Gauls in fighting, that, when several of their bucklers had been by one stroke of the (Roman) javelins pierced through and pinned fast together, as the point of the iron had bent itself, they could neither pluck it out, nor, with their left hand entangled, fight with sufficient ease; so that many, after having long tossed their arm about, chose rather to cast away the buckler from their hand, and to fight with their person unprotected. At length, worn out with wounds, they began to give way, and, as there was in the neighborhood a mountain about a mile off, to betake themselves thither. When the mountain had been gained, and our men were advancing up, the Boii and Tulingi, who with about 15,000 men closed the enemy's line of march and served as a guard to their rear, having assailed our men on the exposed flank as they advanced [prepared] to surround them; upon seeing which, the Helvetii who had betaken themselves to the mountain, began to press on again and renew the battle. The Romans having faced about, advanced to the attack in two divisions; the first and second line, to withstand those who had been defeated and driven off the field; the third to receive those who were just arriving.

1:26 Thus, was the contest long and vigorously carried on with

re frumentaria intercludi posse confiderent, commutato consilio atque itinere converso nostros a novissimo agmine insequi ac lacessere coeperunt.

Postquam id animum advertit, copias suas Caesar in proximum collem subduxit equitatumque, qui sustineret hostium petum, misit. Ipse interim in colle medio triplicem aciem instruxit legionum quattuor veteranarum; in summo iugo duas legiones quas in Gallia citeriore proxime conscripserat et omnia auxilia conlocavit, ita ut supra se totum montem hominibus compleret; impedimenta sarcinasque in unum locum conferri et eum ab iis qui in superiore acie constiterant muniri iussit. Helvetii cum omnibus suis carris secuti impedimenta in unum locum contulerunt; ipsi confertissima acie, reiecto nostro equitatu, phalange facta sub primam nostram aciem successerunt.

Caesar primum suo, deinde omnium ex conspectu remotis equis, ut aequato omnium periculo spem fugae tolleret, cohortatus suos proelium commisit. Milites loco superiore pilis missis facile hostium phalangem perfregerunt. Ea disiecta gladiis destrictis in eos impetum fecerunt. Gallis magno ad pugnam erat impedimento quod pluribus eorum scutis uno ictu pilorum transfixis et conligatis, cum ferrum se inflexisset, neque evellere neque sinistra impedita satis commode pugnare poterant, multi ut diu iactato bracchio praeoptarent scutum manu emittere et nudo corpore pugnare. Tandem vulneribus defessi et pedem referre et, quod mons suberit circiter mille passuum spatio, eo se recipere coeperunt. Capto monte et succedentibus nostris, Boi et Tulingi, qui hominum milibus circiter XV agmen hostium claudebant et novissimis praesidio erant, ex itinere nostros ab latere aperto adgressi circumvenire, et id conspicati Helvetii, qui in montem sese receperant, rursus instare et proelium redintegrare coeperunt. Romani conversa signa bipertito intulerunt: prima et secunda acies, ut victis ac submotis resisteret, tertia, ut venientes sustineret.

Ita ancipiti proelio diu atque acriter pugnatum est.

doubtful success. When they could no longer withstand the attacks of our men, the one division, as they had begun to do, betook themselves to the mountain; the other repaired to their baggage and wagons. For during the whole of this battle, although the fight lasted from the seventh hour [i.e. 12 (noon) 1 P. M.] to eventide, no one could see an enemy with his back turned. The fight was carried on also at the baggage till late in the night, for they had set wagons in the way as a rampart, and from the higher ground kept throwing weapons upon our men, as they came on, and some from between the wagons and the wheels kept darting their lances and javelins from beneath, and wounding our men. After the fight had lasted some time, our men gained possession of their baggage and camp. There the daughter and one of the sons of Orgetorix was taken. After the battle about 130,000 men [of the enemy] remained alive, who marched incessantly during the whole of that night; and after a march discontinued for no part of the night, arrived in the territories of the Lingones on the fourth day, while our men, having stopped for three days, both on account of the wounds of the soldiers and the burial of the slain, had not been able to follow them. Caesar sent letters and messengers to the Lingones [with orders] that they should not assist them with corn or with any thing else; for that if they should assist them, he would regard them in the same light as the Helvetii. After the three days' interval he began to follow them himself with all his forces.

1:27 The Helvetii, compelled by the want of every thing, sent embassadors to him about a surrender. When these had met him on the way and had thrown themselves at his feet, and speaking in suppliant tone had with tears sued for peace, and [when] he had ordered them to await his arrival, in the place, where they then were, they obeyed his commands. When Caesar arrived at that place, he demanded hostages, their arms, and the slaves who had deserted to them. While those things are being sought for and got together, after a night's interval, about 6000 men of that canton which is called the Verbigene, whether terrified by fear, lest after delivering up their arms, they should suffer punishment, or else induced by the hope of safety, because they supposed that, amid so vast a multitude of those who had surrendered themselves, their flight might either be concealed or entirely overlooked, having at night-fall departed out of the camp of the Helvetii, hastened to the Rhine and the territories of the Germans.

1:28 But when Caesar discovered this, he commanded those through whose territory they had gone, to seek them out and to bring them back again, if they meant to be acquitted before him; and considered them, when brought back, in the light of

Diutius cum sustinere nostrorum impetus non possent, alteri se, ut coeperant, in montem receperunt, alteri ad impedimenta et carros suos se contulerunt. Nam hoc toto proelio, cum ab hora septima ad vesperum pugnatum sit, aversum hostem videre nemo potuit. Ad multam noctem etiam ad impedimenta pugnatum est, propterea quod pro vallo carros obiecerunt et e loco superiore in nostros venientes tela coiciebant et non nulli inter carros rotasque mataras ac tragulas subiciebant nostrosque vulnerabant. Diu cum esset pugnatum, impedimentis castrisque nostri potiti sunt. Ibi Orgetorigis filia atque unus e filiis captus est. Ex eo proelio circiter hominum milia CXXX superfuerunt eaque tota nocte continenter ierunt [nullam partem noctis itinere intermisso]; in fines Lingonum die quarto pervenerunt, cum et propter vulnera militum et propter sepulturam occisorum nostri [triduum morati] eos sequi non potuissent. Caesar ad Lingonas litteras nuntiosque misit, ne eos frumento neve alia re iuvarent: qui si iuvissent, se eodem loco quo Helvetios habiturum. Ipse triduo intermisso cum omnibus copiis eos sequi coepit.

Helvetii omnium rerum inopia adducti legatos de deditione ad eum miserunt. Qui cum eum in itinere convenissent seque ad pedes proiecissent suppliciterque locuti flentes pacem petissent, atque eos in eo loco quo tum essent suum adventum expectare iussisset, paruerunt. Eo postquam Caesar pervenit, obsides, arma, servos qui ad eos perfugissent, poposcit. Dum ea conquiruntur et conferuntur, [nocte intermissa] circiter hominum milia VI eius pagi qui Verbigenus appellatur, sive timore perterriti, ne armis traditis supplicio adficerentur, sive spe salutis inducti, quod in tanta multitudine dediticiorum suam fugam aut occultari aut omnino ignorari posse existimarent, prima nocte e castris Helvetiorum egressi ad Rhenum finesque Germanorum contenderunt.

Quod ubi Caesar resciit, quorum per fines ierant his uti conquirerent et reducerent, si sibi purgati esse vellent, imperavit; reductos in hostium numero habuit; reliquos omnes obsidibus, armis, perfugis traditis in

15

enemies; he admitted all the rest to a surrender, upon their delivering up the hostages, arms, and deserters. He ordered the Helvetii, the Tulingi, and the Latobrigi, to return to their territories from which they had come, and as there was at home nothing whereby they might support their hunger, all the productions of the earth having been destroyed, he commanded the Allobroges to let them have a plentiful supply of corn; and ordered them to rebuild the towns and villages which they had burned. This he did, chiefly, on this account, because he was unwilling that the country, from which the Helvetii had departed, should be untenanted, lest the Germans, who dwell on the other side of the Rhine, should, on account of the excellence of the lands, cross over from their own territories into those of the Helvetii, and become borderers upon the province of Gaul and the Allobroges. He granted the petition of the Aedui, that they might settle the Boii, in their own (i. e. in the Aeduan) territories, as these were known to be of distinguished valor, to whom they gave lands, and whom they afterward admitted to the same state of rights and freedom as themselves.

1:29 In the camp of the Helvetii, lists were found, drawn up in Greek characters, and were brought to Caesar, in which an estimate had been drawn up, name by name, of the number which had gone forth from their country of those who were able to bear arms; and likewise the boys, the old men, and the women, separately. Of all which items the total was: Of the Helvetii [lit. of the heads of the Helvetii] 263,000; Of the Tulingi 36,000; Of the Latobrigi 14,000; Of the Rauraci 23,000; Of the Boii 32,000. The sum of all amounted to 368,000. Out of these, such as could bear arms, [amounted] to about 92,000. When the census of those who returned home was taken, as Caesar had commanded, the number was found to be 110,000.

1:30 When the war with the Helvetii was concluded, embassadors from almost all parts of Gaul, the chiefs of states, assembled to congratulate Caesar, [saying] that they were well aware, that, although he had taken vengeance on the Helvetii in war, for the old wrong done by them to the Roman people, yet that circumstance had happened no less to the benefit of the land of Gaul than of the Roman people, because the Helvetii, while their affairs were most flourishing, had quitted their country with the design of making war upon the whole of Gaul, and seizing the government of it, and selecting, out of a great abundance, that spot for an abode, which they should judge to be the most convenient and most productive of all Gaul, and hold the rest of the states as tributaries. They requested that they might be allowed to proclaim an assembly of the whole of Gaul for a particular day, and to do that with Caesar's

deditionem accepit. Helvetios, Tulingos, Latobrigos in fines suos, unde erant profecti, reverti iussit, et, quod omnibus frugibus amissis domi nihil erat quo famem tolerarent, Allobrogibus imperavit ut iis frumenti copiam facerent; ipsos oppida vicosque, quos incenderant, restituere iussit. Id ea maxime ratione fecit, quod noluit eum locum unde Helvetii discesserant vacare, ne propter bonitatem agrorum Germani, qui trans Rhenum incolunt, ex suis finibus in Helvetiorum fines transirent et finitimi Galliae provinciae Allobrogibusque essent. Boios petentibus Haeduis, quod egregia virtute erant cogniti, ut in finibus suis conlocarent, concessit; quibus illi agros dederunt quosque postea in parem iuris libertatisque condicionem atque ipsi erant receperunt.

In castris Helvetiorum tabulae repertae sunt litteris Graecis confectae et ad Caesarem relatae, quibus in tabulis nominatim ratio confecta erat, qui numerus domo exisset eorum qui arma ferre possent, et item separatim, quot pueri, senes mulieresque. [Quarum omnium rerum] summa erat capitum Helvetiorum milium CCLXIII, Tulingorum milium XXXVI, Latobrigorum XIIII, Rauracorum XXIII, Boiorum XXXII; ex his qui arma ferre possent ad milia nonaginta duo. Summa omnium fuerunt ad milia CCCLXVIII. Eorum qui domum redierunt censu habito, ut Caesar imperaverat, repertus est numerus milium C et X.

Bello Helvetiorum confecto totius fere Galliae legati, principes civitatum, ad Caesarem gratulatum convenerunt: intellegere sese, tametsi pro veteribus Helvetiorum iniuriis populi Romani ab his poenas bello repetisset, tamen eam rem non minus ex usu [terrae] Galliae quam populi Romani accidisse, propterea quod eo consilio florentissimis rebus domos suas Helvetii reliquissent uti toti Galliae bellum inferrent imperioque potirentur, locumque domicilio ex magna copia deligerent quem ex omni Gallia oportunissimum ac fructuosissimum iudicassent, reliquasque civitates stipendiarias haberent. Petierunt uti sibi concilium totius Galliae in diem certam indicere idque Caesaris facere voluntate liceret: sese habere quasdam res quas ex communi consensu ab

permission, [stating] that they had some things which, with the general consent, they wished to ask of him. This request having been granted, they appointed a day for the assembly, and ordained by an oath with each other, that no one should disclose [their deliberations] except those to whom this [office] should be assigned by the general assembly.

1:31 When that assembly was dismissed, the same chiefs of states, who had before been to Caesar, returned, and asked that they might be allowed to treat with him privately (in secret) concerning the safety of themselves and of all. That request having been obtained, they all threw themselves in tears at Caesar's feet, [saying] that they no less begged and earnestly desired that what they might say should not be disclosed, than that they might obtain those things which they wished for; inasmuch as they saw, that, if a disclosure was made, they should be put to the greatest tortures. For these Divitiacus the Aeduan spoke and told him: "That there were two parties in the whole of Gaul: that the Aedui stood at the head of one of these, the Arverni of the other. After these had been violently struggling with one another for the superiority for many years, it came to pass that the Germans were called in for hire by the Arverni and the Sequani. That about 15,000 of them [i.e. of the Germans] had at first crossed the Rhine: but after that these wild and savage men had become enamored of the lands and the refinement and the abundance of the Gauls, more were brought over, that there were now as many as 120,000 of them in Gaul: that with these the Aedui and their dependents had repeatedly struggled in arms--that they had been routed, and had sustained a great calamity--had lost all their nobility, all their senate, all their cavalry. And that broken by such engagements and calamities, although they had formerly been very powerful in Gaul, both from their own valor and from the Roman people's hospitality and friendship, they were now compelled to give the chief nobles of their state, as hostages to the Sequani, and to bind their state by an oath, that they would neither demand hostages in return, nor supplicate aid from the Roman people, nor refuse to be forever under their sway and empire. That he was the only one out of all the state of the Aedui, who could not be prevailed upon to take the oath or to give his children as hostages. On that account he had fled from his state and had gone to the senate at Rome to beseech aid, as he alone was bound neither by oath nor hostages. But a worse thing had befallen the victorious Sequani than the vanquished Aedui, for Ariovistus the king of the Germans, had settled in their territories, and had seized upon a third of their land, which was the best in the whole of Gaul, and was now ordering them to depart from another third part, because a few

eo petere vellent. Ea re permissa diem concilio constituerunt et iure iurando ne quis enuntiaret, nisi quibus communi consilio mandatum esset, inter se sanxerunt.

Eo concilio dimisso, idem princeps civitatum qui ante fuerant ad Caesarem reverterunt petieruntque uti sibi secreto in occulto de sua omniumque salute cum eo agere liceret. Ea re impetrata sese omnes flentes Caesari ad pedes proiecerunt: non minus se id contendere et laborare ne ea quae dixissent enuntiarentur quam uti ea quae vellent impetrarent, propterea quod, si enuntiatum esset, summum in cruciatum se venturos viderent. Locutus est pro his Diviciacus Haeduus: Galliae totius factiones esse duas; harum alterius principatum tenere Haeduos, alterius Arvernos. Hi cum tantopere de potentatu inter se multos annos contenderent, factum esse uti ab Arvernis Sequanisque Germani mercede arcesserentur. Horum primo circiter milia XV Rhenum transisse; postea quam agros et cultum et copias Gallorum homines feri ac barbari adamassent, traductos plures; nunc esse in Gallia ad C et XX milium numerum. Cum his Haeduos eorumque clientes semel atque iterum armis contendisse; magnam calamitatem pulsos accepisse, omnem nobilitatem, omnem senatum, omnem equitatum amisisse. Quibus proeliis calamitatibusque fractos, qui et sua virtute et populi Romani hospitio atque amicitia plurimum ante in Gallia potuissent, coactos esse Sequanis obsides dare nobilissimos civitatis et iure iurando civitatem obstringere sese neque obsides repetituros neque auxilium a populo Romano imploraturos neque recusaturos quo minus perpetuo sub illorum dicione atque imperio essent. Unum se esse ex omni civitate Haeduorum qui adduci non potuerit ut iuraret aut liberos suos obsides daret. Ob eam rem se ex civitate profugisse et Romam ad senatum venisse auxilium postulatum, quod solus neque iure iurando neque obsidibus teneretur. Sed peius victoribus Sequanis quam Haeduis victis accidisse, propterea quod Ariovistus, rex Germanorum, in eorum finibus consedisset tertiamque partem agri Sequani, qui esset optimus totius Galliae, occupavisset et nunc de altera parte tertia Sequanos decedere iuberet, propterea quod

months previously 24,000 men of the Harudes had come to him, for whom room and settlements must be provided. The consequence would be, that in a few years they would all be driven from the territories of Gaul, and all the Germans would cross the Rhine; for neither must the land of Gaul be compared with the land of the Germans, nor must the habit of living of the latter be put on a level with that of the former. Moreover, [as for] Ariovistus, no sooner did he defeat the forces of the Gauls in a battle which took place at Magetobria, than [he began] to lord it haughtily and cruelly, to demand as hostages the children of all the principal nobles, and wreak on them every kind of cruelty, if every thing was not done at his nod or pleasure; that he was a savage, passionate, and reckless man, and that his commands could no longer be borne. Unless there was some aid in Caesar and the Roman people, the Gauls must all do the same thing that the Helvetii have done, [viz.] emigrate from their country, and seek another dwelling place, other settlements remote from the Germans, and try whatever fortune may fall to their lot. If these things were to be disclosed to Ariovistus, [Divitiacus adds] that he doubts not that he would inflict the most severe punishment on all the hostages who are in his possession, [and says] that Caesar could, either by his own influence and by that of his army, or by his late victory, or by name of the Roman people, intimidate him, so as to prevent a greater number of Germans being brought over the Rhine, and could protect all Gaul from the outrages of Ariovistus.

1:32 When this speech had been delivered by Divitiacus, all who were present began with loud lamentation to entreat assistance of Caesar. Caesar noticed that the Sequani were the only people of all who did none of those things which the others did, but, with their heads bowed down, gazed on the earth in sadness. Wondering what was the reason of this conduct, he inquired of themselves. No reply did the Sequani make, but silently continued in the same sadness. When he had repeatedly inquired of them and could not elicit any answer at all, the same Divitiacus the Aeduan answered, that--"the lot of the Sequani was more wretched and grievous than that of the rest, on this account, because they alone durst not even in secret complain or supplicate aid; and shuddered at the cruelty of Ariovistus [even when] absent, just as if he were present; for, to the rest, despite of every thing there was an opportunity of flight given; but all tortures must be endured by the Sequani, who had admitted Ariovistus within their territories, and whose towns were all in his power."

1:33 Caesar, on being informed of these things, cheered the minds of the Gauls with his words, and promised that this affair should be an object of his concern, [saying] that he had great

paucis mensibus ante Harudum milia hominum XXIIII ad eum venissent, quibus locus ac sedes pararentur. Futurum esse paucis annis uti omnes ex Galliae finibus pellerentur atque omnes Germani Rhenum transirent; neque enim conferendum esse Gallicum cum Germanorum agro neque hanc consuetudinem victus cum illa comparandam. Ariovistum autem, ut semel Gallorum copias proelio vicerit, quod proelium factum sit ad Magetobrigam, superbe et crudeliter imperare, obsides nobilissimi cuiusque liberos poscere et in eos omnia exempla cruciatusque edere, si qua res non ad nutum aut ad voluntatem eius facta sit. Hominem esse barbarum, iracundum, temerarium: non posse eius imperia, diutius sustineri. Nisi quid in Caesare populoque Romano sit auxilii, omnibus Gallis idem esse faciendum quod Helvetii fecerint, ut domo emigrent, aliud domicilium, alias sedes, remotas a Germanis, petant fortunamque, quaecumque accidat, experiantur. Haec si enuntiata Ariovisto sint, non dubitare quin de omnibus obsidibus qui apud eum sint gravissimum supplicium sumat. Caesarem vel auctoritate sua atque exercitus vel recenti victoria vel nomine populi Romani deterrere posse ne maior multitudo Germanorum Rhenum traducatur, Galliamque omnem ab Ariovisti iniuria posse defendere.

Hac oratione ab Diviciaco habita omnes qui aderant magno fletu auxilium a Caesare petere coeperunt. Animadvertit Caesar unos ex omnibus Sequanos nihil earum rerum facere quas ceteri facerent sed tristes capite demisso terram intueri. Eius rei quae causa esset miratus ex ipsis quaesiit. Nihil Sequani respondere, sed in eadem tristitia taciti permanere. Cum ab his saepius quaereret neque ullam omnino vocem exprimere posset, idem Diviacus Haeduus respondit: hoc esse miseriorem et graviorem fortunam Sequanorum quam reliquorum, quod soli ne in occulto quidem queri neque auxilium implorare auderent absentisque Ariovisti crudelitatem, velut si cora adesset, horrerent, propterea quod reliquis tamen fugae facultas daretur, Sequanis vero, qui intra fines suos Ariovistum recepissent, quorum oppida omnia in potestate eius essent, omnes cruciatus essent perferendi.

His rebus cognitis Caesar Gallorum animos verbis confirmavit pollicitusque est sibi eam rem curae futuram; magnam se habere spem et beneficio suo et

hopes that Ariovistus, induced both by his kindness and his power, would put an end to his oppression. After delivering this speech, he dismissed the assembly; and, besides those statements, many circumstances induced him to think that this affair ought to be considered and taken up by him; especially as he saw that the Aedui, styled [as they had been] repeatedly by the senate "brethren" and "kinsmen," were held in the thraldom and dominion of the Germans, and understood that their hostages were with Ariovistus and the Sequani, which in so mighty an empire [as that] of the Roman people he considered very disgraceful to himself and the republic. That, moreover, the Germans should by degrees become accustomed to cross the Rhine, and that a great body of them should come into Gaul, he saw [would be] dangerous to the Roman people, and judged, that wild and savage men would not be likely to restrain themselves, after they had possessed themselves of all Gaul, from going forth into the province and thence marching into Italy (as the Cimbri and Teutones had done before them), particularly as the Rhone [was the sole barrier that] separated the Sequani from our province. Against which events he thought he ought to provide as speedily as possible. Moreover, Ariovistus, for his part, had assumed to himself such pride and arrogance, that he was felt to be quite insufferable.

1:34 He therefore determined to send embassadors to Ariovistus to demand of him to name some intermediate spot for a conference between the two, [saying] that he wished to treat him on state-business and matters of the highest importance to both of them. To this embassy Ariovistus replied, that if he himself had had need of any thing from Caesar, he would have gone to him; and that if Caesar wanted any thing from him he ought to come to him. That, besides, neither dare he go without an army into those parts of Gaul which Caesar had possession of, nor could he, without great expense and trouble, draw his army together to one place; that to him, moreover, it appeared strange, what business either Caesar or the Roman people at all had in his own Gaul, which he had conquered in war.

1:35 When these answers were reported to Caesar, he sends embassadors to him a second time with this message. "Since, after having been treated with so much kindness by himself and the Roman people (as he had in his consulship been styled 'king and friend' by the senate), he makes this recompense to [Caesar] himself and the Roman people, [viz.] that when invited to a conference he demurs, and does not think that it concerns him to advise and inform himself about an object of mutual interest, these are the things which he requires of him; first, that he do not any more bring over any body of men across the

auctoritate adductum Ariovistum finem iniuriis facturum. Hac oratione habita, concilium dimisit. Et secundum ea multae res eum hortabantur quare sibi eam rem cogitandam et suscipiendam putaret, in primis quod Haeduos, fratres consanguineosque saepe numero a senatu appellatos, in servitute atque in dicione videbat Germanorum teneri eorumque obsides esse apud Ariovistum ac Sequanos intellegebat; quod in tanto imperio populi Romani turpissimum sibi et rei publicae esse arbitrabatur. Paulatim autem Germanos consuescere Rhenum transire et in Galliam magnam eorum multitudinem venire populo Romano periculosum videbat, neque sibi homines feros ac barbaros temperaturos existimabat quin, cum omnem Galliam occupavissent, ut ante Cimbri Teutonique fecissent, in provinciam exirent atque inde in Italiam contenderent [, praesertim cum Sequanos a provincia nostra Rhodanus divideret]; quibus rebus quam maturrime occurrendum putabat. Ipse autem Ariovistus tantos sibi spiritus, tantam arrogantiam sumpserat, ut ferendus non videretur.

Quam ob rem placuit ei ut ad Ariovistum legatos mitteret, qui ab eo postularent uti aliquem locum medium utrisque conloquio deligeret: velle sese de re publica et summis utriusque rebus cum eo agere. Ei legationi Ariovistus respondit: si quid ipsi a Caesare opus esset, sese ad eum venturum fuisse; si quid ille se velit, illum ad se venire oportere. Praeterea se neque sine exercitu in eas partes Galliae venire audere quas Caesar possideret, neque exercitum sine magno commeatu atque molimento in unum locum contrahere posse. Sibi autem mirum videri quid in sua Gallia, quam bello vicisset, aut Caesari aut omnino populo Romano negotii esset.

His responsis ad Caesarem relatis, iterum ad eum Caesar legatos cum his mandatis mittit: quoniam tanto suo populique Romani beneficio adfectus, cum in consulatu suo rex atque amicus a senatu appellatus esset, hanc sibi populoque Romano gratiam referret ut in conloquium venire invitatus gravaretur neque de communi re dicendum sibi et cognoscendum putaret, haec esse quae ab eo postularet: primum ne quam multitudinem hominum amplius trans Rhenum in Galliam traduceret; deinde

19

Rhine into Gaul; in the next place, that he restore the hostages, which he has from the Aedui, and grant the Sequani permission to restore to them with his consent those hostages which they have, and that he neither provoke the Aedui by outrage nor make war upon them or their allies; if he would accordingly do this," [Caesar says] that "he himself and the Roman people will entertain a perpetual feeling of favor and friendship toward him; but that if he [Caesar] does not obtain [his desires] that he (forasmuch as in the consulship of Marcus Messala and Marcus Piso the senate had decreed that, whoever should have the administration of the province of Gaul should, as far as he could do so consistently with the interests of the republic, protect the Aedui and the other friends of the Roman people), will not overlook the wrongs of the Aedui."

1:36 To this Ariovistus replied, that "the right of war was, that they who had conquered should govern those whom they had conquered, in what manner they pleased; that in that way the Roman people were wont to govern the nations which they had conquered, not according to the dictation of any other, but according to their own discretion. If he for his part did not dictate to the Roman people as to the manner in which they were to exercise their right, he ought not to be obstructed by the Roman people in his right; that the Aedui, inasmuch as they had tried the fortune of war and had engaged in arms and been conquered, had become tributaries to him; that Caesar was doing a great injustice, in that by his arrival he was making his revenues less valuable to him; that he should not restore their hostages to the Aedui, but should not make war wrongfully either upon them or their allies, if they abided by that which had been agreed on, and paid their tribute annually: if they did not continue to do that, the Roman people's name of 'brothers' would avail them naught. As to Caesar's threatening him, that he would not overlook the wrongs of the Aedui, [he said] that no one had ever entered into a contest with him [Ariovistus] without utter ruin to himself. That Caesar might enter the lists when he chose; he would feel what the invincible Germans, well-trained [as they were] beyond all others to arms, who for fourteen years had not been beneath a roof, could achieve by their valor."

1:37 At the same time that this message was delivered to Caesar, embassadors came from the Aedui and the Treviri; from the Aedui to complain that the Harudes, who had lately been brought over into Gaul, were ravaging their territories; that they had not been able to purchase peace from Ariovistus, even by giving hostages: and from the Treviri, [to state] that a hundred cantons of the Suevi had encamped on the banks of the Rhine, and were attempting to cross it; that the brothers,

obsides quos haberet ab Haeduis redderet Sequanisque permitteret ut quos illi haberent voluntate eius reddere illis liceret; neve Haeduos iniuria lacesseret neve his sociisque eorum bellum inferret. Si id ita fecisset, sibi populoque Romano perpetuam gratiam atque amicitiam cum eo futuram; si non impetraret, sese, quoniam M. Messala, M. Pisone consulibus senatus censuisset uti quicumque Galliam provinciam obtineret, quod commodo rei publicae lacere posset, Haeduos ceterosque amicos populi Romani defenderet, se Haeduorum iniurias non neglecturum.

Ad haec Ariovistus respondit: ius esse belli ut qui vicissent iis quos vicissent quem ad modum vellent imperarent. Item populum Romanum victis non ad alterius praescriptum, sed ad suum arbitrium imperare consuesse. Si ipse populo Romano non praescriberet quem ad modum suo iure uteretur, non oportere se a populo Romano in suo iure impediri. Haeduos sibi, quoniam belli fortunam temptassent et armis congressi ac superati essent, stipendiarios esse factos. Magnam Caesarem iniuriam facere, qui suo adventu vectigalia sibi deteriora faceret. Haeduis se obsides redditurum non esse neque his neque eorum sociis iniuria bellum inlaturum, si in eo manerent quod convenisset stipendiumque quotannis penderent; si id non fecissent, longe iis fraternum nomen populi Romani afuturum. Quod sibi Caesar denuntiaret se Haeduorum iniurias non neglecturum, neminem secum sine sua pernicie contendisse. Cum vellet, congrederetur: intellecturum quid invicti Germani, exercitatissimi in armis, qui inter annos XIIII tectum non subissent, virtute possent.

Haec eodem tempore Caesari mandata referebantur et legati ab Haeduis et a Treveris veniebant: Haedui questum quod Harudes, qui nuper in Galliam transportati essent, fines eorum popularentur: sese ne obsidibus quidem datis pacem Ariovisti redimere potuisse; Treveri autem, pagos centum Sueborum ad ripas Rheni consedisse, qui Rhemum transire conarentur; his praeesse Nasuam et Cimberium

Nasuas and Cimberius, headed them. Being greatly alarmed at these things, Caesar thought that he ought to use all dispatch, lest, if this new band of Suevi should unite with the old troops of Ariovistus, he [Ariovistus] might be less easily withstood. Having therefore, as quickly as he could, provided a supply of corn, he hastened to Ariovistus by forced marches.

1:38 When he had proceeded three days' journey, word was brought to him that Ariovistus was hastening with all his forces to seize on Vesontio, which is the largest town of the Sequani, and had advanced three days' journey from its territories. Caesar thought that he ought to take the greatest precautions lest this should happen, for there was in that town a most ample supply of every thing which was serviceable for war; and so fortified was it by the nature of the ground, as to afford a great facility for protracting the war, inasmuch as the river Doubs almost surrounds the whole town, as though it were traced round it with a pair of compasses. A mountain of great height shuts in the remaining space, which is not more than 600 feet, where the river leaves a gap, in such a manner that the roots of that mountain extend to the river's bank on either side. A wall thrown around it makes a citadel of this [mountain], and connects it with the town. Hither Caesar hastens by forced marches by night and day, and, after having seized the town, stations a garrison there.

1:39 While he is tarrying a few days at Vesontio, on account of corn and provisions; from the inquiries of our men and the reports of the Gauls and traders (who asserted that the Germans were men of huge stature, of incredible valor and practice in arms-that oftentimes they, on encountering them, could not bear even their countenance, and the fierceness of their eyes)-so great a panic on a sudden seized the whole army, as to discompose the minds and spirits of all in no slight degree. This first arose from the tribunes of the soldiers, the prefects and the rest, who, having followed Caesar from the city [Rome] from motives of friendship, had no great experience in military affairs. And alleging, some of them one reason, some another, which they said made it necessary for them to depart, they requested that by his consent they might be allowed to withdraw; some, influenced by shame, stayed behind in order that they might avoid the suspicion of cowardice. These could neither compose their countenance, nor even sometimes check their tears: but hidden in their tents, either bewailed their fate, or deplored with their comrades the general danger. Wills were sealed universally throughout the whole camp. By the expressions and cowardice of these men, even those who possessed great experience in the camp, both soldiers and centurions, and those [the decurions] who were in command of

fratres. Quibus rebus Caesar vehementer commotus maturandum sibi existimavit, ne, si nova manus Sueborum cum veteribus copiis Ariovisti sese coniunxisset, minus facile resisti posset. Itaque re frumentaria quam celerrime potuit comparata magnis itineribus ad Ariovistum contendit.

Cum tridui viam processisset, nuntiatum est ei Ariovistum cum suis omnibus copiis ad occupandum Vesontionem, quod est oppidum maximum Sequanorum, contendere [triduique viam a suis finibus processisse]. Id ne accideret, magnopere sibi praecavendum Caesar existimabat. Namque omnium rerum quae ad bellum usui erant summa erat in eo oppido facultas, idque natura loci sic muniebatur ut magnam ad ducendum bellum daret facultatem, propterea quod flumen [alduas] Dubis ut circino circumductum paene totum oppidum cingit, reliquum spatium, quod est non amplius pedum MDC, qua flumen intermittit, mons continet magna altitudine, ita ut radices eius montis ex utraque parte ripae fluminis contingant, hunc murus circumdatus arcem efficit et cum oppido coniungit. Huc Caesar magnis nocturnis diurnisque itineribus contendit occupatoque oppido ibi praesidium conlocat.

Dum paucos dies ad Vesontionem rei frumentariae commeatusque causa moratur, ex percontatione nostrorum vocibusque Gallorum ac mercatorum, qui ingenti magnitudine corporum Germanos, incredibili virtute atque exercitatione in armis esse praedicabant (saepe numero sese cum his congressos ne vultum quidem atque aciem oculorum dicebant ferre potuisse), tantus subito timor omnem exercitum occupavit ut non mediocriter omnium mentes animosque perturbaret. Hic primum ortus est a tribunis militum, praefectis, reliquisque qui ex urbe amicitiae causa Caesarem secuti non magnum in re militari usum habebant: quorum alius alia causa inlata, quam sibi ad proficiscendum necessariam esse diceret, petebat ut eius voluntate discedere liceret; non nulli pudore adducti, ut timoris suspicionem vitarent, remanebant. Hi neque vultum fingere neque interdum lacrimas tenere poterant: abditi in tabernaculis aut suum fatum querebantur aut cum familiaribus suis commune periculum miserabantur. Vulgo totis castris testamenta obsignabantur. Horum vocibus ac timore paulatim etiam ii qui magnum in castris usum habebant, milites

the cavalry, were gradually disconcerted. Such of them as wished to be considered less alarmed, said that they did not dread the enemy, but feared the narrowness of the roads and the vastness of the forests which lay between them and Ariovistus, or else that the supplies could not be brought up readily enough. Some even declared to Caesar, that when he gave orders for the camp to be moved and the troops to advance, the soldiers would not be obedient to the command, nor advance in consequence of their fear.

1:40 When Caesar observed these things, having called a council, and summoned to it the centurions of all the companies, he severely reprimanded them, "particularly, for supposing that it belonged to them to inquire or conjecture, either in what direction they were marching, or with what object. That Ariovistus, during his [Caesar's] consulship, had most anxiously sought after the friendship of the Roman people; why should any one judge that he would so rashly depart from his duty? He for his part was persuaded, that, when his demands were known and the fairness of the terms considered, he would reject neither his nor the Roman people's favor. But even if, driven on by rage and madness, he should make war upon them, what after all were they afraid of?-or why should they despair either of their own valor or of his zeal? Of that enemy a trial had been made within our fathers' recollection, when, on the defeat of the Cimbri and Teutones by Caius Marius, the army was regarded as having deserved no less praise than their commander himself. It had been made lately, too, in Italy, during the rebellion of the slaves, whom, however, the experience and training which they had received from us, assisted in some respect. From which a judgment might be formed of the advantages which resolution carries with it inasmuch as those whom for some time they had groundlessly dreaded when unarmed, they had afterward vanquished, when well armed and flushed with success. In short, that these were the same men whom the Helvetii, in frequent encounters, not only in their own territories, but also in theirs [the German], have generally vanquished, and yet can not have been a match for our army. If the unsuccessful battle and flight of the Gauls disquieted any, these, if they made inquiries, might discover that, when the Gauls had been tired out by the long duration of the war, Ariovistus, after he had many months kept himself in his camp and in the marshes, and had given no opportunity for an engagement, fell suddenly upon them, by this time despairing of a battle and scattered in all directions, and was victorious more through stratagem and cunning than valor. But though there had been room for such stratagem against savage and unskilled men, not even [Ariovistus] himself expected that

centurionesque quique equitatui praeerant, perturbabantur. Qui se ex his minus timidos existimari volebant, non se hostem vereri, sed angustias itineris et magnitudinem silvarum quae intercederent inter ipsos atque Ariovistum, aut rem frumentariam, ut satis commode supportari posset, timere dicebant. Non nulli etiam Caesari nuntiabant, cum castra moveri ac signa ferri iussisset, non fore dicto audientes milites neque propter timorem signa laturos.

Haec cum animadvertisset, convocato consilio omniumque ordinum ad id consilium adhibitis centurionibus, vehementer eos incusavit: primum, quod aut quam in partem aut quo consilio ducerentur sibi quaerendum aut cogitandum putarent. Ariovistum se consule cupidissime populi Romani amicitiam adpetisse; cur hunc tam temere quisquam ab officio discessurum iudicaret? Sibi quidem persuaderi cognitis suis poslulatis atque aequitate condicionum perspecta eum neque suam neque populi Romani gratiam repudiaturum. Quod si furore atque amentia impulsum bellum intulisset, quid tandem vererentur? Aut cur de sua virtute aut de ipsius diligentia desperarent? Factum eius hostis periculum patrum nostrorum memoria Cimbris et Teutonis a C. Mario pulsis [cum non minorem laudem exercitus quam ipse imperator meritus videbatur]; factum etiam nuper in Italia servili tumultu, quos tamen aliquid usus ac disciplina, quam a nobis accepissent, sublevarint. Ex quo iudicari posse quantum haberet in se boni constantia, propterea quod quos aliquam diu inermes sine causa timuissent hos postea armatos ac victores superassent. Denique hos esse eosdem Germanos quibuscum saepe numero Helvetii congressi non solum in suis sed etiam in illorum finibus plerumque superarint, qui tamen pares esse nostro exercitui non potuerint. Si quos adversum proelium et fuga Gallorum commoveret, hos, si quaererent, reperire posse diuturnitate belli defatigatis Gallis Ariovistum, cum multos menses castris se ac paludibus tenuisset neque sui potestatem fecisset, desperantes iam de pugna et dispersos subito adortum magis ratione et consilio quam virtute vicisse. Cui rationi contra homines barbaros atque imperitos locus fuisset, hac ne ipsum quidem sperare nostros exercitus capi posse. Qui suum timorem in rei frumentariae simulationem angustiasque itineris conferrent, facere arroganter, cum aut de officio imperatoris desperare

thereby our armies could be entrapped. That those who ascribed their fear to a pretense about the [deficiency of] supplies and the narrowness of the roads, acted presumptuously, as they seemed either to distrust their general's discharge of his duty, or to dictate to him. That these things were his concern; that the Sequani, the Leuci, and the Lingones were to furnish the corn; and that it was already ripe in the fields; that as to the road they would soon be able to judge for themselves. As to its being reported that the soldiers would not be obedient to command, or advance, he was not at all disturbed at that; for he knew, that in the case of all those whose army had not been obedient to command, either upon some mismanagement of an affair, fortune had deserted them, or, that upon some crime being discovered, covetousness had been clearly proved [against them]. His integrity had been seen throughout his whole life, his good fortune in the war with the Helvetii. That he would therefore instantly set about what he had intended to put off till a more distant day, and would break up his camp the next night, in the fourth watch, that he might ascertain, as soon as possible, whether a sense of honor and duty, or whether fear had more influence with them. But that, if no one else should follow, yet he would go with only the tenth legion, of which he had no misgivings, and it should be his praetorian cohort." This legion Caesar had both greatly favored, and in it, on account of its valor, placed the greatest confidence.

1:41 Upon the delivery of this speech, the minds of all were changed in a surprising manner, and the highest ardor and eagerness for prosecuting the war were engendered; and the tenth legion was the first to return thanks to him, through their military tribunes, for his having expressed this most favorable opinion of them; and assured him that they were quite ready to prosecute the war. Then, the other legions endeavored, through their military tribunes and the centurions of the principal companies, to excuse themselves to Caesar, [saying] that they had never either doubted or feared, or supposed that the determination of the conduct of the war was theirs and not their general's. Having accepted their excuse, and having had the road carefully reconnoitered by Divitiacus, because in him of all others he had the greatest faith [he found] that by a circuitous route of more than fifty miles he might lead his army through open parts; he then set out in the fourth watch, as he had said [he would]. On the seventh day, as he did not discontinue his march, he was informed by scouts that the forces of Ariovistus were only four and twenty miles distant from ours.

1:42 Upon being apprized of Caesar's arrival, Ariovistus sends embassadors to him, [saying] that what he had before requested as to a conference, might now, as far as his

aut praescribere viderentur. Haec sibi esse curae; frumentum Sequanos, Leucos, Lingones subministrare, iamque esse in agris frumenta matura; de itinere ipsos brevi tempore iudicaturos. Quod non fore dicto audientes neque signa laturi dicantur, nihil se ea re commoveri: scire enim, quibuscumque exercitus dicto audiens non fuerit, aut male re gesta fortunam defuisse aut aliquo facinore comperto avaritiam esse convictam. Suam innocentiam perpetua vita, felicitatem Helvetiorum bello esse perspectam. Itaque se quod in longiorem diem conlaturus fuisset repraesentaturum et proxima nocte de quarta, vigilia castra moturum, ut quam primum intellegere posset utrum apud eos pudor atque officium an timor plus valeret. Quod si praeterea nemo sequatur, tamen se cum sola decima legione iturum, de qua non dubitet, sibique eam praetoriam cohortem futuram. Huic legioni Caesar et indulserat praecipue et propter virtutem confidebat maxime.

Hac oratione habita mirum in modum conversae sunt omnium mentes summaque alacritas et cupiditas belli gerendi innata est, princepsque X. legio per tribunos militum ei gratias egit quod de se optimum iudicium fecisset, seque esse ad bellum gerendum paratissimam confirmavit. Deinde reliquae legiones cum tribunis militum et primorum ordinum centurionibus egerunt uti Caesari satis facerent: se neque umquam dubitasse neque timuisse neque de summa belli suum iudicium sed imperatoris esse existimavisse. Eorum satisfactione accepta et itinere exquisito per Diviciacum, quod ex Gallis ei maximam fidem habebat, ut milium amplius quinquaginta circuitu locis apertis exercitum duceret, de quarta vigilia, ut dixerat, profectus est. Septimo die, cum iter non intermitteret, ab exploratoribus certior factus est Ariovisti copias a nostris milia passuum IIII et XX abesse.

Cognito Caesaris adventu Ariovistus legatos ad eum mittit: quod antea de conloquio postulasset, id per se fieri licere, quoniam propius accessisset seque id sine

permission went, take place, since he [Caesar] had approached nearer, and he considered that he might now do it without danger. Caesar did not reject the proposal and began to think that he was now returning to a rational state of mind as he spontaneously proffered that which he had previously refused to him when requesting it; and was in great hopes that, in consideration of his own and the Roman people's great favors toward him, the issue would be that he would desist from his obstinacy upon his demands being made known. The fifth day after that was appointed as the day of conference. Meanwhile, as ambassadors were being often sent to and fro between them, Ariovistus demanded that Caesar should not bring any foot-soldier with him to the conference, [saying] that "he was afraid of being ensnared by him through treachery; that both should come accompanied by cavalry; that he would not come on any other condition." Caesar, as he neither wished that the conference should, by an excuse thrown in the way, be set aside, nor durst trust his life to the cavalry of the Gauls, decided that it would be most expedient to take away from the Gallic cavalry all their horses, and thereon to mount the legionary soldiers of the tenth legion, in which he placed the greatest confidence, in order that he might have a body-guard as trustworthy as possible, should there be any need for action. And when this was done, one of the soldiers of the tenth legion said, not without a touch of humor, "that Caesar did more for them than he had promised; he had promised to have the tenth legion in place of his praetorian cohort; but he now converted them into horse."

1:43 There was a large plain, and in it a mound of earth of considerable size. This spot was at nearly an equal distance from both camps. Thither, as had been appointed, they came for the conference. Caesar stationed the legion, which he had brought [with him] on horseback, 200 paces from this mound. The cavalry of Ariovistus also took their stand at an equal distance. Ariovistus then demanded that they should confer on horseback, and that, besides themselves, they should bring with them ten men each to the conference. When they were come to the place, Caesar, in the opening of his speech, detailed his own and the senate's favors toward him [Ariovistus], in that he had been styled king, in that [he had been styled] friend, by the senate-in that very considerable presents had been sent him; which circumstance he informed him had both fallen to the lot of few, and had usually been bestowed in consideration of important personal services; that he, although he had neither an introduction, nor a just ground for the request, had obtained these honors through the kindness and munificence of himself [Caesar] and the senate.

periculo facere posse existimaret. Non respuit condicionem Caesar iamque eum ad sanitatem reverti arbitrabatur, cum id quod antea petenti denegasset ultro polliceretur, magnamque in spem veniebat pro suis tantis populique Romani in eum beneficiis cognitis suis postulatis fore uti pertinacia desisteret. Dies conloquio dictus est ex eo die quintus. Interim saepe cum legati ultro citroque inter eos mitterentur, Ariovistus postulavit ne quem peditem ad conloquium Caesar adduceret: vereri se ne per insidias ab eo circumveniretur; uterque cum equitatu veniret: alia ratione sese non esse venturum. Caesar, quod neque conloquium interposita causa tolli volebat neque salutem suam Gallorum equitatui committere audebat, commodissimum esse statuit omnibus equis Gallis equitibus detractis eo legionarios milites legionis X., cui quam maxime confidebat, imponere, ut praesidium quam amicissimum, si quid opus facto esset, haberet. Quod cum fieret, non inridicule quidam ex militibus X. legionis dixit: plus quam pollicitus esset Caesarem facere; pollicitum se in cohortis praetoriae loco X. legionem habiturum ad equum rescribere.

Planities erat magna et in ea tumulus terrenus satis grandis. Hic locus aequum fere spatium a castris Ariovisti et Caesaris aberat. Eo, ut erat dictum, ad conloquium venerunt. Legionem Caesar, quam equis devexerat, passibus CC ab eo tumulo constituit. Item equites Ariovisti pari intervallo constiterunt. Ariovistus ex equis ut conloquerentur et praeter se denos ad conloquium adducerent postulavit. Ubi eo ventum est, Caesar initio orationis sua senatusque in eum beneficia commemoravit, quod rex appellatus esset a senatu, quod amicus, quod munera amplissime missa; quam rem et paucis contigisse et pro magnis hominum officiis consuesse tribui docebat; illum, cum neque aditum neque causam postulandi iustam haberet, beneficio ac liberalitate sua ac senatus ea praemia consecutum. Docebat etiam quam veteres quamque iustae causae necessitudinis ipsis cum Haeduis intercederent, quae senatus consulta quotiens quamque honorifica in eos facta essent, ut

He informed him too, how old and how just were the grounds of connection that existed between themselves [the Romans] and the Aedui, what decrees of the senate had been passed in their favor, and how frequent and how honorable; how from time immemorial the Aedui had held the supremacy of the whole of Gaul; even [said Caesar] before they had sought our friendship; that it was the custom of the Roman people to desire not only that its allies and friends should lose none of their property, but be advanced in influence, dignity, and honor: who then could endure that what they had brought with them to the friendship of the Roman people should be torn from them?" He then made the same demands which he had commissioned the embassadors to make, that [Ariovistus] should not make war either upon the Aedui or their allies, that he should restore the hostages; that if he could not send back to their country any part of the Germans, he should at all events suffer none of them any more to cross the Rhine.

1:44 Ariovistus briefly replied to the demands of Caesar; but expatiated largely on his own virtues, "that he had crossed the Rhine not of his own accord, but on being invited and sent for by the Gauls; that he had not left home and kindred without great expectations and great rewards; that he had settlements in Gaul, granted by the Gauls themselves; that the hostages had been given by their good-will; that he took by right of war the tribute which conquerors are accustomed to impose on the conquered; that he had not made war upon the Gauls, but the Gauls upon him; that all the states of Gaul came to attack him, and had encamped against him; that all their forces had been routed and beaten by him in a single battle; that if they chose to make a second trial, he was ready to encounter them again; but if they chose to enjoy peace, it was unfair to refuse the tribute, which of their own free-will they had paid up to that time. That the friendship of the Roman people ought to prove to him an ornament and a safeguard, not a detriment; and that he sought it with that expectation. But if through the Roman people the tribute was to be discontinued, and those who surrendered to be seduced from him, he would renounce the friendship of the Roman people no less heartily than he had sought it. As to his leading over a host of Germans into Gaul, that he was doing this with a view of securing himself, not of assaulting Gaul: that there was evidence of this, in that he did not come without being invited, and in that he did not make war, but merely warded it off. That he had come into Gaul before the Roman people. That never before this time did a Roman army go beyond the frontiers of the province of Gaul. What [said he] does [Caesar] desire?- why come into his [Ariovistus] domains?-that this was his province of Gaul, just as that is ours.

omni tempore totius Galliae principatum Haedui tenuissent, prius etiam quam nostram amicitiam adpetissent. Populi Romani hanc esse consuetudinem, ut socios atque amicos non modo sui nihil deperdere, sed gratia, dignitate, honore auctiores velit esse; quod vero ad amicitiam populi Romani attulissent, id iis eripi quis pati posset? Postulavit deinde eadem quae legatis in mandatis dederat: ne aut Haeduis aut eorum sociis bellum inferret, obsides redderet, si nullam partem Germanorum domum remittere posset, at ne quos amplius Rhenum transire pateretur.

Ariovistus ad postulata Caesaris pauca respondit, de suis virtutibus multa praedicavit: transisse Rhenum sese non sua sponte, sed rogatum et arcessitum a Gallis; non sine magna spe magnisque praemiis domum propinquosque reliquisse; sedes habere in Gallia ab ipsis concessas, obsides ipsorum voluntate datos; stipendium capere iure belli, quod victores victis imponere consuerint. Non sese Gallis sed Gallos sibi bellum intulisse: omnes Galliae civitates ad se oppugnandum venisse ac contra se castra habuisse; eas omnes copias a se uno proelio pulsas ac superatas esse. Si iterum experiri velint, se iterum paratum esse decertare; si pace uti velint, iniquum esse de stipendio recusare, quod sua voluntate ad id tempus pependerint. Amicitiam populi Romani sibi ornamento et praesidio, non detrimento esse oportere, atque se hac spe petisse. Si per populum Romanum stipendium remittatur et dediticii subtrahantur, non minus libenter sese recusaturum populi Romani amicitiam quam adpetierit. Quod multitudinem Germanorum in Galliam traducat, id se sui muniendi, non Galliae oppugnandae causa facere; eius rei testimonium esse quod nisi rogatus non venerit et quod bellum non intulerit sed defenderit. Se prius in Galliam venisse quam populum Romanum. Numquam ante hoc tempus exercitum populi Romani Galliae provinciae finibus egressum. Quid sibi vellet? Cur in suas possessiones veniret? Provinciam suam hanc esse Galliam, sicut illam nostram. Ut ipsi concedi non oporteret, si in nostros fines impetum

As it ought not to be pardoned in him, if he were to make an attack upon our territories; so, likewise, that we were unjust, to obstruct him in his prerogative. As for Caesar's saying that the Aedui had been styled 'brethren' by the senate, he was not so uncivilized nor so ignorant of affairs, as not to know that the Aedui in the very last war with the Allobroges had neither rendered assistance to the Romans, nor received any from the Roman people in the struggles which the Aedui had been maintaining with him and with the Sequani. He must feel suspicious, that Caesar, though feigning friendship as the reason for his keeping an army in Gaul, was keeping it with the view of crushing him. And that unless he depart and withdraw his army from these parts, he shall regard him not as a friend, but as a foe; and that, even if he should put him to death, he should do what would please many of the nobles and leading men of the Roman people; he had assurance of that from themselves through their messengers, and could purchase the favor and the friendship of them all by his [Caesar's] death. But if he would depart and resign to him the free possession of Gaul, he would recompense him with a great reward, and would bring to a close whatever wars he wished to be carried on, without any trouble or risk to him."

1:45 Many things were stated by Caesar to the effect [to show]; "why he could not waive the business, and that neither his nor the Roman people's practice would suffer him to abandon most meritorious allies, nor did he deem that Gaul belonged to Ariovistus rather than to the Roman people; that the Arverni and the Ruteni had been subdued in war by Quintus Fabius Maximus, and that the Roman people had pardoned them and had not reduced them into a province or imposed a tribute upon them. And if the most ancient period was to be regarded-then was the sovereignty of the Roman people in Gaul most just: if the decree of the Senate was to be observed, then ought Gaul to be free, which they [the Romans] had conquered in war, and had permitted to enjoy its own laws."

1:46 While these things are being transacted in the conference it was announced to Caesar that the cavalry of Ariovistus were approaching nearer the mound, and were riding up to our men, and casting stones and weapons at them. Caesar made an end of his speech and betook himself to his men; and commanded them that they should by no means return a weapon upon the enemy. For though he saw that an engagement with the cavalry would be without any danger to his chosen legion, yet he did not think proper to engage, lest, after the enemy were routed, it might be said that they had been insnared by him under the sanction of a conference. When it was spread abroad among the common soldiery with what haughtiness Ariovistus had

faceret, sic item nos esse iniquos, quod in suo iure se interpellaremus. Quod fratres a senatu Haeduos appellatos diceret, non se tam barbarum neque tam imperitum esse rerum ut non sciret neque bello Allobrogum proximo Haeduos Romanis auxilium tulisse neque ipsos in iis contentionibus quas Haedui secum et cum Sequanis habuissent auxilio populi Romani usos esse. Debere se suspicari simulata Caesarem amicitia, quod exercitum in Gallia habeat, sui opprimendi causa habere. Qui nisi decedat atque exercitum deducat ex his regionibus, sese illum non pro amico sed pro hoste habiturum. Quod si eum interfecerit, multis sese nobilibus principibusque populi Romani gratum esse facturum (id se ab ipsis per eorum nuntios compertum habere), quorum omnium gratiam atque amicitiam eius morte redimere posset. Quod si decessisset et liberam possessionem Galliae sibi tradidisset, magno se illum praemio remuneraturum et quaecumque bella geri vellet sine ullo eius labore et periculo confecturum.

Multa a Caesare in eam sententiam dicta sunt quare negotio desistere non posset: neque suam neque populi Romani consuetudinem pati ut optime meritos socios desereret, neque se iudicare Galliam potius esse Ariovisti quam populi Romani. Bello superatos esse Arvernos et Rutenos a Q. Fabio Maximo, quibus populus Romanus ignovisset neque in provinciam redegisset neque stipendium posuisset. Quod si antiquissimum quodque tempus spectari oporteret, populi Romani iustissimum esse in Gallia imperium; si iudicium senatus observari oporteret, liberam debere esse Galliam, quam bello victam suis legibus uti voluisset.

Dum haec in conloquio geruntur, Caesari nuntiatum est equites Ariovisti propius tumulum accedere et ad nostros adequitare, lapides telaque in nostros coicere. Caesar loquendi finem fecit seque ad suos recepit suisque imperavit ne quod omnino telum in hostes reicerent. Nam etsi sine ullo periculo legionis delectae cum equitatu proelium fore videbat, tamen committendum non putabat ut, pulsis hostibus, dici posset eos ab se per fidem in conloquio circumventos. Postea quam in vulgus militum elatum est qua arrogantia in conloquio Ariovistus usus omni Gallia Romanis interdixisset, impetumque in nostros

behaved at the conference, and how he had ordered the Romans to quit Gaul, and how his cavalry had made an attack upon our men, and how this had broken off the conference, a much greater alacrity and eagerness for battle was infused into our army.

1:47 Two days after, Ariovistus sends embassadors to Caesar, to state "that he wished to treat with him about those things which had been begun to be treated of between them, but had not been concluded;" [and to beg] that "he would either again appoint a day for a conference; or, if he were not willing to do that, that he would send one of his [officers] as an embassador to him." There did not appear to Caesar any good reason for holding a conference; and the more so as the day before the Germans could not be restrained from casting weapons at our men. He thought he should not without great danger send to him as embassador one of his [Roman] officers, and should expose him to savage men. It seemed [therefore] most proper to send to him C. Valerius Procillus, the son of C. Valerius Caburus, a young man of the highest courage and accomplishments (whose father had been presented with the freedom of the city by C. Valerius Flaccus), both on account of his fidelity and on account of his knowledge of the Gallic language, which Ariovistus, by long practice, now spoke fluently; and because in his case the Germans would have no motive for committing violence; and [as his colleague] M. Mettius, who had shared the hospitality of Ariovistus. He commissioned them to learn what Ariovistus had to say, and to report to him. But when Ariovistus saw them before him in his camp, he cried out in the presence of his army, "Why were they come to him? Was it for the purpose of acting as spies?" He stopped them when attempting to speak, and cast them into chains.

1:48 The same day he moved his camp forward and pitched under a hill six miles from Caesar's camp. The day following he led his forces past Caesar's camp, and encamped two miles beyond him; with this design that he might cut off Caesar from the corn and provisions, which might be conveyed to him from the Sequani and the Aedui. For five successive days from that day, Caesar drew out his forces before the camp, and put them in battle order, that, if Ariovistus should be willing to engage in battle, an opportunity might not be wanting to him. Ariovistus all this time kept his army in camp: but engaged daily in cavalry skirmishes. The method of battle in which the Germans had practiced themselves was this. There were 6,000 horse, and as many very active and courageous foot, one of whom each of the horse selected out of the whole army for his own protection. By these [foot] they were constantly accompanied in their

eius equites fecissent, eaque res conloquium ut diremisset, multo maior alacritas studiumque pugnandi maius exercitui iniectum est.

Biduo post Ariovistus ad Caesarem legatos misit: velle se de iis rebus quae inter eos egi coeptae neque perfectae essent agere cum eo: uti aut iterum conloquio diem constitueret aut, si id minus vellet, ex suis legatis aliquem ad se mitteret. Conloquendi Caesari causa visa non est, et eo magis quod pridie eius diei Germani retineri non potuerant quin tela in nostros coicerent. Legatum ex suis sese magno cum periculo ad eum missurum et hominibus feris obiecturum existimabat. Commodissimum visum est C. Valerium Procillum, C. Valerii Caburi filium, summa virtute et humanitate adulescentem, cuius pater a C. Valerio Flacco civitate donatus erat, et propter fidem et propter linguae Gallicae scientiam, qua multa iam Ariovistus longinqua consuetudine utebatur, et quod in eo peccandi Germanis causa non esset, ad eum mittere, et una M. Metium, qui hospitio Ariovisti utebatur. His mandavit quae diceret Ariovistus cognoscerent et ad se referrent. Quos cum apud se in castris Ariovistus conspexisset, exercitu suo praesente conclamavit: quid ad se venirent? an speculandi causa? Conantes dicere prohibuit et in catenas coniecit.

Eodem die castra promovit et milibus passuum VI a Caesaris castris sub monte consedit. Postridie eius diei praeter castra Caesaris suas copias traduxit et milibus passuum duobus ultra eum castra fecit eo consilio uti frumento commeatuque qui ex Sequanis et Haeduis supportaretur Caesarem intercluderet. Ex eo die dies continuos V Caesar pro castris suas copias produxit et aciem instructam habuit, ut, si vellet Ariovistus proelio contendere, ei potestas non deesset. Ariovistus his omnibus diebus exercitum castris continuit, equestri proelio cotidie contendit. Genus hoc erat pugnae, quo se Germani exercuerant: equitum milia erant VI, totidem numero pedites velocissimi ac fortissimi, quos ex omni copia singuli singulos suae salutis causa delegerant: cum

engagements; to these the horse retired; these on any emergency rushed forward; if any one, upon receiving a very severe wound, had fallen from his horse, they stood around him: if it was necessary to advance further than usual, or to retreat more rapidly, so great, from practice, was their swiftness, that, supported by the manes of the horses, they could keep pace with their speed.

1:49 Perceiving that Ariovistus kept himself in camp, Caesar, that he might not any longer be cut off from provisions, chose a convenient position for a camp beyond that place in which the Germans had encamped, at about 600 paces from them, and having drawn up his army in three lines, marched to that place. He ordered the first and second lines to be under arms; the third to fortify the camp. This place was distant from the enemy about 600 paces, as has been stated. Thither Ariovistus sent light troops, about 16,000 men in number, with all his cavalry; which forces were to intimidate our men, and hinder them in their fortification. Caesar nevertheless, as he had before arranged, ordered two lines to drive off the enemy: the third to execute the work. The camp being fortified, he left there two legions and a portion of the auxiliaries; and led back the other four legions into the larger camp.

1:50 The next day, according to his custom, Caesar led out his forces from both camps, and having advanced a little from the larger one, drew up his line of battle, and gave the enemy an opportunity of fighting. When he found that they did not even then come out [from their intrenchments,] he led back his army into camp about noon. Then at last Ariovistus sent part of his forces to attack the lesser camp. The battle was vigorously maintained on both sides till the evening. At sunset, after many wounds had been inflicted and received, Ariovistus led back his forces into camp. When Caesar inquired of his prisoners, wherefore Ariovistus did not come to an engagement, he discovered this to be the reason-that among the Germans it was the custom for their matrons to pronounce from lots and divination, whether it were expedient that the battle should be engaged in or not; that they had said, "that it was not the will of heaven that the Germans should conquer, if they engaged in battle before the new moon."

1:51 The day following, Caesar left what seemed sufficient as a guard for both camps; [and then] drew up all the auxiliaries in sight of the enemy, before the lesser camp, because he was not very powerful in the number of legionary soldiers, considering the number of the enemy; that [thereby] he might make use of his auxiliaries for appearance. He himself, having drawn up his army in three lines, advanced to the camp of the

his in proeliis versabantur, ad eos se equites recipiebant; hi, si quid erat durius, concurrebant, si qui graviore vulnere accepto equo deciderat, circumsistebant; si quo erat longius prodeundum aut celerius recipiendum, tanta erat horum exercitatione celeritas ut iubis sublevati equorum cursum adaequarent.

Ubi eum castris se tenere Caesar intellexit, ne diutius commeatu prohiberetur, ultra eum locum, quo in loco Germani consederant, circiter passus DC ab his, castris idoneum locum delegit acieque triplici instructa ad eum locum venit. Primam et secundam aciem in armis esse, tertiam castra munire iussit. Hic locus ab hoste circiter passus DC, uti dictum est, aberat. Eo circiter hominum XVI milia expedita cum omni equitatu Ariovistus misit, quae copiae nostros terrerent et munitione prohiberent. Nihilo setius Caesar, ut ante constituerat, duas acies hostem propulsare, tertiam opus perficere iussit. Munitis castris duas ibi legiones reliquit et partem auxiliorum, quattuor reliquas legiones in castra maiora reduxit.

Proximo die instituto suo Caesar ex castris utrisque copias suas eduxit paulumque a maioribus castris progressus aciem instruxit hostibusque pugnandi potestatem fecit. Ubi ne tum quidem eos prodire intellexit, circiter meridiem exercitum in castra reduxit. Tum demum Ariovistus partem suarum copiarum, quae castra minora oppugnaret, misit. Acriter utrimque usque ad vesperum pugnatum est. Solis occasu suas copias Ariovistus multis et inlatis et acceptis vulneribus in castra reduxit. Cum ex captivis quaereret Caesar quam ob rem Ariovistus proelio non decertaret, hanc reperiebat causam, quod apud Germanos ea consuetudo esset ut matres familiae eorum sortibus et vaticinationibus declararent utrum proelium committi ex usu esset necne; eas ita dicere: non esse fas Germanos superare, si ante novam lunam proelio contendissent.

Postridie eius diei Caesar praesidio utrisque castris quod satis esse visum est reliquit, alarios omnes in conspectu hostium pro castris minoribus constituit, quod minus multitudine militum legionariorum pro hostium numero valebat, ut ad speciem alariis uteretur; ipse triplici instructa acie usque ad castra hostium accessit. Tum demum necessario Germani

enemy. Then at last of necessity the Germans drew their forces out of camp, and disposed them canton by canton, at equal distances, the Harudes, Marcomanni, Tribocci, Vangiones, Nemetes, Sedusii, Suevi; and surrounded their whole army with their chariots and wagons, that no hope might be left in flight. On these they placed their women, who, with disheveled hair and in tears, entreated the soldiers, as they went forward to battle, not to deliver them into slavery to the Romans.

1:52 Caesar appointed over each legion a lieutenant and a questor, that every one might have them as witnesses of his valor. He himself began the battle at the head of the right wing, because he had observed that part of the enemy to be the least strong. Accordingly our men, upon the signal being given, vigorously made an attack upon the enemy, and the enemy so suddenly and rapidly rushed forward, that there was no time for casting the javelins at them. Throwing aside [therefore] their javelins, they fought with swords hand to hand. But the Germans, according to their custom, rapidly forming a phalanx, sustained the attack of our swords. There were found very many of our soldiers who leaped upon the phalanx, and with their hands tore away the shields, and wounded the enemy from above. Although the army of the enemy was routed on the left wing and put to flight, they [still] pressed heavily on our men from the right wing, by the great number of their troops. On observing which, P. Crassus, a young man, who commanded the cavalry-as he was more disengaged than those who were employed in the fight-sent the third line as a relief to our men who were in distress.

1:53 Thereupon the engagement was renewed, and all the enemy turned their backs, nor did they cease to flee until they arrived at the river Rhine, about fifty miles from that place. There some few, either relying on their strength, endeavored to swim over, or, finding boats, procured their safety. Among the latter was Ariovistus, who meeting with a small vessel tied to the bank, escaped in it; our horse pursued and slew all the rest of them. Ariovistus had two wives, one a Suevan by nation, whom he brought with him from home; the other a Norican, the sister of king Vocion, whom he had married in Gaul, she having been sent [thither for that purpose] by her brother. Both perished in that flight. Of their two daughters, one was slain, the other captured. C. Valerius Procillus, as he was being dragged by his guards in the fight, bound with a triple chain, fell into the hands of Caesar himself, as he was pursuing the enemy with his cavalry. This circumstance indeed afforded Caesar no less pleasure than the victory itself; because he saw a man of the first rank in the province of Gaul, his intimate acquaintance and friend, rescued from the hand of the enemy, and restored to

suas copias castris eduxerunt generatimque constituerunt paribus intervallis, Harudes, Marcomanos, Tribocos, Vangiones, Nemetes, Sedusios, Suebos, omnemque aciem suam raedis et carris circumdederunt, ne qua spes in fuga relinqueretur. Eo mulieres imposuerunt, quae ad proelium proficiscentes milites passis manibus flentes implorabant ne se in servitutem Romanis traderent.

Caesar singulis legionibus singulos legatos et quaestorem praefecit, uti eos testes suae quisque virtutis haberet; ipse a dextro cornu, quod eam partem minime firmam hostium esse animadverterat, proelium commisit. Ita nostri acriter in hostes signo dato impetum fecerunt itaque hostes repente celeriterque procurrerunt, ut spatium pila in hostes coiciendi non daretur. Relictis pilis comminus gladiis pugnatum est. At Germani celeriter ex consuetudine sua phalange facta impetus gladiorum exceperunt. Reperti sunt complures nostri qui in phalanga insilirent et scuta manibus revellerent et desuper vulnerarent. Cum hostium acies a sinistro cornu pulsa atque in fugam coniecta esset, a dextro cornu vehementer multitudine suorum nostram aciem premebant. Id cum animadvertisset P. Crassus adulescens, qui equitatui praeerat, quod expeditior erat quam ii qui inter aciem versabantur, tertiam aciem laborantibus nostris subsidio misit.

Ita proelium restitutum est, atque omnes hostes terga verterunt nec prius fugere destiterunt quam ad flumen Rhenum milia passuum ex eo loco circiter L pervenerunt. Ibi perpauci aut viribus confisi tranare contenderunt aut lintribus inventis sibi salutem reppererunt. In his fuit Ariovistus, qui naviculam deligatam ad ripam nactus ea profugit; reliquos omnes consecuti equites nostri interfecerunt. Duae fuerunt Ariovisti uxores, una Sueba natione, quam domo secum eduxerat, altera Norica, regis Voccionis soror, quam in Gallia duxerat a fratre missam: utraque in ea fuga periit; duae filiae: harum altera occisa, altera capta est. C. Valerius Procillus, cum a custodibus in fuga trinis catenis vinctus traheretur, in ipsum Caesarem hostes equitatu insequentem incidit. Quae quidem res Caesari non minorem quam ipsa victoria voluptatem attulit, quod hominem honestissimum provinciae Galliae, suum familiarem et hospitem, ereptum ex manibus hostium sibi restitutum

him, and that fortune had not diminished aught of the joy and exultation [of that day] by his destruction. He [Procillus] said that, in his own presence, the lots had been thrice consulted respecting him, whether he should immediately be put to death by fire, or be reserved for another time: that by the favor of the lots he was uninjured. M. Mettius, also, was found and brought back to him [Caesar.]

1:54 This battle having been reported beyond the Rhine, the Suevi, who had come to the banks of that river, began to return home, when the Ubii, who dwelt nearest to the Rhine, pursuing them, while much alarmed, slew a great number of them. Caesar having concluded two very important wars in one campaign, conducted his army into winter quarters among the Sequani, a little earlier than the season of the year required. He appointed Labienus over the winter-quarters, and set out in person for Hither Gaul to hold the assizes.

videbat neque eius calamitate de tanta voluptate et gratulatione quicquam fortuna deminuerat. Is se praesente de se ter sortibus consultum dicebat, utrum igni statim necaretur an in aliud tempus reservaretur: sortium beneficio se esse incolumem. Item M. Metius repertus et ad eum reductus est.

Hoc proelio trans Rhenum nuntiato, Suebi, qui ad ripas Rheni venerant, domum reverti coeperunt; quos ubi qui proximi Rhenum incolunt perterritos senserunt, insecuti magnum ex iis numerum occiderunt. Caesar una aestate duobus maximis bellis confectis maturius paulo quam tempus anni postulabat in hiberna in Sequanos exercitum deduxit; hibernis Labienum praeposuit; ipse in citeriorem Galliam ad conventus agendos profectus est.

Gallic Wars Book 2 (57 B.C.E.)

2:1 While Caesar was in winter quarters in Hither Gaul, as we have shown above, frequent reports were brought to him, and he was also informed by letters from Labienus, that all the Belgae, who we have said are a third part of Gaul, were entering into a confederacy against the Roman people, and giving hostages to one another; that the reasons of the confederacy were these-first, because they feared that, after all [Celtic] Gaul was subdued, our army would be led against them; secondly, because they were instigated by several of the Gauls; some of whom as [on the one hand] they had been unwilling that the Germans should remain any longer in Gaul, so [on the other] they were dissatisfied that the army of the Roman people should pass the winter in it, and settle there; and others of them, from a natural instability and fickleness of disposition, were anxious for a revolution; [the Belgae were instigated] by several, also, because the government in Gaul was generally seized upon by the more powerful persons and by those who had the means of hiring troops, and they could less easily effect this object under our dominion.

2:2 Alarmed by these tidings and letters, Caesar levied two new legions in Hither Gaul, and, at the beginning of summer, sent Q. Pedius, his lieutenant, to conduct them further into Gaul. He, himself, as soon as there began to be plenty of forage, came to the army. He gives a commission to the Senones and the other Gauls who were neighbors of the Belgae, to learn what is going on among them [i.e. the Belgae], and inform him of these matters. These all uniformly reported that troops were being raised, and that an army was being collected in one place. Then, indeed, he thought that he ought not to hesitate about proceeding toward them, and having provided supplies, moves his camp, and in about fifteen days arrives at the territories of the Belgae.

2:3 As he arrived there unexpectedly and sooner than any one anticipated, the Remi, who are the nearest of the Belgae to [Celtic] Gaul, sent to him Iccius and Antebrogius, [two of] the principal persons of the state, as their embassadors: to tell him that they surrendered themselves and all their possessions to the protection and disposal of the Roman people: and that they had neither combined with the rest of the Belgae, nor entered into any confederacy against the Roman people: and were prepared to give hostages, to obey his commands, to receive him into their towns, and to aid him with corn and other things; that all the rest of the Belgae were in arms; and that the Germans, who dwell on this side of the Rhine, had joined themselves to them; and that so

Cum esset Caesar in citeriore Gallia [in hibernis], ita uti supra demonstravimus, crebri ad eum rumores adferebantur litterisque item Labieni certior fiebat omnes Belgas, quam tertiam esse Galliae partem dixeramus, contra populum Romanum coniurare obsidesque inter se dare. Coniurandi has esse causas: primum quod vererentur ne, omni pacata Gallia, ad eos exercitus noster adduceretur; deinde quod ab non nullis Gallis sollicitarentur, partim qui, ut Germanos diutius in Gallia versari noluerant, ita populi Romani exercitum hiemare atque inveterascere in Gallia moleste ferebant, partim qui mobilitate et levitate animi novis imperiis studebant; ab non nullis etiam quod in Gallia a potentioribus atque iis qui ad conducendos homines facultates habebant vulgo regna occupabantur; qui minus facile eam rem imperio nostro consequi poterant.

His nuntiis litterisque commotus Caesar duas legiones in citeriore Gallia novas conscripsit et inita aestate in ulteriorem Galliam qui deduceret Q. Pedium legatum misit. Ipse, cum primum pabuli copia esse inciperet, ad exercitum venit. Dat negotium Senonibus reliquisque Gallis qui finitimi Belgis erant uti ea quae apud eos gerantur cognoscant seque de his rebus certiorem faciant. Hi constanter omnes nuntiaverunt manus cogi, exercitum in unum locum conduci. Tum vero dubitandum non existimavit quin ad eos proficisceretur. Re frumentaria provisa castra movet diebusque circiter XV ad fines Belgarum pervenit.

Eo cum de improviso celeriusque omnium opinione venisset, Remi, qui proximi Galliae ex Belgis sunt, ad eum legatos Iccium et Andebrogium, primos civitatis, miserunt, qui dicerent se suaque omnia in fidem atque potestatem populi Romani permittere, neque se cum reliquis Belgis consensisse neque contra populum Romanum coniurasse, paratosque esse et obsides dare et imperata facere et oppidis recipere et frumento ceterisque rebus iuvare; reliquos omnes Belgas in armis esse, Germanosque qui cis Rhenum incolant sese cum

great was the infatuation of them all, that they could not restrain even the Suessiones, their own brethren and kinsmen, who enjoy the same rights, and the, same laws, and who have one government and one magistracy [in common] with themselves, from uniting with them.

2:4 When Caesar inquired of them what states were in arms, how powerful they were, and what they could do, in war, he received the following information: that the greater part of the Belgae were sprung, from the Germans, and that having crossed the Rhine at an early period, they had settled there, on account of the fertility of the country, and had driven out the Gauls who inhabited those regions; and that they were the only people who, in the memory of our fathers, when all Gaul was overrun, had prevented the Teutones and the Cimbri from entering their territories; the effect of which was, that, from the recollection of those events, they assumed to themselves great authority and haughtiness in military matters. The Remi said, that they had known accurately every thing respecting their number, because being united to them by neighborhood and by alliances, they had learned what number each state had in the general council of the Belgae promised for that war. That the Bellovaci were the most powerful among them in valor, influence, and the number of men; that these could muster 100,000 armed men, [and had] promised 60,000 picked men out of that number, and demanded for themselves the command of the whole war. That the Suessiones were their nearest neighbors and possessed a very extensive and fertile country; that among them, even in our own memory, Divitiacus, the most powerful man of all Gaul, had been king; who had held the government of a great part of these regions, as well as of Britain; that their king at present was Galba; that the direction of the whole war was conferred by the consent of all, upon him, on account of his integrity and prudence; that they had twelve towns; that they had promised 50,000 armed men; and that the Nervii, who are reckoned the most warlike among them, and are situated at a very great distance, [had promised] as many; the Atrebates 15,000; the Ambiani, 10,000; the Morini, 25,000; the Menapii, 9,000; the Caleti, 10,000; the Velocasses and the Veromandui as many; the Aduatuci 19,000; that the Condrusi, the Eburones, the Caeraesi, the Paemani, who are called by the common name of Germans [had promised], they thought, to the number of 40,000.

2:5 Caesar, having encouraged the Remi, and addressed them courteously, ordered the whole senate to assemble before him, and the children of their chief men to be brought to him as hostages; all which commands they punctually performed by the day [appointed]. He, addressing himself to Divitiacus, the Aeduan,

his coniunxisse, tantumque esse eorum omnium furorem ut ne Suessiones quidem, fratres consanguineosque suos, qui eodem iure et isdem legibus utantur, unum imperium unumque magistratum cum ipsis habeant, deterrere potuerint quin cum iis consentirent.

Cum ab iis quaereret quae civitates quantaeque in armis essent et quid in bello possent, sic reperiebat: plerosque Belgos esse ortos a Germanis Rhenumque antiquitus traductos propter loci fertilitatem ibi consedisse Gallosque qui ea loca incolerent expulisse, solosque esse qui, patrum nostrorum memoria omni Gallia vexata, Teutonos Cimbrosque intra suos fines ingredi prohibuerint; qua ex re fieri uti earum rerum memoria magnam sibi auctoritatem magnosque spiritus in re militari sumerent. De numero eorum omnia se habere explorata Remi dicebant, propterea quod propinquitatibus adfinitatibus quo coniuncti quantam quisque multitudinem in communi Belgarum concilio ad id bellum pollicitus sit cognoverint. Plurimum inter eos Bellovacos et virtute et auctoritate et hominum numero valere: hos posse conficere armata milia centum, pollicitos ex eo numero electa milia LX totiusque belli imperium sibi postulare. Suessiones suos esse finitimos; fines latissimos feracissimosque agros possidere. Apud eos fuisse regem nostra etiam memoria Diviciacum, totius Galliae potentissimum, qui cum magnae partis harum regionum, tum etiam Britanniae imperium obtinuerit; nunc esse regem Galbam: ad hunc propter iustitiam prudentiamque summam totius belli omnium voluntate deferri; oppida habere numero XII, polliceri milia armata L; totidem Nervios, qui maxime feri inter ipsos habeantur longissimeque absint; XV milia Atrebates, Ambianos X milia, Morinos XXV milia, Menapios VII milia, Caletos X milia, Veliocasses et Viromanduos totidem, Atuatucos XVIIII milia; Condrusos, Eburones, Caerosos, Paemanos, qui uno nomine Germani appellantur, arbitrari ad XL milia.

Caesar Remos cohortatus liberaliterque oratione prosecutus omnem senatum ad se convenire principumque liberos obsides ad se adduci iussit. Quae omnia ab his diligenter ad diem facta sunt. Ipse Diviciacum Haeduum magnopere cohortatus

with great earnestness, points out how much it concerns the republic and their common security, that the forces of the enemy should be divided, so that it might not be necessary to engage with so large a number at one time. [He asserts] that this might be affected if the Aedui would lead their forces into the territories of the Bellovaci, and begin to lay waste their country. With these instructions he dismissed him from his presence. After he perceived that all the forces of the Belgae, which had been collected in one place, were approaching toward him, and learned from the scouts whom he had sent out, and [also] from the Remi, that they were then not far distant, he hastened to lead his army over the Aisne, which is on the borders of the Remi, and there pitched his camp. This position fortified one side of his camp by the banks of the river, rendered the country which lay in his rear secure from the enemy, and furthermore insured that provisions might without danger be brought to him by the Remi and the rest of the states. Over that river was a bridge: there he places a guard; and on the other side of the river he leaves Q. Titurius Sabinus, his lieutenant, with six cohorts. He orders him to fortify a camp with a rampart twelve feet in height, and a trench eighteen feet in breadth.

2:6 There was a town of the Remi, by name Bibrax, eight miles distant from this camp. This the Belgae on their march began to attack with great vigor. [The assault] was with difficulty sustained for that day. The Gauls' mode of besieging is the same as that of the Belgae: when after having drawn a large number of men around the whole of the fortifications, stones have begun to be cast against the wall on all sides, and the wall has been stripped of its defenders, [then], forming a testudo, they advance to the gates and undermine the wall: which was easily effected on this occasion; for while so large a number were casting stones and darts, no one was able to maintain his position upon the wall. When night had put an end to the assault, Iccius, who was then in command of the town, one of the Remi, a man of the highest rank and influence among his people, and one of those who had come to Caesar as embassador [to sue] for peace, sends messengers to him, [to report] "That, unless assistance were sent to him he could not hold out any longer."

2:7 Thither, immediately after midnight, Caesar, using as guides the same persons who had come to him as messengers from Iccius, sends some Numidian and Cretan archers, and some Balearian slingers as a relief to the towns-people, by whose arrival both a desire to resist together with the hope of [making good their] defense, was infused into the Remi, and, for the same reason, the hope of gaining the town, abandoned the enemy. Therefore, after staying a short time before the town, and laying waste the country of the Remi, when all the villages and buildings

docet quanto opere rei publicae communisque salutis intersit manus hostium distineri, ne cum tanta multitudine uno tempore confligendum sit. Id fieri posse, si suas copias Haedui in fines Bellovacorum introduxerint et eorum agros populari coeperint. His datis mandatis eum a se dimittit. Postquam omnes Belgarum copias in unum locum coactas ad se venire vidit neque iam longe abesse ab iis quos miserat exploratoribus et ab Remis cognovit, flumen Axonam, quod est in extremis Remorum finibus, exercitum traducere maturavit atque ibi castra posuit. Quae res et latus unum castrorum ripis fluminis muniebat et post eum quae erant tuta ab hostibus reddebat et commeatus ab Remis reliquisque civitatibus ut sine periculo ad eum portari possent efficiebat. In eo flumine pons erat. Ibi praesidium ponit et in altera parte fluminis Q. Titurium Sabinum legatum cum sex cohortibus relinquit; castra in altitudinem pedum XII vallo fossaque duodeviginti pedum muniri iubet.

Ab his castris oppidum Remorum nomine Bibrax aberat milia passuum VIII. Id ex itinere magno impetu Belgae oppugnare coeperunt. Aegre eo die sustentatum est. Gallorum eadem atque Belgarum oppugnatio est haec: ubi circumiecta multitudine hominum totis moenibus undique in murum lapides iaci coepti sunt murusque defensoribus nudatus est, testudine facta portas succedunt murumque subruunt. Quod tum facile fiebat. Nam cum tanta multitudo lapides ac tela coicerent, in muro consistendi potestas erat nulli. Cum finem oppugnandi nox fecisset, Iccius Remus, summa nobilitate et gratia inter suos, qui tum oppido praeerat, unus ex iis qui legati de pace ad Caesarem venerant, nuntium ad eum mittit, nisi subsidium sibi submittatur, sese diutius sustinere non posse.

Eo de media nocte Caesar isdem ducibus usus qui nuntii ab Iccio venerant, Numidas et Cretas sagittarios et funditores Baleares subsidio oppidanis mittit; quorum adventu et Remis cum spe defensionis studium propugnandi accessit et hostibus eadem de causa spes potiundi oppidi discessit. Itaque paulisper apud oppidum morati agrosque Remorum depopulati, omnibus vicis aedificiisque quo adire potuerant incensis, ad

which they could approach had been burned, they hastened with all their forces to the camp of Caesar, and encamped within less than two miles [of it]; and their camp, as was indicated by the smoke and fires, extended more than eight miles in breadth.

2:8 Caesar at first determined to decline a battle, as well on account of the great number of the enemy as their distinguished reputation for valor: daily, however, in cavalry actions, he strove to ascertain by frequent trials, what the enemy could effect by their prowess and what our men would dare. When he perceived that our men were not inferior, as the place before the camp was naturally convenient and suitable for marshaling an army (since the hill where the camp was pitched, rising gradually from the plain, extended forward in breadth as far as the space which the marshaled army could occupy, and had steep declines of its side in either direction, and gently sloping in front gradually sank to the plain); on either side of that hill he drew a cross trench of about four hundred paces, and at the extremities of that trench built forts, and placed there his military engines, lest, after he had marshaled his army, the enemy, since they were so powerful in point of number, should be able to surround his men in the flank, while fighting. After doing this, and leaving in the camp the two legions which he had last raised, that, if there should be any occasion, they might be brought as a reserve, he formed the other six legions in order of battle before the camp. The enemy, likewise, had drawn up their forces which they had brought out of the camp.

2:9 There was a marsh of no great extent between our army and that of the enemy. The latter were waiting to see if our men would pass this; our men, also, were ready in arms to attack them while disordered, if the first attempt to pass should be made by them. In the mean time battle was commenced between the two armies by a cavalry action. When neither army began to pass the marsh, Caesar, upon the skirmishes of the horse [proving] favorable to our men, led back his forces into the camp. The enemy immediately hastened from that place to the river Aisne, which it has been stated was behind our camp. Finding a ford there, they endeavored to lead a part of their forces over it; with the design, that, if they could, they might carry by storm the fort which Q. Titurius, Caesar's lieutenant, commanded, and might cut off the bridge; but, if they could not do that, they should lay waste the lands of the Remi, which were of great use to us in carrying on the war, and might hinder our men from foraging.

2:10 Caesar, being apprized of this by Titurius, leads all his cavalry and light-armed Numidians, slingers and archers, over the

castra Caesaris omnibus copiis contenderunt et a milibus passuum minus duobus castra posuerunt; quae castra, ut fumo atque ignibus significabatur, amplius milibus passuum VIII latitudinem patebant.

Caesar primo et propter multitudinem hostium et propter eximiam opinionem virtutis proelio supersedere statuit; cotidie tamen equestribus proeliis quid hostis virtute posset et quid nostri auderent periclitabatur. Ubi nostros non esse inferiores intellexit, loco pro castris ad aciem instruendam natura oportuno atque idoneo, quod is collis ubi castra posita erant paululum ex planitie editus tantum adversus in latitudinem patebat quantum loci acies instructa occupare poterat, atque ex utraque parte lateris deiectus habebat et in fronte leniter fastigatus paulatim ad planitiem redibat, ab utroque latere eius collis transversam fossam obduxit circiter passuum CCCC et ad extremas fossas castella constituit ibique tormenta conlocavit, ne, cum aciem instruxisset, hostes, quod tantum multitudine poterant, ab lateribus pugnantes suos circumvenire possent. Hoc facto, duabus legionibus quas proxime conscripserat in castris relictis ut, si quo opus esset, subsidio duci possent, reliquas VI legiones pro castris in acie constituit. Hostes item suas copias ex castris eductas instruxerunt.

Palus erat non magna inter nostrum atque hostium exercitum. Hanc si nostri transirent hostes expectabant; nostri autem, si ab illis initium transeundi fieret, ut impeditos adgrederentur, parati in armis erant. Interim proelio equestri inter duas acies contendebatur. Ubi neutri transeundi initium faciunt, secundiore equitum proelio nostris Caesar suos in castra reduxit. Hostes protinus ex eo loco ad flumen Axonam contenderunt, quod esse post nostra castra demonstratum est. Ibi vadis repertis partem suarum copiarum traducere conati sunt eo consilio ut, si possent, castellum, cui praeerat Q. Titurius legatus, expugnarent pontemque interscinderent; si minus potuissent, agros Remorum popularentur, qui magno nobis usui ad bellum gerendum erant, commeatuque nostros prohiberent.

[Caesar] certior factus ab Titurio omnem equitatum et levis armaturae Numidas, funditores

bridge, and hastens toward them. There was a severe struggle in that place. Our men, attacking in the river the disordered enemy, slew a great part of them. By the immense number of their missiles they drove back the rest, who, in a most courageous manner were attempting to pass over their bodies, and surrounded with their cavalry, and cut to pieces those who had first crossed the river. The enemy, when they perceived that their hopes had deceived them both with regard to their taking the town by storm and also their passing the river, and did not see our men advance to a more disadvantageous place for the purpose of fighting, and when provisions began to fail them, having called a council, determined that it was best for each to return to his country, and resolved to assemble from all quarters to defend those into whose territories the Romans should first march an army; that they might contend in their own rather than in a foreign country, and might enjoy the stores of provision which they possessed at home. Together with other causes, this consideration also led them to that resolution, viz: that they had learned that Divitiacus and the Aedui were approaching the territories of the Bellovaci. And it was impossible to persuade the latter to stay any longer, or to deter them from conveying succor to their own people.

2:11 That matter being determined on, marching out of their camp at the second watch, with great noise and confusion, in no fixed order, nor under any command, since each sought for himself the foremost place in the journey, and hastened to reach home, they made their departure appear very like a flight. Caesar, immediately learning this through his scouts, [but] fearing an ambuscade, because he had not yet discovered for what reason they were departing, kept his army and cavalry within the camp. At daybreak, the intelligence having been confirmed by the scouts, he sent forward his cavalry to harass their rear; and gave the command of it to two of his lieutenants, Q. Pedius, and L. Aurunculeius Cotta. He ordered T. Labienus, another of his lieutenants, to follow them closely with three legions. These, attacking their rear, and pursuing them for many miles, slew a great number of them as they were fleeing; while those in the rear with whom they had come up, halted, and bravely sustained the attack of our soldiers; the van, because they appeared to be removed from danger, and were not restrained by any necessity or command, as soon as the noise was heard, broke their ranks, and, to a man, rested their safety in flight. Thus without any risk [to themselves] our men killed as great a number of them as the length of the day allowed; and at sunset desisted from the pursuit, and betook themselves into the camp, as they had been commanded.

sagittariosque pontem traducit atque ad eos contendit. Acriter in eo loco pugnatum est. Hostes impeditos nostri in flumine adgressi magnum eorum numerum occiderunt; per eorum corpora reliquos audacissime transire conantes multitudine telorum reppulerunt primosque, qui transierant, equitatu circumventos interfecerunt. Hostes, ubi et de expugnando oppido et de flumine transeundo spem se fefellisse intellexerunt neque nostros in locum iniquiorum progredi pugnandi causa viderunt atque ipsos res frumentaria deficere coepit, concilio convocato constituerunt optimum esse domum suam quemque reverti, et quorum in fines primum Romani exercitum introduxissent, ad eos defendendos undique convenirent, ut potius in suis quam in alienis finibus decertarent et domesticis copiis rei frumentariae uterentur. Ad eam sententiam cum reliquis causis haec quoque ratio eos deduxit, quod Diviciacum atque Haeduos finibus Bellovacorum adpropinquare cognoverant. His persuaderi ut diutius morarentur neque suis auxilium ferrent non poterat.

Ea re constituta, secunda vigilia magno cum, strepitu ac tumultu castris egressi nullo certo ordine neque imperio, cum sibi quisque primum itineris locum peteret et domum pervenire properaret, fecerunt ut consimilis fugae profectio videretur. Hac re statim Caesar per speculatores cognita insidias veritus, quod qua de causa discederent nondum perspexerat, exercitum equitatumque castris continuit. Prima luce, confirmata re ab exploratoribus, omnem equitatum, qui novissimum agmen moraretur, praemisit. His Q. Pedium et L. Aurunculeium Cottam legatos praefecit; T. Labienum legatum cum legionibus tribus subsequi iussit. Hi novissimos adorti et multa milia passuum prosecuti magnam multitudinem eorum fugientium conciderunt, cum ab extremo agmine, ad quos ventum erat, consisterent fortiterque impetum nostrorum militum sustinerent, priores, quod abesse a periculo viderentur neque ulla necessitate neque imperio continerentur, exaudito clamore perturbatis ordinibus omnes in fuga sibi praesidium ponerent. Ita sine ullo periculo tantam eorum multitudinem nostri interfecerunt quantum fuit diei spatium; sub occasum solis sequi

2:12 On the day following, before the enemy could recover from their terror and flight, Caesar led his army into the territories of the Suessiones, which are next to the Remi, and having accomplished a long march, hastens to the town named Noviodunum. Having attempted to take it by storm on his march, because he heard that it was destitute of [sufficient] defenders, he was not able to carry it by assault, on account of the breadth of the ditch and the height of the wall, though few were defending it. Therefore, having fortified the camp, he began to bring up the vineae, and to provide whatever things were necessary for the storm. In the mean time the whole body of the Suessiones, after their flight, came the next night into the town. The vineae having been quickly brought up against the town, a mound thrown up, and towers built, the Gauls, amazed by the greatness of the works, such as they had neither seen nor heard of before, and struck also by the dispatch of the Romans, send embassadors to Caesar respecting a surrender, and succeed in consequence of the Remi requesting that they [the Suessiones] might be spared.

2:13 Caesar, having received as hostages the first men of the state, and even the two sons of king Galba himself; and all the arms in the town having been delivered up, admitted the Suessiones to a surrender, and led his army against the Bellovaci. Who, when they had conveyed themselves and all their possessions into the town Galled Bratuspantium, and Caesar with his army was about five miles distant from that town, all the old men, going out of the town, began to stretch out their hands to Caesar, and to intimate by their voice that they would throw themselves on his protection and power, nor would contend in arms against the Roman people. In like manner, when he had come up to the town, and there pitched his camp, the boys and the women from the wall, with outstretched hands, after their custom, begged peace from the Romans.

2:14 For these Divitiacus pleads (for after the departure of the Belgae, having dismissed the troops of the Aedui, he had returned to Caesar). "The Bellovaci had at all times been in the alliance and friendship of the Aeduan state; that they had revolted from the Aedui and made war upon the Roman people, being urged thereto by their nobles, who said that the Aedui, reduced to slavery by Caesar, were suffering every indignity and insult. That they who had been the leaders of that plot, because they perceived how great a calamity they had brought upon the state, had fled into Britain. That not only the Bellovaci, but also the Aedui, entreated him to use his [accustomed] clemency and lenity toward them [the Bellovaci]: which if he did, he would increase the influence of the

destiterunt seque in castra, ut erat imperatum, receperunt.

Postridie eius diei Caesar, prius quam se hostes ex terrore ac fuga reciperent, in fines Suessionum, qui proximi Remis erant, exercitum duxit et magno itinere [confecto] ad oppidum Noviodunum contendit. Id ex itinere oppugnare conatus, quod vacuum ab defensoribus esse audiebat, propter latitudinem fossae murique altitudinem paucis defendentibus expugnare non potuit. Castris munitis vineas agere quaeque ad oppugnandum usui erant comparare coepit. Interim omnis ex fuga Suessionum multitudo in oppidum proxima nocte convenit. Celeriter vineis ad oppidum actis, aggere iacto turribusque constitutis, magnitudine operum, quae neque viderant ante Galli neque audierant, et celeritate Romanorum permoti legatos ad Caesarem de deditione mittunt et petentibus Remis ut conservarentur impetrant.

Caesar, obsidibus acceptis primis civitatis atque ipsius Galbae regis duobus filiis armisque omnibus ex oppido traditis, in deditionem Suessiones accipit exercitumque in Bellovacos ducit. Qui cum se suaque omnia in oppidum Bratuspantium contulissent atque ab eo oppido Caesar cum exercitu circiter milia passuum V abesset, omnes maiores natu ex oppido egressi manus ad Caesarem tendere et voce significare coeperunt sese in eius fidem ac potestatem venire neque contra populum Romanum armis contendere. Item, cum ad oppidum accessisset castraque ibi poneret, pueri mulieresque ex muro passis manibus suo more pacem ab Romanis petierunt.

Pro his Diviciacus (nam post discessum Belgarum dimissis Haeduorum copiis ad eum reverterat) facit verba: Bellovacos omni tempore in fide atque amicitia civitatis Haeduae fuisse; impulsos ab suis principibus, qui dicerent Haeduos a Caesare in servitutem redacto. Omnes indignitates contumeliasque perferre, et ab Haeduis defecisse et populo Romano bellum intulisse. Qui eius consilii principes fuissent, quod intellegerent quantam calamitatem civitati intulissent, in Britanniam profugisse. Petere non solum Bellovacos, sed etiam pro his Haeduos, ut sua

Aedui among all the Belgae, by whose succor and resources they had been accustomed to support themselves whenever any wars occurred."

2:15 Caesar said that on account of his respect for Divitiacus and the Aeduans, he would receive them into his protection, and would spare them; but, because the state was of great influence among the Belgae, and pre-eminent in the number of its population, he demanded 600 hostages. When these were delivered, and all the arms in the town collected, he went from that place into the territories of the Ambiani, who, without delay, surrendered themselves and all their possessions. Upon their territories bordered the Nervii, concerning whose character and customs when Caesar inquired he received the following information:--That there was no access for merchants to them; that they suffered no wine and other things tending to luxury to be imported; because, they thought that by their use the mind is enervated and the courage impaired: that they were a savage people and of great bravery: that they upbraided and condemned the rest of the Belgae who had surrendered themselves to the Roman people and thrown aside their national courage: that they openly declared they would neither send embassadors, nor accept any condition of peace."

2:16 After he had made three days march through their territories, he discovered from some prisoners, that the river Sambre was not more than ten miles from his camp; that all the Nervii had stationed themselves on the other side of that river, and together with the Atrebates and the Veromandui, their neighbors, were there awaiting the arrival of the Romans; for they had persuaded both these nations to try the same fortune of war [as themselves]: that the forces of the Aduatuci were also expected by them, and were on their march; that they had put their women, and those who through age appeared useless for war, in a place to which there was no approach for an army, on account of the marshes.

2:17 Having learned these things, he sends forward scouts and centurions to choose a convenient place for the camp. And as a great many of the surrounding Belgae and other Gauls, following Caesar, marched with him; some of these, as was afterwards learned from the prisoners, having accurately observed, during those days, the army's method of marching, went by night to the Nervii, and informed them that a great number of baggage-trains passed between the several legions, and that there would be no difficulty, when the first legion had come into the camp, and the other legions were at a great distance, to attack that legion while

clementia ac mansuetudine in eos utatur. Quod si fecerit, Haeduorum auctoritatem apud omnes Belgas amplificaturum, quorum auxiliis atque opibus, si qua bella inciderint, sustentare consuerint.

Caesar honoris Diviciaci atque Haeduorum causa sese eos in fidem recepturum et conservaturum dixit, et quod erat civitas magna inter Belgas auctoritate atque hominum multitudine praestabat, DC obsides poposcit. His traditis omnibusque armis ex oppido conlatis, ab eo loco in fines Ambianorum pervenit; qui se suaque omnia sine mora dediderunt. Eorum fines Nervii attingebant. Quorum de natura moribusque Caesar cum quaereret, sic reperiebat: nullum esse aditum ad eos mercatoribus; nihil pati vini reliquarumque rerum ad luxuriam pertinentium inferri, quod his rebus relanguescere animos eorum et remitti virtutem existimarent; esse homines feros magnaeque virtutis; increpitare atque incusare reliquos Belgas, qui se populo Romano dedidissent patriamque virtutem proiecissent; confirmare sese neque legatos missuros neque ullam condicionem pacis accepturos.

Cum per eorum fines triduum iter fecisset, inveniebat ex captivis Sabim flumen a castris suis non amplius milibus passuum X abesse; trans id flumen omnes Nervios consedisse adventumque ibi Romanorum expectare una cum Atrebatibus et Viromanduis, finitimis suis (nam his utrisque persuaserant uti eandem belli fortunam experirentur); expectari etiam ab iis Atuatucorum copias atque esse in itinere; mulieres quique per aetatem ad pugnam inutiles viderentur in eum locum coniecisse quo propter paludes exercitui aditus non esset.

His rebus cognitis, exploratores centurionesque praemittit qui locum castris idoneum deligant. Cum ex dediticiis Belgis reliquisque Gallis complures Caesarem secuti una iter facerent, quidam ex his, ut postea ex captivis cognitum est, eorum dierum consuetudine itineris nostri exercitus perspecta, nocte ad Nervios pervenerunt atque his demonstrarunt inter singulas legiones impedimentorum magnum numerum intercedere, neque esse quicquam negotii, cum prima legio in

under baggage, which being routed, and the baggage-train seized, it would come to pass that the other legions would not dare to stand their ground. It added weight also to the advice of those who reported that circumstance, that the Nervii, from early times, because they were weak in cavalry, (for not even at this time do they attend to it, but accomplish by their infantry whatever they can,) in order that they might the more easily obstruct the cavalry of their neighbors if they came upon them for the purpose of plundering, having cut young trees, and bent them, by means of their numerous branches [extending] on to the sides, and the quick-briars and thorns springing up between them, had made these hedges present a fortification like a wall, through which it was not only impossible to enter, but even to penetrate with the eye. Since [therefore] the march of our army would be obstructed by these things, the Nervii thought that the advice ought not to be neglected by them.

2:18 The nature of the ground which our men had chosen for the camp was this: A hill, declining evenly from the top, extending to the river Sambre, which we have mentioned above: from this river there arose a [second] hill of like ascent, on the other side and opposite to the former, and open for about 200 paces at the lower part; but in the upper part, woody, (so much so) that it was not easy to see through it into the interior. Within these woods the enemy kept themselves in concealment; a few troops of horse-soldiers appeared on the open ground, along the river. The depth of the river was about three feet.

2:19 Caesar, having sent his cavalry on before, followed close after them with all his forces; but the plan and order of the march was different from that which the Belgae had reported to the Nervii. For as he was approaching the enemy, Caesar, according to his custom, led on [as the van six legions unencumbered by baggage; behind them he had placed the baggage-trains of the whole army; then the two legions which had been last raised closed the rear, and were a guard for the baggage-train. Our horse, with the slingers and archers, having passed the river, commenced action with the cavalry of the enemy. While they from time to time betook themselves into the woods to their companions, and again made an assault out of the wood upon our men, who did not dare to follow them in their retreat further than the limit to which the plain and open parts extended, in the mean time the six legions which had arrived first, having measured out the work, began to fortify the camp. When the first part of the baggage train of our army was seen by those who lay hid in the woods, which had been agreed on among them as the time for commencing action, as soon as they had arranged their line of

castra venisset reliquaeque legiones magnum spatium abessent, hanc sub sarcinis adoriri; qua pulsa impedimentisque direptis, futurum ut reliquae contra consistere non auderent. Adiuvabat etiam eorum consilium qui rem deferebant quod Nervii antiquitus, cum equitatu nihil possent (neque enim ad hoc tempus ei rei student, sed quicquid possunt, pedestribus valent copiis), quo facilius finitimorum equitatum, si praedandi causa ad eos venissent, impedirent, teneris arboribus incisis atque inflexis crebrisque in latitudinem ramis enatis [et] rubis sentibusque interiectis effecerant ut instar muri hae saepes munimentum praeberent, quo non modo non intrari sed ne perspici quidem posset. His rebus cum iter agminis nostri impediretur, non omittendum sibi consilium Nervii existimaverunt.

Loci natura erat haec, quem locum nostri castris delegerant. Collis ab summo aequaliter declivis ad flumen Sabim, quod supra nominavimus, vergebat. Ab eo flumine pari acclivitate collis nascebatur adversus huic et contrarius, passus circiter CC infimus apertus, ab superiore parte silvestris, ut non facile introrsus perspici posset. Intra eas silvas hostes in occulto sese continebant; in aperto loco secundum flumen paucae stationes equitum videbantur. Fluminis erat altitudo pedum circiter trium.

Caesar equitatu praemisso subsequebatur omnibus copiis; sed ratio ordoque agminis aliter se habebat ac Belgae ad Nervios detulerant. Nam quod hostibus adpropinquabat, consuetudine sua Caesar VI legiones expeditas ducebat; post eas totius exercitus impedimenta conlocarat; inde duae legiones quae proxime conscriptae erant totum agmen claudebant praesidioque impedimentis erant. Equites nostri cum funditoribus sagittariisque flumen transgressi cum hostium equitatu proelium commiserunt. Cum se illi identidem in silvis ad suos reciperent ac rursus ex silva in nostros impetum facerent, neque nostri longius quam quem ad finem porrecta [ac] loca aperta pertinebant cedentes insequi auderent, interim legiones VI quae primae venerant, opere dimenso, castra munire coeperunt. Ubi prima impedimenta nostri exercitus ab iis qui in silvis abditi latebant visa sunt, quod tempus inter eos

battle and formed their ranks within the woods, and had encouraged one another, they rushed out suddenly with all their forces and made an attack upon our horse. The latter being easily routed and thrown into confusion, the Nervii ran down to the river with such incredible speed that they seemed to be in the woods, the river, and close upon us almost at the same time. And with the same speed they hastened up the hill to our camp, and to those who were employed in the works.

2:20 Caesar had every thing to do at one time: the standard to be displayed, which was the sign when it was necessary to run to arms; the signal to be given by the trumpet; the soldiers to be called off from the works; those who had proceeded some distance for the purpose of seeking materials for the rampart, to be summoned; the order of battle to be formed; the soldiers to be encouraged; the watchword to be given. A great part of these arrangements was prevented by the shortness of time and the sudden approach and charge of the enemy. Under these difficulties two things proved of advantage; [first] the skill and experience of the soldiers, because, having been trained by former engagements, they could suggest to themselves what ought to be done, as conveniently as receive information from others; and [secondly] that Caesar had forbidden his several lieutenants to depart from the works and their respective legions, before the camp was fortified. These, on account of the near approach and the speed of the enemy, did not then wait for any command from Caesar, but of themselves executed whatever appeared proper.

2:21 Caesar, having given the necessary orders, hastened to and fro into whatever quarter fortune carried him, to animate the troops, and came to the tenth legion. Having encouraged the soldiers with no further speech than that "they should keep up the remembrance of their wonted valor, and not be confused in mind, but valiantly sustain the assault of the enemy ;" as the latter were not further from them than the distance to which a dart could be cast, he gave the signal for commencing battle. And having gone to another quarter for the purpose of encouraging [the soldiers], he finds them fighting. Such was the shortness of the time, and so determined was the mind of the enemy on fighting, that time was wanting not only for affixing the military insignia, but even for putting on the helmets and drawing off the covers from the shields. To whatever part any one by chance came from the works (in which he had been employed), and whatever standards he saw first, at these he stood, lest in seeking his own company he should lose the time for fighting.

2:22 The army having been marshaled, rather as the nature of the

committendi proelii convenerat, ut intra silvas aciem ordinesque constituerant atque ipsi sese confirmaverant, subito omnibus copiis provolaverunt impetumque in nostros equites fecerunt. His facile pulsis ac proturbatis, incredibili celeritate ad flumen decucurrerunt, ut paene uno tempore et ad silvas et in flumine [et iam in manibus nostris] hostes viderentur. Eadem autem celeritate adverso colle ad nostra castra atque eos qui in opere occupati erant contenderunt.

Caesari omnia uno tempore erant agenda: vexillum proponendum, quod erat insigne, cum ad arma concurri oporteret; signum tuba dandum; ab opere revocandi milites; qui paulo longius aggeris petendi causa processerant arcessendi; acies instruenda; milites cohortandi; signum dandum. Quarum rerum magnam partem temporis brevitas et incursus hostium impediebat. His difficultatibus duae res erant subsidio, scientia atque usus militum, quod superioribus proeliis exercitati quid fieri oporteret non minus commode ipsi sibi praescribere quam ab aliis doceri poterant, et quod ab opere singulisque legionibus singulos legatos Caesar discedere nisi munitis castris vetuerat. Hi propter propinquitatem et celeritatem hostium nihil iam Caesaris imperium expectabant, sed per se quae videbantur administrabant.

Caesar, necessariis rebus imperatis, ad cohortandos milites, quam [in] partem fors obtulit, decucurrit et ad legionem decimam devenit. Milites non longiore oratione cohortatus quam uti suae pristinae virtutis memoriam retinerent neu perturbarentur animo hostiumque impetum fortiter sustinerent, quod non longius hostes aberant quam quo telum adigi posset, proelii committendi signum dedit. Atque in alteram item cohortandi causa profectus pugnantibus occurrit. Temporis tanta fuit exiguitas hostiumque tam paratus ad dimicandum animus ut non modo ad insignia accommodanda sed etiam ad galeas induendas scutisque tegimenta detrahenda tempus defuerit. Quam quisque ab opere in partem casu devenit quaeque prima signa conspexit, ad haec constitit, ne in quaerendis suis pugnandi tempus dimitteret.

Instructo exercitu magis ut loci natura [deiectusque

ground and the declivity of the hill and the exigency of the time, than as the method and order of military matters required; while the legions in the different places were withstanding the enemy, some in one quarter, some in another, and the view was obstructed by the very thick hedges intervening, as we have before remarked, neither could proper reserves be posted, nor could the necessary measures be taken in each part, nor could all the commands be issued by one person. Therefore, in such an unfavorable state of affairs, various events of fortune followed.

2:23 The soldiers of the ninth and tenth legions, as they had been stationed on the left part of the army, casting their weapons, speedily drove the Atrebates (for that division had been opposed to them,) who were breathless with running and fatigue, and worn out with wounds, from the higher ground into the river; and following them as they were endeavoring to pass it, slew with their swords a great part of them while impeded (therein). They themselves did not hesitate to pass the river; and having advanced to a disadvantageous place, when the battle was renewed, they [nevertheless] again put to flight the enemy, who had returned and were opposing them. In like manner, in another quarter two different legions, the eleventh and the eighth, having routed the Veromandui, with whom they had engaged, were fighting from the higher ground upon the very banks of the river. But, almost the whole camp on the front and on the left side being then exposed, since the twelfth legion was posted in the right wing, and the seventh at no great distance from it, all the Nervii, in a very close body, with Boduognatus, who held the chief command, as their leader, hastened toward that place; and part of them began to surround the legions on their unprotected flank, part to make for the highest point of the encampment.

2:24 At the same time our horsemen, and light-armed infantry, who had been with those, who, as I have related, were routed by the first assault of the enemy, as they were betaking themselves into the camp, met the enemy face to face, and again sought flight into another quarter; and the camp-followers who from the Decuman Gate, and from the highest ridge of the hill had seen our men pass the river as victors, when, after going out for the purposes of plundering, they looked back and saw the enemy parading in our camp, committed themselves precipitately to flight; at the same time there arose the cry and shout of those who came with the baggage-train: and they (affrighted), were carried some one way, some another. By all these circumstances the cavalry of the Treviri were much alarmed, (whose reputation for courage is extraordinary among the Gauls, and who had come to Caesar, being sent by their state as auxiliaries), and, when they saw our camp filled with a large number of the enemy, the legions hard pressed and almost held surrounded, the camp-retainers,

collis] et necessitas temporis quam ut rei militaris ratio atque ordo postulabat, cum diversae legiones aliae alia in parte hostibus resisterent saepibusque densissimis, ut ante demonstravimus, interiectis prospectus impediretur, neque certa subsidia conlocari neque quid in quaque parte opus esset providere neque ab uno omnia imperia administrari poterant. Itaque in tanta rerum iniquitate fortunae quoque eventus varii sequebantur.

Legionis VIIII. et X. milites, ut in sinistra parte aciei constiterant, pilis emissis cursu ac lassitudine exanimatos vulneribusque confectos Atrebates (nam his ea pars obvenerat) celeriter ex loco superiore in flumen compulerunt et transire conantes insecuti gladiis magnam partem eorum impeditam interfecerunt. Ipsi transire flumen non dubitaverunt et in locum iniquum progressi rursus resistentes hostes redintegrato proelio in fugam coniecerunt. Item alia in parte diversae duae legiones, XI. et VIII., profligatis Viromanduis, quibuscum erant congressae, ex loco superiore in ipsis fluminis ripis proeliabantur. At totis fere castris a fronte et a sinistra parte nudatis, cum in dextro cornu legio XII. et non magno ab ea intervallo VII. constitisset, omnes Nervii confertissimo agmine duce Boduognato, qui summam imperii tenebat, ad eum locum contenderunt; quorum pars ab aperto latere legiones circumvenire, pars summum castrorum locum petere coepit.

Eodem tempore equites nostri levisque armaturae pedites, qui cum iis una fuerant, quos primo hostium impetu pulsos dixeram, cum se in castra reciperent, adversis hostibus occurrebant ac rursus aliam in partem fugam petebant; et calones, qui ab decumana porta ac summo iugo collis nostros victores flumen transire conspexerant, praedandi causa egressi, cum respexissent et hostes in nostris castris versari vidissent, praecipites fugae sese mandabant. Simul eorum qui cum impedimentis veniebant clamor fremitusque oriebatur, aliique aliam in partem perterriti ferebantur. Quibus omnibus rebus permoti equites Treveri, quorum inter Gallos virtutis opinio est singularis, qui auxilii causa a civitate missi ad Caesarem venerant, cum multitudine hostium castra [nostra] compleri,

horsemen, slingers, and Numidians fleeing on all sides divided and scattered, they, despairing of our affairs, hastened home, and related to their state that the Romans were routed and conquered, [and] that the enemy were in possession of their camp and baggage-train.

2:25 Caesar proceeded, after encouraging the tenth legion, to the right wing; where he perceived that his men were hard pressed, and that in consequence of the standards of the twelfth legion being collected together in one place, the crowded soldiers were a hinderance to themselves in the fight; that all the centurions of the fourth cohort were slain, and the standard-bearer killed, the standard itself lost, almost all the centurions of the other cohorts either wounded or slain, and among them the chief centurion of the legion P. Sextius Baculus, a very valiant man, who was so exhausted by many and severe wounds, that he was already unable to support himself; he likewise perceived that the rest were slackening their efforts, and that some, deserted by those in the rear, were retiring from the battle and avoiding the weapons; that the enemy [on the other hand] though advancing from the lower ground, were not relaxing in front, and were [at the same time] pressing hard on both flanks; he also perceived that the affair was at a crisis, and that there was not any reserve which could be brought up, having therefore snatched a shield from one of the soldiers in the rear (for he himself had come without a shield), he advanced to the front of the line, and addressing the centurions by name, and encouraging the rest of the soldiers, he ordered them to carry forward the standards, and extend the companies, that they might the more easily use their swords. On his arrival, as hope was brought to the soldiers and their courage restored, while every one for his own part, in the sight of his general, desired to exert his utmost energy, the impetuosity of the enemy was a little checked.

2:26 Caesar, when he perceived that the seventh legion, which stood close by him, was also hard pressed by the enemy, directed the tribunes of the soldiers to effect a junction of the legions gradually, and make their charge upon the enemy with a double front; which having been done, since they brought assistance the one to the other, nor feared lest their rear should be surrounded by the enemy, they began to stand their ground more boldly, and to fight more courageously. In the mean time, the soldiers of the two legions which had been in the rear of the army, as a guard for the baggage-train, upon the battle being reported to them, quickened their pace, and were seen by the enemy on the top of the hill; and Titus Labienus, having gained possession of the camp of the enemy, and observed from the higher ground what was going on

legiones premi et paene circumventas teneri, calones, equites, funditores, Numidas diversos dissipatosque in omnes partes fugere vidissent, desperatis nostris rebus domum contenderunt: Romanos pulsos superatosque, castris impedimentisque eorum hostes potitos civitati renuntiaverunt.

Caesar ab X. legionis cohortatione ad dextrum cornu profectus, ubi suos urgeri signisque in unum locum conlatis XII. legionis confertos milites sibi ipsos ad pugnam esse impedimento vidit, quartae cohortis omnibus centurionibus occisis signiferoque interfecto, signo amisso, reliquarum cohortium omnibus fere centurionibus aut vulneratis aut occisis, in his primipilo P. Sextio Baculo, fortissimo viro, multis gravibusque vulneribus confecto, ut iam se sustinere non posset, reliquos esse tardiores et non nullos ab novissimis deserto loco proelio excedere ac tela vitare, hostes neque a fronte ex inferiore loco subeuntes intermittere et ab utroque latere instare et rem esse in angusto vidit, neque ullum esse subsidium quod submitti posset, scuto ab novissimis [uni] militi detracto, quod ipse eo sine scuto venerat, in primam aciem processit centurionibusque nominatim appellatis reliquos cohortatus milites signa inferre et manipulos laxare iussit, quo facilius gladiis uti possent. Cuius adventu spe inlata militibus ac redintegrato animo, cum pro se quisque in conspectu imperatoris etiam in extremis suis rebus operam navare cuperet, paulum hostium impetus tardatus est.

Caesar, cum VII. legionem, quae iuxta constiterat, item urgeri ab hoste vidisset, tribunos militum monuit ut paulatim sese legiones coniungerent et conversa signa in hostes inferrent. Quo facto cum aliis alii subsidium ferrent neque timerent ne aversi ab hoste circumvenirentur, audacius resistere ac fortius pugnare coeperunt. Interim milites legionum duarum quae in novissimo agmine praesidio impedimentis fuerant, proelio nuntiato, cursu incitato in summo colle ab hostibus conspiciebantur, et T. Labienus castris hostium potitus et ex loco superiore quae res in nostris castris gererentur conspicatus X. legionem subsidio

in our camp, sent the tenth legion as a relief to our men, who, when they had learned from the flight of the horse and the sutlers in what position the affair was, and in how great danger the camp and the legion and the commander were involved, left undone nothing [which tended] to dispatch.

2:27 By their arrival, so great a change of matters was made, that our men, even those who had fallen down exhausted with wounds, leaned on their shields, and renewed the fight: then the camp-retainers, though unarmed, seeing the enemy completely dismayed, attacked [them though] armed; the horsemen too, that they might by their valor blot the disgrace of their flight, thrust themselves before the legionary soldiers in all parts of the battle. But the enemy, even in the last hope of safety, displayed such great courage, that when the foremost of them had fallen, the next stood upon them prostrate, and fought from their bodies; when these were overthrown, and their corpses heaped up together, those who survived cast their weapons against our men [thence], as from a mound, and returned our darts which had fallen short between [the armies]; so that it ought not to be concluded, that men of such great courage had injudiciously dared to pass a very broad river, ascend very high banks, and come up to a very disadvantageous place; since their greatness of spirit had rendered these actions easy, although in themselves very difficult.

2:28 This battle being ended, and the nation and name of the Nervii being almost reduced to annihilation, their old men, whom together with the boys and women we have stated to have been collected together in the fenny places and marshes, on this battle having been reported to them, since they were convinced that nothing was an obstacle to the conquerors, and nothing safe to the conquered, sent embassadors to Caesar by the consent of all who remained, and surrendered themselves to him; and in recounting the calamity of their state, said that their senators were reduced from 600 to three; that from 60,000 men they [were reduced] to scarcely 500 who could bear arms; whom Caesar, that he might appear to use compassion toward the wretched and the suppliant, most carefully spared; and ordered them to enjoy their own territories and towns, and commanded their neighbors that they should restrain themselves and their dependents from offering injury or outrage [to them].

2:29 When the Aduatuci, of whom we have written above, were coming up with all their forces to the assistance of the Nervii, upon this battle being reported to them, they returned home after they were on the march; deserting all their towns and forts, they conveyed together all their possessions into one town, eminently fortified by nature. While this town had on all sides around it very high rocks and precipices, there was left on one side a gently

nostris misit. Qui cum ex equitum et calonum fuga quo in loco res esset quantoque in periculo et castra et legiones et imperator versaretur cognovissent, nihil ad celeritatem sibi reliqui fecerunt.

Horum adventu tanta rerum commutatio est facta ut nostri, etiam qui vulneribus confecti procubuissent, scutis innixi proelium redintegrarent, calones perterritos hostes conspicati etiam inermes armatis occurrerent, equites vero, ut turpitudinem fugae virtute delerent, omnibus in locis pugnae se legionariis militibus praeferrent. At hostes, etiam in extrema spe salutis, tantam virtutem praestiterunt ut, cum primi eorum cecidissent, proximi iacentibus insisterent atque ex eorum corporibus pugnarent, his deiectis et coacervatis cadaveribus qui superessent ut ex tumulo tela in nostros conicerent et pila intercepta remitterent: ut non nequiquam tantae virtutis homines iudicari deberet ausos esse transire latissimum flumen, ascendere altissimas ripas, subire iniquissimum locum; quae facilia ex difficillimis animi magnitudo redegerat.

Hoc proelio facto et prope ad internecionem gente ac nomine Nerviorum redacto, maiores natu, quos una cum pueris mulieribusque in aestuaria ac paludes coniectos dixeramus, hac pugna nuntiata, cum victoribus nihil impeditum, victis nihil tutum arbitrarentur, omnium qui supererant consensu legatos ad Caesarem miserunt seque ei dediderunt; et in commemoranda civitatis calamitate ex DC ad tres senatores, ex hominum milibus LX vix ad D, qui arma ferre possent, sese redactos esse dixerunt. Quos Caesar, ut in miseros ac supplices usus misericordia videretur, diligentissime conservavit suisque finibus atque oppidis uti iussit et finitimis imperavit ut ab iniuria et maleficio se suosque prohiberent.

Atuatuci, de quibus supra diximus, cum omnibus copiis auxilio Nerviis venirent, hac pugna nuntiata ex itinere domum reverterunt; cunctis oppidis castellisque desertis sua omnia in unum oppidum egregie natura munitum contulerunt. Quod cum ex omnibus in circuitu partibus altissimas rupes deiectusque haberet, una ex parte leniter acclivis

ascending approach, of not more than 200 feet in width; which place they had fortified with a very lofty double wall: besides, they had placed stones of great weight and sharpened stakes upon the walls. They were descended from the Cimbri and Teutones, who, when they were marching into our province and Italy, having deposited on this side the river Rhine such of their baggage-trains as they could not drive or convey with them, left 6,000 of their men as a guard and defense for them. These having, after the destruction of their countrymen, been harassed for many years by their neighbors, while one time they waged war offensively, and at another resisted it when waged against them, concluded a peace with the consent of all, and chose this place as their settlement.

2:30 And on the first arrival of our army they made frequent sallies from the town, and contended with our men in trifling skirmishes; afterward, when hemmed in by a rampart of twelve feet [in height], and fifteen miles in circuit, they kept themselves within the town. When, vineae having been brought up and a mound raised, they observed that a tower also was being built at a distance, they at first began to mock the Romans from their wall, and to taunt them with the following speeches. "For what purpose was so vast a machine constructed at so great a distance? With what hands," or "with what strength did they, especially [as they were] men of such very small stature" (for our shortness of stature, in comparison to the great size of their bodies, is generally a subject of much contempt to the men of Gaul) "trust to place against their walls a tower of such great weight."

2:31 But when they saw that it was being moved, and was approaching their walls, startled by the new and unaccustomed sight, they sent embassadors to Caesar [to treat] about peace; who spoke in the following manner: "That they did not believe the Romans waged war without divine aid, since they were able to move forward machines of such a height with so great speed, and thus fight from close quarters; that they resigned themselves and all their possessions to [Caesar's] disposal: that they begged and earnestly entreated one thing, viz., that if perchance, agreeable to his clemency and humanity, which they had heard of from others, he should resolve that the Aduatuci were to be spared, he would not deprive them of their arms; that all their neighbors were enemies to them and envied their courage, from whom they could not defend themselves if their arms were delivered up: that it was better for them, if they should be reduced to that state, to suffer any fate from the Roman people, than to be tortured to death by those among whom they had been accustomed to rule."

2:32 To these things Caesar replied, "That he, in accordance with his custom, rather than owing to their desert, should spare the

aditus in latitudinem non amplius pedum CC relinquebatur; quem locum duplici altissimo muro munierant; tum magni ponderis saxa et praeacutas trabes in muro conlocabant. Ipsi erant ex Cimbris Teutonisque prognati, qui, cum iter in provinciam nostram atque Italiam facerent, iis impedimentis quae secum agere ac portare non poterant citra flumen Rhenum depositis custodiam [ex suis] ac praesidium VI milia hominum una reliquerant. Hi post eorum obitum multos annos a finitimis exagitati, cum alias bellum inferrent, alias inlatum defenderent, consensu eorum omnium pace facta hunc sibi domicilio locum delegerant.

Ac primo adventu exercitus nostri crebras ex oppido excursiones faciebant parvulisque proeliis cum nostris contendebant; postea vallo pedum XII in circuitu quindecim milium crebrisque castellis circummuniti oppido sese continebant. Ubi vineis actis aggere extructo turrim procul constitui viderunt, primum inridere ex muro atque increpitare vocibus, quod tanta machinatio a tanto spatio institueretur: quibusnam manibus aut quibus viribus praesertim homines tantulae staturae (nam plerumque omnibus Gallis prae magnitudine corporum quorum brevitas nostra contemptui est) tanti oneris turrim in muro sese posse conlocare confiderent?

Ubi vero moveri et adpropinquare muris viderunt, nova atque inusitata specie commoti legatos ad Caesarem de pace miserunt, qui ad hunc modum locuti; non se existimare Romanos sine ope divina bellum gerere, qui tantae altitudinis machinationes tanta celeritate promovere possent; se suaque omnia eorum potestati permittere dixerunt. Unum petere ac deprecari: si forte pro sua clementia ac mansuetudine, quam ipsi ab aliis audirent, statuisset Atuatucos esse conservandos, ne se armis despoliaret. Sibi omnes fere finitimos esse inimicos ac suae virtuti invidere; a quibus se defendere traditis armis non possent. Sibi praestare, si in eum casum deducerentur, quamvis fortunam a populo Romano pati quam ab his per cruciatum interfici inter quos dominari consuessent.

Ad haec Caesar respondit: se magis consuetudine sua quam merito eorum civitatem conservaturum,

state, if they should surrender themselves before the battering-ram should touch the wall; but that there was no condition of surrender, except upon their arms being delivered up; that he should do to them that which he had done in the case of the Nervii, and would command their neighbors not to offer any injury to those who had surrendered to the Roman people." The matter being reported to their countrymen, they said that they would execute his commands. Having cast a very large quantity of their arms from the wall into the trench that was before the town, so that the heaps of arms almost equalled the top of the wall and the rampart, and nevertheless having retained and concealed, as we afterward discovered, about a third part in the town, the gates were opened, and they enjoyed peace for that day.

2:33 Toward evening Caesar ordered the gates to be shut, and the soldiers to go out of the town, lest the towns-people should receive any injury from them by night. They [the Aduatuci], by a design before entered into, as we afterwards understood, because they believed that, as a surrender had been made, our men would dismiss their guards, or at least would keep watch less carefully, partly with those arms which they had retained and concealed, partly with shields made of bark or interwoven wickers, which they had hastily covered over with skins, (as the shortness of time required) in the third watch, suddenly made a sally from the town with all their forces [in that direction] in which the ascent to our fortifications seemed the least difficult. The signal having been immediately given by fires, as Caesar had previously commended, a rush was made thither [i. e. by the Roman soldiers] from the nearest fort; and the battle was fought by the enemy as vigorously as it ought to be fought by brave men, in the last hope of safety, in a disadvantageous place, and against those who were throwing their weapons from a rampart and from towers; since all hope of safety depended on their courage alone. About 4,000 of the men having been slain, the rest were forced back into the town. The day after, Caesar, after breaking open the gates, which there was no one then to defend, and sending in our soldiers, sold the whole spoil of that town. The number of 53,000 persons was reported to him by those who had bought them.

2:34 At the same time he was informed by P. Crassus, whom he had sent with one legion against the Veneti, the Unelli, the Osismii, the Curiosolitae, the Sesuvii, the Aulerci, and the Rhedones, which are maritime states, and touch upon the [Atlantic] ocean, that all these nations were brought under the dominion and power of the Roman people.

2:35 These things being achieved, [and] all Gaul being subdued, so high an opinion of this war was spread among the barbarians, that embassadors were sent to Caesar by those nations who dwelt

si prius quam murum aries attigisset se dedidissent; sed deditionis nullam esse condicionem nisi armis traditis. Se id quod in Nerviis fecisset facturum finitimisque imperaturum ne quam dediticiis populi Romani iniuriam inferrent. Re renuntiata ad suos illi se quae imperarentur facere dixerunt. Armorum magna multitudine de muro in fossam, quae erat ante oppidum, iacta, sic ut prope summam muri aggerisque altitudinem acervi armorum adaequarent, et tamen circiter parte tertia, ut postea perspectum est, celata atque in oppido retenta, portis patefactis eo die pace sunt usi.

Sub vesperum Caesar portas claudi militesque ex oppido exire iussit, ne quam noctu oppidani a militibus iniuriam acciperent. Illi ante inito, ut intellectum est, consilio, quod deditione facta nostros praesidia deducturos aut denique indiligentius servaturos crediderant, partim cum iis quae retinuerant et celaverant armis, partim scutis ex cortice factis aut viminibus intextis, quae subito, ut temporis exiguitas postulabat, pellibus induxerant, tertia vigilia, qua minime arduus ad nostras munitiones accensus videbatur, omnibus copiis repente ex oppido eruptionem fecerunt. Celeriter, ut ante Caesar imperaverat, ignibus significatione facta, ex proximis castellis eo concursum est, pugnatumque ab hostibus ita acriter est ut a viris fortibus in extrema spe salutis iniquo loco contra eos qui ex vallo turribusque tela iacerent pugnari debuit, cum in una virtute omnis spes consisteret. Occisis ad hominum milibus IIII reliqui in oppidum reiecti sunt. Postridie eius diei refractis portis, cum iam defenderet nemo, atque intromissis militibus nostris, sectionem eius oppidi universam Caesar vendidit. Ab iis qui emerant capitum numerus ad eum relatus est milium LIII.

Eodem tempore a P. Crasso, quem cum legione una miserat ad Venetos, Venellos, Osismos, Coriosolitas, Esuvios, Aulercos, Redones, quae sunt maritimae civitates Oceanumque attingunt, certior factus est omnes eas civitates in dicionem potestatemque populi Romani esse redactas.

His rebus gestis omni Gallia pacata, tanta huius belli ad barbaros opinio perlata est uti ab iis nationibus quae trans Rhenum incolerent

beyond the Rhine, to promise that they would give hostages and execute his commands. Which embassies Caesar, because he was hastening into Italy and Illyricum, ordered to return to him at the beginning of the following summer. He himself, having led his legions into winter quarters among the Carnutes, the Andes, and the Turones, which states were close to those regions in which he had waged war, set out for Italy; and a thanksgiving of fifteen days was decreed for those achievements, upon receiving Caesar's letter; [an honor] which before that time had been conferred on none.

legationes ad Caesarem mitterentur, quae se obsides daturas, imperata facturas pollicerentur. Quas legationes Caesar, quod in Italiam Illyricumque properabat, inita proxima aestate ad se reverti iussit. Ipse in Carnutes, Andes, Turonos quaeque civitates propinquae iis locis erant ubi bellum gesserat, legionibus in hiberna deductis, in Italiam profectus est. Ob easque res ex litteris Caesaris dierum XV supplicatio decreta est, quod ante id tempus accidit nulli.

Gallic Wars Book 3 (56 B.C.E.)

3:1 When Caesar was setting out for Italy, he sent Servius Galba with the twelfth legion and part of the cavalry, against the Nantuates, the Veragri, and Seduni, who extend from the territories of the Allobroges, and the lake of Geneva, and the River Rhone to the top of the Alps. The reason for sending him was, that he desired that the pass along the Alps, through which [the Roman] merchants had been accustomed to travel with great danger, and under great imposts, should be opened. He permitted him, if he thought it necessary, to station the legion in these places, for the purpose of wintering. Galba having fought some successful battles and stormed several of their forts, upon embassadors being sent to him from all parts and hostages given and a peace concluded, determined to station two cohorts among the Nantuates, and to winter in person with the other cohorts of that legion in a village of the Veragri, which is called Octodurus; and this village being situated in a valley, with a small plain annexed to it, is bounded on all sides by very high mountains. As this village was divided into two parts by a river, he granted one part of it to the Gauls, and assigned the other, which had been left by them unoccupied, to the cohorts to winter in. He fortified this [latter] part with a rampart and a ditch.

3:2 When several days had elapsed in winter quarters, and he had ordered corn to be brought in he was suddenly informed by his scouts that all the people had gone off in the night from that part of the town which he had given up to the Gauls, and that the mountains which hung over it were occupied by a very large force of the Seduni and Veragri. It had happened for several reasons that the Gauls suddenly formed the design of renewing the war and cutting off that legion. First, because they despised a single legion, on account of its small number, and that not quite full (two cohorts having been detached, and several individuals being absent, who had been dispatched for the purpose of seeking provision); then, likewise, because they thought that on account of the disadvantageous character of the situation, even their first attack could not be sustained [by us] when they would rush from the mountains into the valley, and discharge their weapons upon us. To this was added, that they were indignant that their children were torn from them under the title of hostages, and they were persuaded that the Romans designed to seize upon the summits of the Alps, and unite those parts to the neighboring province [of Gaul], not only to secure the passes, but also a constant possession.

3:3 Having received these tidings, Galba, since the works of the

Cum in Italiam proficisceretur Caesar, Ser. Galbam cum legione XII et parte equitatus in Nantuates, Veragros Sedunosque misit, qui a finibus Allobrogum et lacu Lemanno et flumine Rhodano ad summas Alpes pertinent. Causa mittendi fuit quod iter per Alpes, quo magno cum periculo magnisque cum portoriis mercatores ire consuerant, patefieri volebat. Huic permisit, si opus esse arbitraretur, uti in his locis legionem hiemandi causa conlocaret. Galba secundis aliquot proeliis factis castellisque compluribus eorum expugnatis, missis ad eum undique legatis obsidibusque datis et pace facta, constituit cohortes duas in Nantuatibus conlocare et ipse cum reliquis eius legionis cohortibus in vico Veragrorum, qui appellatur Octodurus hiemare; qui vicus positus in valle non magna adiecta planitie altissimis montibus undique continetur. Cum hic in duas partes flumine divideretur, alteram partem eius vici Gallis [ad hiemandum] concessit, alteram vacuam ab his relictam cohortibus attribuit. Eum locum vallo fossaque munivit.

Cum dies hibernorum complures transissent frumentumque eo comportari iussisset, subito per exploratores certior factus est ex ea parte vici, quam Gallis concesserat, omnes noctu discessisse montesque qui impenderent a maxima multitudine Sedunorum et Veragrorum teneri. Id aliquot de causis acciderat, ut subito Galli belli renovandi legionisque opprimendae consilium caperent: primum, quod legionem neque eam plenissimam detractis cohortibus duabus et compluribus singillatim, qui commeatus petendi causa missi erant, absentibus propter paucitatem despiciebant; tum etiam, quod propter iniquitatem loci, cum ipsi ex montibus in vallem decurrerent et tela coicerent, ne primum quidem impetum suum posse sustineri existimabant. Accedebat quod suos ab se liberos abstractos obsidum nomine dolebant, et Romanos non solum itinerum causa sed etiam perpetuae possessionis culmina Alpium occupare conari et ea loca finitimae provinciae adiungere sibi persuasum habebant.

His nuntiis acceptis Galba, cum neque opus

winter-quarters and the fortifications were not fully completed, nor was sufficient preparation made with regard to corn and other provisions (since, as a surrender had been made, and hostages received, he had thought he need entertain no apprehension of war), speedily summoning a council, began to anxiously inquire their opinions. In which council, since so much sudden danger had happened contrary to the general expectation, and almost all the higher places were seen already covered with a multitude of armed men, nor could [either] troops come to their relief, or provisions be brought in, as the passes were blocked up [by the enemy]; safety being now nearly despaired of, some opinions of this sort were delivered: that, "leaving their baggage, and making a sally, they should hasten away for safety by the same routes by which they had come thither." To the greater part, however, it seemed best, reserving that measure to the last, to await the issue of the matter, and to defend the camp.

3:4 A short time only having elapsed, so that time was scarcely given for arranging and executing those things which they had determined on, the enemy, upon the signal being given, rushed down [upon our men] from all parts, and discharged stones and darts, upon our rampart. Our men at first, while their strength was fresh, resisted bravely, nor did they cast any weapon ineffectually from their higher station. As soon as any part of the camp, being destitute of defenders, seemed to be hard pressed, thither they ran, and brought assistance. But they were over-matched in this, that the enemy when wearied by the long continuance of the battle, went out of the action, and others with fresh strength came in their place; none of which things could be done by our men, owing to the smallness of their number; and not only was permission not given to the wearied [Roman] to retire from the fight, but not even to the wounded [was liberty granted] to quit the post where he had been stationed, and recover.

3:5 When they had now been fighting for more than six hours, without cessation, and not only strength, but even weapons were failing our men, and the enemy were pressing on more rigorously, and had begun to demolish the rampart and to fill up the trench, while our men were becoming exhausted, and the matter was now brought to the last extremity, P. Sextius Baculus, a centurion of the first rank, whom we have related to have been disabled by severe wounds in the engagement with the Nervii, and also C. Volusenus, a tribune of the soldiers, a man of great skill and valor, hasten to Galba, and assure him that the only hope of safety lay in making a sally, and trying the last resource. Whereupon assembling the centurions, he quickly gives orders to the soldiers to discontinue the fight a short time, and only collect the weapons flung [at them], and recruit themselves after their fatigue, and afterward, upon the

hibernorum munitionesque plene essent perfectae neque de frumento reliquoque commeatu satis esset provisum quod deditione facta obsidibusque acceptis nihil de bello timendum existimaverat, consilio celeriter convocato sententias exquirere coepit. Quo in consilio, cum tantum repentini periculi praeter opinionem accidisset ac iam omnia fere superiora loca multitudine armatorum completa conspicerentur neque subsidio veniri neque commeatus supportari interclusis itineribus possent, prope iam desperata salute non nullae eius modi sententiae dicebantur, ut impedimentis relictis eruptione facta isdem itineribus quibus eo pervenissent ad salutem contenderent. Maiori tamen parti placuit, hoc reservato ad extremum casum consilio interim rei eventum experiri et castra defendere.

Brevi spatio interiecto, vix ut iis rebus quas constituissent conlocandis atque administrandis tempus daretur, hostes ex omnibus partibus signo dato decurrere, lapides gaesaque in vallum coicere. Nostri primo integris viribus fortiter propugnare neque ullum frustra telum ex loco superiore mittere, et quaecumque pars castrorum nudata defensoribus premi videbatur, eo occurrere et auxilium ferre, sed hoc superari quod diuturnitate pugnae hostes defessi proelio excedebant, alii integris viribus succedebant; quarum rerum a nostris propter paucitatem fieri nihil poterat, ac non modo defesso ex pugna excedendi, sed ne saucio quidem eius loci ubi constiterat relinquendi ac sui recipiendi facultas dabatur.

Cum iam amplius horis sex continenter pugnaretur, ac non solum vires sed etiam tela nostros deficerent, atque hostes acrius instarent languidioribusque nostris vallum scindere et fossas complere coepissent, resque esset iam ad extremum perducta casum, P. Sextius Baculus, primi pili centurio, quem Nervico proelio compluribus confectum vulneribus diximus, et item C. Volusenus, tribunus militum, vir et consilii magni et virtutis, ad Galbam accurrunt atque unam esse spem salutis docent, si eruptione facta extremum auxilium experirentur. Itaque convocatis centurionibus celeriter milites certiores facit, paulisper intermitterent proelium ac tantum modo

signal being given, sally forth from the camp, and place in their valor all their hope of safety.

3:6 They do what they were ordered; and, making a sudden sally from all the gates [of the camp], leave the enemy the means neither of knowing what was taking place, nor of collecting themselves. Fortune thus taking a turn, [our men] surround on every side, and slay those who had entertained the hope of gaining the camp and having killed more than the third part of an army of more than 30,000 men (which number of the barbarians it appeared certain had come up to our camp), put to flight the rest when panic-stricken, and do not suffer them to halt even upon the higher grounds. All the forces of the enemy being thus routed, and stripped of their arms, [our men] betake themselves to their camp and fortifications. Which battle being finished, inasmuch as Galba was unwilling to tempt fortune again, and remembered that he had come into winter quarters with one design, and saw that he had met with a different state of affairs; chiefly however urged by the want of corn and provision, having the next day burned all the buildings of that village, he hastens to return into the province; and as no enemy opposed or hindered his march, he brought the legion safe into the [country of the] Nantuates, thence into [that of] the Allobroges, and there wintered.

3:7 These things being achieved, while Caesar had every reason to suppose that Gaul was reduced to a state of tranquillity, the Belgae being overcome, the Germans expelled, the Seduni among the Alps defeated, and when he had, therefore, in the beginning of winter, set out for Illyricum, as he wished to visit those nations, and acquire a knowledge of their countries, a sudden war sprang up in Gaul. The occasion of that war was this: P. Crassus, a young man, had taken up his winter quarters with the seventh legion among the Andes, who border upon the [Atlantic] ocean. He, as there was a scarcity of corn in those parts, sent out some officers of cavalry, and several military tribunes among the neighbouring states, for the purpose of procuring corn and provision; in which number T. Terrasidius was sent among the Esubii; M. Trebius Gallus among the Curiosolitae; Q. Velanius, T. Silius, amongst the Veneti.

3:8 The influence of this state is by far the most considerable of any of the countries on the whole sea coast, because the Veneti both have a very great number of ships, with which they have been accustomed to sail to Britain, and [thus] excel the rest in their knowledge and experience of nautical affairs; and as only a few ports lie scattered along that stormy and open sea, of which they are in possession, they hold as tributaries almost all those who are accustomed to traffic in that sea. With them arose the beginning

tela missa exciperent seque ex labore reficerent, post dato signo ex castris erumperent, atque omnem spem salutis in virtute ponerent.

Quod iussi sunt faciunt, ac subito omnibus portis eruptione facta neque cognoscendi quid fieret neque sui colligendi hostibus facultatem relinquunt. Ita commutata fortuna eos qui in spem potiundorum castrorum venerant undique circumventos intercipiunt, et ex hominum milibus amplius XXX, quem numerum barbarorum ad castra venisse constabat, plus tertia parte interfecta reliquos perterritos in fugam coniciunt ac ne in locis quidem superioribus consistere patiuntur. Sic omnibus hostium copiis fusis armisque exutis se intra munitiones suas recipiunt. Quo proelio facto, quod saepius fortunam temptare Galba nolebat atque alio se in hiberna consilio venisse meminerat, aliis occurrisse rebus videbat, maxime frumenti [commeatusque] inopia permotus postero die omnibus eius vici aedificiis incensis in provinciam reverti contendit, ac nullo hoste prohibente aut iter demorante incolumem legionem in Nantuates, inde in Allobroges perduxit ibique hiemavit.

His rebus gestis cum omnibus de causis Caesar pacatam Galliam existimaret, [superatis Belgis, expulsis Germanis, victis in Alpibus Sedunis,] atque ita inita hieme in Illyricum profectus esset, quod eas quoque nationes adire et regiones cognoscere volebat, subitum bellum in Gallia coortum est. Eius belli haec fuit causa. P. Crassus adulescens eum legione VII. proximus mare Oceanum in Andibus hiemabat. Is, quod in his locis inopia frumenti erat, praefectos tribunosque militum complures in finitimas civitates frumenti causa dimisit; quo in numero est T. Terrasidius missus in Esuvios, M. Trebius Gallus in Coriosolites, Q. Velanius cum T. Silio in Venetos.

Huius est civitatis longe amplissima auctoritas omnis orae maritimae regionum earum, quod et naves habent Veneti plurimas, quibus in Britanniam navigare consuerunt, et scientia atque usu rerum nauticarum ceteros antecedunt et in magno impetu maris atque aperto paucis portibus interiectis, quos tenent ipsi, omnes fere qui eo mari uti consuerunt habent vectigales. Ab his fit initium

[of the revolt] by their detaining Silius and Velanius; for they thought that they should recover by their means the hostages which they had given to Crassus. The neighboring people led on by their influence (as the measures of the Gauls are sudden and hasty), detain Trebius and Terrasidius for the same motive; and quickly sending embassadors, by means of their leading men, they enter into a mutual compact to do nothing except by general consent, and abide the same issue of fortune; and they solicit the other states to choose rather to continue in that liberty which they had received from their ancestors, than endure slavery under the Romans. All the sea coast being quickly brought over to their sentiments, they send a common embassy to P. Crassus [to say], "If he wished to receive back his officers, let him send back to them their hostages."

3:9 Caesar, being informed of these things by Crassus, since he was so far distant himself, orders ships of war to be built in the mean time on the river Loire, which flows into the ocean; rowers to be raised from the province; sailors and pilots to be provided. These matters being quickly executed, he himself, as soon as the season of the year permits, hastens to the army. The Veneti, and the other states also, being informed of Caesar's arrival, when they reflected how great a crime they had committed, in that, the embassadors (a character which had among all nations ever been sacred and inviolable) had by them been detained and thrown into prison, resolve to prepare for a war in proportion to the greatness of their danger, and especially to provide those things which appertain to the service of a navy, with the greater confidence, inasmuch as they greatly relied on the nature of their situation. They knew that the passes by land were cut off by estuaries, that the approach by sea was most difficult, by reason of our ignorance of the localities, [and] the small number of the harbors, and they trusted that our army would not be able to stay very long among them, on account of the insufficiency of corn; and again, even if all these things should turn out contrary to their expectation, yet they were very powerful in their navy. They well understood that the Romans neither had any number of ships, nor were acquainted with the shallows, the harbors, or the islands of those parts where they would have to carry on the war; and the navigation was very different in a narrow sea from what it was in the vast and open ocean. Having come to this resolution, they fortify their towns, convey corn into them from the country parts, bring together as many ships as possible to Venetia, where it appeared Caesar would at first carry on the war. They unite to themselves as allies for that war, the Osismii, the Lexovii, the Nannetes, the Ambiliati, the Morini, the Diablintes, and the Menapii; and send for auxiliaries from Britain, which is situated over against those regions.

retinendi Silii atque Velanii, quod per eos suos se obsides, quos Crasso dedissent, recuperaturos existimabant. Horum auctoritate finitimi adducti, ut sunt Gallorum subita et repentina consilia, eadem de causa Trebium Terrasidiumque retinent et celeriter missis legatis per suos principes inter se coniurant nihil nisi communi consilio acturos eundemque omnes fortunae exitum esse laturos, reliquasque civitates sollicitant, ut in ea libertate quam a maioribus acceperint permanere quam Romanorum servitutem perferre malint. Omni ora maritima celeriter ad suam sententiam perducta communem legationem ad P. Crassum mittunt, si velit suos recuperare, obsides sibi remittat.

Quibus de rebus Caesar a Crasso certior factus, quod ipse aberat longius, naves interim longas aedificari in flumine Ligeri, quod influit in Oceanum, remiges ex provincia institui, nautas gubernatoresque comparari iubet. His rebus celeriter administratis ipse, cum primum per anni tempus potuit, ad exercitum contendit. Veneti reliquaeque item civitates cognito Caesaris adventu [certiores facti], simul quod quantum in se facinus admisissent intellegebant, [legatos, quod nomen ad omnes nationes sanctum inviolatumque semper fuisset, retentos ab se et in vincula coniectos,] pro magnitudine periculi bellum parare et maxime ea quae ad usum navium pertinent providere instituunt, hoc maiore spe quod multum natura loci confidebant. Pedestria esse itinera concisa aestuariis, navigationem impeditam propter inscientiam locorum paucitatemque portuum sciebant, neque nostros exercitus propter inopiam frumenti diutius apud se morari posse confidebant; ac iam ut omnia contra opinionem acciderent, tamen se plurimum navibus posse, [quam] Romanos neque ullam facultatem habere navium, neque eorum locorum ubi bellum gesturi essent vada, portus, insulas novisse; ac longe aliam esse navigationem in concluso mari atque in vastissimo atque apertissimo Oceano perspiciebant. His initis consiliis oppida muniunt, frumenta ex agris in oppida comportant, naves in Venetiam, ubi Caesarem primum bellum gesturum constabat, quam plurimas possunt cogunt. Socios sibi ad id bellum Osismos, Lexovios, Namnetes, Ambiliatos, Morinos, Diablintes, Menapios

3:10 There were these difficulties which we have mentioned above, in carrying on the war, but many things, nevertheless, urged Caesar to that war;-the open insult offered to the state in the detention of the Roman knights, the rebellion raised after surrendering, the revolt after hostages were given, the confederacy of so many states, but principally, lest if, [the conduct of] this part was overlooked, the other nations should think that the same thing was permitted them. Wherefore, since he reflected that almost all the Gauls were fond of revolution, and easily and quickly excited to war; that all men likewise, by nature, love liberty and hate the condition of slavery, he thought he ought to divide and more widely distribute his army, before more states should join the confederation.

3:11 He therefore sends T. Labienus, his lieutenant, with the cavalry to the Treviri, who are nearest to the river Rhine. He charges him to visit the Remi and the other Belgians, and to keep them in their allegiance and repel the Germans (who were said to have been summoned by the Belgae to their aid,) if they attempted to cross the river by force in their ships. He orders P. Crassus to proceed into Aquitania with twelve legionary cohorts and a great number of the cavalry, lest auxiliaries should be sent into Gaul by these states, and such great nations be united. He sends Q. Titurius Sabinus his lieutenant, with three legions, among the Unelli, the Curiosolitae, and the Lexovii, to take care that their forces should be kept separate from the rest. He appoints D. Brutus, a young man, over the fleet and those Gallic vessels which he had ordered to be furnished by the Pictones and the Santoni, and the other provinces which remained at peace; and commands him to proceed toward the Veneti, as soon as he could. He himself hastens thither with the land forces.

3:12 The sites of their towns were generally such that, being placed on extreme points [of land] and on promontories, they neither had an approach by land when the tide had rushed in from the main ocean, which always happens twice in the space of twelve hours; nor by ships, because, upon the tide ebbing again, the ships were likely to be dashed upon the shoals. Thus, by either circumstance, was the storming of their towns rendered difficult; and if at any time perchance the Veneti overpowered by the greatness of our works, (the sea having been excluded by a mound and large dams, and the latter being made almost equal in height to the walls of the town) had begun to despair of their fortunes; bringing up a large number of ships, of which they had a very great quantity, they carried off all their property and betook

adsciscunt; auxilia ex Britannia, quae contra eas regiones posita est, arcessunt.

Erant hae difficultates belli gerendi quas supra ostendimus, sed tamen multa Caesarem ad id bellum incitabant: iniuria retentorum equitum Romanorum, rebellio facta post deditionem, defectio datis obsidibus, tot civitatum coniuratio, in primis ne hac parte neglecta reliquae nationes sibi idem licere arbitrarentur. Itaque cum intellegeret omnes fere Gallos novis rebus studere et ad bellum mobiliter celeriterque excitari, omnes autem homines natura libertati studere et condicionem servitutis odisse, prius quam plures civitates conspirarent, partiendum sibi ac latius distribuendum exercitum putavit.

Itaque T. Labienum legatum in Treveros, qui proximi flumini Rheno sunt, cum equitatu mittit. Huic mandat, Remos reliquosque Belgas adeat atque in officio contineat Germanosque, qui auxilio a Belgis arcessiti dicebantur, si per vim navibus flumen transire conentur, prohibeat. P. Crassum cum cohortibus legionariis XII et magno numero equitatus in Aquitaniam proficisci iubet, ne ex his nationibus auxilia in Galliam mittantur ac tantae nationes coniungantur. Q. Titurium Sabinum legatum cum legionibus tribus in Venellos, Coriosolites Lexoviosque mittit, qui eam manum distinendam curet. D. Brutum adulescentem classi Gallicisque navibus, quas ex Pictonibus et Santonis reliquisque pacatis regionibus convenire iusserat, praeficit et, cum primum possit, in Venetos proficisci iubet. Ipse eo pedestribus copiis contendit.

Erant eius modi fere situs oppidorum ut posita in extremis lingulis promunturiisque neque pedibus aditum haberent, cum ex alto se aestus incitavisset, quod [bis] accidit semper horarum XII spatio, neque navibus, quod rursus minuente aestu naves in vadis adflictarentur. Ita utraque re oppidorum oppugnatio impediebatur. Ac si quando magnitudine operis forte superati, extruso mari aggere ac molibus atque his oppidi moenibus adaequatis, suis fortunis desperare coeperant, magno numero navium adpulso, cuius rei summam facultatem habebant, omnia sua deportabant seque in proxima oppida recipiebant:

themselves to the nearest towns; there they again defended themselves by the same advantages of situation. They did this the more easily during a great part of the summer, because our ships were kept back by storms, and the difficulty of sailing was very great in that vast and open sea, with its strong tides and its harbors far apart and exceedingly few in number.

3:13 For their ships were built and equipped after this manner. The keels were somewhat flatter than those of our ships, whereby they could more easily encounter the shallows and the ebbing of the tide: the prows were raised very high, and, in like manner the sterns were adapted to the force of the waves and storms [which they were formed to sustain]. The ships were built wholly of oak, and designed to endure any force and violence whatever; the benches which were made of planks a foot in breadth, were fastened by iron spikes of the thickness of a man's thumb; the anchors were secured fast by iron chains instead of cables, and for sails they used skins and thin dressed leather. These [were used] either through their want of canvas and their ignorance of its application, or for this reason, which is more probable, that they thought that such storms of the ocean, and such violent gales of wind could not be resisted by sails, nor ships of such great burden be conveniently enough managed by them. The encounter of our fleet with these ships' was of such a nature that our fleet excelled in speed alone, and the plying of the oars; other things, considering the nature of the place [and] the violence of the storms, were more suitable and better adapted on their side; for neither could our ships injure theirs with their beaks (so great was their strength), nor on account of their height was a weapon easily cast up to them; and for the same reason they were less readily locked in by rocks. To this was added, that whenever a storm began to rage and they ran before the wind, they both could weather the storm more easily and heave to securely in the shallows, and when left by the tide feared nothing from rocks and shelves: the risk of all which things was much to be dreaded by our ships.

3:14 Caesar, after taking many of their towns, perceiving that so much labor was spent in vain and that the flight of the enemy could not be prevented on the capture of their towns, and that injury could not be done them, he determined to wait for his fleet. As soon as it came up and was first seen by the enemy, about 220 of their ships, fully equipped and appointed with every kind of [naval] implement, sailed forth from the harbor, and drew up opposite to ours; nor did it appear clear to Brutus, who commanded the fleet, or to the tribunes of the soldiers and the centurions, to whom the several ships were assigned, what to do, or what system of tactics to adopt; for they knew that damage could not be done by their

ibi se rursus isdem opportunitatibus loci defendebant. Haec eo facilius magnam partem aestatis faciebant quod nostrae naves tempestatibus detinebantur summaque erat vasto atque aperto mari, magnis aestibus, raris ac prope nullis portibus difficultas navigandi.

Namque ipsorum naves ad hunc modum factae armataeque erant: carinae aliquanto planiores quam nostrarum navium, quo facilius vada ac decessum aestus excipere possent; prorae admodum erectae atque item puppes, ad magnitudinem fluctuum tempestatumque accommodatae; naves totae factae ex robore ad quamvis vim et contumeliam perferendam; transtra ex pedalibus in altitudinem trabibus, confixa clavis ferreis digiti pollicis crassitudine; ancorae pro funibus ferreis catenis revinctae; pelles pro velis alutaeque tenuiter confectae, [hae] sive propter inopiam lini atque eius usus inscientiam, sive eo, quod est magis veri simile, quod tantas tempestates Oceani tantosque impetus ventorum sustineri ac tanta onera navium regi velis non satis commode posse arbitrabantur. Cum his navibus nostrae classi eius modi congressus erat ut una celeritate et pulsu remorum praestaret, reliqua pro loci natura, pro vi tempestatum illis essent aptiora et accommodatiora. Neque enim iis nostrae rostro nocere poterant (tanta in iis erat firmitudo), neque propter altitudinem facile telum adigebatur, et eadem de causa minus commode copulis continebautur. Accedebat ut, cum [saevire ventus coepisset et] se vento dedissent, et tempestatem ferrent facilius et in vadis consisterent tutius et ab aestu relictae nihil saxa et cautes timerent; quarum rerum omnium nostris navibus casus erat extimescendus.

Compluribus expugnatis oppidis Caesar, ubi intellexit frustra tantum laborem sumi neque hostium fugam captis oppidis reprimi neque iis noceri posse, statuit expectandam classem. Quae ubi convenit ac primum ab hostibus visa est, circiter CCXX naves eorum paratissimae atque omni genere armorum ornatissimae profectae ex portu nostris adversae constiterunt; neque satis Bruto, qui classi praeerat, vel tribunis militum centurionibusque, quibus singulae naves erant attributae, constabat quid agerent aut quam

beaks; and that, although turrets were built [on their decks], yet the height of the stems of the barbarian ships exceeded these; so that weapons could not be cast up from [our] lower position with sufficient effect, and those cast by the Gauls fell the more forcibly upon us. One thing provided by our men was of great service, [viz.] sharp hooks inserted into and fastened upon poles, of a form not unlike the hooks used in attacking town walls. When the ropes which fastened the sail-yards to the masts were caught by them and pulled, and our vessel vigorously impelled with the oars, they [the ropes] were severed; and when they were cut away, the yards necessarily fell down; so that as all the hope of the Gallic vessels depended on their sails and rigging, upon these being cut away, the entire management of the ships was taken from them at the same time. The rest of the contest depended on courage; in which our men decidedly had the advantage; and the more so, because the whole action was carried on in the sight of Caesar and the entire army; so that no act, a little more valiant than ordinary, could pass unobserved, for all the hills and higher grounds, from which there was a near prospect of the sea were occupied by our army.

3:15 The sail yards [of the enemy], as we have said, being brought down, although two and [in some cases] three ships [of theirs] surrounded each one [of ours], the soldiers strove with the greatest energy to board the ships of the enemy; and, after the barbarians observed this taking place, as a great many of their ships were beaten, and as no relief for that evil could be discovered, they hastened to seek safety in flight. And, having now turned their vessels to that quarter in which the wind blew, so great a calm and lull suddenly arose, that they could not move out of their place, which circumstance, truly, was exceedingly opportune for finishing the business; for our men gave chase and took them one by one, so that very few out of all the number, [and those] by the intervention of night, arrived at the land, after the battle had lasted almost from the fourth hour till sun-set.

3:16 By this battle the war with the Veneti and the whole of the sea coast was finished; for both all the youth, and all, too, of more advanced age, in whom there was any discretion or rank, had assembled in that battle; and they had collected in that one place whatever naval forces they had anywhere; and when these were lost, the survivors had no place to retreat to, nor means of defending their towns. They accordingly surrendered themselves and all their possessions to Caesar, on whom Caesar thought that punishment should be inflicted the more severely, in order that for the future the rights of embassadors might be more carefully

rationem pugnae insisterent. Rostro enim noceri non posse cognoverant; turribus autem excitatis tamen has altitudo puppium ex barbaris navibus superabat, ut neque ex inferiore loco satis commode tela adigi possent et missa a Gallis gravius acciderent. Una erat magno usui res praeparata a nostris, falces praeacutae insertae adfixaeque longuriis, non absimili forma muralium falcium. His cum funes qui antemnas ad malos destinabant comprehensi adductique erant, navigio remis incitato praerumpebantur. Quibus abscisis antemnae necessario concidebant, ut, cum omnis Gallicis navibus spes in velis armamentisque consisteret, his ereptis omnis usus navium uno tempore eriperetur. Reliquum erat certamen positum in virtute, qua nostri milites facile superabant, atque eo magis quod in conspectu Caesaris atque omnis exercitus res gerebatur, ut nullum paulo fortius factum latere posset; omnes enim colles ac loca superiora, unde erat propinquus despectus in mare, ab exercitu tenebantur.

Deiectis, ut diximus, antemnis, cum singulas binae ac ternae naves circumsteterant, milites summa vi transcendere in hostium naves contendebant. Quod postquam barbari fieri animadverterunt, expugnatis compluribus navibus, cum ei rei nullum reperiretur auxilium, fuga salutem petere contenderunt. Ac iam conversis in eam partem navibus quo ventus ferebat, tanta subito malacia ac tranquillitas exstitit ut se ex loco movere non possent. Quae quidem res ad negotium conficiendum maximae fuit oportunitati: nam singulas nostri consectati expugnaverunt, ut perpaucae ex omni numero noctis interventu ad terram pervenirent, cum ab hora fere IIII usque ad solis occasum pugnaretur.

Quo proelio bellum Venetorum totiusque orae maritimae confectum est. Nam cum omnis iuventus, omnes etiam gravioris aetatis in quibus aliquid consilii aut dignitatis fuit eo convenerant, tum navium quod ubique fuerat in unum locum coegerant; quibus amissis reliqui neque quo se reciperent neque quem ad modum oppida defenderent habebant. Itaque se suaque omnia Caesari dediderunt. In quos eo gravius Caesar vindicandum statuit quo diligentius in reliquum

respected by barbarians; having, therefore, put to death all their senate, he sold the rest for slaves.

3:17 While these things are going on among the Veneti, Q. Titurius Sabinus with those troops which he had received from Caesar, arrives in the territories of the Unelli. Over these people Viridovix ruled, and held the chief command of all those states which had revolted; from which he had collected a large and powerful army. And in those few days, the Aulerci and the Sexovii, having slain their senate because they would not consent to be promoters of the war, shut their gates [against us] and united themselves to Viridovix; a great multitude besides of desperate men and robbers assembled out of Gaul from all quarters, whom the hope of plundering and the love of fighting had called away from husbandry and their daily labor. Sabinus kept himself within his camp, which was in a position convenient for everything; while Viridovix encamped over against him at a distance of two miles, and daily bringing out his forces, gave him an opportunity of fighting; so that Sabinus had now not only come into contempt with the enemy, but also was somewhat taunted by the speeches of our soldiers; and furnished so great a suspicion of his cowardice that the enemy presumed to approach even to the very rampart of our camp. He adopted this conduct for the following reason: because he did not think that a lieutenant ought to engage in battle with so great a force, especially while he who held the chief command was absent, except on advantageous ground or some favorable circumstance presented itself.

3:18 After having established this suspicion of his cowardice, he selected a certain suitable and crafty Gaul, who was one of those whom he had with him as auxiliaries. He induces him by great gifts and promises to go over to the enemy; and informs [him] of what he wished to be done. Who, when he arrives among them as a deserter, lays before them the fears of the Romans; and informs them by what difficulties Caesar himself was harassed, and that the matter was not far removed from this- that Sabinus would the next night privately draw off his army out of the camp and set forth to Caesar for the purpose of carrying [him] assistance, which, when they heard, they a11 cry out together that an opportunity of successfully conducting their enterprise, ought not to be thrown away: that they ought to go to the [Roman] camp. Many things persuaded the Gauls to this measure; the delay of Sabinus during the previous days; the positive assertion of the [pretended] deserter; want of provisions, for a supply of which they had not taken the requisite precautions; the hope springing from the Venetic war; and [also] because in most cases men willingly believe what they wish. Influenced by these things they do not

tempus a barbaris ius legatorum conservaretur. Itaque omni senatu necato reliquos sub corona vendidit.

Dum haec in Venetis geruntur, Q. Titurius Sabinus cum iis copiis quas a Caesare acceperat in fines Venellorum pervenit. His praeerat Viridovix ac summam imperii tenebat earum omnium civitatum quae defecerant, ex quibus exercitum [magnasque copias] coegerat; atque his paucis diebus Aulerci Eburovices Lexoviique, senatu suo interfecto quod auctores belli esse nolebant, portas clauserunt seque cum Viridovice coniunxerunt; magnaque praeterea multitudo undique ex Gallia perditorum hominum latronumque convenerat, quos spes praedandi studiumque bellandi ab agri cultura et cotidiano labore revocabat. Sabinus idoneo omnibus rebus loco castris sese tenebat, cum Viridovix contra eum duorum milium spatio consedisset cotidieque productis copiis pugnandi potestatem faceret, ut iam non solum hostibus in contemptionem Sabinus veniret, sed etiam nostrorum militum vocibus non nihil carperetur; tantamque opinionem timoris praebuit ut iam ad vallum castrorum hostes accedere auderent. Id ea de causa faciebat quod cum tanta multitudine hostium, praesertim eo absente qui summam imperii teneret, nisi aequo loco aut oportunitate aliqua data legato dimicandum non existimabat.

Hac confirmata opinione timoris idoneum quendam hominem et callidum deligit, Gallum, ex iis quos auxilii causa secum habebat. Huic magnis praemiis pollicitationibusque persuadet uti ad hostes transeat, et quid fieri velit edocet. Qui ubi pro perfuga ad eos venit, timorem Romanorum proponit, quibus angustiis ipse Caesar a Venetis prematur docet, neque longius abesse quin proxima nocte Sabinus clam ex castris exercitum educat et ad Caesarem auxilii ferendi causa proficiscatur. Quod ubi auditum est, conclamant omnes occasionem negotii bene gerendi amittendam non esse: ad castra iri oportere. Multae res ad hoc consilium Gallos hortabantur: superiorum dierum Sabini cunctatio, perfugae confirmatio, inopia cibariorum, cui rei parum diligenter ab iis erat provisum, spes Venetici belli, et quod fere libenter homines id quod volunt credunt. His rebus adducti non prius Viridovicem

discharge Viridovix and the other leaders from the council, before they gained permission from them to take up arms and hasten to [our] camp; which being granted, rejoicing as if victory were fully certain, they collected faggots and brushwood, with which to fill up the Roman trenches, and hasten to the camp.

3:19 The situation of the camp was a rising ground, gently sloping from the bottom for about a mile. Thither they proceeded with great speed (in order that as little time as possible might be given to the Romans to collect and arm themselves), and arrived quite out of breath. Sabinus having encouraged his men, gives them the signal, which they earnestly desired. While the enemy were encumbered by reason of the burdens which they were carrying, he orders a sally to be made suddenly from two gates [of the camp]. It happened, by the advantage of situation, by the unskilfulness and the fatigue of the enemy, by the valor of our soldiers, and their experience in former battles, that they could not stand one attack of our men, and immediately turned their backs; and our men with full vigor followed them while disordered, and slew a great number of them; the horse pursuing the rest, left but few, who escaped by flight. Thus at the same time, Sabinus was informed of the naval battle and Caesar of victory gained by Sabinus; and all the states immediately surrendered themselves to Titurius: for as the temper of the Gauls is impetuous and ready to undertake wars, so their mind is weak, and by no means resolute in enduring calamities.

3:20 About the same time, P. Crassus, when he had arrived in Aquitania (which, as has been before said, both from its extent of territory and the great number of its people, is to be reckoned a third part of Gaul,) understanding that he was to wage war in these parts, where a few years before, L. Valerius Praeconinus, the lieutenant had been killed, and his army routed, and from which L. Manilius, the proconsul, had fled with the loss of his baggage, he perceived that no ordinary care must be used by him. Wherefore, having provided corn, procured auxiliaries and cavalry, [and] having summoned by name many valiant men from Tolosa, Carcaso, and Narbo, which are the states of the province of Gaul, that border on these regions [Aquitania], he led his army into the territories of the Sotiates. On his arrival being known, the Sotiates having brought together great forces and [much] cavalry, in which their strength principally lay, and assailing our army on the march, engaged first in a cavalry action, then when their cavalry was routed, and our men pursuing, they suddenly display their infantry forces, which they had placed in ambuscade in a valley. These attacked our men [while] disordered, and renewed the fight.

reliquosque duces ex concilio dimittunt quam ab iis sit concessum arma uti capiant et ad castra contendant. Qua re concessa laeti, ut explorata victoria, sarmentis virgultisque collectis, quibus fossas Romanorum compleant, ad castra pergunt.

Locus erat castrorum editus et paulatim ab imo acclivis circiter passus mille. Huc magno cursu contenderunt, ut quam minimum spatii ad se colligendos armandosque Romanis daretur, exanimatique pervenerunt. Sabinus suos hortatus cupientibus signum dat. Impeditis hostibus propter ea quae ferebant onera subito duabus portis eruptionem fieri iubet. Factum est oportunitate loci, hostium inscientia ac defatigatione, virtute militum et superiorum pugnarum exercitatione, ut ne unum quidem nostrorum impetum ferrent ac statim terga verterent. Quos impeditos integris viribus milites nostri consecuti magnum numerum eorum occiderunt; reliquos equites consectati paucos, qui ex fuga evaserant, reliquerunt. Sic uno tempore et de navali pugna Sabinus et de Sabini victoria Caesar est certior factus, civitatesque omnes se statim Titurio dediderunt. Nam ut ad bella suscipienda Gallorum alacer ac promptus est animus, sic mollis ac minime resistens ad calamitates ferendas mens eorum est.

Eodem fere tempore P. Crassus, cum in Aquitaniam pervenisset, quae [pars], ut ante dictum est, [et regionum latitudine et multitudine hominum] tertia pars Galliae est [aestimanda], cum intellegeret in iis locis sibi bellum gerendum ubi paucis ante annis L. Valerius Praeconinus legatus exercitu pulso interfectus esset atque unde L. Manlius proconsul impedimentis amissis profugisset, non mediocrem sibi diligentiam adhibendam intellegebat. Itaque re frumentaria provisa, auxiliis equitatuque comparato, multis praeterea viris fortibus Tolosa et Carcasone et Narbone, quae sunt civitates Galliae provinciae finitimae, ex his regionibus nominatim evocatis, in Sotiatium fines exercitum introduxit. Cuius adventu cognito Sotiates magnis copiis coactis, equitatuque, quo plurimum valebant, in itinere agmen nostrum adorti primum equestre proelium commiserunt, deinde equitatu suo pulso atque insequentibus nostris subito pedestres copias, quas in convalle in insidiis conlocaverant,

3:21 The battle was long and vigorously contested, since the Sotiates, relying on their former victories, imagined that the safety of the whole of Aquitania rested on their valor; [and] our men, on the other hand, desired it might be seen what they could accomplish without their general and without the other legions, under a very young commander; at length the enemy, worn out with wounds, began to turn their backs, and a great number of them being slain, Crassus began to besiege the [principal] town of the Sotiates on his march. Upon their valiantly resisting, he raised vineae and turrets. They at one time attempting a sally, at another forming mines, to our rampart and vineae (at which the Aquitani are eminently skilled, because in many places among them there are copper mines); when they perceived that nothing could be gained by these operations through the perseverance of our men, they send embassadors to Crassus, and entreat him to admit them to a surrender. Having obtained it, they, being ordered to deliver up their arms, comply.

3:22 And while the attention of our men is engaged in that matter, in another part Adcantuannus, who held the chief command, with 600 devoted followers whom they call soldurii (the conditions of whose association are these,--that they enjoy all the conveniences of life with those to whose friendship they have devoted themselves: if any thing calamitous happen to them, either they endure the same destiny together with them, or commit suicide: nor hitherto, in the, memory of men, has there been found any one who, upon his being slain to whose friendship he had devoted himself, refused to die); Adcantuannus, [Isay] endeavoring to make a sally with these, when our soldiers had rushed together to arms, upon a shout being raised at that part of the, fortification, and a fierce battle had been fought there, was driven back into the town, yet he obtained from Crassus [the indulgence] that he should enjoy the same terms of surrender [as the other inhabitants].

3:23 Crassus, having received their arms and hostages, marched into the territories of the Vocates and the Tarusates. But then, the barbarians being alarmed, because they had heard that a town fortified by the nature of the place and by art, had been taken by us in a few days after our arrival there, began to send embassadors into all quarters, to combine, to give hostages one to another, to raise troops. Embassadors also are sent to those states of Hither Spain which are nearest to Aquitania, and auxiliaries and leaders are summoned from them; on whose arrival they proceed to carry on the war with great confidence, and with a great host of men. They who had been with Q. Sertorius the whole

ostenderunt. Hi nostros disiectos adorti proelium renovarunt.

Pugnatum est diu atque acriter, cum Sotiates superioribus victoriis freti in sua virtute totius Aquitaniae salutem positam putarent, nostri autem quid sine imperatore et sine reliquis legionibus adulescentulo duce efficere possent perspici cuperent; tandem confecti vulneribus hostes terga verterunt. Quorum magno numero interfecto Crassus ex itinere oppidum Sotiatium oppugnare coepit. Quibus fortiter resistentibus vineas turresque egit. Illi alias eruptione temptata, alias cuniculis ad aggerem vineasque actis (cuius rei sunt longe peritissimi Aquitani, propterea quod multis locis apud eos aerariae secturaeque sunt), ubi diligentia nostrorum nihil his rebus profici posse intellexerunt, legatos ad Crassum mittunt seque in deditionem ut recipiat petunt.

Qua re impetrata arma tradere iussi faciunt. Atque in eam rem omnium nostrorum intentis animis alia ex parte oppidi Adiatunnus, qui summam imperii tenebat, cum DC devotis, quos illi soldurios appellant, quorum haec est condicio, ut omnibus in vita commodis una cum iis fruantur quorum se amicitiae dediderint, si quid his per vim accidat, aut eundem casum una ferant aut sibi mortem consciscant; neque adhuc hominum memoria repertus est quisquam qui, eo interfecto cuius se amicitiae devovisset, mortem recusaret---cum his Adiatunnus eruptionem facere conatus clamore ab ea parte munitionis sublato cum ad arma milites concurrissent vehementerque ibi pugnatum esset, repulsus in oppidum tamen uti eadem deditionis condicione uteretur a Crasso impetravit.

Armis obsidibusque acceptis, Crassus in fines Vocatium et Tarusatium profectus est. Tum vero barbari commoti, quod oppidum et natura loci et manu munitum paucis diebus quibus eo ventum erat expugnatum cognoverant, legatos quoque versum dimittere, coniurare, obsides inter se dare, copias parare coeperunt. Mittuntur etiam ad eas civitates legati quae sunt citerioris Hispaniae finitimae Aquitaniae: inde auxilia ducesque arcessuntur. Quorum adventu magna cum auctoritate et magna [cum] hominum multitudine

period [of his war in Spain] and were supposed to have very great skill in military matters, are chosen leaders. These, adopting the practice of the Roman people, begin to select [advantageous] places, to fortify their camp, to cut off our men from provisions, which, when Crassus observes, [and likewise] that his forces, on account of their small number could not safely be separated; that the enemy both made excursions and beset the passes, and [yet] left sufficient guard for their camp; that on that account, corn and provision could not very conveniently be brought up to him, and that the number of the enemy was daily increased, he thought that he ought not to delay in giving battle. This matter being brought to a council, when he discovered that all thought the same thing, he appointed the next day for the fight.

3:24 Having drawn out all his forces at the break of day, and marshaled them in a double line, he posted the auxiliaries in the center, and waited to see what measures the enemy would take. They, although on account of their great number and their ancient renown in war, and the small number of our men, they supposed they might safely fight, nevertheless considered it safer to gain the victory without any wound, by besetting the passes [and] cutting off the provisions: and if the Romans, on account of the want of corn, should begin to retreat, they intended to attack them while encumbered in their march and depressed in spirit [as being assailed while] under baggage. This measure being approved of by the leaders and the forces of the Romans drawn out, the enemy [still] kept themselves in their camp. Crassus having remarked this circumstance, since the enemy, intimidated by their own delay, and by the reputation [i.e. for cowardice arising thence] had rendered our soldiers more eager for fighting, and the remarks of all were heard [declaring] that no longer ought delay to be made in going to the camp, after encouraging his men, he marches to the camp of the enemy, to the great gratification of his own troops.)

3:25 There, while some were filling up the ditch, and others, by throwing a large number of darts, were driving the defenders from the rampart and fortifications, and the auxiliaries, on whom Crassus did not much rely in the battle, by supplying stones and weapons [to the soldiers], and by conveying turf to the mound, presented the appearance and character of men engaged in fighting; while also the enemy were fighting resolutely and boldly, and their weapons, discharged from their higher position, fell with great effect; the horse, having gone round the camp of the enemy, reported to Crassus that the camp was not fortified with equal care on the side of the Decuman gate, and had an easy approach.

bellum gerere conantur. Duces vero ii deliguntur qui una cum Q. Sertorio omnes annos fuerant summamque scientiam rei militaris habere existimabantur. Hi consuetudine populi Romani loca capere, castra munire, commeatibus nostros intercludere instituunt. Quod ubi Crassus animadvertit, suas copias propter exiguitatem non facile diduci, hostem et vagari et vias obsidere et castris satis praesidii relinquere, ob eam causam minus commode frumentum commeatumque sibi supportari, in dies hostium numerum augeri, non cunctandum existimavit quin pugna decertaret. Hac re ad consilium delata, ubi omnes idem sentire intellexit, posterum diem pugnae constituit.

Prima luce productis omnibus copiis duplici acie instituta, auxiliis in mediam aciem coniectis, quid hostes consilii caperent expectabat. Illi, etsi propter multitudinem et veterem belli gloriam paucitatemque nostrorum se tuto dimicaturos existimabant, tamen tutius esse arbitrabantur obsessis viis commeatu intercluso sine vulnere victoria potiri, et si propter inopiam rei frumentariae Romani se recipere coepissent, impeditos in agmine et sub sarcinis infirmiore animo adoriri cogitabant. Hoc consilio probato ab ducibus, productis Romanorum copiis, sese castris tenebant. Hac re perspecta Crassus, cum sua cunctatione atque opinione timoris hostes nostros milites alacriores ad pugnandum effecissent atque omnium voces audirentur expectari diutius non oportere quin ad castra iretur, cohortatus suos omnibus cupientibus ad hostium castra contendit.

Ibi cum alii fossas complerent, alii multis telis coniectis defensores vallo munitionibusque depellerent, auxiliaresque, quibus ad pugnam non multum Crassus confidebat, lapidibus telisque subministrandis et ad aggerem caespitibus comportandis speciem atque opinionem pugnantium praeberent, cum item ab hostibus constanter ac non timide pugnaretur telaque ex loco superiore missa non frustra acciderent, equites circumitis hostium castris Crasso renuntiaverunt non eadem esse diligentia ab decumana porta castra munita facilemque aditum habere.

3:26 Crassus, having exhorted the commanders of the horse to animate their men by great rewards and promises, points out to them what he wished to have done. They, as they had been commanded, having brought out the four cohorts, which, as they had been left as a guard for the camp, were not fatigued by exertion, and having led them round by a some what longer way, lest they could be seen from the camp of the enemy, when the eyes and minds of all were intent upon the battle, quickly arrived at those fortifications which we have spoken of, and, having demolished these, stood in the camp of the enemy before they were seen by them, or it was known what was going on. And then, a shout being heard in that quarter, our men, their strength having been recruited, (which usually occurs on the hope of victory), began to fight more vigorously. The enemy surrounded on all sides, [and] all their affairs being despaired of, made great attempts to cast themselves down over the ramparts and to seek safety in flight. These the cavalry pursued over the very open plains, and after leaving scarcely a fourth part out of the number of 50,000, which it was certain had assembled out of Aquitania and from the Cantabri, returned late at night to the camp.

3:27 Having heard of this battle, the greatest part of Aquitania surrendered itself to Crassus, and of its own accord sent hostages, in which number were the Tarbelli, the Bigerriones, the Preciani, the Vocasates, the Tarusates, the Elurates, the Garites, the Ausci, the Garumni, the Sibuzates, the Cocosates. A few [and those] most remote nations, relying on the time of the year, because winter was at hand, neglected to do this.

3:28 About the same time Caesar, although the summer was nearly past, yet, since, all Gaul being reduced, the Morini and the Menapii alone remained in arms, and had never sent embassadors to him [to make a treaty] of peace, speedily led his army thither, thinking that that war might soon be terminated. They resolved to conduct the war on a very different method from the rest of the Gauls; for as they perceived that the greatest nations [of Gaul] who had engaged in war, had been routed and overcome, and as they possessed continuous ranges of forests and morasses, they removed themselves and all their property thither. When Caesar had arrived at the opening of these forests, and had began to fortify his camp, and no enemy was in the mean time seen, while our men were dispersed on their respective duties, they suddenly rushed out from all parts of the forest, and made an attack on our men. The latter quickly took up arms and drove them back again to their forests; and having killed a great many, lost a few of their own men while pursuing them too far through those intricate places.

Crassus equitum praefectos cohortatus, ut magnis praemiis pollicitationibusque suos excitarent, quid fieri vellet ostendit. Illi, ut erat imperatum, eductis iis cohortibus quae praesidio castris relictae intritae ab labore erant, et longiore itinere circumductis, ne ex hostium castris conspici possent, omnium oculis mentibusque ad pugnam intentis celeriter ad eas quas diximus munitiones pervenerunt atque his prorutis prius in hostium castris constiterunt quam plane ab his videri aut quid rei gereretur cognosci posset. Tum vero clamore ab ea parte audito nostri redintegratis viribus, quod plerumque in spe victoriae accidere consuevit, acrius impugnare coeperunt. Hostes undique circumventi desperatis omnibus rebus se per munitiones deicere et fuga salutem petere contenderunt. Quos equitatus apertissimis campis consectatus ex milium L numero, quae ex Aquitania Cantabrisque convenisse constabat, vix quarta parte relicta, multa nocte se in castra recepit.

Hac audita pugna maxima pars Aquitaniae sese Crasso dedidit obsidesque ultro misit; quo in numero fuerunt Tarbelli, Bigerriones, Ptianii, Vocates, Tarusates, Elusates, Gates, Ausci, Garumni, Sibusates, Cocosates: paucae ultimae nationes anni tempore confisae, quod hiems suberat, id facere neglexerunt.

Eodem fere tempore Caesar, etsi prope exacta iam aestas erat, tamen, quod omni Gallia pacata Morini Menapiique supererant, qui in armis essent neque ad eum umquam legatos de pace misissent, arbitratus id bellum celeriter confici posse eo exercitum duxit; qui longe alia ratione ac reliqui Galli bellum gerere coeperunt. Nam quod intellegebant maximas nationes, quae proelio contendissent, pulsas superatasque esse, continentesque silvas ac paludes habebant, eo se suaque omnia contulerunt. Ad quarum initium silvarum cum Caesar pervenisset castraque munire instituisset neque hostis interim visus esset, dispersis in opere nostris subito ex omnibus partibus silvae evolaverunt et in nostros impetum fecerunt. Nostri celeriter arma ceperunt eosque in silvas repulerunt et compluribus interfectis longius impeditioribus locis secuti paucos ex suis deperdiderunt.

3:29 During the remaining days after this, Caesar began to cut down the forests; and that no attack might be made on the flank of the soldiers, while unarmed and not foreseeing it, he placed together (opposite to the enemy) all that timber which was cut down, and piled it up as a rampart on either flank. When a great space had been, with incredible speed, cleared in a few days, when the cattle [of the enemy] and the rear of their baggage train were already seized by our men, and they themselves were seeking for the thickest parts of the forests, storms of such a kind came on that the work was necessarily suspended, and, through the continuance of the rains, the soldiers could not any longer remain in their tents. Therefore, having laid waste all their country, [and] having burned their villages and houses, Caesar led back his army and stationed them in winter quarters among the Aulerci and Lexovii, and the other states which had made war upon him last.

Reliquis deinceps diebus Caesar silvas caedere instituit, et ne quis inermibus imprudentibusque militibus ab latere impetus fieri posset, omnem eam materiam quae erat caesa conversam ad hostem conlocabat et pro vallo ad utrumque latus extruebat. Incredibili celeritate magno spatio paucis diebus confecto, cum iam pecus atque extrema impedimenta a nostris tenerentur, ipsi densiores silvas peterent, eius modi sunt tempestates consecutae uti opus necessario intermitteretur et continuatione imbrium diutius sub pellibus milites contineri non possent. Itaque vastatis omnibus eorum agris, vicis aedificiisque incensis, Caesar exercitum reduxit et in Aulercis Lexoviisque, reliquis item civitatibus quae proxime bellum fecerant, in hibernis conlocavit.

Gallic Wars Book 4 (55 B.C.E.)

4:1 The following winter (this was the year in which Cn. Pompey and M. Crassus were consuls), those Germans [called] the Usipetes, and likewise the Tenchtheri, with a great number of men, crossed the Rhine, not far from the place at which that river discharges itself into the sea. The motive for crossing [that river] was, that having been for several years harassed by the Suevi, they were constantly engaged in war, and hindered from the pursuits of agriculture. The nation of the Suevi is by far the largest and the most warlike nation of all the Germans. They are said to possess a hundred cantons, from each of which they yearly send from their territories for the purpose of war a thousand armed men: the others who remain at home, maintain [both] themselves and those-engaged in the expedition. The latter again, in their turn, are in arms the year after: the former remain at home. Thus neither husbandry, nor the art and practice of war are neglected. But among them there exists no private and separate land; nor are they permitted to remain more than one year in one place for the purpose of residence. They do not live much on corn, but subsist for the most part on milk and flesh, and are much [engaged] in hunting; which circumstance must, by the nature of their food, and by their daily exercise and the freedom of their life (for having from boyhood been accustomed to no employment, or discipline, they do nothing at all contrary to their inclination), both promote their strength and render them men of vast stature of body. And to such a habit have they brought themselves, that even in the coldest parts they wear no clothing whatever except skins, by reason of the scantiness of which, a great portion of their body is bare, and besides they bathe in open rivers.

4:2 Merchants have access to them rather that they may have persons to whom they may sell those things which they have taken in war, than because they need any commodity to be imported to them. Moreover, even as to laboring cattle, in which the Gauls take the greatest pleasure, and which they procure at a great price, the Germans do not employ such as are imported, but those poor and ill-shaped animals, which belong to their country; these, however, they render capable of the greatest labor by daily exercise. In cavalry actions they frequently leap from their horses and fight on foot; and train their horses to stand still in the very spot on which they leave them, to which they retreat with great activity when there is occasion; nor, according to their practice, is any thing regarded as more unseemly, or more unmanly, than to use housings. Accordingly, they have the courage, though they be themselves but few, to advance against any number whatever of horse mounted with housings. They on no account permit wine to

Ea quae secuta est hieme, qui fuit annus Cn. Pompeio, M. Crasso consulibus, Usipetes Germani et item Tencteri magna [cum] multitudine hominum flumen Rhenum transierunt, non longe a mari, quo Rhenus influit. Causa transeundi fuit quod ab Suebis complures annos exagitati bello premebantur et agri cultura prohibebantur. Sueborum gens est longe maxima et bellicosissima Germanorum omnium. Hi centum pagos habere dicuntur, ex quibus quotannis singula milia armatorum bellandi causa ex finibus educunt. Reliqui, qui domi manserunt, se atque illos alunt; hi rursus in vicem anno post in armis sunt, illi domi remanent. Sic neque agri cultura nec ratio atque usus belli intermittitur. Sed privati ac separati agri apud eos nihil est, neque longius anno remanere uno in loco colendi causa licet. Neque multum frumento, sed maximam partem lacte atque pecore vivunt multum sunt in venationibus; quae res et cibi genere et cotidiana exercitatione et libertate vitae, quod a pueris nullo officio aut disciplina adsuefacti nihil omnino contra voluntatem faciunt, et vires alit et immani corporum magnitudine homines efficit. Atque in eam se consuetudinem adduxerunt ut locis frigidissimis neque vestitus praeter pelles habeant quicquam, quarum propter exiguitatem magna est corporis pars aperta, et laventur in fluminibus.

Mercatoribus est aditus magis eo ut quae bello ceperint quibus vendant habeant, quam quo ullam rem ad se importari desiderent. Quin etiam iumentis, quibus maxime Galli delectantur quaeque impenso parant pretio, Germani importatis non utuntur, sed quae sunt apud eos nata, parva atque deformia, haec cotidiana exercitatione summi ut sint laboris efficiunt. Equestribus proeliis saepe ex equis desiliunt ac pedibus proeliantur, equos eodem remanere vestigio adsuefecerunt, ad quos se celeriter, cum usus est, recipiunt: neque eorum moribus turpius quicquam aut inertius habetur quam ephippiis uti. Itaque ad quemvis numerum ephippiatorum equitum quamvis pauci adire audent. Vinum omnino ad se importari non patiuntur, quod ea re

be imported to them, because they consider that men degenerate in their powers of enduring fatigue, and are rendered effeminate by that commodity.

4:3 They esteem it their greatest praise as a nation, that the lands about their territories lie unoccupied to a very great extent, inasmuch as [they think] that by this circumstance is indicated, that a great number of nations can not withstand their power; and thus on one side of the Suevi the lands are said to lie desolate for about six hundred miles. On the other side they border on the Ubii, whose state was large and flourishing, considering the condition of the Germans, and who are somewhat more refined than those of the same race and the rest [of the Germans], and that because they border on the Rhine, and are much resorted to by merchants, and are accustomed to the manners of the Gauls, by reason of their approximity to them. Though the Suevi, after making the attempt frequently and in several wars, could not expel this nation from their territories, on account of the extent and population of their state, yet they made them tributaries, and rendered them less distinguished and powerful [than they had ever been].

4:4 In the same condition were the Usipetes and the Tenchtheri (whom we have mentioned above), who, for many years, resisted the power of the Suevi, but being at last driven from their possessions, and having wandered through many parts of Germany, came to the Rhine, to districts which the Menapii inhabited, and where they had lands, houses, and villages on either side of the river. The latter people, alarmed by the arrival of so great a multitude, removed from those houses which they had on the other side of the river, and having placed guards on this side the Rhine, proceeded to hinder the Germans from crossing. They, finding themselves, after they had tried all means, unable either to force a passage on account of their deficiency in shipping, or cross by stealth on account of the guards of the Menapii, pretended to return to their own settlements and districts; and, after having proceeded three days' march, returned; and their cavalry having performed the whole of this journey in one night, cut off the Menapii, who were ignorant of, and did not expect [their approach, and] who, having moreover been informed of the departure of the Germans by their scouts, had, without apprehension, returned to their villages beyond the Rhine. Having slain these, and seized their ships, they crossed the river before that part of the Menapii, who were at peace in their settlements over the Rhine, were apprized of [their intention]; and seizing all their houses, maintained themselves upon their provisions during the rest of the winter.

4:5 Caesar, when informed of these matters, fearing the fickle disposition of the Gauls, who are easily prompted to take up

ad laborem ferendum remollescere homines atque effeminari arbitrantur.

Publice maximam putant esse laudem quam latissime a suis finibus vacare agros: hac re significari magnum numerum civitatum suam vim sustinere non posse. Itaque una ex parte a Suebis circiter milia passuum C agri vacare dicuntur. Ad alteram partem succedunt Ubii, quorum fuit civitas ampla atque florens, ut est captus Germanorum; ii paulo, quamquam sunt eiusdem generis, sunt ceteris humaniores, propterea quod Rhenum attingunt multum ad eos mercatores ventitant et ipsi propter propinquitatem [quod] Gallicis sunt moribus adsuefacti. Hos cum Suebi multis saepe bellis experti propter amplitudinem gravitatem civitatis finibus expellere non potuissent, tamen vectigales sibi fecerunt ac multo humiliores infirmiores redegerunt.

In eadem causa fuerunt Usipetes et Tencteri, quos supra diximus; qui complures annos Sueborum vim sustinuerunt, ad extremum tamen agris expulsi et multis locis Germaniae triennium vagati ad Rhenum pervenerunt, quas regiones Menapii incolebant. Hi ad utramque ripam fluminis agros, aedificia vicosque habebant; sed tantae multitudinis adventu perterriti ex iis aedificiis quae trans flumen habuerant demigraverant, et cis Rhenum dispositis praesidiis Germanos transire prohibebant. Illi omnia experti, cum neque vi contendere propter inopiam navium neque clam transire propter custodias Menapiorum possent, reverti se in suas sedes regionesque simulaverunt et tridui viam progressi rursus reverterunt atque omni hoc itinere una nocte equitatu confecto inscios inopinantes Menapios oppresserunt, qui de Germanorum discessu per exploratores certiores facti sine metu trans Rhenum in suos vicos remigraverant. His interfectis navibus eorum occupatis, prius quam ea pars Menapiorum quae citra Rhenum erat certior fieret, flumen transierunt atque omnibus eorum aedificiis occupatis reliquam partem hiemis se eorum copiis aluerunt.

His de rebus Caesar certior factus et infirmitatem Gallorum veritus, quod sunt in consiliis capiendis

resolutions, and much addicted to change, considered that nothing was to be intrusted to them; for it is the custom of that people to compel travelers to stop, even against their inclination, and inquire what they may have heard, or may know, respecting any matter; and in towns the common people throng around merchants and force them to state from what countries they come, and what affairs they know of there. They often engage in resolutions concerning the most important matters, induced by these reports and stories alone; of which they must necessarily instantly repent, since they yield to mere unauthorized reports; and since most people give to their questions answers framed agreeably to their wishes.

4:6 Caesar, being aware of their custom, in order that he might not encounter a more formidable war, sets forward to the army earlier in the year than he was accustomed to do. When he had arrived there, he discovered that those things, which he had suspected would occur, had taken place; that embassies had been sent to the Germans by some of the states, and that they had been entreated to leave the Rhine, and had been promised that all things which they desired should be provided by the Gauls. Allured by this hope, the Germans were then making excursions to greater distances, and had advanced to the territories of the Eburones and the Condrusi, who are under the protection of the Treviri. After summoning the chiefs of Gaul, Caesar thought proper to pretend ignorance of the things which he had discovered; and having conciliated and confirmed their minds, and ordered some cavalry to be raised, resolved to make war against the Germans.

4:7 Having provided corn and selected his cavalry, he began to direct his march toward those parts in which he heard the Germans were. When he was distant from them only a few days' march, embassadors came to him from their state, whose speech was as follows: "That the Germans neither make war upon the Roman people first, nor do they decline, if they are provoked, to engage with them in arms; for that this was the custom of the Germans handed down to them from their forefathers, -to resist whatsoever people make war upon them and not to avert it by entreaty; this, however, they confessed,--that they had come hither reluctantly, having been expelled from their country. If the Romans were disposed to accept their friendship, they might be serviceable allies to them; and let them either assign them lands, or permit them to retain those which they had acquired by their arms; that they are inferior to the Suevi alone, to whom not even the immortal gods can show themselves equal; that there was none at all besides on earth whom they could not conquer."

4:8 To these remarks Caesar replied in such terms as he thought proper; but the conclusion of his speech was, "That he could make

mobiles et novis plerumque rebus student, nihil his committendum existimavit. Est enim hoc Gallicae consuetudinis, uti et viatores etiam invitos consistere cogant et quid quisque eorum de quaque re audierit aut cognoverit quaerant et mercatores in oppidis vulgus circumsistat quibus ex regionibus veniant quas ibi res cognoverint pronuntiare cogat. His rebus atque auditionibus permoti de summis saepe rebus consilia ineunt, quorum eos in vestigio paenitere necesse est, cum incertis rumoribus serviant et pleri ad voluntatem eorum ficta respondeant.

Qua consuetudine cognita Caesar, ne graviori bello, occurreret, maturius quam consuerat ad exercitum proficiscitur. Eo cum venisset, ea quas fore suspicatus erat facta cognovit: missas legationes ab non nullis civitatibus ad Germanos invitatos eos uti ab Rheno discederent: omnia quae[que] postulassent ab se fore parata. Qua spe adducti Germani latius iam vagabantur et in fines Eburonum et Condrusorum, qui sunt Treverorum clientes, pervenerant. Principibus Gallice evocatis Caesar ea quae cognoverat dissimulanda sibi existimavit, eorumque animis permulsis et confirmatis equitatu imperato bellum cum Germanis gerere constituit.

Re frumentaria comparata equitibusque delectis iter in ea loca facere coepit, quibus in locis esse Germanos audiebat. A quibus cum paucorum dierum iter abesset, legati ab iis venerunt, quorum haec fuit oratio: Germanos neque priores populo Romano bellum inferre neque tamen recusare, si lacessantur, quin armis contendant, quod Germanorum consuetudo [haec] sit a maioribus tradita, Quicumque bellum inferant, resistere neque deprecari. Haec tamen dicere venisse invitos, eiectos domo; si suam gratiam Romani velint, posse iis utiles esse amicos; vel sibi agros attribuant vel patiantur eos tenere quos armis possederint: sese unis Suebis concedere, quibus ne di quidem immortales pares esse possint; reliquum quidem in terris esse neminem quem non superare possint.

Ad haec Caesar quae visum est respondit; sed exitus fuit orationis: sibi nullam cum iis amicitiam

no alliance with them, if they continued in Gaul; that it was not probable that they who were not able to defend their own territories, should get possession of those of others, nor were there any lands lying waste in Gaul, which could be given away, especially to so great a number of men, without doing wrong [to others]; but they might, if they were desirous, settle in the territories of the Ubii; whose embassadors were then with him, and were complaining of the aggressions of the Suevi, and requesting assistance from him; and that he would obtain this request from them."

4:9 The embassadors said that they would report these things to their country men; and, after having deliberated on the matter, would return to Caesar after the third day, they begged that he would not in the mean time advance his camp nearer to them. Caesar said that he could not grant them even that; for he had learned that they had sent a great part of their cavalry over the Meuse to the Ambivariti, some days before, for the purpose of plundering and procuring forage. He supposed that they were then waiting for these horse, and that the delay was caused on this account.

4:10 The Meuse rises from mount Le Vosge, which is in the territories of the Lingones; and, having received a branch of the Rhine, which is called the Waal, forms the island of the Batavi, and not more than eighty miles from it it falls into the ocean. But the Rhine takes its source among the Lepontii, who inhabit the Alps, and is carried with a rapid current for a long distance through the territories of the Sarunates, Helvetii, Sequani, Mediomatrici, Tribuci, and Treviri, and when it approaches the ocean, divides into several branches; and, having formed many and extensive islands, a great part of which are inhabited by savage and barbarous nations (of whom there are some who are supposed to live on fish and the eggs of sea-fowl), flows into the ocean by several mouths.

4:11 When Caesar was not more than twelve miles distant from the enemy, the embassadors return to him, as had been arranged; who meeting him on the march, earnestly entreated him not to advance any further. When they could not obtain this, they begged him to send on a dispatch to those who had marched in advance of the main army, and forbid them to engage; and grant them permission to send embassadors to the Ubii, and if the princes and senate of the latter would give them security by oath, they assured Caesar that they would accept such conditions as might be proposed by him; and requested that he would give them the space of three days for negociating these affairs. Caesar thought that these things tended to the self-same point [as their other

esse posse, si in Gallia remanerent; neque verum esse, qui suos fines tueri non potuerint alienos occupare; neque ullos in Gallia vacare agros qui dari tantae praesertim multitudini sine iniuria possint; sed licere, si velint, in Ubiorum finibus considere, quorum sint legati apud se et de Sueborum iniuriis querantur et a se auxilium petant: hoc se Ubiis imperaturus.

Legati haec se ad suos relaturos dixerunt et re deliberata post diem tertium ad Caesarem reversuros: interea ne propius se castra moveret petierunt. Ne id quidem Caesar ab se impetrari posse dixit. Cognoverat enim magnam partem equitatus ab iis aliquot diebus ante praedandi frumentandi causa ad Ambivaritos trans Mosam missam: hos expectari equites atque eius rei causa moram interponi arbitrabatur.

[Mosa profluit ex monte Vosego, qui est in finibus Lingonum, et parte quadam ex Rheno recepta, quae appellatur Vacalus insulam efficit Batavorum, in Oceanum influit neque longius ab Oceano milibus passuum LXXX in Rhenum influit. Rhenus autem oritur ex Lepontiis, qui Alpes incolunt, et longo spatio per fines Nantuatium, Helvetiorum, Sequanorum, Mediomatricorum, Tribocorum, Treverorum citatus fertur et, ubi Oceano adpropinquavit, in plures diffluit partes multis ingentibus insulis effectis, quarum pars magna a feris barbaris nationibus incolitur, ex quibus sunt qui piscibus atque ovis avium vivere existimantur, multis capitibus in Oceanum influit.]

Caesar cum ab hoste non amplius passuum XII milibus abesset, ut erat constitutum, ad eum legati revertuntur; qui in itinere congressi magnopere ne longius progrederetur orabant. Cum id non impetrassent, petebant uti ad eos [equites] qui agmen antecessissent praemitteret eos pugna prohiberet, sibique ut potestatem faceret in Ubios legatos mittendi; quorum si principes ac senatus sibi iure iurando fidem fecisset, ea condicione quae a Caesare ferretur se usuros ostendebant: ad has res conficiendas sibi tridui spatium daret. Haec omnia Caesar eodem illo pertinere

proposal]; [namely] that, in consequence of a delay of three days intervening, their horse, which were at a distance, might return; however, he said, that he would not that day advance further than four miles for the purpose of procuring water; he ordered that they should assemble at that place in as large a number as possible, the following day, that he might inquire into their demands. In the mean time he sends messengers to the officers who had marched in advance with all the cavalry, to order them not to provoke the enemy to an engagement, and if they themselves were assailed, to sustain the attack until he came up with the army.

4:12 But the enemy, as soon as they saw our horse, the number of which was 5000, whereas they themselves had not more than 800 horse, because those which had gone over the Meuse for the purpose of foraging had not returned, while our men had no apprehensions, because their embassadors had gone away from Caesar a little before, and that day had been requested by them as a period of truce, made an onset on our men, and soon threw them into disorder. When our men, in their turn, made a stand, they, according to their practice, leaped from their horses to their feet, and stabbing our horses in the belly and overthrowing a great many of our men, put the rest to flight, and drove them forward so much alarmed that they did not desist from their retreat till they had come in sight of our army. In that encounter seventy-four of our horse were slain; among them, Piso, an Aquitanian, a most valiant man, and descended from a very illustrious family; whose grandfather had held the sovereignty of his state, and had been styled friend by our senate. He, while he was endeavoring to render assistance to his brother who was surrounded by the enemy, and whom he rescued from danger, was himself thrown from his horse, which was wounded under him, but still opposed [his antagonists] with the greatest intrepidity, as long as he was able to maintain the conflict. When at length he fell, surrounded on all sides and after receiving many wounds, and his brother, who had then retired from the fight, observed it from a distance, he spurred on his horse, threw himself upon the enemy, and was killed.

4:13 After this engagement, Caesar considered that neither ought embassadors to be received to audience, nor conditions be accepted by him from those who, after having sued for peace by way of stratagem and treachery, had made war without provocation. And to wait until the enemy's forces were augmented and their cavalry had returned, he concluded, would be the greatest madness; and knowing the fickleness of the Gauls, he felt how much influence the enemy had already acquired among them by this one skirmish. He [therefore] deemed that no time for concerting measures ought to be afforded them. After having resolved on those things and communicated his plans to his

arbitrabatur ut tridui mora interposita equites eorum qui abessent reverterentur; tamen sese non longius milibus passuum IIII aquationis causa processurum eo die dixit: huc postero die quam frequentissimi convenirent, ut de eorum postulatis cognosceret. Interim ad praefectos, qui cum omni equitatu antecesserant, mittit qui nuntiarent ne hostes proelio lacesserent, et si ipsi lacesserentur, sustinerent quoad ipse cum exercitu propius accessisset.

At hostes, ubi primum nostros equites conspexerunt, quorum erat V milium numerus, cum ipsi non amplius DCCC equites haberent, quod ii qui frumentandi causa erant trans Mosam profecti nondum redierant, nihil timentibus nostris, quod legati eorum paulo ante a Caesare discesserant atque is dies indutiis erat ab his petitus, impetu facto celeriter nostros perturbaverunt; rursus his resistentibus consuetudine sua ad pedes desiluerunt subfossis equis compluribus nostris deiectis reliquos in fugam coniecerunt atque ita perterritos egerunt ut non prius fuga desisterent quam in conspectum agminis nostri venissent. In eo proelio ex equitibus nostris interficiuntur IIII et LXX, in his vir fortissimus Piso Aquitanus, amplissimo genere natus, cuius avus in civitate sua regnum obtinuerat amicus a senatu nostro appellatus. Hic cum fratri intercluso ab hostibus auxilium ferret, illum ex periculo eripuit, ipse equo vulnerato deiectus, quoad potuit, fortissime restitit; cum circumventus multis vulneribus acceptis cecidisset atque id frater, qui iam proelio excesserat, procul animadvertisset, incitato equo se hostibus obtulit atque interfectus est.

Hoc facto proelio Caesar neque iam sibi legatos audiendos neque condiciones accipiendas arbitrabatur ab iis qui per dolum atque insidias petita pace ultro bellum intulissent; expectare vero dum hostium copiae augerentur equitatus reverteretur summae dementiae esse iudicabat, et cognita Gallorum infirmitate quantum iam apud eos hostes uno proelio auctoritatis essent consecuti sentiebat; quibus ad consilia capienda nihil spatii dandum existimabat. His constitutis rebus et consilio cum legatis et quaestore

lieutenants and quaestor in order that he might not suffer any opportunity for engaging to escape him, a very seasonable event occurred, namely, that on the morning of the next day, a large body of Germans, consisting of their princes and old men, came to the camp to him to practice the same treachery and dissimulation; but, as they asserted, for the purpose of acquitting themselves for having engaged in a skirmish the day before, contrary to what had been agreed and to what indeed, they themselves had requested; and also if they could by any means obtain a truce by deceiving him. Caesar, rejoicing that they had fallen into his power, ordered them to be detained. He then drew all his forces out of the camp, and commanded the cavalry, because he thought they were intimidated by the late skirmish, to follow in the rear.

4:14 Having marshalled his army in three lines, and in a short time performed a march of eight miles, he arrived at the camp of the enemy before the Germans could perceive what was going on; who being suddenly alarmed by all the circumstances, both by the speediness of our arrival and the absence of their own officers, as time was afforded neither for concerting measures nor for seizing their arms, are perplexed as to whether it would be better to lead out their forces against the enemy, or to defend their camp, or seek their safety by flight. Their consternation being made apparent by their noise and tumult, our soldiers, excited by the treachery of the preceding day, rushed into the camp: such of them as could readily get their arms, for a short time withstood our men, and gave battle among their carts and baggage wagons; but the rest of the people, [consisting] of boys and women (for they had left their country and crossed the Rhine with all their families) began to fly in all directions; in pursuit of whom Caesar sent the cavalry.

4:15 The Germans when, upon hearing a noise behind them, [they looked and] saw that their families were being slain, throwing away their arms and abandoning their standards, fled out of the camp, and when they had arrived at the confluence of the Meuse and the Rhine, the survivors despairing of further escape, as a great number of their countrymen had been killed, threw themselves into the river and there perished, overcome by fear, fatigue, and the violence of the stream. Our soldiers, after the alarm of so great a war, for the number of the enemy amounted to 430,000, returned to their camp, all safe to a man, very few being even wounded. Caesar granted those whom he had detained in the camp liberty of departing. They however, dreading revenge and torture from the Gauls, whose lands they had harassed, said that they desired to remain with him. Caesar granted them permission.

communicato, ne quem diem pugnae praetermitteret, oportunissima res accidit, quod postridie eius diei mane eadem et perfidia et simulatione usi Germani frequentes, omnibus principibus maioribusque natu adhibitis, ad eum in castra venerunt, simul, ut dicebatur, sui purgandi causa, quod contra atque esset dictum et ipsi petissent, proelium pridie commisissent, simul ut, si quid possent, de indutiis fallendo impetrarent. Quos sibi Caesar oblatos gavisus illos retineri iussit; ipse omnes copias castris D eduxit equitatumque, quod recenti proelio perterritum esse existimabat, agmen subsequi iussit.

Acie triplici instituta et celeriter VIII milium itinere confecto, prius ad hostium castra pervenit quam quid ageretur Germani sentire possent. Qui omnibus rebus subito perterriti et celeritate adventus nostri et discessu suorum, neque consilii habendi neque arma capiendi spatio dato perturbantur, copiasne adversus hostem ducere an castra defendere an fuga salutem petere praestaret. Quorum timor cum fremitu et concursu significaretur, milites nostri pristini diei perfidia incitati in castra inruperunt. Quo loco qui celeriter arma capere potuerunt paulisper nostris restiterunt atque inter carros impedimentaque proelium commiserunt; at reliqua multitudo puerorum mulierumque (nam cum omnibus suis domo excesserant Rhenum transierant) passim fugere coepit, ad quos consectandos Caesar equitatum misit.

Germani post tergum clamore audito, cum suos interfiei viderent, armis abiectis signis militaribus relictis se ex castris eiecerunt, et cum ad confluentem Mosae et Rheni pervenissent, reliqua fuga desperata, magno numero interfecto, reliqui se in flumen praecipitaverunt atque ibi timore, lassitudine, vi fluminis oppressi perierunt. Nostri ad unum omnes incolumes, perpaucis vulneratis, ex tanti belli timore, cum hostium numerus capitum CCCCXXX milium fuisset, se in castra receperunt. Caesar iis quos in castris retinuerat discedendi potestatem fecit. Illi supplicia cruciatusque Gallorum veriti, quorum agros vexaverant, remanere se apud eum velle dixerunt. His Caesar libertatem concessit.

4:16 The German war being finished, Caesar thought it expedient for him to cross the Rhine, for many reasons; of which this was the most weighty, that, since he saw the Germans were so easily urged to go into Gaul, he desired they should have their fears for their own territories, when they discovered that the army of the Roman people both could and dared pass the Rhine. There was added also, that portion of the cavalry of the Usipetes and the Tenchtheri, which I have above related to have crossed the Meuse for the purpose of plundering and procuring forage, and was not present at the engagement, had betaken themselves, after the retreat of their countrymen, across the Rhine into the territories of the Sigambri, and united themselves to them. When Caesar sent embassadors to them, to demand that they should give up to him those who had made war against him and against Gaul, they replied, "That the Rhine bounded the empire of the Roman people; if he did not think it just for the Germans to pass over into Gaul against his consent, why did he claim that any thing beyond the Rhine should be subject to his dominion or power?" The Ubii, also, who alone, out of all the nations lying beyond the Rhine, had sent embassadors to Caesar, and formed an alliance and given hostages, earnestly entreated "that he would bring them assistance, because they were grievously oppressed by the Suevi; or, if he was prevented from doing so by the business of the commonwealth, he would at least transport his army over the Rhine; that that would be sufficient for their present assistance and their hope for the future; that so great was the name and the reputation of his army, even among the most remote nations of the Germans, arising from the defeat of Ariovistus and this last battle which was fought, that they might be safe under the fame and friendship of the Roman people." They promised a large number of ships for transporting the army.

4:17 Caesar, for those reasons which I have mentioned, had resolved to cross the Rhine; but to cross by ships he neither deemed to be sufficiently safe, nor considered consistent with his own dignity or that of the Roman people. Therefore, although the greatest difficulty in forming a bridge was presented to him, on account of the breadth, rapidity, and depth of the river, he nevertheless considered that it ought to be attempted by him, or that his army ought not otherwise to be led over. He devised this plan of a bridge. He joined together at the distance of two feet, two piles, each a foot and a half thick, sharpened a little at the lower end, and proportioned in length, to the depth of the river. After he had, by means of engines, sunk these into the river, and fixed them at the bottom, and then driven them in with rammers, not quite perpendicularly, dike a stake, but bending forward and sloping, so as to incline in the direction of the current of the river;

Germanico bello confecto multis de causis Caesar statuit sibi Rhenum esse transeundum; quarum illa fuit iustissima quod, cum videret Germanos tam facile impelli ut in Galliam venirent, suis quoque rebus eos timere voluit, cum intellegerent et posse et audere populi Romani exercitum Rhenum transire. Accessit etiam quod illa pars equitatus Usipetum et Tencterorum, quam supra commemoravi praedandi frumentandi causa Mosam transisse neque proelio interfuisse, post fugam suorum se trans Rhenum in fines Sugambrorum receperat seque cum his coniunxerat. Ad quos cum Caesar nuntios misisset, qui postularent eos qui sibi Galliae bellum intulissent sibi dederent, responderunt: populi Romani imperium Rhenum finire; si se invito Germanos in Galliam transire non aequum existimaret, cur sui quicquam esse imperii aut potestatis trans Rhenum postularet? Ubii autem, qui uni ex Transrhenanis ad Caesarem legatos miserant, amicitiam fecerant, obsides dederant, magnopere orabant ut sibi auxilium ferret, quod graviter ab Suebis premerentur; vel, si id facere occupationibus rei publicae prohiberetur, exercitum modo Rhenum transportaret: id sibi ad auxilium spemque reliqui temporis satis futurum. Tantum esse nomen atque opinionem eius exercitus Ariovisto pulso et hoc novissimo proelio facto etiam ad ultimas Germanorum nationes, uti opinione et amicitia populi Romani tuti esse possint. Navium magnam copiam ad transportandum exercitum pollicebantur.

Caesar his de causis quas commemoravi Rhenum transire decrevat; sed navibus transire neque satis tutum esse arbitrabatur neque suae neque populi Romani dignitatis esse statuebat. Itaque, etsi summa difficultas faciendi pontis proponebatur propter latitudinem, rapiditatem altitudinemque fluminis, tamen id sibi contendendum aut aliter non traducendum exercitum existimabat. Rationem pontis hanc instituit. Tigna bina sesquipedalia. paulum ab imo praeacuta dimensa ad altitudinem fluminis intervallo pedum duorum inter se iungebat. Haec cum machinationibus immissa in flumen defixerat fistucisque adegerat, non sublicae modo derecte ad perpendiculum, sed prone ac fastigate, ut secundum naturam fluminis

he also placed two [other piles] opposite to these, at the distance of forty feet lower down, fastened together in the same manner, but directed against the force and current of the river. Both these, moreover, were kept firmly apart by beams two feet thick (the space which the binding of the piles occupied), laid in at their extremities between two braces on each side, and in consequence of these being in different directions and fastened on sides the one opposite to the other, so great was the strength of the work, and such the arrangement of the materials, that in proportion as the greater body of water dashed against the bridge, so much the closer were its parts held fastened together. These beams were bound together by timber laid over them, in the direction of the length of the bridge, and were [then] covered over with laths and hurdles; and in addition to this, piles were driven into the water obliquely, at the lower side of the bridge, and these, serving as buttresses, and being connected with every portion of the work, sustained the force of the stream: and there were others also above the bridge, at a moderate distance; that if trunks of trees or vessels were floated down the river by the barbarians for the purpose of destroying the work, the violence of such things might be diminished by these defenses, and might not injure the bridge.

4:18 Within ten days after the timber began to be collected, the whole work was completed, and the whole army led over. Caesar, leaving a strong guard at each end of the bridge, hastens into the territories of the Sigambri. In the mean time, embassadors from several nations come to him, whom, on their suing for peace and alliance, he answers in a courteous manner, and orders hostages to be brought to him. But the Sigambri, at the very time the bridge was begun to be built, made preparations for a flight (by the advice of such of the Tenchtheri and Usipetes as they had among them), and quitted their territories, and conveyed away all their possessions, and concealed themselves in deserts and woods.

4:19 Caesar, having remained in their territories a few days, and burned all their villages and houses, and cut down their corn, proceeded into the territories of the Ubii; and having promised them his assistance, if they were ever harassed by the Suevi, he learned from them these particulars: that the Suevi, after they had by means of their scouts found that the bridge was being built, had called a council, according to their custom, and sent orders to all parts of their state to remove from the towns and convey their children, wives, and all their possessions into the woods, and that all who could bear arms should assemble in one place; that the place thus chosen was nearly the centre of those regions which the Suevi possessed; that in this spot they had resolved to await the arrival of the Romans, and give them battle there. When

procumberent, iis item contraria duo ad eundem modum iuncta intervallo pedum quadragenum ab inferiore parte contra vim atque impetu fluminis conversa statuebat. Haec utraque insuper bipedalibus trabibus immissis, quantum eorum tignorum iunctura distabat, binis utrimque fibulis ab extrema parte distinebantur; quibus disclusis atque in contrariam partem revinctis, tanta erat operis firmitudo atque ea rerum natura ut, quo maior vis aquae se incitavisset, hoc artius inligata tenerentur. Haec derecta materia iniecta contexebantur ac longuriis cratibusque consternebantur; ac nihilo setius sublicae et ad inferiorem partem fluminis oblique agebantur, quae pro ariete subiectae et cum omni opere coniunctae vim fluminis exciperent, et aliae item supra pontem mediocri spatio, ut, si arborum trunci sive naves deiciendi operis causa essent a barbaris missae, his defensoribus earum rerum vis minueretur neu ponti nocerent.

Diebus X, quibus materia coepta erat comportari, omni opere effecto exercitus traducitur. Caesar ad utramque partem pontis firmo praesidio relicto in fines Sugambrorum contendit. Interim a compluribus civitatibus ad eum legati veniunt; quibus pacem atque amicitiam petentibus liberaliter respondet obsidesque ad se adduci iubet. At Sugambri, ex eo tempore quo pons institui coeptus est fuga comparata, hortantibus iis quos ex Tencteris atque Usipetibus apud se habebant, finibus suis excesserant suaque omnia exportaverant seque in solitudinem ac silvas abdiderant.

Caesar paucos dies in eorum finibus moratus, omnibus vicis aedificiisque incensis frumentisque succisis, se in fines Ubiorum recepit atque his auxilium suum pollicitus, si a Suebis premerentur, haec ab iis cognovit: Suebos, postea quam per exploratores pontem fieri comperissent, more suo concilio habito nuntios in omnes partes dimisisse, uti de oppidis demigrarent, liberos, uxores suaque omnia in silvis deponerent atque omnes qui arma ferre possent unum in locum convenirent. Hunc esse delectum medium fere regionum earum quas Suebi obtinerent; hic Romanorum adventum expectare atque ibi decertare constituisse. Quod

Caesar discovered this, having already accomplished all these things on account of which he had resolved to lead his army over, namely, to strike fear into the Germans, take vengeance on the Sigambri, and free the Ubii from the invasion of the Suevi, having spent altogether eighteen days beyond the Rhine, and thinking he had advanced far enough to serve both honor and interest, he returned into Gaul, and cut down the bridge.

4:20 During the short part of summer which remained, Caesar, although in these countries, as all Gaul lies toward the north, the winters are early, nevertheless resolved to proceed into Britain, because he discovered that in almost all the wars with the Gauls succors had been furnished to our enemy from that country; and even if the time of year should be insufficient for carrying on the war, yet he thought it would be of great service to him if he only entered the island, and saw into the character of the people, and got knowledge of their localities, harbors, and landing-places, all which were for the most part unknown to the Gauls. For neither does any one except merchants generally go thither, nor even to them was any portion of it known, except the sea-coast and those parts which are opposite to Gaul. Therefore, after having called up to him the merchants from all parts, he could learn neither what was the size of the island, nor what or how numerous were the nations which inhabited it, nor what system of war they followed, nor what customs they used, nor what harbors were convenient for a great number of large ships.

4:21 He sends before him Caius Volusenus with a ship of war, to acquire a knowledge of these particulars before he in person should make a descent into the island, as he was convinced that this was a judicious measure. He commissioned him to thoroughly examine into all matters, and then return to him as soon as possible. He himself proceeds to the Morini with all his forces. He orders ships from all parts of the neighboring countries, and the fleet which the preceding summer he had built for the war with the Veneti, to assemble in this place. In the mean time, his purpose having been discovered, and reported to the Britons by merchants, embassadors come to him from several states of the island, to promise that they will give hostages, and submit to the government of the Roman people. Having given them an audience, he after promising liberally, and exhorting them to continue in that purpose, sends them back to their own country, and [dispatches] with them Commius, whom, upon subduing the Atrebates, he had created king there, a man whose courage and conduct he esteemed, and who he thought would be faithful to him, and whose influence ranked highly in those countries. He orders him to visit as many

ubi Caesar comperit, omnibus iis rebus confectis, quarum rerum causa exercitum traducere constituerat, ut Germanis metum iniceret, ut Sugambros ulcisceretur, ut Ubios obsidione liberaret, diebus omnino XVIII trans Rhenum consumptis, satis et ad laudem et ad utilitatem profectum arbitratus se in Galliam recepit pontemque rescidit.

Exigua parte aestatis reliqua Caesar, etsi in his locis, quod omnis Gallia ad septentriones vergit, maturae sunt hiemes, tamen in Britanniam proficisci contendit, quod omnibus fere Gallicis bellis hostibus nostris inde subministrata auxilia intellegebat, et si tempus anni ad bellum gerendum deficeret, tamen magno sibi usui fore arbitrabatur, si modo insulam adiisset, genus hominum perspexisset, loca, portus, aditus cognovisset; quae omnia fere Gallis erant incognita. Neque enim temere praeter mercatores illo adit quisquam, neque his ipsis quicquam praeter oram maritimam atque eas regiones quae sunt contra Galliam notum est. Itaque vocatis ad se undique mercatoribus, neque quanta esset insulae magnitudo neque quae aut quantae nationes incolerent, neque quem usum belli haberent aut quibus institutis uterentur, neque qui essent ad maiorem navium multitudinem idonei portus reperire poterat.

Ad haec cognoscenda, prius quam periculum faceret, idoneum esse arbitratus C. Volusenum cum navi longa praemittit. Huic mandat ut exploratis omnibus rebus ad se quam primum revertatur. Ipse cum omnibus copiis in Morinos proficiscitur, quod inde erat brevissimus in Britanniam traiectus. Huc naves undique ex finitimis regionibus et quam superiore aestate ad Veneticum bellum fecerat classem iubet convenire. Interim, consilio eius cognito et per mercatores perlato ad Britannos, a compluribus insulae civitatibus ad eum legati veniunt, qui polliceantur obsides dare atque imperio populi Romani obtemperare. Quibus auditis, liberaliter pollicitus hortatusque ut in ea sententia permanerent, eos domum remittit et cum iis una Commium, quem ipse Atrebatibus superatis regem ibi constituerat, cuius et virtutem et consilium probabat et quem sibi fidelem esse arbitrabatur cuiusque auctoritas

states as he could, and persuade them to embrace the protection of the Roman people, and apprize them that he would shortly come thither. Volusenus, having viewed the localities as far as means could be afforded one who dared not leave his ship and trust himself to barbarians, returns to Caesar on the fifth day, and reports what he had there observed.

4:22 While Caesar remains in these parts for the purpose of procuring ships, embassadors come to him from a great portion of the Morini, to plead their excuse respecting their conduct on the late occasion; alleging that it was as men uncivilized, and as those who were unacquainted with our custom, that they had made war upon the Roman people, and promising to perform what he should command. Caesar, thinking that this had happened fortunately enough for him, because he neither wished to leave an enemy behind him, nor had an opportunity for carrying on a war, by reason of the time of year, nor considered that employment in such trifling matters was to be preferred to his enterprise on Britain, imposes a large number of hostages; and when these were brought, he received them to his protection. Having collected together, and provided about eighty transport ships, as many as he thought necessary for conveying over two legions, he assigned such [ships] of war as he had besides to the quaestor, his lieutenants, and officers of cavalry. There were in addition to these eighteen ships of burden which were prevented, eight miles from that place, by winds, from being able to reach the same port. These he distributed among the horse; the rest of the army, he delivered to Q. Titurius Sabinus and L. Aurunculeius Cotta, his lieutenants, to lead into the territories of the Menapii and those cantons of the Morini from which embassadors had not come to him. He ordered P. Sulpicius Rufus, his lieutenant, to hold possession of the harbor, with such a garrison as he thought sufficient.

4:23 These matters being arranged, finding the weather favorable for his voyage, he set sail about the third watch, and ordered the horse to march forward to the further port, and there embark and follow him. As this was performed rather tardily by them, he himself reached Britain with the first squadron of ships, about the fourth hour of the day, and there saw the forces of the enemy drawn up in arms on all the hills. The nature of the place was this: the sea was confined by mountains so close to it that a dart could be thrown from their summit upon the shore. Considering this by no means a fit place for disembarking, he remained at anchor till the ninth hour, for the other ships to arrive there. Having in the mean time assembled the lieutenants and military tribunes, he told

in his regionibus magni habebatur, mittit. Huic imperat quas possit adeat civitates horteturque ut populi Romani fidem sequantur seque celeriter eo venturum nuntiet. Volusenus perspectis regionibus omnibus quantum ei facultatis dari potuit, qui navi egredi ac se barbaris committere non auderet, V. die ad Caesarem revertitur quaeque ibi perspexisset renuntiat.

Dum in his locis Caesar navium parandarum causa moratur, ex magna parte Morinorum ad eum legati venerunt, qui se de superioris temporis consilio excusarent, quod homines barbari et nostrae consuetudinis imperiti bellum populo Romano fecissent, seque ea quae imperasset facturos pollicerentur. Hoc sibi Caesar satis oportune accidisse arbitratus, quod neque post tergum hostem relinquere volebat neque belli gerendi propter anni tempus facultatem habebat neque has tantularum rerum occupationes Britanniae anteponendas iudicabat, magnum iis numerum obsidum imperat. Quibus adductis eos in fidem recipit. Navibus circiter LXXX onerariis coactis contractisque, quot satis esse ad duas transportandas legiones existimabat, quod praeterea navium longarum habebat quaestori, legatis praefectisque distribuit. Huc accedebant XVIII onerariae naves, quae ex eo loco a milibus passuum VIII vento tenebantur quo minus in eundem portum venire possent: has equitibus tribuit. Reliquum exercitum Q. Titurio Sabino et L. Aurunculeio Cottae legatis in Menapios atque in eos pagos Morinorum a quibus ad eum legati non venerant ducendum dedit. P. Sulpicium Rufum legatum cum eo praesidio quod satis esse arbitrabatur portum tenere iussit.

His constitutis rebus, nactus idoneam ad navigandum tempestatem III. fere vigilia solvit equitesque in ulteriorem portum progredi et naves conscendere et se sequi iussit. A quibus cum paulo tardius esset administratum, ipse hora diei circiter IIII. cum primis navibus Britanniam attigit atque ibi in omnibus collibus eitas hostium copias armatas conspexit. Cuius loci haec erat natura atque ita montibus angustis mare continebatur, uti ex locis superioribus in litus telum adigi posset. Hunc ad egrediendum nequaquam idoneum locum arbitratus, dum reliquae naves eo convenirent ad

them both what he had learned from Volusenus, and what he wished to be done; and enjoined them (as the principle of military matters, and especially as maritime affairs, which have a precipitate and uncertain action, required) that all things should be performed by them at a nod and at the instant. Having dismissed them, meeting both with wind and tide favorable at the same time, the signal being given and the anchor weighed, he advanced about seven miles from that place, and stationed his fleet over against an open and level shore.

4:24 But the barbarians, upon perceiving the design of the Romans, sent forward their cavalry and charioteers, a class of warriors of whom it is their practice to make great use in their battles, and following with the rest of their forces, endeavored to prevent our men landing. In this was the greatest difficulty, for the following reasons, namely, because our ships, on account of their great size, could be stationed only in deep water; and our soldiers, in places unknown to them, with their hands embarrassed, oppressed with a large and heavy weight of armor, had at the same time to leap from the ships, stand amid the waves, and encounter the enemy; whereas they, either on dry ground, or advancing a little way into the water, free in all their limbs in places thoroughly known to them, could confidently throw their weapons and spur on their horses, which were accustomed to this kind of service. Dismayed by these circumstances and altogether untrained in this mode of battle, our men did not all exert the same vigor and eagerness which they had been wont to exert in engagements on dry ground.

4:25 When Caesar observed this, he ordered the ships of war, the appearance of which was somewhat strange to the barbarians and the motion more ready for service, to be withdrawn a little from the transport vessels, and to be propelled by their oars, and be stationed toward the open flank of the enemy, and the enemy to be beaten off and driven away, with slings, arrows, and engines: which plan was of great service to our men; for the barbarians being startled by the form of our ships and the motions of our oars and the nature of our engines, which was strange to them, stopped, and shortly after retreated a little. And while our men were hesitating [whether they should advance to the shore], chiefly on account of the depth of the sea, he who carried the eagle of the tenth legion, after supplicating the gods that the matter might turn out favorably to the legion, exclaimed, "Leap, fellow soldiers, unless you wish to betray your eagle to the enemy. I, for my part, will perform my duty to the commonwealth and my general." When he had said this with a loud voice, he leaped from the ship and proceeded to bear the eagle toward the enemy. Then our men, exhorting one another that so great a disgrace should not be incurred, all leaped from the ship. When those in the nearest

horam nonam in ancoris expectavit. Interim legatis tribunisque militum convocatis et quae ex Voluseno cognovisset et quae fieri vellet ostendit monuitque, ut rei militaris ratio, maximeque ut maritimae res postularent, ut, cum celerem atque instabilem motum haberent, ad nutum et ad tempus D omnes res ab iis administrarentur. His dimissis, et VII ab eo loco progressus aperto ac plano litore naves constituit.

At barbari, consilio Romanorum cognito praemisso equitatu et essedariis, quo plerumque genere in proeliis uti consuerunt, reliquis copiis subsecuti nostros navibus egredi prohibebant. Erat ob has causas summa difficultas, quod naves propter magnitudinem nisi in alto constitui non poterant, militibus autem, ignotis locis, impeditis manibus, magno et gravi onere armorum oppressis simul et de navibus desiliendum et in auctibus consistendum et cum hostibus erat pugnandum, cum illi aut ex arido aut paulum in aquam progressi omnibus membris expeditis, notissimis locis, audacter tela coicerent et equos insuefactos incitarent. Quibus rebus nostri perterriti atque huius omnino generis pugnae imperiti, non eadem alacritate ac studio quo in pedestribus uti proeliis consuerant utebantur.

Quod ubi Caesar animadvertit, naves longas, quarum et species erat barbaris inusitatior et motus ad usum expeditior, paulum removeri ab onerariis navibus et remis incitari et ad latus apertum hostium constitui atque inde fundis, sagittis, tormentis hostes propelli ac submoveri iussit; quae res magno usui nostris fuit. Nam et navium figura et remorum motu et inusitato genere tormentorum permoti barbari constiterunt ac paulum modo pedem rettulerunt. Atque nostris militibus cunctantibus, maxime propter altitudinem maris, qui X legionis aquilam gerebat, obtestatus deos, ut ea res legioni feliciter eveniret, ' desilite', inquit, ' milites, nisi vultis aquilam hostibus prodere; ego certe meum rei publicae atque imperatori officium praestitero.' Hoc cum voce magna dixisset, se ex navi proiecit atque in hostes aquilam ferre coepit. Tum nostri cohortati inter se, ne tantum dedecus admitteretur, universi ex navi desiluerunt. Hos item ex proximis primi navibus

vessels saw them, they speedily followed and approached the enemy.

4:26 The battle was maintained vigorously on both sides. Our men, however, as they could neither keep their ranks, nor get firm footing, nor follow their standards, and as one from one ship and another from another assembled around whatever standards they met, were thrown into great confusion. But the enemy, who were acquainted with all the shallows, when from the shore they saw any coming from a ship one by one, spurred on their horses, and attacked them while embarrassed; many surrounded a few, others threw their weapons upon our collected forces on their exposed flank. When Caesar observed this, he ordered the boats of the ships of war and the spy sloops to be filled with soldiers, and sent them up to the succor of those whom he had observed in distress. Our men, as soon as they made good their footing on dry ground, and all their comrades had joined them, made an attack upon the enemy, and put them to flight, but could not pursue them very far, because the horse had not been able to maintain their course at sea and reach the island. This alone was wanting to Caesar's accustomed success.

4:27 The enemy being thus vanquished in battle, as soon as they recovered after their flight, instantly sent embassadors to Caesar to negotiate about peace. They promised to give hostages and perform what he should command. Together with these embassadors came Commius the Altrebatian, who, as I have above said, had been sent by Caesar into Britain. Him they had seized upon when leaving his ship, although in the character of embassador he bore the general's commission to them, and thrown into chains: then after the battle was fought, they sent him back, and in suing for peace cast the blame of that act upon the common people, and entreated that it might be pardoned on account of their indiscretion. Caesar, complaining, that after they had sued for peace, and had voluntarily sent embassadors into the continent for that purpose, they had made war without a reason, said that he would pardon their indiscretion, and imposed hostages, a part of whom they gave immediately; the rest they said they would give in a few days, since they were sent for from remote places. In the mean time they ordered their people to return to the country parts, and the chiefs assembled from all quarter, and proceeded to surrender themselves and their states to Caesar.

4:28 A peace being established by these proceedings four days after we had come into Britain, the eighteen ships, to which reference has been made above, and which conveyed the cavalry,

cum conspexissent, subsecuti hostibus adpropinquaverunt.

Pugnatum est ab utrisque acriter. Nostri tamen, quod neque ordines servare neque firmiter insistere neque signa subsequi poterant atque alius alia ex navi quibuscumque signis occurrerat se adgregabat, magnopere perturbabantur; hostes vero, notis omnibus vadii, ubi ex litore aliquos singulares ex navi egredientes conspexerant, incitatis equis impeditos adoriebantur, plures paucos circumsistebant, alii ab latere aperto in universos tela coiciebant. Quod cum animadvertisset Caesar, scaphas longarum navium, item speculatoria navigia militibus compleri iussit, et quos laborantes conspexerat, his subsidia submittebat. Nostri, simul in arido constiterunt, suis omnibus consecutis, in hostes impetum fecerunt atque eos in fugam dederunt; neque longius prosequi potuerunt, quod equites cursum tenere atque insulam capere non potuerant. Hoc unum ad pristinam fortunam Caesari defuit.

Hostes proelio superati, simul atque se ex fuga receperunt, statim ad Caesarem legatos de pace miserunt; obsides sese daturos quaeque imperasset facturos polliciti sunt. Una cum his legatis Commius Atrebas venit, quem supra demonstraveram a Caesare in Britanniam praemissum. Hunc illi e navi egressum, cum ad eos oratoris modo Caesaris mandata deferret, comprehenderant atque in vincula coniecerant; tum proelio facto remiserunt et in petenda pace eius rei culpam in multitudinem contulerunt et propter imprudentiam ut ignosceretur petiverunt. Caesar questus quod, cum ultro in continentem legatis missis pacem ab se petissent, bellum sine causa intulissent, ignoscere se imprudentiae dixit obsidesque imperavit; quorum illi partem statim dederunt, partem ex longinquioribus locis arcessitam paucis diebus sese daturos dixerunt. Interea suos in agros remigrare iusserunt, principesque undique convenire et se civitatesque suas Caesari commendare coeperunt.

His rebus pace confirmata, post diem quartum quam est in Britanniam ventum naves XVIII, de quibus supra demonstratum est, quae equites

set sail from the upper port with a gentle gale, when, however, they were approaching Britain and were seen from the camp, so great a storm suddenly arose that none of them could maintain their course at sea; and some were taken back to the same port from which they had started;-others, to their great danger, were driven to the lower part of the island, nearer to the west; which, however, after having cast anchor, as they were getting filled with water, put out to sea through necessity in a stormy night, and made for the continent.

4:29 It happened that night to be full moon, which usually occasions very high tides in that ocean; and that circumstance was unknown to our men. Thus, at the same time, the tide began to fill the ships of war which Caesar had provided to convey over his army, and which he had drawn up on the strand; and the storm began to dash the ships of burden which were riding at anchor against each other; nor was any means afforded our men of either managing them or of rendering any service. A great many ships having been wrecked, inasmuch as the rest, having lost their cables, anchors, and other tackling, were unfit for sailing, a great confusion, as would necessarily happen, arose throughout the army; for there were no other ships in which they could be conveyed back, and all things which are of service in repairing vessels were wanting, and, corn for the winter had not been provided in those places, because it was understood by all that they would certainly winter in Gaul.

4:30 On discovering these things the chiefs of Britain, who had come up after the battle was fought to perform those conditions which Caesar had imposed, held a conference, when they perceived that cavalry, and ships, and corn were wanting to the Romans, and discovered the small number of our soldiers from the small extent of the camp (which, too, was on this account more limited than ordinary, because Caesar had conveyed over his legions without baggage), and thought that the best plan was to renew the war, and cut off our men from corn and provisions and protract the affair till winter; because they felt confident, that, if they were vanquished or cut off from a return, no one would afterward pass over into Britain for the purpose of making war. Therefore, again entering into a conspiracy, they began to depart from the camp by degrees and secretly bring up their people from the country parts.

4:31 But Caesar, although he had not as yet discovered their measures, yet, both from what had occurred to his ships, and from the circumstance that they had neglected to give the promised

sustulerant, ex superiore portu leni vento solverunt. Quae cum adpropinquarent Britanniae et ex castris viderentur, tanta tempestas subito coorta est ut nulla earum cursum tenere posset, sed aliae eodem unde erant profectae referrentur, aliae ad inferiorem partem insulae, quae est propius solis occasum, magno suo cum periculo deicerentur; quae tamen ancoris iactis cum fluctibus complerentur, necessario adversa nocte in altum provectae continentem petierunt.

Eadem nocte accidit ut esset luna plena, qui dies a maritimos aestus maximos in Oceano efficere consuevit, nostrisque id erat incognitum. Ita uno tempore et longas naves, [quibus Caesar exercitum transportandum curaverat,] quas Caesar in aridum subduxerat, aestus complebat, et onerarias, quae ad ancoras erant deligatae, tempestas adflictabat, neque ulla nostris facultas aut administrandi aut auxiliandi dabatur. Compluribus navibus fractis, reliquae cum essent funibus, ancoris reliquisque armamentis amissis ad navigandum inutiles, magna, id quod necesse erat accidere, totius exercitus perturbatio facta est. Neque enim naves erant aliae quibus reportari possent, et omnia deerant quae ad reficiendas naves erant usui, et, quod omnibus constabat hiemari in Gallia oportere, frumentum in his locis in hiemem provisum non erat.

Quibus rebus cognitis, principes Britanniae, qui post proelium ad Caesarem convenerant, inter se conlocuti, cum et equites et naves et frumentum Romanis deesse intellegerent et paucitatem militum ex castrorum exiguitate cognoscerent, quae hoc erant etiam angustior quod sine impedimentis Caesar legiones transportaverat, optimum factu esse duxerunt rebellione facta frumento commeatuque nostros prohibere et rem in hiemem producere, quod his superatis aut reditu interclusis neminem postea belli inferendi causa in Britanniam transiturum confidebant. Itaque rursus coniuratione facta paulatim ex castris discedere et suos clam ex agris deducere coeperunt.

At Caesar, etsi nondum eorum consilia cognoverat, tamen et ex eventu navium suarum et ex eo quod obsides dare intermiserant fore id quod

hostages, suspected that the thing would come to pass which really did happen. He therefore provided remedies against all contingencies; for he daily conveyed corn from the country parts into the camp, used the timber and brass of such ships as were most seriously damaged for repairing the rest, and ordered whatever things besides were necessary for this object to be brought to him from the continent. And thus, since that business was executed by the soldiers with the greatest energy, he effected that, after the loss of twelve ships, a voyage could be made well enough in the rest.

4:32 While these things are being transacted, one legion had been sent to forage, according to custom, and no suspicion of war had arisen as yet, and some of the people remained in the country parts, others went backward and forward to the camp, they who were on duty at the gates of the camp reported to Caesar that a greater dust than was usual was seen in that direction in which the legion had marched. Caesar, suspecting that which was [really the case],--that some new enterprise was undertaken by the barbarians, ordered the two cohorts which were on duty, to march into that quarter with him, and two other cohorts to relieve them on duty; the rest to be armed and follow him immediately. When he had advanced some little way from the camp, he saw that his men were overpowered by the enemy and scarcely able to stand their ground, and that, the legion being crowded together, weapons were being cast on them from all sides. For as all the corn was reaped in every part with the exception of one, the enemy, suspecting that our men would repair to that, had concealed themselves in the woods during the night. Then attacking them suddenly, scattered as they were, and when they had laid aside their arms, and were engaged in reaping, they killed a small number, threw the rest into confusion, and surrounded them with their cavalry and chariots.

4:33 Their mode of fighting with their chariots is this: firstly, they drive about in all directions and throw their weapons and generally break the ranks of the enemy with the very dread of their horses and the noise of their wheels; and when they have worked themselves in between the troops of horse, leap from their chariots and engage on foot. The charioteers in the mean time withdraw some little distance from the battle, and so place themselves with the chariots that, if their masters are overpowered by the number of the enemy, they may have a ready retreat to their own troops. Thus they display in battle the speed of horse, [together with] the firmness of infantry; and by daily practice and exercise attain to such expertness that they are accustomed, even on a declining and steep place, to check their horses at full speed, and manage and turn them in an instant and run along the pole, and stand on

accidit suspicabatur. Itaque ad omnes casus subsidia comparabat. Nam et frumentum ex agris cotidie in castra conferebat et, quae gravissime adflictae erant naves, earum materia atque aere ad reliquas reficiendas utebatur et quae ad eas res erant usui ex continenti comportari iubebat. Itaque, cum summo studio a militibus administraretur, XII navibus amissis, reliquis ut navigari satis commode posset effecit.

Dum ea geruntur, legione ex consuetudine una frumentatum missa, quae appellabatur VII, neque ulla ad id tempus belli suspicione interposita, cum pars hominum in agris remaneret, pars etiam in castra ventitaret, ii qui pro portis castrorum in statione erant Caesari nuntiaverunt pulverem maiorem quam consuetudo ferret in ea parte videri quam in partem legio iter fecisset. Caesar id quod erat suspicatus aliquid novi a barbaris initum consilii, cohortes quae in statione erant secum in eam partem proficisci, ex reliquis duas in stationem succedere, reliquas armari et confestim sese subsequi iussit. Cum paulo longius a castris processisset, suos ab hostibus premi atque aegre sustinere et conferta legione ex omnibus partibus tela coici animadvertit. Nam quod omni ex reliquis partibus demesso frumento pars una erat reliqua, suspicati hostes huc nostros esse venturos noctu in silvis delituerant; tum dispersos depositis armis in metendo occupatos Subito adorti paucis interfectis reliquos incertis ordinibus perturbaverant, simul equitatu atque essedis circumdederant.

Genus hoc est ex essedis pugnae. Primo per omnes partes perequitant et tela coiciunt atque ipso terrore equorum et strepitu rotarum ordines plerumque perturbant, et cum se inter equitum turmas insinuaverunt, ex essedis desiliunt et pedibus proeliantur. Aurigae interim paulatim ex proelio excedunt atque ita currus conlocant ut, si illi a multitudine hostium premantur, expeditum ad quos receptum habeant. Ita mobilitatem equitum, stabilitatem peditum in proeliis praestant, ac tantum usu cotidiano et exercitatione efficiunt uti in declivi ac praecipiti loco incitatos equos sustinere et brevi moderari ac flectere et per temonem percurrere et in iugo insistere et se inde in currus

the yoke, and thence betake themselves with the greatest celerity to their chariots again.

4:34 Under these circumstances, our men being dismayed by the novelty of this mode of battle, Caesar most seasonably brought assistance; for upon his arrival the enemy paused, and our men recovered from their fear; upon which thinking the time unfavorable for provoking the enemy and coming to an action, he kept himself in his own quarter, and, a short time having intervened, drew back the legions into the camp. While these things are going on, and all our men engaged, the rest of the Britons, who were in the fields, departed. Storms then set in for several successive days, which both confined our men to the camp and hindered the enemy from attacking us. In the mean time the barbarians dispatched messengers to all parts, and reported to their people the small number of our soldiers, and how good an opportunity was given for obtaining spoil and for liberating themselves forever, if they should only drive the Romans from their camp. Having by these means speedily got together a large force of infantry and of cavalry they came up to the camp.

4:35 Although Caesar anticipated that the same thing which had happened on former occasions would then occur-that, if the enemy were routed, they would escape from danger by their speed; still, having got about thirty horse, which Commius the Atrebatian, of whom mention has been made, had brought over with him [from Gaul], he drew up the legions in order of battle before the camp. When the action commenced, the enemy were unable to sustain the attack of our men long, and turned their backs; our men pursued them as far as their speed and strength permitted, and slew a great number of them; then, having destroyed and burned every thing far and wide, they retreated to their camp.

4:36 The same day, embassadors sent by the enemy came to Caesar to negotiate a peace. Caesar doubled the number of hostages which he had before demanded; and ordered that they should be brought over to the continent, because, since the time of the equinox was near, he did not consider that, with his ships out of repair, the voyage ought to be deferred till winter. Having met with favorable weather, he set sail a little after midnight, and all his fleet arrived safe at the continent, except two of the ships of burden which could not make the same port which the other ships did, and were carried a little lower down.

4:37 When our soldiers, about 300 in number, had been drawn out of these two ships, and were marching to the camp, the Morini,

citissime recipere consuerint.

Quibus rebus perturbatis nostris [novitate pugnae] tempore oportunissimo Caesar auxilium tulit: namque eius adventu hostes constiterunt, nostri se ex timore receperunt. Quo facto, ad lacessendum hostem et committendum proelium alienum esse tempus arbitratus suo se loco continuit et brevi tempore intermisso in castra legiones reduxit. Dum haec geruntur, nostris omnibus occupatis qui erant in agris reliqui discesserunt. Secutae sunt continuos complures dies tempeststes, quae et nostros in castris continerent et hostem a pugna prohiberent. Interim barbari nuntios in omnes partes dimiserunt paucitatemque nostrorum militum suis praedicaverunt et quanta praedae faciendae atque in perpetuum sui liberandi facultas daretur, si Romanos castris expulissent, demonstraverunt. His rebus celeriter magna multitudine peditatus equitatusque coacta ad castra venerunt.

Caesar, etsi idem quod superioribus diebus acciderat fore videbat, ut, si essent hostes pulsi, celeritate periculum effugerent, tamen nactus equites circiter XXX, quos Commius Atrebas, de quo ante dictum est, secum transportaverat, legiones in acie pro castris constituit. Commisso proelio diutius nostrorum militum impetum hostes ferre non potuerunt ac terga verterunt. Quos tanto spatio secuti quantum cursu et viribus efficere potuerunt, complures ex iis occiderunt, deinde omnibus longe lateque aedificiis incensis se in castra receperunt.

Eodem die legati ab hostibus missi ad Caesarem de pace venerunt. His Caesar numerum obsidum quem ante imperaverat duplicavit eosque in continentem adduci iussit, quod propinqua die aequinoctii infirmis navibus hiemi navigationem subiciendam non existimabat. Ipse idoneam tempestatem nactus paulo post mediam noctem naves solvit, quae omnes incolumes ad continentem pervenerunt; sed ex iis onerariae duae eosdem portus quos reliquae capere non potuerunt et paulo infra delatae sunt.

Quibus ex navibus cum essent eiti milites circiter CCC atque in castra contenderent, Morini, quos

whom Caesar, when setting forth for Britain, had left in a state of peace, excited by the hope of spoil, at first surrounded them with a small number of men, and ordered them to lay down their arms, if they did not wish to be slain; afterward however, when they, forming a circle, stood on their defense, a shout was raised and about 6000 of the enemy soon assembled; which being reported, Caesar sent all the cavalry in the camp as a relief to his men. In the mean time our soldiers sustained the attack of the enemy, and fought most valiantly for more than four hours, and, receiving but few wounds themselves, slew several of them. But after our cavalry came in sight, the enemy, throwing away their arms, turned their backs, and a great number of them were killed.

4:38 The day following Caesar sent Labienus, his lieutenant, with those legions which he had brought back from Britain, against the Morini, who had revolted; who, as they had no place to which they might retreat, on account of the drying up of their marshes (which they had availed themselves of as a place of refuge the preceding year), almost all fell into the power of Labienus. In the mean time Caesar's lieutenants, Q. Titurius and L. Cotta, who had led the legions into the territories of the Menapii, having laid waste all their lands, cut down their corn and burned their houses, returned to Caesar because the Menapii had all concealed themselves in their thickest woods. Caesar fixed the winter quarters of all the legions among the Belgae. Thither only two British states sent hostages; the rest omitted to do so. For these successes, a thanksgiving of twenty days was decreed by the senate upon receiving Caesar's letter.

Caesar in Britanniam proficiscens pacatos reliquerat, spe praedae adducti primo non ita magno suorum numero circumsteterunt ac, si sese interfici nollent, arma ponere iusserunt. Cum illi orbe facto sese defenderent, celeriter ad clamorem hominum circiter milia VI convenerunt; qua re nuntiata, Caesar omnem ex castris equitatum suis auxilio misit. Interim nostri milites impetum hostium sustinuerunt atque amplius horis IIII fortissime pugnaverunt et paucis vulneribus acceptis complures ex iis occiderunt. Postea vero quam equitatus noster in conspectum venit, hostes abiectis armis terga verterunt magnusque eorum numerus est occisus.

Caesar postero die T. Labienum legatum cum iis legionibus quas ex Britannia reduxerat in Morinos qui rebellionem fecerant misit. Qui cum propter siccitates paludum quo se reciperent non haberent, quo perfugio superiore anno erant usi, omnes fere in potestatem Labieni venerunt. At Q. Titurius et L. Cotta legati, qui in Menapiorum fines legiones duxerant, omnibus eorum agris vastatis, frumentis succisis, aedificiis incensis, quod Menapii se omnes in densissimas silvas abdiderant, se ad Caesarem receperunt. Caesar in Belgis omnium legionum hiberna constituit. Eo duae omnino civitates ex Britannia obsides miserunt, reliquae neglexerunt. His rebus gestis ex litteris Caesaris dierum XX supplicatio a senatu decreta est.

Gallic Wars Book 5 (54 B.C.E.)

5:1 Lucius Domitius and Appius Claudius being consuls, Caesar, when departing from his winter quarters into Italy, as he had been accustomed to do yearly, commands the lieutenants whom he appointed over the legions to take care that during the winter as many ships as possible should be built, and the old repaired. He plans the size and shape of them. For dispatch of lading, and for drawing them on shore, he makes them a little lower than those which we have been accustomed to use in our sea; and that so much the more, because he knew that, on account of the frequent changes of the tide, less swells occurred there; for the purpose of transporting burdens and a great number of horses, [he makes them] a little broader than those which we use in other seas. All these he orders to be constructed for lightness and expedition, to which object their lowness contributes greatly. He orders those things which are necessary for equipping ships to be brought thither from Spain. He himself, on the assizes of Hither Gaul being concluded, proceeds into Illyricum, because he heard that the part of the province nearest them was being laid waste by the incursions of the Pirustae. When he had arrived there, he levies soldiers upon the states, and orders them to assemble at an appointed place. Which circumstance having been reported [to them], the Pirustae send embassadors to him to inform him that no part of those proceedings was done by public deliberation, and assert that they were ready to make compensation by all means for the injuries [inflicted]. Caesar, accepting their defense, demands hostages, and orders them to be brought to him on a specified day, and assures them that unless they did so he would visit their state with war. These being brought to him on the day which he had ordered, he appoints arbitrators between the states, who should estimate the damages and determine the reparation.

5:2 These things being finished, and the assizes being concluded, he returns into Hither Gaul, and proceeds thence to the army. When he had arrived there, having made a survey of the winter quarter, he finds that, by the extraordinary ardor of the soldiers, amid the utmost scarcity of all materials, about six hundred ships of that kind which we have described above and twenty-eight ships of war, had been built, and were not far from that state, that they might be launched in a few days. Having commended the soldiers and those who had presided over the work, he informs them what he wishes to be done, and orders all the ships to assemble at port Itius, from which port he had learned that the passage into Britain was shortest, [being only] about thirty miles from the continent. He left what seemed a sufficient number of soldiers for that design; he

L. Domitio Ap. Claudio consulibus, discedens ab hibernis Caesar in Italiam, ut quotannis facere consuerat, legatis imperat quos legionibus praefecerat uti quam plurimas possent hieme naves aedificandas veteresque reficiendas curarent. Earum modum formamque demonstrat. Ad celeritatem onerandi subductionesque paulo facit humiliores quam quibus in nostro mari uti consuevimus, atque id eo magis, quod propter crebras commutationes aestuum minus magnos ibi fluctus fieri cognoverat; ad onera, ad multitudinem iumentorum transportandam paulo latiores quam quibus in reliquis utimur maribus. Has omnes actuarias imperat fieri, quam ad rem multum humilitas adiuvat. Ea quae sunt usui ad armandas naves ex Hispania apportari iubet. Ipse conventibus Galliae citeribris peractis in Illyricum proficiscitur, quod a Pirustis finitimam partem provinciae incursionibus vastari audiebat. Eo cum venisset, civitatibus milites imperat certumque in locum convenire iubet. Qua re nuntiata Pirustae legatos ad eum mittunt qui doceant nihil earum rerum publico factum consilio, seseque paratos esse demonstrant omnibus rationibus de iniuriis satisfacere. Accepta oratione eorum Caesar obsides imperat eosque ad certam diem adduci iubet; nisi ita fecerint, sese bello civitatem persecuturum demonstrat. Eis ad diem adductis, ut imperaverat, arbitros inter civitates dat qui litem aestiment poenamque constituant.

His confectis rebus conventibusque peractis, in citeriorem Galliam revertitur atque inde ad exercitum proficiscitur. Eo cum venisset, circuitis omnibus hibernis, singulari militum studio in summa omnium rerum inopia circiter sescentas eius generis cuius supra demonstravimus naves et longas XXVIII invenit instructas neque multum abesse ab eo quin paucis diebus deduci possint. Collaudatis militibus atque eis qui negotio praefuerant, quid fieri velit ostendit atque omnes ad portum Itium convenire iubet, quo ex portu commodissimum in Britanniam traiectum esse cognoverat, circiter milium passuum XXX

himself proceeds into the territories of the Treviri with four legions without baggage, and 800 horse, because they neither came to the general diets [of Gaul], nor obeyed his commands, and were moreover, said to be tampering with the Germans beyond the Rhine.

5:3 This state is by far the most powerful of all Gaul in cavalry, and has great forces of infantry, and as we have remarked above, borders on the Rhine. In that state, two persons, Indutiomarus and Cingetorix, were then contending with each other for the supreme power; one of whom, as soon as the arrival of Caesar and his legions was known, came to him; assures him that he and all his party would continue in their allegiance, and not revolt from the alliance of the Roman people, and informs him of the things which were going on among the Treviri. But Indutiomarus began to collect cavalry and infantry, and make preparations for war, having concealed those who by reason of their age could not be under arms, in the forest Arduenna, which is of immense size, [and] extends from the Rhine across the country of the Treviri to the frontiers of the Remi. But after that, some of the chief persons of the state, both influenced by their friendship for Cingetorix, and alarmed at the arrival of our army, came to Caesar and began to solicit him privately about their own interests, since they could not provide for the safety of the state; Indutiomarus, dreading lest he should be abandoned by all, sends embassadors to Caesar, to declare that he absented himself from his countrymen, and refrained from coming to him on this account, that he might the more easily keep the state in its allegiance, lest on the departure of all the nobility the commonalty should, in their indiscretion, revolt. And thus the whole state was at his control; and that he, if Caesar would permit, would come to the camp to him, and would commit his own fortunes and those of the state to his good faith.

5:4 Caesar, though he discerned from what motive these things were said, and what circumstances deterred him from his meditated plan, still, in order that he might not be compelled to waste the summer among the Treviri, while all things were prepared for the war with Britain, ordered Indutiomarus to come to him with 200 hostages. When they were brought, [and] among them his son and near relations, whom he had demanded by name, he consoled Indutiomarus, and enjoined him to continue in his allegiance; yet, nevertheless, summoning to him the chief men of the Treviri, he reconciled them individually to Cingetorix: this he both thought should be done by him in justice to the merits of the latter, and also judged that it was of great importance that the influence of one whose singular attachment toward him he had

transmissum a continenti: huic rei quod satis esse visum est militum reliquit. Ipse cum legionibus expeditis IIII et equitibus DCCC in fines Treverorum proficiscitur, quod hi neque ad concilia veniebant neque imperio parebant Germanosque Transrhenanos sollicitare dicebantur.

Haec civitas longe plurimum totius Galliae equitatu valet magnasque habet copias peditum Rhenumque, ut supra demonstravimus, tangit. In ea civitate duo de principatu inter se contendebant, Indutiomarus et Cingetorix; e quibus alter, simul atque de Caesaris legionumque adventu cognitum est, ad eum venit, se suosque omnes in officio futuros neque ab amicitia populi Romani defecturos confirmavit quaeque in Treveris gererentur ostendit. At Indutiomarus equitatum peditatumque cogere, eisque qui per aetatem in armis esse non poterant in silvam Arduennam abditis, quae ingenti magnitudine per medios fines Treverorum a flumine Rheno ad initium Remorum pertinet, bellum parare instituit. Sed posteaquam nonnulli principes ex ea civitate et familiaritate Cingetorigis adducti et adventu nostri exercitus perterriti ad Caesarem venerunt et de suis privatim rebus ab eo petere coeperunt, quoniam civitati consulere non possent, veritus ne ab omnibus desereretur Indutiomarus legatos ad Caesarem mittit: sese idcirco ab suis discedere atque ad eum venire noluisse, quo facilius civitatem in officio contineret, ne omnis nobilitatis discessu plebs propter imprudentiam laberetur: itaque esse civitatem in sua potestate, seseque, si Caesar permitteret, ad eum in castra venturum, suas civitatisque fortunas eius fidei permissurum.

Caesar, etsi intellegebat qua de causa ea dicerentur quaeque eum res ab instituto consilio deterreret, tamen, ne aestatem in Treveris consumere cogeretur omnibus ad Britannicum bellum rebus comparatis, Indutiomarum ad se cum CC obsidibus venire iussit. His adductis, in eis filio propinquisque eius omnibus, quos nominatim evocaverat, consolatus Indutiomarum hortatusque est uti in officio maneret; nihilo tamen setius principibus Treverorum ad se convocatis hos singillatim Cingetorigi conciliavit, quod cum merito eius a se fieri intellegebat, tum magni interesse arbitrabatur eius auctoritatem inter suos quam

fully seen, should prevail as much as possible among his people. Indutiomarus was very much offended at this act, [seeing that] his influence was diminished among his countrymen; and he, who already before had borne a hostile mind toward us, was much more violently inflamed against us through resentment at this.

5:5 These matters being settled, Caesar went to port Itius with the legions. There he discovers that forty ships, which had been built in the country of the Meldi, having been driven back by a storm, had been unable to maintain their course, and had returned to the same port from which they had set out; he finds the rest ready for sailing, and furnished with every thing. In the same place, the cavalry of the whole of Gaul, in number 4,000, assembles, and [also] the chief persons of all the states; he had determined to leave in Gaul a very few of them, whose fidelity toward him he had clearly discerned, and take the rest with him as hostages; because he feared a commotion in Gaul when he should be absent.

5:6 There was together with the others, Dumnorix, the Aeduan, of whom we have made previous mention. Him, in particular, he had resolved to have with him, because he had discovered him to be fond of change, fond of power, possessing great resolution, and great influence among the Gauls. To this was added, that Dumnorix had before said in an assembly of Aeduans, that the sovereignty of the state had been made over to him by Caesar; which speech the Aedui bore with impatience and yet dared not send embassadors to Caesar for the purpose of either rejecting or deprecating [that appointment]. That fact Caesar had learned from his own personal friends. He at first strove to obtain by every entreaty that he should be left in Gaul; partly, because, being unaccustomed to sailing, he feared the sea; partly because he said he was prevented by divine admonitions. After he saw that this request was firmly refused him, all hope of success being lost, he began to tamper with the chief persons of the Gauls, to call them apart singly and exhort them to remain on the continent; to agitate them with the fear that it was not without reason that Gaul should be stripped of all her nobility; that it was Caesar's design, to bring over to Britain and put to death all those whom he feared to slay in the sight of Gaul, to pledge his honor to the rest, to ask for their oath that they would by common deliberation execute what they should perceive to be necessary for Gaul. These things were reported to Caesar by several persons.

5:7 Having learned this fact, Caesar, because he had conferred so much honor upon the Aeduan state, determined that Dumnorix should be restrained and deterred by whatever means he could; and that, because he perceived his insane designs to be

plurimum valere, cuius tam egregiam in se voluntatem perspexisset. Id tulit factum graviter Indutiomarus, suam gratiam inter suos minui, et, qui iam ante inimico in nos animo fuisset, multo gravius hoc dolore exarsit.

His rebus constitutis Caesar ad portum Itium cum legionibus pervenit. Ibi cognoscit LX naves, quae in Meldis factae erant, tempestate reiectas cursum tenere non potuisse atque eodem unde erant profectae revertisse; reliquas paratas ad navigandum atque omnibus rebus instructas invenit. Eodem equitatus totius Galliae convenit, numero milium quattuor, principesque ex omnibus civitatibus; ex quibus perpaucos, quorum in se fidem perspexerat, relinquere in Gallia, reliquos obsidum loco secum ducere decreverat, quod, cum ipse abesset, motum Galliae verebatur.

Erat una cum ceteris Dumnorix Aeduus, de quo ante ab nobis dictum est. Hunc secum habere in primis constituerat, quod eum cupidum rerum novarum, cupidum imperi, magni animi, magnae inter Gallos auctoritatis cognoverat. Accedebat huc quod in concilio Aeduorum Dumnorix dixerat sibi a Caesare regnum civitatis deferri; quod dictum Aedui graviter ferebant, neque recusandi aut deprecandi causa legatos ad Caesarem mittere audebant. Id factum ex suis hospitibus Caesar cognoverat. Ille omnibus primo precibus petere contendit ut in Gallia relinqueretur, partim quod insuetus navigandi mare timeret, partim quod religionibus impediri sese diceret. Posteaquam id obstinate sibi negari vidit, omni spe impetrandi adempta principes Galliae sollicitare, sevocare singulos hortarique coepit uti in continenti remanerent: metu territare: non sine causa fieri, ut Gallia omni nobilitate spoliaretur; id esse consilium Caesaris, ut quos in conspectu Galliae interficere vereretur, hos omnes in Britanniam traductos necaret; fidem reliquis interponere, iusiurandum poscere, ut quod esse ex usu Galliae intellexissent communi consilio administrarent. Haec a compluribus ad Caesarem deferebantur.

Qua re cognita Caesar, quod tantum civitati Aeduae dignitatis tribuebat, coercendum atque deterrendum quibuscumque rebus posset Dumnorigem statuebat; quod longius eius

proceeding further and further, care should be taken lest he might be able to injure him and the commonwealth. Therefore, having stayed about twenty-five days in that place, because the north wind, which usually blows a great part of every season, prevented the voyage, he exerted himself to keep Dumnorix in his allegiance [and] nevertheless learn all his measures: having at length met with favorable weather, he orders the foot soldiers and the horse to embark in the ships. But, while the minds of all were occupied, Dumnorix began to take his departure from the camp homeward with the cavalry of the Aedui, Caesar being ignorant of it. Caesar, on this matter being reported to him, ceasing from his expedition and deferring all other affairs, sends a great part of the cavalry to pursue him, and commands that he be brought back; he orders that if he use violence and do not submit, that he be slain; considering that Dumnorix would do nothing as a rational man while he himself was absent, since he had disregarded his command even when present. He, however, when recalled, began to resist and defend himself with his hand, and implore the support of his people, often exclaiming that "he was free and the subject of a free state." They surround and kill the man as they had been commanded; but the Aeduan horsemen all return to Caesar.

5:8 When these things were done [and] Labienus, left on the continent with three legions and 2,000 horse, to defend the harbors and provide corn, and discover what was going on in Gaul, and take measures according to the occasion and according to the circumstance; he himself, with five legions and a number of horse, equal to that which he was leaving on the continent, set sail at sun-set, and [though for a time] borne forward by a gentle south-west wind, he did not maintain his course, in consequence of the wind dying away about midnight, and being carried on too far by the tide, when the sun rose, espied Britain passed on his left. Then, again, following the change of tide, he urged on with the oars that he might make that part of the island in which he had discovered the preceding summer, that there was the best landing-place, and in this affair the spirit of our soldiers was very much to be extolled; for they with the transports and heavy ships, the labor of rowing not being [for a moment] discontinued, equaled the speed of the ships of war. All the ships reached Britain nearly at mid-day; nor was there seen a [single] enemy in that place, but, as Caesar afterward found from some prisoners, though large bodies of troops had assembled there, yet being alarmed by the great number of our ships, more than eight hundred of which, including the ships of the preceding year, and those private vessels which each had built for his own convenience, had appeared at one time,

amentiam progredi videbat, prospiciendum, ne quid sibi ac rei publicae nocere posset. Itaque dies circiter XXV in eo loco commoratus, quod Corus ventus navigationem impediebat, qui magnam partem omnis temporis in his locis flare consuevit, dabat operam ut in officio Dumnorigem contineret, nihilo tamen setius omnia eius consilia cognosceret: tandem idoneam nactus tempestatem milites equitesque conscendere in naves iubet. At omnium impeditis animis Dumnorix cum equitibus Aeduorum a castris insciente Caesare domum discedere coepit. Qua re nuntiata Caesar intermissa profectione atque omnibus rebus postpositis magnam partem equitatus ad eum insequendum mittit retrahique imperat; si vim faciat neque pareat, interfici iubet, nihil hunc se absente pro sano facturum arbitratus, qui praesentis imperium neglexisset. Ille enim revocatus resistere ac se manu defendere suorumque fidem implorare coepit, saepe clamitans liberum se liberaeque esse civitatis. Illi, ut erat imperatum, circumsistunt hominem atque interficiunt: at equites Aedui ad Caesarem omnes revertuntur.

His rebus gestis, Labieno in continente cum tribus legionibus et equitum milibus duobus relicto ut portus tueretur et rem frumentariam provideret quaeque in Gallia gererentur cognosceret consiliumque pro tempore et pro re caperet, ipse cum quinque legionibus et pari numero equitum, quem in continenti reliquerat, ad solis occasum naves solvit et leni Africo provectus media circiter nocte vento intermisso cursum non tenuit, et longius delatus aestu orta luce sub sinistra Britanniam relictam conspexit. Tum rursus aestus commutationem secutus remis contendit ut eam partem insulae caperet, qua optimum esse egressum superiore aestate cognoverat. Qua in re admodum fuit militum virtus laudanda, qui vectoriis gravibusque navigiis non intermisso remigandi labore longarum navium cursum adaequarunt. Accessum est ad Britanniam omnibus navibus meridiano fere tempore, neque in eo loco hostis est visus; sed, ut postea Caesar ex captivis cognovit, cum magnae manus eo convenissent, multitudine navium perterritae, quae cum annotinis privatisque quas sui quisque commodi fecerat

they had quitted the coast and concealed themselves among the higher points.

5:9 Caesar, having disembarked his army and chosen a convenient place for the camp, when he discovered from the prisoners in what part the forces of the enemy had lodged themselves, having left ten cohorts and 300 horse at the sea, to be a guard to the ships, hastens to the enemy, at the third watch, fearing the less for the ships, for this reason because he was leaving them fastened at anchor upon an even and open shore; and he placed Q. Atrius over the guard of the ships. He himself, having advanced by night about twelve miles, espied the forces of the enemy. They, advancing to the river with their cavalry and chariots from the higher ground, began to annoy our men and give battle. Being repulsed by our cavalry, they concealed themselves in woods, as they had secured a place admirably fortified by nature and by art, which, as it seemed, they had before prepared on account of a civil war; for all entrances to it were shut up by a great number of felled trees. They themselves rushed out of the woods to fight here and there, and prevented our men from entering their fortifications. But the soldiers of the seventh legion, having formed a testudo and thrown up a rampart against the fortification, took the place and drove them out of the woods, receiving only a few wounds. But Caesar forbade his men to pursue them in their flight any great distance; both because he was ignorant of the nature of the ground, and because, as a great part of the day was spent, he wished time to be left for the fortification of the camp.

5:10 The next day, early in the morning, he sent both foot-soldiers and horse in three divisions on an expedition to pursue those who had fled. These having advanced a little way, when already the rear [of the enemy] was in sight, some horse came to Caesar from Quintus Atrius, to report that the preceding night, a very great storm having arisen, almost all the ships were dashed to pieces and cast upon the shore, because neither the anchors and cables could resist, nor could the sailors and pilots sustain the violence of the storm; and thus great damage was received by that collision of the ships.

5:11 These things being known [to him], Caesar orders the legions and cavalry to be recalled and to cease from their march; he himself returns to the ships: he sees clearly before him almost the same things which he had heard of from the messengers and by letter, so that, about forty ships being lost, the remainder seemed capable of being repaired with much labor. Therefore he selects workmen from the legions, and orders others to be sent for from

amplius octingentae uno erant visae tempore, a litore discesserant ac se in superiora loca abdiderant.

Caesar eito exercitu et loco castris idoneo capto, ubi ex captivis cognovit quo in loco hostium copiae consedissent, cohortibus decem ad mare relictis et equitibus trecentis, qui praesidio navibus essent, de tertia vigilia ad hostes contendit, eo minus veritus navibus, quod in litore molli atque aperto deligatas ad ancoram relinquebat, et praesidio navibus Q. Atrium praefecit. Ipse noctu progressus milia passuum circiter XII hostium copias conspicatus est. Illi equitatu atque essedis ad flumen progressi ex loco superiore nostros prohibere et proelium committere coeperuut. Repulsi ab equitatu se in silvas abdiderunt, locum nacti egregie et natura et opere munitum, quem domestici belli, ut videbantur, causa iam ante praeparaverant: nam crebris arboribus succisis omnes introitus erant praeclusi. Ipsi ex silvis rari propugnabant nostrosque intra munitiones ingredi prohibebant. At milites legionis septimae, testudine facta et aggere ad munitiones adiecto, locum ceperunt eosque ex silvis expulerunt paucis vulneribus acceptis. Sed eos fugientes longius Caesar prosequi vetuit, et quod loci naturam ignorabat, et quod magna parte diei consumpta munitioni castrorum tempus relinqui volebat.

Postridie eius diei mane tripertito milites equitesque in expeditionem misit, ut eos qui fugerant persequerentur. His aliquantum itineris progressis, cum iam extremi essent in prospectu, equites a Quinto Atrio ad Caesarem venerunt, qui nuntiarent superiore nocte maxima coorta tempestate prope omnes naves adflictas atque in litore eiectas esse, quod neque ancorae funesque subsisterent, neque nautae gubernatoresque vim tempestatis pati possent; itaque ex eo concursu navium magnum esse incommodum acceptum.

His rebus cognitis Caesar legiones equitatumque revocari atque in itinere resistere iubet, ipse ad naves revertitur; eadem fere quae ex nuntiis litterisque cognoverat coram perspicit, sic ut amissis circiter XL navibus reliquae tamen refici posse magno negotio viderentur. Itaque ex legionibus fabros deligit et ex continenti alios

the continent; he writes to Labienus to build as many ships as he could with those legions which were with him. He himself, though the matter was one of great difficulty and labor, yet thought it to be most expedient for all the ships to be brought up on shore and joined with the camp by one fortification. In these matters he employed about ten days, the labor of the soldiers being unremitting even during the hours of night. The ships having been brought up on shore and the camp strongly fortified, he left the same forces as he did before as a guard for the ships; he sets out in person for the same place that he had returned from. When he had come thither, greater forces of the Britons had already assembled at that place, the chief command and management of the war having been intrusted to Cassivellaunus, whose territories a river, which is called the Thames, separates, from the maritime states at about eighty miles from the sea. At an earlier period perpetual wars had taken place between him and the other states; but, greatly alarmed by our arrival, the Britons had placed him over the whole war and the conduct of it.

5:12 The interior portion of Britain is inhabited by those of whom they say that it is handed down by tradition that they were born in the island itself: the maritime portion by those who had passed over from the country of the Belgae for the purpose of plunder and making war; almost all of whom are called by the names of those states from which being sprung they went thither, and having waged war, continued there and began to cultivate the lands. The number of the people is countless, and their buildings exceedingly numerous, for the most part very like those of the Gauls: the number of cattle is great. They use either brass or iron rings, determined at a certain weight, as their money. Tin is produced in the midland regions; in the maritime, iron; but the quantity of it is small: they employ brass, which is imported. There, as in Gaul, is timber of every description, except beech and fir. They do not regard it lawful to eat the hare, and the cock, and the goose; they, however, breed them for amusement and pleasure. The climate is more temperate than in Gaul, the colds being less severe.

5:13 The island is triangular in its form, and one of its sides is opposite to Gaul. One angle of this side, which is in Kent, whither almost all ships from Gaul are directed, [looks] to the east; the lower looks to the south. This side extends about 500 miles. Another side lies toward Spain and the west, on which part is Ireland, less, as is reckoned, than Britain, by one half: but the passage [from it] into Britain is of equal distance with that from Gaul. In the middle of this voyage, is an island, which is called

arcessi iubet; Labieno scribit, ut quam plurimas posset eis legionibus, quae sunt apud eum, naves instituat. Ipse, etsi res erat multae operae ac laboris, tamen commodissimum esse statuit omnes naves subduci et cum castris una munitione coniungi. In his rebus circiter dies X consumit ne nocturnis quidem temporibus ad laborem militum intermissis. Subductis navibus castrisque egregie munitis easdem copias, quas ante, praesidio navibus reliquit: ipse eodem unde redierat proficiscitur. Eo cum venisset, maiores iam undique in eum locum copiae Britannorum convenerant summa imperi bellique administrandi communi consilio permissa Cassivellauno, cuius fines a maritimis civitatibus fiumen dividit, quod appellatur Tamesis, a mari circiter milia passuum LXXX. Huic superiore tempore cum reliquis civitatibus continentia bella intercesserant; sed nostro adventu permoti Britanni hunc toti bello imperioque praefecerant.

Britanniae pars interior ab eis incolitur quos natos in insula ipsi memoria proditum dicunt, maritima ab eis, qui praedae ac belli inferendi causa ex Belgio transierunt (qui omnes fere eis nominibus civitatum appellantur, quibus orti ex civitatibus eo pervenerunt) et bello illato ibi permanserunt atque agros colere coeperunt. Hominum est infinita multitudo creberrimaque aedificia fere Gallicis consimilia, pecorum magnus numerus. Vtuntur aut aere aut nummo aureo aut taleis ferreis ad certum pondus examinatis pro nummo. Nascitur ibi plumbum album in mediterraneis regionibus, in maritimis ferrum, sed eius exigua est copia; aere utuntur importato. Materia cuiusque generis ut in Gallia est, praeter fagum atque abietem. Leporem et gallinam et anserem gustare fas non putant; haec tamen alunt animi voluptatisque causa. Loca sunt temperatiora quam in Gallia, remissioribus frigoribus.

Insula natura triquetra, cuius unum latus est contra Galliam. Huius lateris alter angulus, qui est ad Cantium, quo fere omnes ex Gallia naves appelluntur, ad orientem solem, inferior ad meridiem spectat. Hoc pertinet circiter mila passuum quingenta. Alterum vergit ad Hispaniam atque occidentem solem; qua ex parte est Hibernia, dimidio minor, ut aestimatur, quam

Mona: many smaller islands besides are supposed to lie [there], of which islands some have written that at the time of the winter solstice it is night there for thirty consecutive days. We, in our inquiries about that matter, ascertained nothing, except that, by accurate measurements with water, we perceived the nights to be shorter there than on the continent. The length of this side, as their account states, is 700 miles. The third side is toward the north, to which portion of the island no land is opposite; but an angle of that side looks principally toward Germany. This side is considered to be 800 miles in length. Thus the whole island is [about] 2,000 miles in circumference.

5:14 The most civilized of all these nations are they who inhabit Kent, which is entirely a maritime district, nor do they differ much from the Gallic customs. Most of the inland inhabitants do not sow corn, but live on milk and flesh, and are clad with skins. All the Britains, indeed, dye themselves with wood, which occasions a bluish color, and thereby have a more terrible appearance in fight. They wear their hair long, and have every part of their body shaved except their head and upper lip. Ten and even twelve have wives common to them, and particularly brothers among brothers, and parents among their children; but if there be any issue by these wives, they are reputed to be the children of those by whom respectively each was first espoused when a virgin.

5:15 The horse and charioteers of the enemy contended vigorously in a skirmish with our cavalry on the march; yet so that our men were conquerors in all parts, and drove them to their woods and hills; but, having slain a great many, they pursued too eagerly, and lost some of their men. But the enemy, after some time had elapsed, when our men were off their guard, and occupied in the fortification of the camp, rushed out of the woods, and making an attack upon those who were placed on duty before the camp, fought in a determined manner; and two cohorts being sent by Caesar to their relief, and these severally the first of two legions, when these had taken up their position at a very small distance from each other, as our men were disconcerted by the unusual mode of battle, the enemy broke through the middle of them most courageously, and retreated thence in safety. That day, Q. Laberius Durus, a tribune of the soldiers, was slain. The enemy, since more cohorts were sent against them, were repulsed.

Britannia, sed pari spatio transmissus atque ex Gallia est in Britanniam. In hoc medio cursu est insula, quae appellatur Mona: complures praeterea minores subiectae insulae existimantur, de quibus insulis nonnulli scripserunt dies continuos triginta sub bruma esse noctem. Nos nihil de eo percontationibus reperiebamus, nisi certis ex aqua mensuris breviores esse quam in continenti noctes videbamus. Huius est longitudo lateris, ut fert illorum opinio, septingentorum milium. Tertium est contra septentriones; cui parti nulla est obiecta terra, sed eius angulus lateris maxime ad Germaniam spectat. Hoc milia passuum octingenta in longitudinem esse existimatur. Ita omnis insula est in circuitu vicies centum milium passuum.

Ex his omnibus longe sunt humanissimi qui Cantium incolunt, quae regio est maritima omnis, neque multum a Gallica differunt consuetudine. Interiores plerique frumenta non serunt, sed lacte et carne vivunt pellibusque sunt vestiti. Omnes vero se Britanni vitro inficiunt, quod caeruleum efficit colorem, atque hoc horridiores sunt in pugna aspectu; capilloque sunt promisso atque omni parte corporis rasa praeter caput et labrum superius. Vxores habent deni duodenique inter se communes et maxime fratres cum fratribus parentesque cum liberis; sed qui sunt ex his nati, eorum habentur liberi, quo primum virgo quaeque deducta est.

Equites hostium essedariique acriter proelio cum equitatu nostro in itinere conflixerunt, tamen ut nostri omnibus partibus superiores fuerint atque eos in silvas collesque compulerint; sed compluribus interfectis cupidius insecuti nonnullos ex suis amiserunt. At illi intermisso spatio imprudentibus nostris atque occupatis in munitione castrorum subito se ex statione pro castris collocati, acriter pugnaverunt, duabusque missis subsidio cohortibus a Caesare atque eis primis legionum duarum, cum hae perexiguo intermisso loci spatio inter se constitissent, novo genere pugnae perterritis nostris per medios audacissime perruperunt seque inde incolumes receperunt. Eo die Quintus Laberius Durus, tribunus militum, interficitur. Illi pluribus submissis cohortibus repelluntur.

5:16 In the whole of this method of fighting since the engagement took place under the eyes of all and before the camp, it was perceived that our men, on account of the weight of their arms, inasmuch as they could neither pursue [the enemy when] retreating, nor dare quit their standards, were little suited to this kind of enemy; that the horse also fought with great danger, because they [the Britons] generally retreated even designedly, and, when they had drawn off our men a short distance from the legions, leaped from their chariots and fought on foot in unequal [and to them advantageous] battle. But the system of cavalry engagement is wont to produce equal danger, and indeed the same, both to those who retreat and to those who pursue. To this was added, that they never fought in close order, but in small parties and at great distances, and had detachments placed [in different parts], and then the one relieved the other, and the vigorous and fresh succeeded the wearied.

5:17 The following day the enemy halted on the hills, a distance from our camp, and presented themselves in small parties, and began to challenge our horse to battle with less spirit than the day before. But at noon, when Caesar had sent three legions, and all the cavalry, with C. Trebonius, the lieutenant, for the purpose of foraging, they flew upon the foragers suddenly from all quarters, so that they did not keep off [even] from the standards and the legions. Our men making an attack on them vigorously, repulsed them; nor did they cease to pursue them until the horse, relying on relief, as they saw the legions behind them, drove the enemy precipitately before them, and slaying a great number of them, did not give them the opportunity either of rallying, or halting, or leaping from their chariots. Immediately after this retreat, the auxiliaries who had assembled from all sides, departed; nor after that time did the enemy ever engage with us in very large numbers.

5:18 Caesar, discovering their design, leads his army into the territories of Cassivellaunus to the river Thames; which river can be forded in one place only and that with difficulty. When he had arrived there, he perceives that numerous forces of the enemy were marshaled on the other bank of the river; the bank also was defended by sharp stakes fixed in front, and stakes of the same kind fixed under the water were covered by the river. These things being discovered from [some] prisoners and deserters, Caesar, sending forward the cavalry, ordered the legions to follow them immediately. But the soldiers advanced with such speed and such ardor, though they stood above the water by their heads only, that the enemy could not sustain the attack of the legions and of the horse, and quitted the banks, and committed themselves to flight.

Toto hoc in genere pugnae, cum sub oculis omnium ac pro castris dimicaretur, intellectum est nostros propter gravitatem armorum, quod neque insequi cedentes possent neque ab signis discedere auderent, minus aptos esse ad huius generis hostem, equites autem magno cum periculo proelio dimicare, propterea quod illi etiam consulto plerumque cederent et, cum paulum ab legionibus nostros removissent, ex essedis desilirent et pedibus dispari proelio contenderent. Equestris autem proeli ratio et cedentibus et insequentibus par atque idem periculum inferebat. Accedebat huc ut numquam conferti sed rari magnisque intervallis proeliarentur stationesque dispositas haberent, atque alios alii deinceps exciperent, integrique et recentes defetigatis succederent.

Postero die procul a castris hostes in collibus constiterunt rarique se ostendere et lenius quam pridie nostros equites proelio lacessere coeperunt. Sed meridie, cum Caesar pabulandi causa tres legiones atque omnem equitatum cum Gaio Trebonio legato misisset, repente ex omnibus partibus ad pabulatores advolaverunt, sic uti ab signis legionibusque non absisterent. Nostri acriter in eos impetu facto reppulerunt neque finem sequendi fecerunt, quoad subsidio confisi equites, cum post se legiones viderent, praecipites hostes egerunt magnoque eorum numero interfecto neque sui colligendi neque consistendi aut ex essedis desiliendi facultatem dederunt. Ex hac fuga protinus, quae undique convenerant, auxilia discesserunt, neque post id tempus umquam summis nobiscum copiis hostes contenderunt.

Caesar cognito consilio eorum ad flumen Tamesim in fines Cassivellauni exercitum duxit; quod flumen uno omnino loco pedibus, atque hoc aegre, transiri potest. Eo cum venisset, animum advertit ad alteram fluminis ripam magnas esse copias hostium instructas. Ripa autem erat acutis sudibus praefixis munita, eiusdemque generis sub aqua defixae sudes flumine tegebantur. His rebus cognitis a captivis perfugisque Caesar praemisso equitatu confestim legiones subsequi iussit. Sed ea celeritate atque eo impetu milites ierunt, cum capite solo ex aqua exstarent, ut hostes impetum legionum atque equitum sustinere non possent

5:19 Cassivellaunus, as we have stated above, all hope [rising out] of battle being laid aside, the greater part of his forces being dismissed, and about 4,000 charioteers only being left, used to observe our marches and retire a little from the road, and conceal himself in intricate and woody places, and in those neighborhoods in which he had discovered we were about to march, he used to drive the cattle and the inhabitants from the fields into the woods; and, when our cavalry, for the sake of plundering and ravaging the more freely, scattered themselves among the fields, he used to send out charioteers from the woods by all the well-known roads and paths, and to the great danger of our horse, engage with them; and this source of fear hindered them from straggling very extensively. The result was, that Caesar did not allow excursions to be made to a great distance from the main body of the legions, and ordered that damage should be done to the enemy in ravaging their lands, and kindling fires only so far as the legionary soldiers could, by their own exertion and marching, accomplish it.

5:20 In the mean time, the Trinobantes, almost the most powerful state of those parts, from which the young man, Mandubratius embracing the protection of Caesar had come to the continent of Gaul to [meet] him (whose father, Imanuentius, had possessed the sovereignty in that state, and had been killed by Cassivellaunus; he himself had escaped death by flight), send embassadors to Caesar, and promise that they will surrender themselves to him and perform his commands; they entreat him to protect Mandubratius from the violence of Cassivellaunus, and send to their state some one to preside over it, and possess the government. Caesar demands forty hostages from them, and corn for his army, and sends Mandubratius to them. They speedily performed the things demanded, and sent hostages to the number appointed, and the corn.

5:21 The Trinobantes being protected and secured from any violence of the soldiers, the Cenimagni, the Segontiaci, the Ancalites, the Bibroci, and the Cassi, sending embassies, surrendered themselves to Caesar. From them he learns that the capital town of Cassivellaunus was not far from that place, and was defended by woods and morasses, and a very large number of men and of cattle had been collected in it. (Now the Britons, when they have fortified the intricate woods, in which they are wont to assemble for the purpose of avoiding the incursion of an enemy, with an intrenchment and a rampart, call them a town.) Thither he proceeds with his legions: he finds the place admirably fortified by nature and art; he, however, undertakes to attack it in two directions. The enemy, having remained only a short time, did not sustain the attack of our soldiers, and hurried away on the

ripasque dimitterent ac se fugae mandarent.

Cassivellaunus, ut supra demonstravimus, omni deposita spe contentionis dimissis amplioribus copiis milibus circiter quattuor essedariorum relictis itinera nostra servabat paulumque ex via excedebat locisque impeditis ac silvestribus sese occultabat, atque eis regionibus quibus nos iter facturos cognoverat pecora atque homines ex agris in silvas compellebat et, cum equitatus noster liberius praedandi vastandique causa se in agros eiecerat, omnibus viis semitisque essedarios ex silvis emittebat et magno cum periculo nostrorum equitum cum eis confligebat atque hoc metu latius vagari prohibebat. Relinquebatur ut neque longius ab agmine legionum discedi Caesar pateretur, et tantum in agris vastandis incendiisque faciendis hostibus noceretur, quantum labore atque itinere legionarii milites efficere poterant.

Interim Trinobantes, prope firmissima earum regionum civitas, ex qua Mandubracius adulescens Caesaris fidem secutus ad eum in continentem Galliam venerat, cuius pater in ea civitate regnum obtinuerat interfectusque erat a Cassivellauno, ipse fuga mortem vitaverat, legatos ad Caesarem mittunt pollicenturque sese ei dedituros atque imperata facturos; petunt, ut Mandubracium ab iniuria Cassivellauni defendat atque in civitatem mittat, qui praesit imperiumque obtineat. His Caesar imperat obsides quadraginta frumentumque exercitui Mandubraciumque ad eos mittit. Illi imperata celeriter fecerunt, obsides ad numerum frumentumque miserunt.

Trinobantibus defensis adque ab omni militum niuria prohibitis Cenimagni, Segontiaci, Ancalites, Bibroci, Cassi legationibus missis sese Caesari dedumt. Ab his cognoscit non longe ex eo loco oppidum Cassivellauni abesse silvis paludibusque munitum, quo satis magnus hominum pecorisque numerus onvenerit. Oppidum autem Britanni vocant, cum silvas impeditas vallo atque fossa munierunt, quo incursionis hostium vitandae causa convenire consuerunt. Eo proficiscitur cum legionibus: locum reperit egregie natura atque opere munitum; tamen hunc duabus ex partibus oppugnare contendit. Hostes paulisper morati militum nostrorum impetum non tulerunt seseque

83

other side of the town. A great amount of cattle was found there, and many of the enemy were taken and slain in their flight.

5:22 While these things are going forward in those places, Cassivellaunus sends messengers into Kent, which, we have observed above, is on the sea, over which districts four several kings reigned, Cingetorix, Carvilius, Taximagulus and Segonax, and commands them to collect all their forces, and unexpectedly assail and storm the naval camp. When they had come to the camp, our men, after making a sally, slaying many of their men, and also capturing a distinguished leader named Lugotorix, brought back their own men in safety. Cassivellaunus, when this battle was reported to him as so many losses had been sustained, and his territories laid waste, being alarmed most of all by the desertion of the states, sends embassadors to Caesar [to treat] about a surrender through the mediation of Commius the Atrebatian. Caesar, since he had determined to pass the winter on the continent, on account of the sudden revolts of Gaul, and as much of the summer did not remain, and he perceived that even that could be easily protracted, demands hostages, and prescribes what tribute Britain should pay each year to the Roman people; he forbids and commands Cassivellaunus that he wage not war against Mandubratius or the Trinobantes.

5:23 When he had received the hostages, he leads back the army to the sea, and finds the ships repaired. After launching these, because he had a large number of prisoners, and some of the ships had been lost in the storm, he determines to convey back his army at two embarkations. And it so happened, that out of so large a number of ships, in so many voyages, neither in this nor in the previous year was any ship missing which conveyed soldiers; but very few out of those which were sent back to him from the continent empty, as the soldiers of the former convoy had been disembarked, and out of those (sixty in number) which Labienus had taken care to have built, reached their destination; almost all the rest were driven back, and when Caesar had waited for them for some time in vain, lest he should be debarred from a voyage by the season of the year, inasmuch as the equinox was at hand, he of necessity stowed his soldiers the more closely, and, a very great calm coming on, after he had weighed anchor at the beginning of the second watch, he reached land at break of day and brought in all the ships in safety.

5:24 The ships having been drawn up and a general assembly of the Gauls held at Samarobriva, because the corn that year had not

alia ex parte oppidi eiecerunt. Magnus ibi numerus pecoris repertus, multique in fuga sunt comprehensi atque interfecti.

Dum haec in his locis geruntur, Cassivellaunus ad Cantium, quod esse ad mare supra demonstravimus, quibus regionibus quattuor reges praeerant, Cingetorix, Carvilius, Taximagulus, Segovax, nuntios mittit atque eis imperat uti coactis omnibus copiis castra navalia de improviso adoriantur atque oppugent. Ei cum ad castra venissent, nostri eruptione facta multis eorum interfectis, capto etiam nobili duce Lugotorige suos incolumes reduxerunt. Cassivellaunus hoc proelio nuntiato tot detrimentis acceptis, vastatis finibus, maxime etiam permotus defectione civitatum legatos per Atrebatem Commium de deditione ad Caesarem mittit. Caesar, cum constituisset hiemare in continenti propter repentinos Galliae motus, neque multum aestatis superesset, atque id facile extrahi posse intellegeret, obsides imperat et quid in annos singulos vectigalis populo Romano Britannia penderet constituit; interdicit atque imperat Cassivellauno, ne Mandubracio neu Trinobantibus noceat.

Obsidibus acceptis exercitum reducit ad mare, naves invenit refectas. His deductis, quod et captivorum magnum numerum habebat, et nonnullae tempestate deperierant naves, duobus commeatibus exercitum reportare instituit. Ac sic accidit, uti ex tanto navium numero tot navigationibus neque hoc neque superiore anno ulla omnino navis, quae milites portaret, desideraretur; at ex eis, quae inanes ex continenti ad eum remitterentur et prioris commeatus eitis militibus et quas postea Labienus faciendas curaverat numero LX, perpaucae locum caperent, reliquae fere omnes reicerentur. Quas cum aliquamdiu Caesar frustra exspectasset, ne anni tempore a navigatione excluderetur, quod aequinoctium suberat, necessario angustius milites collocavit ac summa tranquillitate consecuta, secunda inita cum solvisset vigilia, prima luce terram attigit omnesque incolumes naves perduxit.

Subductis navibus concilioque Gallorum Samarobrivae peracto, quod eo anno frumentum

prospered in Gaul by reason of the droughts, he was compelled to station his army in its winter-quarters differently from the former years, and to distribute the legions among several states: one of them he gave to C. Fabius, his lieutenant, to be marched into the territories of the Morini; a second to Q. Cicero, into those of the Nervii; a third to L. Roscius, into those of the Essui; a fourth he ordered to winter with T. Labienus among the Remi in the confines of the Treviri; he stationed three in Belgium; over these he appointed M. Crassus, his questor, and L. Munatius Plancus and C. Trebonius, his lieutenants. One legion which he had raised last on the other side of the Po, and five cohorts, he sent among the Eburones, the greatest portion of whom lie between the Meuse and the Rhine, [and] who were under the government of Ambiorix and Cativolcus. He ordered Q. Titurius Sabinus and L. Aurunculeius Cotta, his lieutenants, to take command of these soldiers. The legions being distributed in this manner, he thought he could most easily remedy the scarcity of corn and yet the winter-quarters of all these legions (except that which he had given to L. Roscius, to be led into the most peaceful and tranquil neighborhood) were comprehended within [about] 100 miles. He himself in the mean while, until he had stationed the legions and knew that the several winter-quarters were fortified, determined to stay in Gaul.

5:25 There was among the Carnutes a man named Tasgetius, born of very high rank, whose ancestors had held the sovereignty in his state. To him Caesar had restored the position of his ancestors, in consideration of his prowess and attachment toward him, because in all his wars he had availed himself of his valuable services. His personal enemies had killed him when in the third year of his reign, many even of his own state being openly promoters [of that act] This event is related to Caesar. He fearing, because several were involved in the act, that the state might revolt at their instigation, orders Lucius Plancus, with a legion, to proceed quickly from Belgium to the Carnutes, and winter there, and arrest and send to him the persons by whose instrumentality he should discover that Tasgetius was slain. In the mean time, he was apprised by all the lieutenants and questors to whom he had assigned the legions, that they had arrived in winter-quarters, and that the place for the quarters was fortified.

5:26 About fifteen days after they had come into winter-quarters, the beginning of a sudden insurrection and revolt arose from Ambiorix and Cativolcus, who, though they had met with Sabinus and Cotta at the borders of their kingdom, and had conveyed corn into our winter-quarters, induced by the messages of Indutiomarus, one of the Treviri, excited their people, and after

in Gallia propter siccitates angustius provenerat, coactus est aliter ac superioribus annis exercitum in hibernis collocare legionesque in plures civitates distribuere. Ex quibus unam in Morinos ducendam Gaio Fabio legato dedit, alteram in Nervios Quinto Ciceroni, tertiam in Esubios Lucio Roscio; quartam in Remis cum Tito Labieno in confinio Treverorum hiemare iussit. Tres in Belgis collocavit: eis Marcum Crassum quaestorem et Lucium Munatium Plancum et Gaium Trebonium legatos praefecit. Vnam legionem, quam proxime trans Padum conscripserat, et cohortes V in Eburones, quorum pars maxima est inter Mosam ac Rhenum, qui sub imperio Ambiorigis et Catuvolci erant, misit. Eis militibus Quintum Titurium Sabinum et Lucium Aurunculeium Cottam legatos praeesse iussit. Ad hunc modum distributis legionibus facillime inopiae frumentariae sese mederi posse existimavit. Atque harum tamen omnium legionum hiberna praeter eam, quam Lucio Roscio im pacatissimam et quietissimam partem ducendam dederat, milibus passuum centum continebantur. Ipse interea, quoad legiones collocatas munitaque hiberna cognovisset, in Gallia morari constituit.

Erat in Carnutibus summo loco natus Tasgetius, cuius maiores in sua civitate regnum obtinuerant. Huic Caesar pro eius virtute atque in se benevolentia, quod in omnibus bellis singulari eius opera fuerat usus, maiorum locum restituerat. Tertium iam hunc annum regnantem inimici, multis palam ex civitate eius auctoribus, eum interfecerunt. Defertur ea res ad Caesarem. Ille veritus, quod ad plures pertinebat, ne civitas eorum impulsu deficeret, Lucium Plancum cum legione ex Belgio celeriter in Carnutes proficisci iubet ibique hiemare quorumque opera cognoverat Tasgetium interfectum, hos comprehensos ad se mittere. Interim ab omnibus legatis quaestoreque, quibus legiones tradiderat, certior factus est in hiberna perventum locumque hibernis esse munitum.

Diebus circiter XV, quibus in hiberna ventum est, initium repentini tumultus ac defectionis ortum est ab Ambiorige et Catuvolco; qui, cum ad fines regni sui Sabino Cottaeque praesto fuissent frumentumque in hiberna comportavissent, Indutiomari Treveri nuntiis impulsi suos

having suddenly assailed the soldiers engaged in procuring wood, came with a large body to attack the camp. When our men had speedily taken up arms and had ascended the rampart, and sending out some Spanish horse on one side, had proved conquerors in a cavalry action, the enemy, despairing of success, drew off their troops from the assault. Then they shouted, according to their custom, that some of our men should go forward to a conference, [alleging] that they had some things which they desired to say respecting the common interest, by which they trusted their disputes could be removed.

5:27 C. Arpineius, a Roman knight, the intimate friend of Q. Titurius, and with him, Q. Junius, a certain person from Spain, who already on previous occasions, had been accustomed to go to Ambiorix, at Caesar's mission, is sent to them for the purpose of a conference: before them Ambiorix spoke to this effect: "That he confessed, that for Caesar's kindness toward him, he was very much indebted to him, inasmuch as by his aid he had been freed from a tribute which he had been accustomed to pay to the Aduatuci, his neighbors; and because his own son and the son of his brother had been sent back to him, whom, when sent in the number of hostages, the Aduatuci had detained among them in slavery and in chains; and that he had not done that which he had done in regard to the attacking of the camp, either by his own judgment or desire, but by the compulsion of his state; and that his government was of that nature, that the people had as much authority over him as he over the people. To the state moreover the occasion of the war was this-that it could not withstand the sudden combination of the Gauls; that he could easily prove this from his own weakness, since he was not so little versed in affairs as to presume that with his forces he could conquer the Roman people; but that it was the common resolution of Gaul; that that day was appointed for the storming of all Caesar's winter-quarters, in order that no legion should be able to come to the relief of another legion, that Gauls could not easily deny Gauls, especially when a measure seemed entered into for recovering their common freedom. Since he had performed his duty to them on the score of patriotism [he said], he has now regard to gratitude for the kindness of Caesar; that he warned, that he prayed Titurius by the claims of hospitality, to consult for his and his soldiers' safely; that a large force of the Germans had been hired and had passed the Rhine; that it would arrive in two days: that it was for them to consider whether they thought fit, before the nearest people perceived it, to lead off their soldiers when drawn out of winter-quarters, either to Cicero or to Labienus; one of whom was about fifty miles distant from them, the other rather more; that this he promised and confirmed by oath, that he would give them a safe

concitaverunt subitoque oppressis lignatoribus magna manu ad castra oppugnatum venerunt. Cum celeriter nostri arma cepissent vallumque adscendissent atque una ex parte Hispanis equitibus emissis equestri proelio superiores fuissent, desperata re hostes suos ab oppugnatione reduxerunt. Tum suo more conclamaverunt, uti aliqui ex nostris ad colloquium prodiret: habere sese, quae de re communi dicere vellent, quibus rebus controversias minui posse sperarent.

Mittitur ad eos colloquendi causa Gaius Arpineius, eques Romanus, familiaris Quinti Tituri, et Quintus Iunius ex Hispania quidam, qui iam ante missu Caesaris ad Ambiorigem ventitare consuerat; apud quos Ambiorix ad hunc modum locutus est: Sese pro Caesaris in se beneficiis plurimum ei confiteri debere, quod eius opera stipendio liberatus esset, quod Aduatucis, finitimis suis, pendere consuesset, quodque ei et filius et fratris filius ab Caesare remissi essent, quos Aduatuci obsidum numero missos apud in servitute et catenis tenuissent; neque id, quod fecerit de oppugnatione castrorum, aut iudicio aut voluntate sua fecisse, sed coactu civitatis, suaque esse eiusmodi imperia, ut non minus haberet iuris in se multitudo quam ipse in multitudinem. Civitati porro hanc fuisse belli causam, quod repentinae Gallorum coniurationi resistere non potuerit. Id se facile ex humilitate sua probare posse, quod non adeo sit imperitus rerum ut suis copiis populum Romanum superari posse confidat. Sed esse Galliae commune consilium: omnibus hibernis Caesaris oppugnandis hunc esse dictum diem, ne qua legio alterae legioni subsidio venire posset. Non facile Gallos Gallis negare potuisse, praesertim cum de recuperanda communi libertate consilium initum videretur. Quibus quoniam pro pietate satisfecerit, habere nunc se rationem offici pro beneficiis Caesaris: monere, orare Titurium pro hospitio, ut suae ac militum saluti consulat. Magnam manum Germanorum conductam Rhenum transisse; hanc adfore biduo. Ipsorum esse consilium, velintne priusquam finitimi sentiant eductos ex hibernis milites aut ad Ciceronem aut ad Labienum deducere, quorum alter milia passuum circiter quinquaginta, alter paulo amplius ab eis absit. Illud

passage through his territories; and when he did that, he was both consulting for his own state, because it would be relieved from the winter-quarters, and also making a requital to Caesar for his obligations."

5:28 Arpineius and Junius relate to the lieutenants what they had heard. They, greatly alarmed by the unexpected affair, though those things were spoken by an enemy, still thought they were not to be disregarded; and they were especially influenced by this consideration, that it was scarcely credible that the obscure and humble state of the Eburones had dared to make war upon the Roman people of their own accord. Accordingly, they refer the matter to a council, and a great controversy arises among them. L. Aurunculeius, and several tribunes of the soldiers and the centurions of the first rank, were of opinion "that nothing should be done hastily, and that they should not depart from the camp without Caesar's orders;" they declared, "that any forces of the Germans, however great, might be encountered by fortified winter-quarters; that this fact was a proof [of it]; that they had sustained the first assault of the Germans most valiantly, inflicting many wounds upon them; that they were not distressed for corn; that in the mean time relief would come both from the nearest winter-quarters and from Caesar; lastly, they put the query, "what could be more undetermined, more undignified, than to adopt measures respecting the most important affairs on the authority of an enemy?"

5:29 In opposition to those things, Titurius exclaimed, "That they would do this too late, when greater forces of the enemy, after a junction with the Germans, should have assembled; or when some disaster had been received in the neighboring winter-quarters; that the opportunity for deliberating was short; that he believed that Caesar had set forth into Italy, as the Carnutes would not otherwise have taken the measure of slaying Tasgetius, nor would the Eburones, if he had been present, have come to the camp with so great defiance of us; that he did not regard the enemy, but the fact, as the authority; that the Rhine was near; that the death of Ariovistus and our previous victories were subjects of great indignation to the Germans; that Gaul was inflamed, that after having received so many defeats she was reduced under the sway of the Roman people, her pristine glory in military matters being extinguished." Lastly, "who would persuade himself of this, that Ambiorix had resorted to a design of that nature without sure grounds? That his own opinion was safe on either side; if there be nothing very formidable, they would go without danger to the nearest legion; if all Gaul conspired with the Germans, their only safety lay in dispatch. What issue would the advice of Cotta and of those who differed from him, have? from which, if immediate

se polliceri et iureiurando confirmare tutum iter per fines daturum. Quod cum faciat, et civitati sese consulere, quod hibernis levetur, et Caesari pro eius meritis gratiam referre. Hac oratione habita discedit Ambiorix.

Arpineius et Iunius, quae audierunt, ad legatoc deferunt. Illi repentina re perturbati, etsi ab hoste ea dicebantur, tamen non neglegenda existimabant maximeque hac re permovebantur, quod civitatem ignobilem atque humilem Eburonum sua sponte populo Romano bellum facere ausam vix erat credendum. Itaque ad consilium rem deferunt magnaque inter eos exsistit controversia. Lucius Aurunculeius compluresque tribuni militum et primorum ordinum centuriones nihil temere agendum neque ex hibernis iniussu Caesaris discedendum existimabant: quantasvis [magnas] copias etiam Germanorum sustineri posse munitis hibernis docebant: rem esse testimonio, quod primum hostium impetum multis ultro vulneribus illatis fortissime sustinuerint: re frumentaria non premi; interea et ex proximis hibernis et a Caesare conventura subsidia: postremo quid esse levius aut turpius, quam auctore hoste de summis rebus capere consilium?

Contra ea Titurius sero facturos clamitabat, cum maiores manus hostium adiunctis Germanis convenissent aut cum aliquid calamitatis in proximis hibernis esset acceptum. Brevem consulendi esse occasionem. Caesarem arbitrari profectum in Italiam; neque aliter Calnutcs interficiendi Tasgeti consilium fuisse capturos, neque Eburones, si ille adesset, tanta contemptione nostri ad castra venturos esse. Non hostem auctorem, sed rem spectare: subesse Rhenum; magno esse Germanis dolori Ariovisti mortem et superiores nostras victorias; ardere Galliam tot contumeliis acceptis sub populi Romani imperium redactam superiore gloria rei militaris exstincta. Postremo quis hoc sibi persuaderet, sine certa re Ambiorigem ad eiusmodi consilium descendisse? Suam sententiam in utramque partem esse tutam: si nihil esset durius, nullo cum periculo ad proximam legionem perventuros; si Gallia omnis cum Germanis consentiret, unam esse in celeritate positam salutem. Cottae quidem

danger was not to be dreaded, yet certainly famine, by a protracted siege, was."

5:30 This discussion having been held on the two sides, when opposition was offered strenuously by Cotta and the principal officers, "Prevail," said Sabinus, "if so you wish it;" and he said it with a louder voice, that a great portion of the soldiers might hear him; "nor am I the person among you," he said, "who is most powerfully alarmed by the danger of death; these will be aware of it, and then, if any thing disastrous shall have occurred, they will demand a reckoning at your hands; these, who, if it were permitted by you, united three days hence with the nearest winter-quarters, may encounter the common condition of war with the rest, and not, as if forced away and separated far from the rest, perish either by the sword or by famine."

5:31 They rise from the council, detain both, and entreat, that "they do not bring the matter into the greatest jeopardy by their dissension and obstinacy; the affair was an easy one, if only they all thought and approved of the same thing, whether they remain or depart; on the other hand, they saw no security in dissension." The matter is prolonged by debate till midnight. At last Cotta, being overruled, yields his assent; the opinion of Sabinus prevails. It is proclaimed that they will march at day-break; the remainder of the night is spent without sleep, since every soldier was inspecting his property, [to see] what he could carry with him, and what, out of the appurtenances of the winter-quarters, he would be compelled to leave; every reason is suggested to show why they could not stay without danger, and how that danger would be increased by the fatigue of the soldiers and their want of sleep. At break of day they quit the camp, in a very extended line and with a very large amount of baggage, in such a manner as men who were convinced that the advice was given by Ambiorix, not as an enemy, but as most friendly [toward them].

5:32 But the enemy, after they had made the discovery of their intended departure by the noise during the night and their not retiring to rest, having placed an ambuscade in two divisions in the woods, in a suitable and concealed place, two miles from the camp, waited for the arrival of the Romans: and when the greater part of the line of march had descended into a considerable valley, they suddenly presented themselves on either side of that valley, and began both to harass the rear and hinder the van from ascending, and to give battle in a place exceedingly disadvantageous to our men.

5:33 Then at length Titurius, as one who had provided nothing beforehand, was confused, ran to and fro, and set about arranging his troops; these very things, however, he did timidly and in such a

atque eorum, qui dissentirent, consilium quem habere exitum? In quo si non praesens periculum, at certe longinqua obsidione fames esset timenda.

Hac in utramque partem disputatione habita, cum a Cotta primisque ordinibus acriter resisteretur, "Vincite," inquit, "si ita vultis," Sabinus, et id clariore voce, ut magna pars militum exaudiret; "neque is sum," inquit, "qui gravissime ex vobis mortis periculo terrear: hi sapient; si gravius quid acciderit, abs te rationem reposcent, qui, si per te liceat, perendino die cum proximis hibernis coniuncti communem cum reliquis belli casum sustineant, non reiecti et relegati longe ab ceteris aut ferro aut fame intereant."

Consurgitur ex consilio; comprehendunt utrumque et orant, ne sua dissensione et pertinacia rem in summum periculum deducat: facilem esse rem, seu maneant, seu proficiscantur, si modo unum omnes sentiant ac probent; contra in dissensione nullam se salutem perspicere. Res disputatione ad mediam noctem perducitur. Tandem dat Cotta permotus manus: superat sententia Sabini. Pronuntiatur prima luce ituros. Consumitur vigiliis reliqua pars noctis, cum sua quisque miles circumspiceret, quid secum portare posset, quid ex instrumento hibernorum relinquere cogeretur. Omnia excogitantur, quare nec sine periculo maneatur, et languore militum et vigiliis periculum augeatur. Prima luce sic ex castris proficiscuntur, ut quibus esset persuasum non ab hoste, sed ab homine amicissimo Ambiorige consilium datum, longissimo agmine maximisque impedimentis.

At hostes, posteaquam ex nocturno fremitu vigiliisque de profectione eorum senserunt, collocatis insidiis bipertito in silvis opportuno atque occulto loco a milibus passuum circiter duobus Romanorum adventum exspectabant, et cum se maior pars agminis in magnam convallem demisisset, ex utraque parte eius vallis subito se ostenderunt novissimosque premere et primos prohibere ascensu atque iniquissimo nostris loco proelium committere coeperunt.

Tum demum Titurius, qui nihil ante providisset, trepidare et concursare cohortesque disponere, haec tamen ipsa timide atque ut eum omnia

manner that all resources seemed to fail him: which generally happens to those who are compelled to take council in the action itself. But Cotta, who had reflected that these things might occur on the march, and on that account had not been an adviser of the departure, was wanting to the common safety in no respect; both in addressing and encouraging the soldiers, he performed the duties of a general, and in the battle those of a soldier. And since they [Titurius and Cotta] could less easily perform every thing by themselves, and provide what was to be done in each place, by reason of the length of the line of march, they ordered [the officers] to give the command that they should leave the baggage and form themselves into an orb, which measure, though in a contingency of that nature it was not to be condemned, still turned out unfortunately; for it both diminished the hope of our soldiers and rendered the enemy more eager for the fight, because it appeared that this was not done without the greatest fear and despair. Besides that happened, which would necessarily be the case, that the soldiers for the most part quitted their ensigns and hurried to seek and carry off from the baggage whatever each thought valuable, and all parts were filled with uproar and lamentation.

5:34 But judgment was not wanting to the barbarians; for their leaders ordered [the officers] to proclaim through the ranks "that no man should quit his place; that the booty was theirs, and for them was reserved whatever the Romans should leave; therefore let them consider that all things depended on their victory. Our men were equal to them in fighting, both in courage and in number, and though they were deserted by their leader and by fortune, yet they still placed all hope of safety in their valor, and as often as any cohort sallied forth on that side, a great number of the enemy usually fell. Ambiorix, when he observed this, orders the command to be issued that they throw their weapons from a distance and do not approach too near, and in whatever direction the Romans should make an attack, there give way (from the lightness of their appointments and from their daily practice no damage could be done them); [but] pursue them when betaking themselves to their standards again.

5:35 Which command having been most carefully obeyed, when any cohort had quitted the circle and made a charge, the enemy fled very precipitately. In the mean time, that part of the Roman army, of necessity, was left unprotected, and the weapons received on their open flank. Again, when they had begun to return to that place from which they had advanced, they were surrounded both by those who had retreated and by those who stood next them; but if, on the other hand, they wish to keep their place, neither was an opportunity left for valor, nor could they, being crowded together, escape the weapons cast by so large a body of

deficere viderentur; quod plerumque eis accidere consuevit, qui in ipso negotio consilium capere coguntur. At Cotta, qui cogitasset haec posse in itinere accidere atque ob eam causam profectionis auctor non fuisset, nulla in re communi saluti deerat et in appellandis cohortandisque militibus imperatoris et in pugna militis officia praestabat. Cum propter longitudinem agminis minus facile omnia per se obire et, quid quoque loco faciendum esset, providere possent, iusserunt pronuntiare, ut impedimenta relinquerent atque in orbem consisterent. Quod consilium etsi in eiusmodi casu reprehendendum non est, tamen incommode accidit: nam et nostris militibus spem minuit et hostes ad pugnam alacriores effecit, quod non sine summo timore et desperatione id factum videbatur. Praeterea accidit, quod fieri necesse erat, ut vulgo milites ab signis discederent, quae quisque eorum carissima haberet, ab impedimentis petere atque arripere properaret, clamore et fletu omnia complerentur.

At barbaris consilium non defuit. Nam duces eorum tota acie pronuntiare iusserunt, ne quis ab loco discederet: illorum esse praedam atque illis reservari quaecumque Romani reliquissent: proinde omnia in victoria posita existimarent. Erant et virtute et studio pugnandi pares; nostri, tametsi ab duce et a fortuna deserebantur, tamen omnem spem salutis in virtute ponebant, et quotiens quaeque cohors procurrerat, ab ea parte magnus numerus hostium cadebat. Qua re animadversa Ambiorix pronuntiari iubet, ut procul tela coniciant neu propius accedant et, quam in partem Romani impetum fecerint, cedant (levitate armorum et cotidiana exercitatione nihil eis noceri posse), rursus se ad signa recipientes insequantur.

Quo praecepto ab eis diligentissime observato, cum quaepiam cohors ex orbe excesserat atque impetum fecerat, hostes velocissime refugiebant. Interim eam partem nudari necesse erat et ab latere aperto tela recipi. Rursus cum in eum locum unde erant egressi reverti coeperant, et ab eis qui cesserant et ab eis qui proximi steterant circumveniebantur; sin autem locum tenere vellent, nec virtuti locus relinquebatur, neque ab tanta multitudine coniecta tela conferti vitare poterant.

men. Yet, though assailed by so many disadvantages, [and] having received many wounds, they withstood the enemy, and, a great portion of the day being spent, though they fought from daybreak till the eighth hour, they did nothing which was unworthy of them. At length, each thigh of T. Balventius, who the year before had been chief centurion, a brave man and one of great authority, is pierced with a javelin; Q. Lucanius, of the same rank, fighting most valiantly, is slain while he assists his son when surrounded by the enemy; L. Cotta, the lieutenant, when encouraging all the cohorts and companies, is wounded full in the mouth by a sling.

5:36 Much troubled by these events, Q. Titurius, when he had perceived Ambiorix in the distance encouraging his men, sends to him his interpreter, Cn. Pompey, to beg that he would spare him and his soldiers. He, when addressed, replied, "If he wishes to confer with him, it was permitted; that he hoped what pertained to the safety of the soldiers could be obtained from the people; that to him however certainly no injury would be done, and that he pledged his faith to that effect." He consults with Cotta, who had been wounded, whether it would appear right to retire from battle, and confer with Ambiorix; [saying] that he hoped to be able to succeed respecting his own and the soldiers' safety. Cotta says he will not go to an armed enemy, and in that perseveres.

5:37 Sabinus orders those tribunes of the soldiers whom he had at the time around him, and the centurions of the first ranks, to follow him, and when he had approached near to Ambiorix, being ordered to throw down his arms, he obeys the order and commands his men to do the same. In the mean time, while they treat upon the terms, and a longer debate than necessary is designedly entered into by Ambiorix, being surrounded by degrees, he is slain. Then they, according to their custom, shout out "Victory," and raise their war-cry, and, making an attack on our men, break their ranks. There L. Cotta, while fighting, is slain, together with the greater part of the soldiers; the rest betake themselves to the camp, from which they had marched forth, and one of them, L. Petrosidius, the standard bearer, when he was overpowered by the great number of the enemy, threw the eagle within the intrenchments and is himself slain while fighting with the greatest courage before the camp. They with difficulty sustain the attack till night; despairing of safety, they all to a man destroy themselves in the night. A few escaping from the battle, made their way to Labienus at winter-quarters, after wandering at random through the woods, and inform him of these events

Tamen tot incommodis conflictati, multis vulneribus acceptis resistebant et magna parte diei consumpta, cum a prima luce ad horam octavam pugnaretur, nihil quod ipsis esset indignum committebant. Tum Tito Balventio, qui superiore anno primum pilum duxerat, viro forti et magnae auctoritatis, utrumque femur tragula traicitur; Quintus Lucanius, eiusdem ordinis, fortissime pugnans, dum circumvento filio subvenit, interficitur; Lucius Cotta legatus omnes cohortes ordinesque adhortans in adversum os funda vulneratur.

His rebus permotus Quintus Titurius, cum procul Ambiorigem suos cohortantem conspexisset, interpretem suum Gnaeum Pompeium ad eum mittit rogatum ut sibi militibusque parcat. Ille appellatus respondit: si velit secum colloqui, licere; sperare a multitudine impetrari posse, quod ad militum salutem pertineat; ipsi vero nihil nocitum iri, inque eam rem se suam fidem interponere. Ille cum Cotta saucio communicat, si videatur, pugna ut excedant et cum Ambiorige una colloquantur: sperare ab eo de sua ac militum salute impetrari posse. Cotta se ad armatum hostem iturum negat atque in eo perseverat.

Sabinus quos in praesentia tribunos militum circum se habebat et primorum ordinum centuriones se sequi iubet et, cum propius Ambiorigem accessisset, iussus arma abicere imperatum facit suisque ut idem faciant imperat. Interim, dum de condicionibus inter se agunt longiorque consulto ab Ambiorige instituitur sermo, paulatim circumventus interficitur. Tum vero suo more victoriam conclamant atque ululatum tollunt impetuque in nostros facto ordines perturbant. Ibi Lucius Cotta pugnans interficitur cum maxima parte militum. Reliqui se in castra recipiunt unde erant egressi. Ex quibus Lucius Petrosidius aquilifer, cum magna multitudine hostium premeretur, aquilam intra vallum proiecit; ipse pro castris fortissime pugnans occiditur. Illi aegre ad noctem oppugnationem sustinent; noctu ad unum omnes desperata salute se ipsi interficiunt. Pauci ex proelio lapsi incertis itineribus per silvas ad Titum Labienum legatum in hiberna perveniunt atque eum de rebus gestis certiorem faciunt.

5:38 Elated by this victory, Ambiorix marches immediately with his cavalry to the Aduatuci, who bordered on his kingdom; he halts neither day nor night, and orders the infantry to follow him closely. Having related the exploit and roused the Aduatuci, the next day he arrived among the Nervii, and entreats "that they should not throw away the opportunity of liberating themselves forever and of punishing the Romans for those wrongs which they had received from them;" [he tells them] "that two lieutenants have been slain, and that a large portion of the army has perished; that it was not a matter of difficulty for the legion which was wintering with Cicero to be cut off, when suddenly assaulted; he declares himself ready to cooperate in that design. He easily gains over the Nervii by this speech.

5:39 Accordingly, messengers having been forthwith dispatched to the Centrones, the Grudii, the Levaci, the Pleumoxii, and the Geiduni, all of whom are under their government, they assemble as large bodies as they can, and rush unexpectedly to the winter-quarters of Cicero, the report of the death of Titurius not having as yet been conveyed to him. That also occurred to him, which was the consequence of a necessary work-that some soldiers who had gone off into the woods for the purpose of procuring timber and therewith constructing fortifications, were intercepted by the sudden arrival of [the enemy's] horse. These having been entrapped, the Eburones, the Nervii, and the Aduatici and all their allies and dependents, begin to attack the legion: our men quickly run together to arms and mount the rampart; they sustained the attack that day with great difficulty, since the enemy placed all their hope in dispatch, and felt assured that, if they obtained this victory, they would be conquerors forever.

5:40 Letters are immediately sent to Caesar by Cicero, great rewards being offered [to the messengers] if they carried them through. All these passes having been beset, those who were sent are intercepted. During the night as many as 120 towers are raised with incredible dispatch out of the timber which they had collected for the purpose of fortification: the things which seemed necessary to the work are completed. The following day the enemy, having collected far greater forces, attack the camp [and] fill up the ditch. Resistance is made by our men in the same manner as the day before; this same thing is done afterward during the remaining days. The work is carried on incessantly in the night: not even to the sick, or wounded, is opportunity given for rest: whatever things are required for resisting the assault of the next day are provided during the night: many stakes burned at the end, and a large number of mural pikes are procured: towers are built up, battlements and parapets are formed of interwoven hurdles. Cicero himself, though he was in very weak health, did not leave himself the night-time for repose, so that he was forced to spare

Hac victoria sublatus Ambiorix statim cum equitatu in Aduatucos, qui erant eius regno finitimi, proficiscitur; neque noctem neque diem intermittit peditatumque subsequi iubet. Re demonstrata Aduatucisque concitatis postero die in Nervios pervenit hortaturque, ne sui in perpetuum liberandi atque ulciscendi Romanos pro eis quas acceperint iniuriis occasionem dimittant: interfectos esse legatos duos magnamque partem exercitus interisse demonstrat; nihil esse negoti subito oppressam legionem quae cum Cicerone hiemet interfici; se ad eam rem profitetur adiutorem. Facile hac oratione Nerviis persuadet.

Itaque confestim dimissis nuntiis ad Ceutrones, Grudios, Levacos, Pleumoxios, Geidumnos, qui omnes sub eorum imperio sunt, quam maximas manus possunt cogunt et de improviso ad Ciceronis hiberna advolant nondum ad eum fama de Tituri morte perlata. Huic quoque accidit, quod fuit necesse, ut nonnulli milites, qui lignationis munitionisque causa in silvas discessissent, repentino equitum adventu interciperentur. His circumventis magna manu Eburones, Nervii, Aduatuci atque horum omnium socii et clientes legionem oppugnare incipiunt. Nostri celeriter ad arma concurrunt, vallum conscendunt. Aegre is dies sustentatur, quod omnem spem hostes in celeritate ponebant atque hanc adepti victoriam in perpetuum se fore victores confidebant.

Mittuntur ad Caesarem confestim ab Cicerone litterae magnis propositis praemiis, si pertulissent: obsessis omnibus viis missi intercipiuntur. Noctu ex materia, quam munitionis causa comportaverant, turres admodum CXX excitantur incredibili celeritate; quae deesse operi videbantur, perficiuntur. Hostes postero die multo maioribus coactis copiis castra oppugnant, fossam complent. Eadem ratione, qua pridie, ab nostris resistitur. Hoc idem reliquis deinceps fit diebus. Nulla pars nocturni temporis ad laborem intermittitur; non aegris, non vulneratis facultas quietis datur. Quaecumque ad proximi diei oppugnationem opus sunt noctu comparantur; multae praeustae sudes, magnus muralium pilorum numerus instituitur; turres contabulantur, pinnae loricaeque ex cratibus attexuntur. Ipse Cicero, cum tenuissima valetudine esset, ne nocturnum quidem sibi tempus ad

himself by the spontaneous movement and entreaties of the soldiers.

5:41 Then these leaders and chiefs of the Nervii, who had any intimacy and grounds of friendship with Cicero, say they desire to confer with him. When permission was granted, they recount the same things which Ambiorix had related to Titurius, namely, "that all Gaul was in arms, that the Germans had passed the Rhine, that the winter-quarters of Caesar and of the others were attacked." They report in addition also, about the death of Sabinus. They point to Ambiorix for the purpose of obtaining credence; "they are mistaken," say they, "if they hoped for any relief from those who distrust their own affairs; that they bear such feelings toward Cicero and the Roman people that they deny them nothing but winter-quarters, and are unwilling that the practice should become constant; that through their [the Nervii's] means it is possible for them [the Romans] to depart from their winter-quarters safely and to proceed without fear into whatever parts they desire." To these Cicero made only one reply: "that it is not the custom of the Roman people to accept any condition from an armed enemy: if they are willing to lay down their arms, they may employ him as their advocate and send embassadors to Caesar: that he believed, from his [Caesar's] justice, they would obtain the things which they might request."

5:42 Disappointed in this hope, the Nervii surround the winter-quarters with a rampart eleven feet high, and a ditch thirteen feet in depth. These military works they had learned from our men in the intercourse of former years, and, having taken some of our army prisoners, were instructed by them: but, as they had no supply of iron tools which are requisite for this service, they were forced to cut the turf with their swords, and to empty out the earth with their hands and cloaks, from which circumstance, the vast number of the men could be inferred; for in less than three hours they completed a fortification of ten miles in circumference; and during the rest of the days they began to prepare and construct towers of the height of the ramparts, and grappling irons, and mantelets, which the same prisoners had taught them.

5:43 On the seventh day of the attack, a very high wind having sprung up, they began to discharge by their slings hot balls made of burned or hardened clay, and heated javelins, upon the huts, which, after the Gallic custom, were thatched with straw. These quickly took fire, and by the violence of the wind, scattered their flames in every part of the camp. The enemy following up their success with a very loud shout, as if victory were already obtained and secured, began to advance their towers and mantelets, and climb the rampart with ladders. But so great was the courage of our soldiers, and such their presence of mind, that though they

quietem relinquebat, ut ultro militum concursu ae vocibus sibi parcere cogeretur.

Tunc duces principesque Nerviorum qui aliquem sermonis aditum causamque amicitiae cum Cicerone habebant colloqui sese velle dicunt. Facta potestate eadem quae Ambiorix cum Titurio egerat commemorant: omnem esse in armis Galliam; Germanos Rhenum transisse; Caesaris reliquorumque hiberna oppugnari. Addunt etiam de Sabini morte: Ambiorigem ostentant fidei faciendae causa. Errare eos dicunt, si quidquam ab his praesidi sperent, qui suis rebus diffidant; sese tamen hoc esse in Ciceronem populumque Romanum animo, ut nihil nisi hiberna recusent atque hanc inveterascere consuetudinem nolint: licere illis incolumibus per se ex hibernis discedere et quascumque in partes velint sine metu proficisci. Cicero ad haec unum modo respondit: non esse consuetudinem populi Romani accipere ab hoste armato condicionem: si ab armis discedere velint, se adiutore utantur legatosque ad Caesarem mittant; sperare pro eius iustitia, quae petierint, impetraturos.

Ab hac spe repulsi Nervii vallo pedum IX et fossa pedum XV hiberna cingunt. Haec et superiorum annorum consuetudine ab nobis cognoverant et, quos clam de exercitu habebant captivos, ab eis docebantur; sed nulla ferramentorum copia quae esset ad hunc usum idonea, gladiis caespites circumcidere, manibus sagulisque terram exhaurire nitebantur. Qua quidem ex re hominum multitudo cognosci potuit: nam minus horis tribus milium pedum XV in circuitu munitionem perfecerunt reliquisque diebus turres ad altitudinem valli, falces testudinesque, quas idem captivi docuerant, parare ac facere coeperunt.

Septimo oppugnationis die maximo coorto vento ferventes fusili ex argilla glandes fundis et fervefacta iacula in casas, quae more Gallico stramentis erant tectae, iacere coeperunt. Hae celeriter ignem comprehenderunt et venti magnitudine in omnem locum castrorum distulerunt. Hostes maximo clamore sicuti parta iam atque explorata victoria turres testudinesque agere et scalis vallum ascendere coeperunt. At tanta militum virtus atque ea praesentia animi fuit,

were scorched on all sides, and harassed by a vast number of weapons, and were aware that their baggage and their possessions were burning, not only did no one quit the rampart for the purpose of withdrawing from the scene, but scarcely did any one even then look behind; and they all fought most vigorously and most valiantly. This day was by far the most calamitous to our men; it had this result, however, that on that day the largest number of the enemy was wounded and slain, since they had crowded beneath the very rampart, and the hindmost did not afford the foremost a retreat. The flame having abated a little, and a tower having been brought up in a particular place and touching the rampart, the centurions of the third cohort retired from the place in which they were standing, and drew off all their men: they began to call on the enemy by gestures and by words, to enter if they wished; but none of them dared to advance. Then stones having been cast from every quarter, the enemy were dislodged, and their tower set on fire.

5:44 In that legion there were two very brave men, centurions, who were now approaching the first ranks, T. Pulfio, and L. Varenus. These used to have continual disputes between them which of them should be preferred, and every year used to contend for promotion with the utmost animosity. When the fight was going on most vigorously before the fortifications, Pulfio, one of them, says, "Why do you hesitate, Varenus? or what [better] opportunity of signalizing your valor do you seek? This very day shall decide our disputes." When he had uttered these words, he proceeds beyond the fortifications, and rushes on that part of the enemy which appeared the thickest. Nor does Varenus remain within the rampart, but respecting the high opinion of all, follows close after. Then, when an inconsiderable space intervened, Pulfio throws his javelin at the enemy, and pierces one of the multitude who was running up, and while the latter was wounded and slain, the enemy cover him with their shields, and all throw their weapons at the other and afford him no opportunity of retreating. The shield of Pulfio is pierced and a javelin is fastened in his belt. This circumstance turns aside his scabbard and obstructs his right hand when attempting to draw his sword: the enemy crowd around him when [thus] embarrassed. His rival runs up to him and succors him in this emergency. Immediately the whole host turn from Pulfio to him, supposing the other to be pierced through by the javelin. Varenus rushes on briskly with his sword and carries on the combat hand to hand, and having slain one man, for a short time drove back the rest: while he urges on too eagerly, slipping into a hollow, he fell. To him, in his turn, when surrounded, Pulfio brings relief; and both having slain a great number, retreat into the

ut, cum undique flamma torrerentur maximaque telorum multitudine premerentur suaque omnia impedimenta atque omnes fortunas conflagrare intellegerent, non modo demigrandi causa de vallo decederet nemo, sed paene ne respiceret quidem quisquam, ac tum omnes acerrime fortissimeque pugnarent. Hic dies nostris longe gravissimus fuit; sed tamen hunc habuit eventum, ut eo die maximus numerus hostium vulneraretur atque interficeretur, ut se sub ipso vallo constipaverant recessumque primis ultimi non dabant. Paulum quidem intermissa flamma et quodam loco turri adacta et contingente vallum tertiae cohortis centuriones ex eo, quo stabant, loco recesserunt suosque omnes removerunt, nutu vocibusque hostes, si introire vellent, vocare coeperunt; quorum progredi ausus est nemo. Tum ex omni parte lapidibus coniectis deturbati, turrisque succensa est.

Erant in ea legione fortissimi viri, centuriones, qui primis ordinibus appropinquarent, Titus Pullo et Lucius Vorenus. Hi perpetuas inter se controversias habebant, quinam anteferretur, omnibusque annis de locis summis simultatibus contendebant. Ex his Pullo, cum acerrime ad munitiones pugnaretur, "Quid dubitas," inquit, " Vorene? aut quem locum tuae probandae virtutis exspectas ? hic dies de nostris controversiis iudicabit." Haec cum dixisset, procedit extra munitiones quaque pars hostium confertissma est visa irrumpit. Ne Vorenus quidem tum sese vallo continet, sed omnium veritus existi mationem subsequitur. Mediocri spatio relicto Pullo pilum in hostes immittit atque unum ex multitudine procurrentem traicit; quo percusso et exanimato hunc scutis protegunt, in hostem tela universi coniciunt neque dant regrediendi facultatem. Transfigitur scutum Pulloni et verutum in balteo defigitur. Avertit hic casus vaginam et gladium educere conanti dextram moratur manum, impeditumque hostes circumsistunt. Succurrit inimicus illi Vorenus et laboranti subvenit. Ad hunc se confestim a Pullone omnis multitudo convertit: illum veruto arbitrantur occisum. Gladio comminus rem gerit Vorenus atque uno interfecto reliquos paulum propellit; dum cupidius instat, in locum deiectus inferiorem concidit. Huic rursus

fortifications amid the highest applause. Fortune so dealt with both in this rivalry and conflict, that the one competitor was a succor and a safeguard to the other, nor could it be determined which of the two appeared worthy of being preferred to the other.

5:45 In proportion as the attack became daily more formidable and violent, and particularly, because, as a great number of the soldiers were exhausted with wounds, the matter had come to a small number of defenders, more frequent letters and messages were sent to Caesar; a part of which messengers were taken and tortured to death in the sight of our soldiers. There was within our camp a certain Nervian, by name Vertico, born in a distinguished position, who in the beginning of the blockade had deserted to Cicero, and had exhibited his fidelity to him. He persuades his slave, by the hope of freedom, and by great rewards, to convey a letter to Caesar. This he carries out bound about his javelin; and mixing among the Gauls without any suspicion by being a Gaul, he reaches Caesar. From him they received information of the imminent danger of Cicero and the legion.

5:46 Caesar having received the letter about the eleventh hour of the day, immediately sends a messenger to the Bellovaci, to M. Crassus, questor there, whose winter-quarters were twenty-five miles distant from him. He orders the legion to set forward in the middle of the night, and come to him with dispatch. Crassus sets out with the messenger. He sends another to C. Fabius, the lieutenant, ordering him to lead forth his legion into the territories of the Atrebates, to which he knew his march must be made. He writes to Labienus to come with his legion to the frontiers of the Nervii, if he could do so to the advantage of the commonwealth: he does not consider that the remaining portion of the army, because it was somewhat further distant, should be waited for; but assembles about 400 horse from the nearest winter-quarters.

5:47 Having been apprised of the arrival of Crassus by the scouts at about the third hour, he advances twenty miles that day. He appoints Crassus over Samarobriva and assigns him a legion, because he was leaving there the baggage of the army, the hostages of the states, the public documents, and all the corn, which he had conveyed thither for passing the winter. Fabius, without delaying a moment, meets him on the march with his legion, as he had been commanded. Labienus, having learned the death of Sabinus and the destruction of the cohorts, as all the forces of the Treviri had come against him, beginning to fear lest, if he made a departure from his winter-quarters, resembling a flight,

circumvento fert subsidium Pullo, atque ambo incolumes compluribus interfectis summa cum laude sese intra munitiones recipiunt. Sic fortuna in contentione et certamine utrumque versavit, ut alter alteri inimicus auxilio salutique esset, neque diiudicari posset, uter utri virtute anteferendus videretur.

Quanto erat in dies gravior atque asperior oppugnatio, et maxime quod magna parte militum confecta vulneribus res ad paucitatem defensorum pervenerat, tanto crebriores litterae nuntiique ad Caesarem mittebantur; quorum pars deprehensa in conspectu nostrorum militum cum cruciatu necabatur. Erat unus intus Nervius nomine Vertico, loco natus honesto, qui a prima obsidione ad Ciceronem perfugerat suamque ei fidem praestiterat. Hic servo spe libertatis magnisque persuadet praemiis, ut litteras ad Caesarem deferat. Has ille in iaculo illigatas effert et Gallus inter Gallos sine ulla suspicione versatus ad Caesarem pervenit. Ab eo de periculis Ciceronis legionisque cognoscitur.

Caesar acceptis litteris hora circiter XI diei statim nuntium in Bellovacos ad M. Crassum quaestorem mittit, cuius hiberna aberant ab eo milia passuum XXV; iubet media nocte legionem proficisci celeriterque ad se venire. Exit cum nuntio Crassus. Alterum ad Gaium Fabium legatum mittit, ut in Atrebatium fines legionem adducat, qua sibi iter faciendum sciebat. Scribit Labieno, si rei publicae commodo facere posset, cum legione ad fines Nerviorum veniat. Reliquam partem exercitus, quod paulo aberat longius, non putat exspectandam; equites circiter quadringentos ex proximis hibernis colligit.

Hora circiter tertia ab antecursoribus de Crassi adventu certior factus eo die milia passuum XX procedit. Crassum Samarobrivae praeficit legionemque attribuit, quod ibi impedimenta exercitus, obsides civitatum, litteras publicas frumentumque omne quod eo tolerandae hiemis causa devexerat relinquebat. Fabius, ut imperatum erat, non ita multum moratus in itinere cum legione occurrit. Labienus interitu Sabini et caede cohortium cognita, cum omnes ad eum Treverorum copiae venissent, veritus, si ex

he should not be able to support the attack of the enemy, particularly since he knew them to be elated by their recent victory, sends back a letter to Caesar, informing him with what great hazard he would lead out his legion from winter-quarters; he relates at large the affairs which had taken place among the Eburones; he informs him that all the infantry and cavalry of the Treviri had encamped at a distance of only three miles from his own camp.

5:48 Caesar, approving of his motives, although he was disappointed in his expectation of three legions, and reduced to two, yet placed his only hopes of the common safety in dispatch. He goes into the territories of the Nervii by long marches. There he learns from some prisoners what things are going on in the camp of Cicero, and in how great jeopardy the affair is. Then with great rewards he induces a certain man of the Gallic horse to convey a letter to Cicero. This he sends written in Greek characters, lest the letter being intercepted, our measures should be discovered by the enemy. He directs him, if he should be unable to enter, to throw his spear with the letter fastened to the thong, inside the fortifications of the camp. He writes in the letter, that he having set out with his legions, will quickly be there: he entreats him to maintain his ancient valor. The Gaul apprehending danger, throws his spear as he has been directed. Is by chance stuck in a tower, and, not being observed by our men for two days, was seen by a certain soldier on the third day: when taken down, it was carried to Cicero. He, after perusing it, reads it out in an assembly of the soldiers, and fills all with the greatest joy. Then the smoke of the fires was seen in the distance, a circumstance which banished all doubt of the arrival of the legions.

5:49 The Gauls, having discovered the matter through their scouts, abandon the blockade, and march toward Caesar with all their forces; these were about 60,000 armed men. Cicero, an opportunity being now afforded, again begs of that Vertico, the Gaul, whom we mentioned above, to convey back a letter to Caesar; he advises him to perform his journey warily; he writes in the letter that the enemy had departed and had turned their entire force against him. When this letter was brought to him about the middle of the night, Caesar apprises his soldiers of its contents, and inspires them with courage for fighting: the following day, at the dawn, he moves his camp, and, having proceeded four miles, he espies the forces of the enemy on the other side of a considerable valley and rivulet. It was an affair of great danger to fight with such large forces in a disadvantageous situation. For the present, therefore, inasmuch as he knew that Cicero was released from the blockade, and thought that he might, on that account, relax his speed, he halted there and fortifies a camp in the most

hibernis fugae similem profectionem fecisset, ut hostium impetum sustinere posset, praesertim quos recenti victoria efferri sciret, litteras Caesari remittit, quanto cum periculo legionem ex hibernis educturus esset; rem gestam in Eburonibus perscribit; docet omnes equitatus peditatusque copias Treverorum tria milia passuum longe ab suis castris consedisse.

Caesar consilio eius probato, etsi opinione trium legionum deiectus ad duas redierat, tamen unum communis salutis auxilium in celeritate ponebat. Venit magnis itineribus in Nerviorum fines. Ibi ex captivis cognoscit, quae apud Ciceronem gerantur, quantoque in periculo res sit. Tum cuidam ex equitibus Gallis magnis praemiis persuadet uti ad Ciceronem epistolam deferat. Hanc Graecis conscriptam litteris mittit, ne intercepta epistola nostra ab hostibus consilia cognoscantur. Si adire non possit, monet ut tragulam cum epistola ad amentum deligata intra munitionem castrorum abiciat. In litteris scribit se cum legionibus profectum celeriter adfore; hortatur ut pristinam virtutem retineat. Gallus periculum veritus, ut erat praeceptum, tragulam mittit. Haec casu ad turrim adhaesit neque ab nostris biduo animadversa tertio die a quodam milite conspicitur, dempta ad Ciceronem defertur. Ille perlectam in conventu militum recitat maximaque omnes laetitia adficit. Tum fumi incendiorum procul videbantur; quae res omnem dubitationem adventus legionum expulit.

Galli re cognita per exploratores obsidionem relinquunt, ad Caesarem omnibus copiis contendunt. Hae erant armata circiter milia LX. Cicero data facultate Gallum ab eodem Verticone, quem supra demonstravimus, repetit, qui litteras ad Caesarem deferat; hunc admonet, iter caute diligenterque faciat: perscribit in litteris hostes ab se discessisse omnemque ad eum multitudinem convertisse. Quibus litteris circiter media nocte Caesar adlatis suos facit certiores eosque ad dimicandum animo confirmat. Postero die luce prima movet castra et circiter milia passuum quattuor progressus trans vallem et rivum multitudinem hostium conspicatur. Erat magni periculi res tantulis copiis iniquo loco dimicare; tum, quoniam obsidione liberatum Ciceronem sciebat, aequo animo remittendum de celeritate

favorable position he can. And this, though it was small in itself, [there being] scarcely 7,000 men, and these too without baggage, still by the narrowness of the passages, he contracts as much as he can, with this object, that he may come into the greatest contempt with the enemy. In the mean while scouts having been sent in all directions, he examines by what most convenient path he might cross the valley.

5:50 That day, slight skirmishes of cavalry having taken place near the river, both armies kept in their own positions: the Gauls, because they were awaiting larger forces which had not then arrived; Caesar, [to see] if perchance by pretense of fear he could allure the enemy toward his position, so that he might engage in battle, in front of his camp, on this side of the valley; if he could not accomplish this, that, having inquired about the passes, he might cross the valley and the river with the less hazard. At daybreak the cavalry of the enemy approaches to the camp and joins battle with our horse. Caesar orders the horse to give way purposely, and retreat to the camp: at the same time he orders the camp to be fortified with a higher rampart in all directions, the gates to be barricaded, and in executing these things as much confusion to be shown as possible, and to perform them under the pretense of fear.

5:51 Induced by all these things, the enemy lead over their forces and draw up their line in a disadvantageous position; and as our men also had been led down from the ramparts, they approach nearer, and throw their weapons into the fortification from all sides, and sending heralds round, order it to be proclaimed that, if "any, either Gaul or Roman, was willing to go over to them before the third hour, it was permitted; after that time there would not be permission;" and so much did they disregard our men, that the gates having been blocked up with single rows of turf as a mere appearance, because they did not seem able to burst in that way, some began to pull down the rampart with their hands, others to fill up the trenches. Then Caesar, making a sally from all the gates, and sending out the cavalry, soon puts the enemy to flight, so that no one at all stood his ground with the intention of fighting; and he slew a great number of them, and deprived all of their arms.

5:52 Caesar, fearing to pursue them very far, because woods and morasses intervened, and also [because] he saw that they suffered no small loss in abandoning their position, reaches Cicero the same day with all his forces safe. He witnesses with surprise the towers, mantelets, and [other] fortifications belonging to the

existimabat: consedit et quam aequissimo loco potest castra communit atque haec, etsi erant exigua per se vix hominum milium septem praesertim nullis cum impedimentis, tamen angustiis viarum quam maxime potest contrahit, eo consilio, ut in summam contemptionem hostibus veniat. Interim speculatoribus in omnes partes dimissis explorat quo commodissime itinere vallem transire possit.

Eo die parvulis equestribus proeliis ad aquam factis utrique sese suo loco continent: Galli, quod ampliores copias, quae nondum convenerant, exspectabant; Caesar, si forte timoris simulatione hostes in suum locum elicere posset, ut citra vallem pro castris proelio contenderet, si id efficere non posset, ut exploratis itineribus minore cum periculo vallem rivumque transiret. Prima luce hostium equitatus ad castra accedit proeliumque cum nostris equitibus committit. Caesar consulto equites cedere seque in castra recipere iubet, simul ex omnibus partibus castra altiore vallo muniri portasque obstrui atque in his administrandis rebus quam maxime concursari et cum simulatione agi timoris iubet.

Quibus omnibus rebus hostes invitati copias traducunt aciemque iniquo loco constituunt, nostris vero etiam de vallo deductis propius accedunt et tela intra munitionem ex omnibus partibus coniciunt praeconibusque circummissis pronuntiari iubent, seu quis Gallus seu Romanus velit ante horam tertiam ad se transire, sine periculo licere; post id tempus non fore potestatem: ac sic nostros contempserunt, ut obstructis in speciem portis singulis ordinibus caespitum, quod ea non posse introrumpere videbantur, alii vallum manu scindere, alii fossas complere inciperent. Tum Caesar omnibus portis eruptione facta equitatuque emisso celeriter hostes in fugam dat, sic uti omnino pugnandi causa resisteret nemo, magnumque ex eis numerum occidit atque omnes armis exuit.

Longius prosequi veritus, quod silvae paludesque intercedebant neque etiam parvulo detrimento illorum locum relinqui videbat, omnibus suis incolumibus copiis eodem die ad Ciceronem pervenit. Institutas turres, testudines

enemy: the legion having been drawn out, he finds that even every tenth soldier had not escaped without wounds. From all these things he judges with what danger and with what great courage matters had been conducted; he commends Cicero according to his desert, and likewise the legion; he addresses individually the centurions and the tribunes of the soldiers, whose valor he had discovered to have been signal. He receives information of the death of Sabinus and Cotta from the prisoners. An assembly being held the following day, he states the occurrence; he consoles and encourages the soldiers; he suggests, that the disaster, which had been occasioned by the misconduct and rashness of his lieutenant, should be borne with a patient mind, because by the favor of the immortal gods and their own valor, neither was lasting joy left to the enemy, nor very lasting grief to them.

5:53 In the mean while the report respecting the victory of Caesar is conveyed to Labienus through the country of the Remi with incredible speed, so that, though he was about sixty miles distant from the winter-quarter of Cicero, and Caesar had arrived there after the ninth hour, before midnight a shout arose at the gates of the camp, by which shout an indication of the victory and a congratulation on the part of the Remi were given to Labienus. This report having been carried to the Treviri, Indutiomarus, who had resolved to attack the camp of Labienus the following day, flies by night and leads back all his forces into the country of the Treviri. Caesar sends back Fabius with his legion to his winter-quarters; he himself determines to winter with three legions near Samarobriva in three different quarters, and, because such great commotions had arisen in Gaul, he resolved to remain during the whole winter with the army himself. For the disaster respecting the death of Sabinus having been circulated among them, almost all the states of Gaul were deliberating about war, sending messengers and embassies into all quarters, inquiring what further measure they should take, and holding councils by night in secluded places. Nor did any period of the whole winter pass over without fresh anxiety to Caesar, or, without his receiving some intelligence respecting the meetings and commotions of the Gauls. Among these, he is informed by L. Roscius, the lieutenant whom he had placed over the thirteenth legion, that large forces of those states of the Gauls, which are called the Armoricae, had assembled for the purpose of attacking him and were not more than eight miles distant; but intelligence respecting the victory of Caesar being carried [to them], had retreated in such a manner that their departure appeared like a flight.

munitionesque hostium admiratur; legione producta cognoscit non decimum quemque esse reliquum militem sine vulnere: ex his omnibus iudicat rebus, quanto cum periculo et quanta cum virtute res sint administratae. Ciceronem pro eius merito legionemque collaudat; centuriones singillatim tribunosquc militum appellat, quorum egregiam fuisse virtutem testimonio Ciceronis cognoverat. De casu Sabini et Cottae certius ex captivis cognoscit. Postero die contione habita rem gestam proponit, milites consolatur et confirmat: quod detrimentum culpa et temeritate legati sit acceptum, hoc aequiore animo ferendum docet, quod beneficio deorum immortalium et virtute eorum expiato incommodo neque hostibus diutina laetatio neque ipsis longior dolor relinquatur.

Interim ad Labienum per Remos incredibili celeritate de victoria Caesaris fama perfertur, ut, cum ab hibernis Ciceronis milia passuum abesset circiter LX, eoque post horam nonam diei Caesar pervenisset, ante mediam noctem ad portas castrorum clamor oreretur, quo clamore significatio victoriae gratulatioque ab Remis Labieno fieret. Hac fama ad Treveros perlata Indutiomarus, qui postero die castra Labieni oppugnare decreverat, noctu profugit copiasque omnes in Treveros reducit. Caesar Fabium cum sua legione remittit in hiberna, ipse cum tribus legionibus circum Samarobrivam trinis hibernis hiemare constituit et, quod tanti motus Galliae exstiterant, totam hiemem ipse ad exercitum manere decrevit. Nam illo incommodo de Sabini morte perlato omnes fere Galliae civitates de bello consultabant, nuntios legationesque in omnes partes dimittebant et quid reliqui consili caperent atque unde initium belli fieret explorabant nocturnaque in locis desertis concilia habebant. Neque ullum fere totius hiemis tempus sine sollicitudine Caesaris intercessit, quin aliquem de consiliis ac motu Gallorum nuntium acciperet. In his ab Lucio Roscio, quem legioni tertiae decimae praefecerat, certior factus est magnas Gallorum copias earum civitatum, quae Armoricae appellantur, oppugnandi sui causa convenisse neque longius milia passuum octo ab hibernis suis afuisse, sed nuntio allato de victoria Caesaris discessisse, adeo ut fugae similis discessus videretur.

5:54 But Caesar, having summoned to him the principal persons of each state, in one case by alarming them, since he declared that he knew what was going on, and in another case by encouraging them, retained a great part of Gaul in its allegiance. The Senones, however, which is a state eminently powerful and one of great influence among the Gauls, attempting by general design to slay Cavarinus, whom Caesar had created king among them (whose brother, Moritasgus, had held the sovereignty at the period of the arrival of Caesar in Gaul, and whose ancestors had also previously held it), when he discovered their plot and fled, pursued him even to the frontiers [of the state], and drove him from his kingdom and his home; and, after having sent embassadors to Caesar for the purpose of concluding a peace, when he ordered all their senate to come to him, did not obey that command. So far did it operate among those barbarian people, that there were found some to be the first to wage war; and so great a change of inclinations did it produce in all, that, except the Aedui and the Remi, whom Caesar had always held in especial honor, the one people for their long standing and uniform fidelity toward the Roman people, the other for their late service in the Gallic war, there was scarcely a state which was not suspected by us. And I do not know whether that ought much to be wondered at, as well for several other reasons, as particularly because they who ranked above all nations for prowess in war, most keenly regretted that they had lost so much of that reputation as to submit to commands from the Roman people.

5:55 But the Triviri and Indutiomarus let no part of the entire winter pass without sending embassadors across the Rhine, importuning the states, promising money, and asserting that, as a large portion of our army had been cut off, a much smaller portion remained. However, none of the German States could be induced to cross the Rhine, since "they had twice essayed it," they said, "in the war with Ariovistus and in the passage of the Tenchtheri there; that fortune was not to be tempted any more." Indutiomarus disappointed in this expectation, nevertheless began to raise troops, and discipline them, and procure horses from the neighboring people, and allure to him by great rewards the outlaws and convicts throughout Gaul. And such great influence had he already acquired for himself in Gaul by these means, that embassies were flocking to him in all directions, and seeking, publicly and privately, his favor and friendship.

5:56 When he perceived that they were coming to him voluntarily; that on the one side the Senones and the Carnutes were stimulated by their consciousness of guilt, on the other side the Nervii and the Aduatuci were preparing war against the Romans,

At Caesar principibus cuiusque civitatis ad se evocatis alias territando, cum se scire quae fierent denuntiaret, alias cohortando magnam partem Galliae in officio tenuit. Tamen Senones, quae est civitas in primis firma et magnae inter Gallos auctoritatis, Cavarinum, quem Caesar apud eos regem constituerat, cuius frater Moritasgus adventu in Galliam Caesaris cuiusque maiores regnum obtinuerant, interficere publico consilio conati, cum ille praesensisset ac profugisset, usque ad fines insecuti regno domoque expulerunt et, missis ad Caesarem satisfaciendi causa legatis, cum is omnem ad se senatum venire iussisset, dicto audientes non fuerunt. Tantum apud homines barbaros valuit esse aliquos repertos principes inferendi belli tantamque omnibus voluntatum commutationem attulit, ut praeter Aeduos et Remos, quos praecipuo semper honore Caesar habuit, alteros pro vetere ac perpetua erga populum Romanum fide, alteros pro recentibus Gallici belli officiis, nulla fere civitas fuerit non suspecta nobis. Idque adeo haud scio mirandumne sit, cum compluribus aliis de causis, tum maxime quod ei, qui virtute belli omnibus gentibus praeferebantur, tantum se eius opinionis deperdidisse ut a populo Romano imperia perferrent gravissime dolebant.

Treveri vero atque Indutiomarus totius hiemis nullum tempus intermiserunt, quin trans Rhenum legatos mitterent, civitates sollicitarent, pecunias pollicerentur, magna parte exercitus nostri interfecta multo minorem superesse dicerent partem. Neque tamen ulli civitati Germanorum persuaderi potuit, ut Rhenum transiret, cum se bis expertos dicerent, Ariovisti bello et Tencterorum transitu: non esse amplius fortunam temptaturos. Hac spe lapsus Indutiomarus nihilo minus copias cogere, exercere, a finitimis equos parare, exules damnatosque tota Gallia magnis praemiis ad se allicere coepit. Ac tantam sibi iam his rebus in Gallia auctoritatem comparaverat ut undique ad eum legationes concurrerent, gratiam atque amicitiam publice privatimque peterent.

Vbi intellexit ultro ad se veniri, altera ex parte Senones Carnutesque conscientia facinoris instigari, altera Nervios Aduatucosque bellum Romanis parare, neque sibi voluntariorum copias

and that forces of volunteers would not be wanting to him if he began to advance from his own territories, he proclaims an armed council (this according to the custom of the Gauls in the commencement of war) at which, by a common law, all the youth were wont to assemble in arms, whoever of them comes last is killed in the sight of the whole assembly after being racked with every torture. In that council he declares Cingetorix, the leader of the other faction, his own son-in-law (whom we have above mentioned, as having embraced the protection of Caesar, and never having deserted him) an enemy and confiscates his property. When these things were finished, he asserts in the council that he, invited by the Senones and the Carnutes, and several other states of Gaul, was about to march thither through the territories of the Remi, devastate their lands, and attack the camp of Labienus: before he does that, he informs them of what he desires to be done.

5:57 Labienus, since he was confining himself within a camp strongly fortified by the nature of the ground and by art, had no apprehensions as to his own and the legion's danger, but was devising that he might throw away no opportunity of conducting the war successfully. Accordingly, the speech of Indutiomarus, which he had delivered in the council, having been made known [to him] by Cingetorix and his allies, he sends messengers to the neighboring states and summons horse from all quarters: he appoints to them a fixed day for assembling. In the mean time, Indutiomarus, with all his cavalry, nearly every day used to parade close to his [Labienus'] camp; at one time, that he might inform himself of the situation of the camp; at another time, for the purpose of conferring with or of intimidating him. Labienus confined his men within the fortifications, and promoted the enemy's belief of his fear by whatever methods he could.

5:58 Since Indutiomarus was daily advancing up to the camp with greater defiance, all the cavalry of the neighboring states which he [Labienus] had taken care to have sent for, having been admitted in one night, he confined all his men within the camp by guards with such great strictness, that that fact could by no means be reported or carried to the Treviri. In the mean while, Indutiomarus, according to his daily practice, advances up to the camp and spends a great part of the day there: his horse cast their weapons, and with very insulting language call out our men to battle. No reply being given by our men, the enemy, when they thought proper, depart toward evening in a disorderly and scattered manner, Labienus unexpectedly sends out all the cavalry by two gates; he gives this command and prohibition, that, when the enemy should be terrified and put to flight (which he foresaw would happen, as it did), they should all make for Indutiomarus, and no one wound any man before he should have seen him slain,

defore, si ex finibus suis progredi coepisset, armatum concilium indicit. Hoc more Gallorum est initium belli, quo lege communi omnes puberes armati convenire consuerunt; qui ex eis novissimus convenit, in conspectu multitudinis omnibus cruciatibus affectus necatur. In eo concilio Cingetorigem, alterius principem factionis, generum suum, quem supra demonstravimus Caesaris secutum fidem ab eo non discessisse, hostem iudicat bonaque eius publicat. His rebus confectis, in concilio pronuntiat arcessitum se a Senonibus et Carnutibus aliisque compluribus Galliae civitatibus; huc iturum per fines Remorum eorumque agros popula turum ac, priusquam id faciat, castra Labieni oppugnaturum. Quae fieri velit praecipit.

Labienus, cum et loci natura et manu munitissumis castris sese teneret, de suo ac legionis periculo nihil timebat; ne quam occasionem rei bene gerendae dimitteret, cogitabat. Itaque a Cingetorige atque eius propinquis oratione Indutiomari cognita, quam in concilio habuerat, nuntios mittit ad finitimas civitates equitesque undique evocat: his certum diem conveniendi dicit. Interim prope cotidie cum omni equitatu Indutiomarus sub castris eius vagabatur, alias ut situm castrorum cognosceret, alias colloquendi aut territandi causa: equites plerumque omnes tela intra vallum coniciebant. Labienus suos intra munitionem continebat timorisque opinionem, quibuscumque poterat rebus, augebat.

Cum maiore in dies contemptione Indutiomarus ad castra accederet, nocte una intromissis equitibus omnium finitimarum civitatum quos arcessendos curaverat, tanta diligentia omnes suos custodiis intra castra continuit, ut nulla ratione ea res enuntiari aut ad Treveros perferri posset. Interim ex consuetudine cotidiana Indutiomarus ad castra accedit atque ibi magnam partem diei consumit; equites tela coniciunt et magna cum contumelia verborum nostros ad pugnam evocant. Nullo ab nostris dato responso, ubi visum est, sub vesperum dispersi ac dissipati discedunt. Subito Labienus duabus portis omnem equitatum emittit; praecipit atque interdicit, proterritis hostibus atque in fugam coniectis (quod fore, sicut accidit, videbat) unum omnes peterent Indutiomarum, neu

because he was unwilling that he should escape, in consequence of gaining time by the delay [occasioned by the pursuit] of the rest. He offers great rewards for those who should kill him: he sends up the cohorts as a relief to the horse. The issue justifies the policy of the man, and since all aimed at one, Indutiomarus is slain, having been overtaken at the very ford of the river, and his head is carried to the camp, the horse, when returning, pursue and slay all whom they can. This affair having been known, all the forces of the Eburones and the Nervii which had assembled, depart; and for a short time after this action, Caesar was less harassed in the government of Gaul.

quis quem prius vulneret, quam illum interfectum viderit, quod mora reliquorum spatium nactum illum effugere nolebat; magna proponit eis qui occiderint praemia; summittit cohortes equitibus subsidio. Comprobat hominis consilium fortuna, et cum unum omnes peterent, in ipso fluminis vado deprehensus Indutiomarus interficitur, caputque eius refertur in castra: redeuntes equites quos possunt consectantur atque occidunt. Hac re cognita omnes Eburonum et Nerviorum quae convenerant copiae discedunt, pauloque habuit post id factum Caesar quietiorem Galliam.

Gallic Wars Book 6 (53 B.C.E.)

6:1 Caesar, expecting for many reasons a greater commotion in Gaul, resolves to hold a levy by the means of M. Silanus C. Antistius Reginus, and T. Sextius, his lieutenants: at the same time he requested Cn. Pompey, the proconsul, that since he was remaining near the city invested with military command for the interests of the commonwealth, he would command those men whom when consul he had levied by the military oath in Cisalpine Gaul, to join their respective corps, and to proceed to him; thinking it of great importance, as far as regarded the opinion which the Gauls would entertain for the future, that that the resources of Italy should appear so great that if any loss should be sustained in war, not only could it be repaired in a short time, but likewise be further supplied by still larger forces. And when Pompey had granted this to the interests of the commonwealth and the claims of friendship, Caesar having quickly completed the levy by means of his lieutenants, after three regiments had been both formed and brought to him before the winter [had] expired, and the number of those cohorts which he had lost under Q. Titurius had been doubled, taught the Gauls, both by his dispatch and by his forces what the discipline and the power of the Roman people could accomplish.

6:2 Indutiomarus having been slain, as we have stated, the government was conferred upon his relatives by the Treviri. They cease not to importune the neighboring Germans and to promise them money: when they could not obtain [their object] from those nearest them, they try those more remote. Having found some states willing to accede to their wishes, they enter into a compact with them by a mutual oath, and give hostages as a security for the money: they attach Ambiorix to them by an alliance and confederacy. Caesar, on being informed of their acts, since he saw that war was being prepared on all sides, that the Nervii, Aduatuci, and Menapii, with the addition of all the Germans on this side of the Rhine were under arms, that the Senones did not assemble according to his command, and were concerting measures with the Carnutes and the neighboring states, that the Germans were importuned by the Treviri in frequent embassies, thought that he ought to take measures for the war earlier [than usual].

6:3 Accordingly, while the winter was not yet ended, having concentrated the four nearest legions, he marched unexpectedly into the territories of the Nervii, and before they could either assemble or retreat, after capturing a large number of cattle and of men, and wasting their lands and giving up that booty to the soldiers, compelled them to enter into a surrender and give him

Multis de causis Caesar maiorem Galliae motum exspectans per Marcum Silanum, Gaium Antistium Reginum, Titum Sextium legatos dilectum habere instituit; simul ab Gnaeo Pompeio proconsule petit, quoniam ipse ad urbem cum imperio rei publicae causa remaneret, quos ex Cisalpina Gallia consulis sacramento rogavisset, ad signa convenire et ad se proficisci iuberet, magni interesse etiam in reliquum tempus ad opinionem Galliae existimans tantas videri Italiae facultates ut, si quid esset in bello detrimenti acceptum, non modo id brevi tempore sarciri, sed etiam maioribus augeri copiis posset. Quod cum Pompeius et rei publicae et amicitiae tribuisset, celeriter confecto per suos dilectu tribus ante exactam hiemem et constitutis et adductis legionibus duplicatoque earum cohortium numero, quas cum Quinto Titurio amiserat, et celeritate et copiis docuit, quid populi Romani disciplina atque opes possent.

Interfecto Indutiomaro, ut docuimus, ad eius propinquos a Treveris imperium defertur. Illi finitimos Germanos sollicitare et pecuniam polliceri non desistunt. Cum ab proximis impetrare non possent, ulteriores temptant. Inventis nonnullis civitatibus iureiurando inter se confirmant obsidibusque de pecunia cavent: Ambiorigem sibi societate et foedere adiungunt. Quibus rebus cognitis Caesar, cum undique bellum parari videret, Nervios, Aduatucos ac Menapios adiunctis Cisrhenanis omnibus Germanis esse in armis, Senones ad imperatum non venire et cum Carnutibus finitimisque civitatibus consilia communicare, a Treveris Germanos crebris legationibus sollicitari, maturius sibi de bello cogitandum putavit.

Itaque nondum hieme confecta proximis quattuor coactis legionibus de improviso in fines Nerviorum contendit et, priusquam illi aut convenire aut profugere possent, magno pecoris atque hominum numero capto atque ea praeda militibus concessa vastatisque agris in deditionem venire atque obsides

hostages. That business having been speedily executed, he again led his legions back into winter-quarters. Having proclaimed a council of Gaul in the beginning of the spring, as he had been accustomed [to do], when the deputies from the rest, except the Senones, the Carnutes, and the Treviri, had come, judging this to be the commencement of war and revolt, that he might appear to consider all things of less consequence [than that war], he transfers the council to Lutetia of the Parisii. These were adjacent to the Senones, and had united their state to them during the memory of their fathers, but were thought to have no part in the present plot. Having proclaimed this from the tribunal, he advances the same day toward the Senones with his legions, and arrives among them by long marches.

6:4 Acco, who had been the author of that enterprise, on being informed of his arrival, orders the people to assemble in the towns; to them, while attempting this, and before it could be accomplished, news is brought that the Romans are close at hand: through necessity they give over their design and send embassadors to Caesar for the purpose of imploring pardon; they make advances to him through the Aedui, whose state was from ancient times under the protection of Rome. Caesar readily grants them pardon, and receives their excuse, at the request of the Aedui, because he thought that the summer season was one for an impending war, not for an investigation. Having imposed one hundred hostages, he delivers these to the Aedui to be held in charge by them. To the same place the Carnutes send embassadors and hostages, employing as their mediators the Remi, under whose protection they were: they receive the same answers. Caesar concludes the council and imposes a levy of cavalry on the states.

6:5 This part of Gaul having been tranquilized, he applies himself entirely both in mind and soul to the war with the Treviri and Ambiorix. He orders Cavarinus to march with him with the cavalry of the Senones, lest any commotion should arise either out of his hot temper, or out of the hatred of the state which he had incurred. After arranging these things, as he considered it certain that Ambiorix would not contend in battle, he watched his other plans attentively. The Menapii bordered on the territories of the Eburones, and were protected by one continued extent of morasses and woods; and they alone out of Gaul had never sent embassadors to Caesar on the subject of peace. Caesar knew that a tie of hospitality subsisted between them and Ambiorix: he also discovered that the latter had entered into an alliance with the Germans by means of the Treviri. Ho thought that these auxiliaries ought to be detached from him before he provoked him to war; lest he, despairing of safety, should either proceed to conceal himself in the territories of the Menapii, or

sibi dare coegit. Eo celeriter confecto negotio rursus in hiberna legiones reduxit. Concilio Galliae primo vere, ut instituerat, indicto, cum reliqui praeter Senones, Carnutes Treverosque venissent, initium belli ac defectionis hoc esse arbitratus, ut omnia postponere videretur, concilium Lutetiam Parisiorum transfert. Confines erant hi Senonibus civitatemque patrum memoria coniunxerant, sed ab hoc consilio afuisse existimabantur. Hac re pro suggestu pronuntiata eodem die cum legionibus in Senones proficiscitur magnisque itineribus eo pervenit.

Cognito eius adventu Acco, qui princeps eius consili fuerat, iubet in oppida multitudinem convenire. Conantibus, priusquam id effici posset, adesse Romanos nuntiatur. Necessario sententia desistunt legatosque deprecandi causa ad Caesarem mittunt: adeunt per Aeduos, quorum antiquitus erat in fide civitas. Libenter Caesar petentibus Aeduis dat veniam excusationemque accipit, quod aestivum tempus instantis belli, non quaestionis esse arbitrabatur. Obsidibus imperatis centum hos Aeduis custodiendos tradit. Eodem Carnutes legatos obsidesque mittunt usi deprecatoribus Renis, quorum erant in clientela: eadem ferunt responsa. Peragit concilium Caesar equitesque imperat civitatibus.

Hac parte Galliae pacata totus et mente et animo in bellum Treverorum et Ambiorigis insistit. Cavarinum cum equitatu Senonum secum proficisci iubet, ne quis aut ex huius iracundia aut ex eo, quod meruerat, odio civitatis motus exsistat. His rebus constitutis, quod pro explorato habebat Ambiorigem proelio non esse concertaturum, reliqua eius consilia animo circumspiciebat. Erant Menapii propinqui Eburonum finibus, perpetuis paludibus silvisque muniti, qui uni ex Gallia de pace ad Caesarem legatos numquam miserant. Cum his esse hospitium Ambiorigi sciebat; item per Treveros venisse Germanis in amicitiam cognoverat. Haec prius illi detrahenda auxilia existimabat quam ipsum bello lacesseret, ne desperata salute aut se in Menapios abderet aut cum Transrhenanis congredi cogeretur. Hoc inito consilio totius exercitus impedimenta ad Labienum in

should be driven to coalesce with the Germans beyond the Rhine. Having entered upon this resolution, he sends the baggage of the whole army to Labienus, in the territories of the Treviri and orders two legions to proceed to him: he himself proceeds against the Menapii with five lightly-equipped legions. They, having assembled no troops, as they relied on the defense of their position, retreat into the woods and morasses, and convey thither all their property.

6:6 Caesar, having divided his forces with C. Fabius, his lieutenant, and M. Crassus his questor, and having hastily constructed some bridges, enters their country in three divisions, burns their houses and villages, and gets possession of a large number of cattle and men. Constrained by these circumstances the Menapii send embassadors to him for the purpose of suing for peace. He, after receiving hostages, assures them that he will consider them in the number of his enemies if they shall receive within their territories either Ambiorix or his embassadors. Having determinately settled these things, he left among the Menapii, Commius the Atrebatian, with some cavalry as a guard; he himself proceeds toward the Treviri.

6:7 While these things are being performed by Caesar, the Treviri, having drawn together large forces of infantry and cavalry, were preparing to attack Labienus and the legion which was wintering in their territories, and were already not further distant from him than a journey of two days, when they learn that two legions had arrived by the order of Caesar. Having pitched their camp fifteen miles off, they resolve to await the support of the Germans. Labienus, having learned the design of the enemy, hoping that through their rashness there would be some opportunity of engaging, after leaving a guard of five cohorts for the baggage, advances against the enemy with twenty-five cohorts and a large body of cavalry, and, leaving the space of a mile between them, fortifies his camp. There was between Labienus and the enemy a river difficult to cross, and with steep banks: this neither did he himself design to cross, nor did he suppose the enemy would cross it. Their hope of auxiliaries was daily increasing. He [Labienus] openly says in a council that "since the Germans are said to be approaching, he would not bring into uncertainty his own and the army's fortunes, and the next day would move his camp at early dawn." These words are quickly carried to the enemy, since out of so large a number of cavalry composed of Gauls, nature compelled some to favor the Gallic interests. Labienus, having assembled the tribunes of the soldiers and principal centurions by night, states what his design is, and, that he may the more easily give the enemy a belief of his fears, he orders the camp to be moved with greater noise and confusion than was usual with the Roman

Treveros mittit duasque legiones ad eum proficisci iubet; ipse cum legionibus expeditis quinque in Menapios proficiscitur. Illi nulla coacta manu loci praesidio freti in silvas paludesque confugiunt suaque eodem conferunt.

Caesar partitis copiis cum Gaio Fabio legato et Marco Crasso quaestore celeriterque effectis pontibus adit tripertito, aedificia vicosque incendit, magno pecoris atque hominum numero potitur. Quibus rebus coacti Menapii legatos ad eum pacis petendae causa mittunt. Ille obsidibus acceptis hostium se habiturum numero confirmat, si aut Ambiorigem aut eius legatos finibus suis recepissent. His confirmatis rebus Commium Atrebatem cum equitatu custodis loco in Menapiis relinquit; ipse in Treveros proficiscitur.

Dum haec a Caesare geruntur, Treveri magnis coactis peditatus equitatusque copiis Labienum cum una legione, quae in eorum finibus hiemaverat, adoriri parabant, iamque ab eo non longius bidui via aberant, cum duas venisse legiones missu Caesaris cognoscunt. Positis castris a milibus passuum XV auxilia Germanorum esspectare constituunt. Labienus hostium cognito consilio sperans temeritate eorum fore aliquam dimicandi facultatem praesidio quinque cohortium impedimentis relicto cum viginti quinque cohortibus magnoque equitatu contra hostem proficiscitur et mille passuum intermisso spatio castra communit. Erat inter Labienum atque hostem difficili transitu flumen ripisque praeruptis. Hoc neque ipse transire habebat in animo neque hostes transituros existi mabat. Augebatur auxiliorum cotidie spes. Loquitur in concilio palam, quoniam Germani appropinquare dicantur, sese suas exercitusque fortunas in dubium non devocaturum et postero die prima luce castra moturum. Celeriter haec ad hostes deferuntur, ut ex magno Gallorum equitum numero nonnullos Gallicis rebus favere natura cogebat. Labienus noctu tribunis militum primisque ordinibus convocatis, quid sui sit consili proponit et, quo facilius hostibus timoris det suspicionem, maiore strepitu et tumultu, quam populi Romani fert consuetudo castra moveri iubet. His

people. By these means he makes his departure [appear] like a retreat. These things, also, since the camps were so near, are reported to the enemy by scouts before daylight.

6:8 Scarcely had the rear advanced beyond the fortifications when the Gauls, encouraging one another "not to cast from their hands the anticipated booty, that it was a tedious thing, while the Romans were panic-stricken, to be waiting for the aid of the Germans, and that their dignity did not suffer them to fear to attack with such great forces so small a band, particularly when retreating and encumbered," do not hesitate to cross the river and give battle in a disadvantageous position. Labienus suspecting that these things would happen, was proceeding quietly, and using the same pretense of a march, in order that he might entice them across the river. Then, having sent forward the baggage some short distance and placed it on a certain eminence, he says, "Soldiers, you have the opportunity you have sought: you hold the enemy in an encumbered and disadvantageous position: display to us, your leaders, the same valor you have ofttimes displayed to your general: imagine that he is present and actually sees these exploits." At the same time he orders the troops to face about toward the enemy and form in line of battle, and, dispatching a few troops of cavalry as a guard for the baggage, he places the rest of the horse on the wings. Our men, raising a shout, quickly throw their javelins at the enemy. They, when, contrary to their expectation, they saw those whom they believed to be retreating, advance toward them with threatening banners, were not able to sustain even the charge, and, being put to flight at the first onslaught, sought the nearest woods; Labienus pursuing them with the cavalry, upon a large number being slain, and several taken prisoners, got possession of the state a few days after; for the Germans, who were coming to the aid of the Treviri, having been informed of their flight, retreated to their homes. The relations of Indutiomarus, who had been the promoters of the revolt, accompanying them, quitted their own state with them. The supreme power and government were delivered to Cingetorix, whom we have stated to have remained firm in his allegiance from the commencement.

6:9 Caesar, after he came from the territories of the Menapii into those of the Treviri, resolved for two reasons to cross the Rhine; one of which was, because they had sent assistance to the Treviri against him; the other, that Ambiorix might not have a retreat among them. Having determined on these matters, he began to build a bridge a little above that place where he had before conveyed over his army. The plan having been known and laid down, the work is accomplished in a few days by the great exertion of the soldiers. Having left a strong guard at the

rebus fugae similem profectionem effecit. Haec quoque per exploratores ante lucem in tanta propinquitate castrorum ad hostes deferuntur.

Vix agmen novissimum extra munitiones processerat, cum Galli cohortati inter se, ne speratam praedam ex manibus dimitterent--longum esse per territis Romanis Germanorum auxilium exspectare, neque suam pati dignitatem ut tantis copiis tam exiguam manum praesertim fugientem atque impeditam adoriri non audeant--flumen transire et iniquo loco committere proelium non dubitant. Quae fore suspicatus Labienus, ut omnes citra flumen eliceret, eadem usus simulatione itineris placide progrediebatur. Tum praemissis paulum impedimentis atque in tumulo quodam collocatis "Habetis," inquit, "milites, quam petistis facultatem: hostem impedito atque iniquo loco tenetis: praestate eandem nobis ducibus virtutem, quam saepe numero imperatori praestitistis, atque illum adesse et haec coram cernere existimate." Simul signa ad hostem converti aciemque dirigi iubet, et paucis turmis praesidio ad impedimenta dimissis reliquos equites ad latera disponit. Celeriter nostri clamore sublato pila in hostes immittunt. Illi, ubi praeter spem quos fugere credebant infestis signis ad se ire viderunt, impetum modo ferre non potuerunt ac primo concursu in fugam coniecti proximas silvas petierunt. Quos Labienus equitatu consectatus, magno numero interfecto, compluribus captis, paucis post diebus civitatem recepit. Nam Germani qui auxilio veniebant percepta Treverorum fuga sese domum receperunt. Cum his propinqui Indutiomari, qui defectionis auctores fuerant, comitati eos ex civitate excesserunt. Cingetorigi, quem ab initio permansisse in officio demonstravimus, principatus atque imperium est traditum.

Caesar, postquam ex Menapiis in Treveros venit, duabus de causis Rhenum transire constituit; quarum una erat, quod auxilia contra se Treveris miserant, altera, ne ad eos Ambiorix receptum haberet. His constitutis rebus paulum supra eum locum quo ante exercitum traduxerat facere pontem instituit. Nota atque instituta ratione magno militum studio paucis diebus opus efficitur. Firmo in Treveris ad pontem praesidio relicto, ne quis ab his subito

bridge on the side of the Treviri, lest any commotion should suddenly arise among them, he leads over the rest of the forces and the cavalry. The Ubii, who before had sent hostages and come to a capitulation, send embassadors to him, for the purpose of vindicating themselves, to assure him that "neither had auxiliaries been sent to the Treviri from their state, nor had they violated their allegiance;" they entreat and beseech him "to spare them, lest, in his common hatred of the Germans, the innocent should suffer the penalty of the guilty: they promise to give more hostages, if he desire them." Having investigated the case, Caesar finds that the auxiliaries had been sent by the Suevi; he accepts the apology of the Ubii, and makes the minute inquiries concerning the approaches and the routes to the territories of the Suevi.

6:10 In the mean time he is informed by the Ubii, a few days after, that the Suevi are drawing all their forces into one place, and are giving orders to those nations which are under their government to send auxiliaries of infantry and of cavalry. Having learned these things, he provides a supply of corn, selects a proper place for his camp, and commands the Ubii to drive off their cattle and carry away all their possessions from the country parts into the towns, hoping that they, being a barbarous and ignorant people, when harassed by the want of provisions, might be brought to an engagement on disadvantageous terms: he orders them to send numerous scouts among the Suevi, and learn what things are going on among them. They execute the orders, and, a few days having intervened, report that all the Suevi, after certain intelligence concerning the army of the Romans had come, retreated with all their own forces and those of their allies, which they had assembled, to the utmost extremities of their territories: that there is a wood there of very great extent, which is called Bacenis; that this stretches a great way into the interior, and, being opposed as a natural barrier, defends from injuries and incursions the Cherusci against the Suevi, and the Suevi against the Cherusci: that at the entrance of that forest the Suevi had determined to await the coming up of the Romans.

6:11 Since we have come to the place, it does not appear to be foreign to our subject to lay before the reader an account of the manners of Gaul and Germany, and wherein these nations differ from each other. In Gaul there are factions not only in all the states, and in all the cantons and their divisions, but almost in each family, and of these factions those are the leaders who are considered according to their judgment to possess the greatest influence, upon whose will and determination the management of all affairs and measures depends. And that seems to have been instituted in ancient times with this view, that no one of the

motus oreretur, reliquas copias equitatumque traducit. Vbii, qui ante obsides dederant atque in deditionem venerant, purgandi sui causa ad eum legatos mittunt, qui doceant neque auxilia ex sua civitate in Treveros missa neque ab se fidem laesam: petunt atque orant ut sibi parcat, ne communi odio Germanorum innocentes pro nocentibus poenas pendant; si amplius obsidum vellet, dare pollicentur. Cognita Caesar causa reperit ab Suebis auxilia missa esse; Vbiorum satisfactionem accipit, aditus viasque in Suebos perquirit.

Interim paucis post diebus fit ab Vbiis certior Suebos omnes in unum locum copias cogere atque eis nationibus quae sub eorum sint imperio denuntiare, ut auxilia peditatus equitatusque mittant. His cognitis rebus rem frumentariam providet, castris idoneum locum deligit; Vbiis imperat ut pecora deducant suaque omnia ex agris in oppida conferant, sperans barbaros atque imperitos homines inopia cibariorum adductos ad iniquam pugnandi condicionem posse deduci; mandat, ut crebros exploratores in Suebos mittant quaeque apud eos gerantur cognoscant. Illi imperata faciunt et paucis diebus intermissis referunt: Suebos omnes, posteaquam certiores nuntii de exercitu Romanorum venerint, cum omnibus suis sociorumque copiis, quas coegissent, penitus ad extremos fines se recepisse: silvam esse ibi infinita magnitudine, quae appellatur Bacenis; hanc longe introrsus pertinere et pro nativo muro obiectam Cheruscos ab Suebis Suebosque ab Cheruscis iniuriis incursionibusque prohibere: ad eius initium silvae Suebos adventum Romanorum exspectare constituisse.

Quoniam ad hunc locum perventum est, non alienum esse videtur de Galliae Germaniaeque moribus et quo differant hae nationes inter sese proponere. In Gallia non solum in omnibus civitatibus atque in omnibus pagis partibusque, sed paene etiam in singulis domibus factiones sunt, earumque factionum principes sunt qui summam auctoritatem eorum iudicio habere existimantur, quorum ad arbitrium iudiciumque summa omnium rerum consiliorumque redeat. Itaque eius rei causa antiquitus institutum

common people should be in want of support against one more powerful; for, none [of those leaders] suffers his party to be oppressed and defrauded, and if he do otherwise, he has no influence among his party. This same policy exists throughout the whole of Gaul; for all the states are divided into two factions.

6:12 When Caesar arrived in Gaul, the Aedui were the leaders of one faction, the Sequani of the other. Since the latter were less powerful by themselves, inasmuch as the chief influence was from of old among the Aedui, and their dependencies were great, they had united to themselves the Germans and Ariovistus, and had brought them over to their party by great sacrifices and promises. And having fought several successful battles and slain all the nobility of the Aedui, they had so far surpassed them in power, that they brought over, from the Aedui to themselves, a large portion of their dependents and received from them the sons of their leading men as hostages, and compelled them to swear in their public character that they would enter into no design against them; and held a portion of the neighboring land, seized on by force, and possessed the sovereignty of the whole of Gaul. Divitiacus urged by this necessity, had proceeded to Rome to the senate, for the purpose of entreating assistance, and had returned without accomplishing his object. A change of affairs ensued on the arrival of Caesar, the hostages were returned to the Aedui, their old dependencies restored, and new acquired through Caesar (because those who had attached themselves to their alliance saw that they enjoyed a better state and a milder government), their other interests, their influence, their reputation were likewise increased, and in consequence, the Sequani lost the sovereignty. The Remi succeeded to their place, and, as it was perceived that they equaled the Aedui in favor with Caesar, those, who on account of their old animosities could by no means coalesce with the Aedui, consigned themselves in clientship to the Remi. The latter carefully protected them. Thus they possessed both a new and suddenly acquired influence. Affairs were then in that position that the Aedui were considered by far the leading people, and the Remi held the second post of honor.

6:13 Throughout all Gaul there are two orders of those men who are of any rank and dignity: for the commonality is held almost in the condition of slaves, and dares to undertake nothing of itself, and is admitted to no deliberation. The greater part, when they are pressed either by debt, or the large amount of their tributes, or the oppression of the more powerful, give themselves up in vassalage to the nobles, who possess over them the same rights without exception as masters over their slaves. But of

videtur, ne quis ex plebe contra potentio rem auxili egeret: suos enim quisque opprimi et circumveniri non patitur, neque, aliter si faciat, ullam inter suos habet auctoritatem. Haec eadem ratio est in summa totius Galliae: namque omnes civitates in partes divisae sunt duas.

Cum Caesar in Galliam venit, alterius factionis principes erant Aedui, alterius Sequani. Hi cum per se minus valerent, quod summa auctoritas antiquitus erat in Aeduis magnaeque eorum erant clientelae, Germanos atque Ariovistum sibi adiunxerant eosque ad se magnis iacturis pollicitationibusque perduxerant. Proeliis vero compluribus factis secundis atque omni nobilitate Aeduorum interfecta tantum potentia antecesserant, ut magnam partem clientium ab Aeduis ad se traducerent obsidesque ab eis principum filios acciperent et publice iurare cogerent nihil se contra Sequanos consili inituros et partem finitimi agri per vim occupatam possiderent Galliaeque totius principatum obtinerent. Qua necessitate adductus Diviciacus auxili petendi causa Romam ad senatum profectus infecta re redierat. Adventu Caesaris facta commutatione rerum, obsidibus Aeduis redditis, veteribus clientelis restitutis, novis per Caesarem comparatis, quod hi, qui se ad eorum amicitiam adgregaverant, meliore condicione atque aequiore imperio se uti videbant, reliquis rebus eorum gratia dignitateque amplificata Sequani principatum dimiserant. In eorum locum Remi successerant: quos quod adaequare apud Caesarem gratia intellegebatur, ei, qui propter veteres inimicitias nullo modo cum Aeduis coniungi poterant, se Remis in clientelam dicabant. Hos illi diligenter tuebantur: ita et novam et repente collectam auctoritatem tene bant. Eo tum statu res erat, ut longe principes haberentur Aedui, secundum locum dignitatis Remi obtinerent.

In omni Gallia eorum hominum, qui aliquo sunt numero atque honore, genera sunt duo. Nam plebes paene servorum habetur loco, quae nihil audet per se, nullo adhibetur consilio. Plerique, cum aut aere alieno aut magnitudine tributorum aut iniuria potentiorum premuntur, sese in servitutem dicant nobilibus: in hos eadem omnia sunt iura, quae dominis in servos. Sed de his duobus generibus

these two orders, one is that of the Druids, the other that of the knights. The former are engaged in things sacred, conduct the public and the private sacrifices, and interpret all matters of religion. To these a large number of the young men resort for the purpose of instruction, and they [the Druids] are in great honor among them. For they determine respecting almost all controversies, public and private; and if any crime has been perpetrated, if murder has been committed, if there be any dispute about an inheritance, if any about boundaries, these same persons decide it; they decree rewards and punishments; if any one, either in a private or public capacity, has not submitted to their decision, they interdict him from the sacrifices. This among them is the most heavy punishment. Those who have been thus interdicted are esteemed in the number of the impious and the criminal: all shun them, and avoid their society and conversation, lest they receive some evil from their contact; nor is justice administered to them when seeking it, nor is any dignity bestowed on them. Over all these Druids one presides, who possesses supreme authority among them. Upon his death, if any individual among the rest is pre-eminent in dignity, he succeeds; but, if there are many equal, the election is made by the suffrages of the Druids; sometimes they even contend for the presidency with arms. These assemble at a fixed period of the year in a consecrated place in the territories of the Carnutes, which is reckoned the central region of the whole of Gaul. Hither all, who have disputes, assemble from every part, and submit to their decrees and determinations. This institution is supposed to have been devised in Britain, and to have been brought over from it into Gaul; and now those who desire to gain a more accurate knowledge of that system generally proceed thither for the purpose of studying it.

6:14 The Druids do not go to war, nor pay tribute together with the rest; they have an exemption from military service and a dispensation in all matters. Induced by such great advantages, many embrace this profession of their own accord, and [many] are sent to it by their parents and relations. They are said there to learn by heart a great number of verses; accordingly some remain in the course of training twenty years. Nor do they regard it lawful to commit these to writing, though in almost all other matters, in their public and private transactions, they use Greek characters. That practice they seem to me to have adopted for two reasons; because they neither desire their doctrines to be divulged among the mass of the people, nor those who learn, to devote themselves the less to the efforts of memory, relying on writing; since it generally occurs to most men, that, in their dependence on writing, they relax their diligence in learning thoroughly, and their employment of the memory. They wish to

alterum est druidum, alterum equitum. Illi rebus divinis intersunt, sacrificia publica ac privata procurant, religiones interpretantur: ad hos magnus adulescentium numerus disciplinae causa concurrit, magnoque hi sunt apud eos honore. Nam fere de omnibus controversiis publicis privatisque constituunt, et, si quod est admissum facinus, si caedes facta, si de hereditate, de finibus controversia est, idem decernunt, praemia poenasque constituunt; si qui aut privatus aut populus eorum decreto non stetit, sacrificiis interdicunt. Haec poena apud eos est gravissima. Quibus ita est interdictum, hi numero impiorum ac sceleratorum habentur, his omnes decedunt, aditum sermonemque defugiunt, ne quid ex contagione incommodi accipiant, neque his petentibus ius redditur neque honos ullus communicatur. His autem omnibus druidibus praeest unus, qui summam inter eos habet auctoritatem. Hoc mortuo aut si qui ex reliquis excellit dignitate succedit, aut, si sunt plures pares, suffragio druidum, nonnumquam etiam armis de principatu contendunt. Hi certo anni tempore in finibus Carnutum, quae regio totius Galliae media habetur, considunt in loco consecrato. Huc omnes undique, qui controversias habent, conveniunt eorumque decretis iudiciisque parent. Disciplina in Britannia reperta atque inde in Galliam translata esse existimatur, et nunc, qui diligentius eam rem cognoscere volunt, plerumque illo discendi causa proficiscuntur.

Druides a bello abesse consuerunt neque tributa una cum reliquis pendunt; militiae vacationem omniumque rerum habent immunitatem. Tantis excitati praemiis et sua sponte multi in disciplinam conveniunt et a parentibus propinquisque mittuntur. Magnum ibi numerum versuum ediscere dicuntur. Itaque annos nonnulli vicenos in disciplina permanent. Neque fas esse existimant ea litteris mandare, cum in reliquis fere rebus, publicis privatisque rationibus Graecis litteris utantur. Id mihi duabus de causis instituisse videntur, quod neque in vulgum disciplinam efferri velint neque eos, qui discunt, litteris confisos minus memoriae studere: quod fere plerisque accidit, ut praesidio litterarum diligentiam in perdiscendo ac memoriam remittant. In primis hoc volunt persuadere, non interire animas,

inculcate this as one of their leading tenets, that souls do not become extinct, but pass after death from one body to another, and they think that men by this tenet are in a great degree excited to valor, the fear of death being disregarded. They likewise discuss and impart to the youth many things respecting the stars and their motion, respecting the extent of the world and of our earth, respecting the nature of things, respecting the power and the majesty of the immortal gods.

6:15 The other order is that of the knights. These, when there is occasion and any war occurs (which before Caesar's arrival was for the most part wont to happen every year, as either they on their part were inflecting injuries or repelling those which others inflected on them), are all engaged in war. And those of them most distinguished by birth and resources, have the greatest number of vassals and dependents about them. They acknowledge this sort of influence and power only.

6:16 The nation of all the Gauls is extremely devoted to superstitious rites; and on that account they who are troubled with unusually severe diseases, and they who are engaged in battles and dangers, either sacrifice men as victims, or vow that they will sacrifice them, and employ the Druids as the performers of those sacrifices; because they think that unless the life of a man be offered for the life of a man, the mind of the immortal gods can not be rendered propitious, and they have sacrifices of that kind ordained for national purposes. Others have figures of vast size, the limbs of which formed of osiers they fill with living men, which being set on fire, the men perish enveloped in the flames. They consider that the oblation of such as have been taken in theft, or in robbery, or any other offense, is more acceptable to the immortal gods; but when a supply of that class is wanting, they have recourse to the oblation of even the innocent.

6:17 They worship as their divinity, Mercury in particular, and have many images of him, and regard him as the inventor of all arts, they consider him the guide of their journeys and marches, and believe him to have great influence over the acquisition of gain and mercantile transactions. Next to him they worship Apollo, and Mars, and Jupiter, and Minerva; respecting these deities they have for the most part the same belief as other nations: that Apollo averts diseases, that Minerva imparts the invention of manufactures, that Jupiter possesses the sovereignty of the heavenly powers; that Mars presides over wars. To him, when they have determined to engage in battle, they commonly vow those things which they shall take in war. When they have conquered, they sacrifice whatever captured animals may have survived the conflict, and collect the other

sed ab aliis post mortem transire ad alios, atque hoc maxime ad virtutem excitari putant metu mortis neglecto. Multa praeterea de sideribus atque eorum motu, de mundi ac terrarum magnitudine, de rerum natura, de deorum immortalium vi ac potestate disputant et iuventuti tradunt.

Alterum genus est equitum. Hi, cum est usus atque aliquod bellum incidit (quod fere ante Caesaris adventum quotannis accidere solebat, uti aut ipsi iniurias inferrent aut illatas propulsarent), omnes in bello versantur, atque eorum ut quisque est genere copiisque amplissimus, ita plurimos circum se ambactos clientesque habet. Hanc unam gratiam potentiamque noverunt.

Natio est omnis Gallorum admodum dedita religionibus, atque ob eam causam, qui sunt adfecti gravioribus morbis quique in proeliis periculisque versantur, aut pro victimis homines immolant aut se immolaturos vovent administrisque ad ea sacrificia druidibus utuntur, quod, pro vita hominis nisi hominis vita reddatur, non posse deorum immortalium numen placari arbitrantur, publiceque eiusdem generis habent instituta sacrificia. Alii immani magnitudine simulacra habent, quorum contexta viminibus membra vivis hominibus complent; quibus succensis circumventi flamma exanimantur homines. Supplicia eorum qui in furto aut in latrocinio aut aliqua noxia sint comprehensi gratiora dis immortalibus esse arbitrantur; sed, cum eius generis copia deficit, etiam ad innocentium supplicia descendunt.

Deum maxime Mercurium colunt. Huius sunt plurima simulacra: hunc omnium inventorem artium ferunt, hunc viarum atque itinerum ducem, hunc ad quaestus pecuniae mercaturasque habere vim maximam arbitrantur. Post hunc Apollinem et Martem et Iovem et Minervam. De his eandem fere, quam reliquae gentes, habent opinionem: Apollinem morbos depellere, Minervam operum atque artificiorum initia tradere, Iovem imperium caelestium tenere, Martem bella regere. Huic, cum proelio dimicare constituerunt, ea quae bello ceperint plerumque devovent: cum superaverunt, animalia capta immolant reliquasque res in unum locum conferunt. Multis in civitatibus harum rerum

things into one place. In many states you may see piles of these things heaped up in their consecrated spots; nor does it often happen that any one, disregarding the sanctity of the case, dares either to secrete in his house things captured, or take away those deposited; and the most severe punishment, with torture, has been established for such a deed.

6:18 All the Gauls assert that they are descended from the god Dis, and say that this tradition has been handed down by the Druids. For that reason they compute the divisions of every season, not by the number of days, but of nights; they keep birthdays and the beginnings of months and years in such an order that the day follows the night. Among the other usages of their life, they differ in this from almost all other nations, that they do not permit their children to approach them openly until they are grown up so as to be able to bear the service of war; and they regard it as indecorous for a son of boyish age to stand in public in the presence of his father.

6:19 Whatever sums of money the husbands have received in the name of dowry from their wives, making an estimate of it, they add the same amount out of their own estates. An account is kept of all this money conjointly, and the profits are laid by: whichever of them shall have survived [the other], to that one the portion of both reverts together with the profits of the previous time. Husbands have power of life and death over their wives as well as over their children: and when the father of a family, born in a more than commonly distinguished rank, has died, his relations assemble, and, if the circumstances of his death are suspicious, hold an investigation upon the wives in the manner adopted toward slaves; and, if proof be obtained, put them to severe torture, and kill them. Their funerals, considering the state of civilization among the Gauls, are magnificent and costly; and they cast into the fire all things, including living creatures, which they suppose to have been dear to them when alive; and, a little before this period, slaves and dependents, who were ascertained to have been beloved by them, were, after the regular funeral rites were completed, burnt together with them.

6:20 Those states which are considered to conduct their commonwealth more judiciously, have it ordained by their laws, that, if any person shall have heard by rumor and report from his neighbors any thing concerning the commonwealth, he shall convey it to the magistrate, and not impart it to any other; because it has been discovered that inconsiderate and inexperienced men were often alarmed by false reports, and driven to some rash act, or else took hasty measures in affairs of the highest importance. The magistrates conceal those things

exstructos tumulos locis consecratis conspicari licet; neque saepe accidit, ut neglecta quispiam religione aut capta apud se occultare aut posita tollere auderet, gravissimumque ei rei supplicium cum cruciatu constitutum est.

Galli se omnes ab Dite patre prognatos praedicant idque ab druidibus proditum dicunt. Ob eam causam spatia omnis temporis non numero dierum sed noctium finiunt; dies natales et mensum et annorum initia sic observant ut noctem dies subsequatur. In reliquis vitae institutis hoc fere ab reliquis differunt, quod suos liberos, nisi cum adoleverunt, ut munus militiae sustinere possint, palam ad se adire non patiuntur filiumque puerili aetate in publico in conspectu patris adsistere turpe ducunt.

Viri, quantas pecunias ab uxoribus dotis nomine acceperunt, tantas ex suis bonis aestimatione facta cum dotibus communicant. Huius omnis pecuniae coniunctim ratio habetur fructusque servantur: uter eorum vita superarit, ad eum pars utriusque cum fructibus superiorum temporum pervenit. Viri in uxores, sicuti in liberos, vitae necisque habent potestatem; et cum paterfamiliae illustriore loco natus decessit, eius propinqui conveniunt et, de morte si res in suspicionem venit, de uxoribus in servilem modum quaestionem habent et, si compertum est, igni atque omnibus tormentis excruciatas interficiunt. Funera sunt pro cultu Gallorum magnifica et sumptuosa; omniaque quae vivis cordi fuisse arbitrantur in ignem inferunt, etiam animalia, ac paulo supra hanc memoriam servi et clientes, quos ab eis dilectos esse constabat, iustis funeribus confectis una cremabantur.

Quae civitates commodius suam rem publicam administrare existimantur, habent legibus sanctum, si quis quid de re publica a finitimis rumore aut fama acceperit, uti ad magistratum deferat neve cum quo alio communicet, quod saepe homines temerarios atque imperitos falsis rumoribus terreri et ad facinus impelli et de summis rebus consilium capere cognitum est. Magistratus quae visa sunt occultant quaeque esse ex usu iudicaverunt multitudini

which require to be kept unknown; and they disclose to the people whatever they determine to be expedient. It is not lawful to speak of the commonwealth, except in council.

6:21 The Germans differ much from these usages, for they have neither Druids to preside over sacred offices, nor do they pay great regard to sacrifices. They rank in the number of the gods those alone whom they behold, and by whose instrumentality they are obviously benefited, namely, the sun, fire, and the moon; they have not heard of the other deities even by report. Their whole life is occupied in hunting and in the pursuits of the military art; from childhood they devote themselves to fatigue and hardships. Those who have remained chaste for the longest time, receive the greatest commendation among their people; they think that by this the growth is promoted, by this the physical powers are increased and the sinews are strengthened. And to have had knowledge of a woman before the twentieth year they reckon among the most disgraceful acts; of which matter there is no concealment, because they bathe promiscuously in the rivers and [only] use skins or small cloaks of deer's hides, a large portion of the body being in consequence naked.

6:22 They do not pay much attention to agriculture, and a large portion of their food consists in milk, cheese, and flesh; nor has any one a fixed quantity of land or his own individual limits; but the magistrates and the leading men each year apportion to the tribes and families, who have united together, as much land as, and in the place in which, they think proper, and the year after compel them to remove elsewhere. For this enactment they advance many reasons-lest seduced by long-continued custom, they may exchange their ardor in the waging of war for agriculture; lest they may be anxious to acquire extensive estates, and the more powerful drive the weaker from their possessions; lest they construct their houses with too great a desire to avoid cold and heat; lest the desire of wealth spring up, from which cause divisions and discords arise; and that they may keep the common people in a contented state of mind, when each sees his own means placed on an equality with [those of] the most powerful.

6:23 It is the greatest glory to the several states to have as wide deserts as possible around them, their frontiers having been laid waste. They consider this the real evidence of their prowess, that their neighbors shall be driven out of their lands and abandon them, and that no one dare settle near them; at the same time they think that they shall be on that account the more secure, because they have removed the apprehension of a sudden incursion. When a state either repels war waged against

produnt. De re publica nisi per concilium loqui non conceditur.

Germani multum ab hac consuetudine differunt. Nam neque druides habent, qui rebus divinis praesint, neque sacrificiis student. Deorum numero eos solos ducunt, quos cernunt et quorum aperte opibus iuvantur, Solem et Vulcanum et Lunam, reliquos ne fama quidem acceperunt. Vita omnis in venationibus atque in studiis rei militaris consistit: ab parvulis labori ac duritiae student. Qui diutissime impuberes permanserunt, maximam inter suos ferunt laudem: hoc ali staturam, ali vires nervosque confirmari putant. Intra annum vero vicesimum feminae notitiam habuisse in turpissimis habent rebus; cuius rei nulla est occultatio, quod et promiscue in fluminibus perluuntur et pellibus aut parvis renonum tegimentis utuntur magna corporis parte nuda.

Agriculturae non student, maiorque pars eorum victus in lacte, caseo, carne consistit. Neque quisquam agri modum certum aut fines habet proprios; sed magistratus ac principes in annos singulos gentibus cognationibusque hominum, qui una coierunt, quantum et quo loco visum est agri attribuunt atque anno post alio transire cogunt. Eius rei multas adferunt causas: ne adsidua consuetudine capti studium belli gerendi agricultura commutent; ne latos fines parare studeant, potentioresque humiliores possessionibus expellant; ne accuratius ad frigora atque aestus vitandos aedificent; ne qua oriatur pecuniae cupiditas, qua ex re factiones dissensionesque nascuntur; ut animi aequitate plebem contineant, cum suas quisque opes cum potentissimis aequari videat.

Civitatibus maxima laus est quam latissime circum se vastatis finibus solitudines habere. Hoc proprium virtutis existimant, expulsos agris finitimos cedere, neque quemquam prope audere consistere; simul hoc se fore tutiores arbitrantur repentinae incursionis timore sublato. Cum bellum civitas aut illa tum defendit aut infert, magistratus, qui ei bello praesint, ut vitae necisque habeant potestatem, deliguntur. In

it, or wages it against another, magistrates are chosen to preside over that war with such authority, that they have power of life and death. In peace there is no common magistrate, but the chiefs of provinces and cantons administer justice and determine controversies among their own people. Robberies which are committed beyond the boundaries of each state bear no infamy, and they avow that these are committed for the purpose of disciplining their youth and of preventing sloth. And when any of their chiefs has said in an assembly "that he will be their leader, let those who are willing to follow, give in their names;" they who approve of both the enterprise and the man arise and promise their assistance and are applauded by the people; such of them as have not followed him are accounted in the number of deserters and traitors, and confidence in all matters is afterward refused them. To injure guests they regard as impious; they defend from wrong those who have come to them for any purpose whatever, and esteem them inviolable; to them the houses of all are open and maintenance is freely supplied.

6:24 And there was formerly a time when the Gauls excelled the Germans in prowess, and waged war on them offensively, and, on account of the great number of their people and the insufficiency of their land, sent colonies over the Rhine. Accordingly, the Volcae Tectosages, seized on those parts of Germany which are the most fruitful [and lie] around the Hercynian forest, (which, I perceive, was known by report to Eratosthenes and some other Greeks, and which they call Orcynia), and settled there. Which nation to this time retains its position in those settlements, and has a very high character for justice and military merit; now also they continue in the same scarcity, indigence, hardihood, as the Germans, and use the same food and dress; but their proximity to the Province and knowledge of commodities from countries beyond the sea supplies to the Gauls many things tending to luxury as well as civilization. Accustomed by degrees to be overmatched and worsted in many engagements, they do not even compare themselves to the Germans in prowess.

6:25 The breadth of this Hercynian forest, which has been referred to above, is to a quick traveler, a journey of nine days. For it can not be otherwise computed, nor are they acquainted with the measures of roads. It begins at the frontiers of the Helvetii, Nemetes, and Rauraci, and extends in a right line along the river Danube to the territories of the Daci and the Anartes; it bends thence to the left in a different direction from the river, and owing to its extent touches the confines of many nations; nor is there any person belonging to this part of Germany who says that he either has gone to the extremity of that forest,

pace nullus est communis magistratus, sed principes regionum atque pagorum inter suos ius dicunt controversiasque minuunt. Latrocinia nullam habent infamiam, quae extra fines cuiusque civitatis fiunt, atque ea iuventutis exercendae ac desidiae minuendae causa fieri praedicant. Atque ubi quis ex principibus in concilio dixit se ducem fore, qui sequi velint, profiteantur, consurgunt ei qui et causam et hominem probant suumque auxilium pollicentur atque ab multitudine collaudantur: qui ex his secuti non sunt, in desertorum ac proditorum numero ducuntur, omniumque his rerum postea fides derogatur. Hospitem violare fas non putant; qui quacumque de causa ad eos venerunt, ab iniuria prohibent, sanctos habent, hisque omnium domus patent victusque communicatur.

Ac fuit antea tempus, cum Germanos Galli virtute superarent, ultro bella inferrent, propter hominum multitudinem agrique inopiam trans Rhenum colonias mitterent. Itaque ea quae fertilissima Germaniae sunt loca circum Hercyniam silvam, quam Eratostheni et quibusdam Graecis fama notam esse video, quam illi Orcyniam appellant, Volcae Tectosages occupaverunt atque ibi consederunt; quae gens ad hoc tempus his sedibus sese continet summamque habet iustitiae et bellicae laudis opinionem. Nunc quod in eadem inopia, egestate, patientia qua Germani permanent, eodem victu et cultu corporis utuntur; Gallis autem provinciarum propinquitas et transmarinarum rerum notitia multa ad copiam atque usus largitur, paulatim adsuefacti superari multisque victi proeliis ne se quidem ipsi cum illis virtute comparant.

Huius Hercyniae silvae, quae supra demonstrata est, latitudo novem dierum iter expedito patet: non enim aliter finiri potest, neque mensuras itinerum noverunt. Oritur ab Helvetiorum et Nemetum et Rauracorum finibus rectaque fluminis Danubi regione pertinet ad fines Dacorum et Anartium; hinc se flectit sinistrorsus diversis ab flumine regionibus multarumque gentium fines propter magnitudinem adtingit; neque quisquam est huius Germaniae, qui se aut adisse ad initium eius silvae dicat, cum dierum iter LX processerit, aut,

though he had advanced a journey of sixty days, or has heard in what place it begins. It is certain that many kinds of wild beast are produced in it which have not been seen in other parts; of which the following are such as differ principally from other animals, and appear worthy of being committed to record.

6:26 There is an ox of the shape of a stag, between whose ears a horn rises from the middle of the forehead, higher and straighter than those horns which are known to us. From the top of this, branches, like palms, stretch out a considerable distance. The shape of the female and of the male is the, same; the appearance and the size of the horns is the same.

6:27 There are also [animals] which are called elks. The shape of these, and the varied color of their skins, is much like roes, but in size they surpass them a little and are destitute of horns, and have legs without joints and ligatures; nor do they lie down for the purpose of rest, nor, if they have been thrown down by any accident, can they raise or lift themselves up. Trees serve as beds to them; they lean themselves against them, and thus reclining only slightly, they take their rest; when the huntsmen have discovered from the footsteps of these animals whither they are accustomed to betake themselves, they either undermine all the trees at the roots, or cut into them so far that the upper part of the trees may appear to be left standing. When they have leant upon them, according to their habit, they knock down by their weight the unsupported trees, and fall down themselves along with them.

6:28 There is a third kind, consisting of those animals which are called uri. These are a little below the elephant in size, and of the appearance, color, and shape of a bull. Their strength and speed are extraordinary; they spare neither man nor wild beast which they have espied. These the Germans take with much pains in pits and kill them. The young men harden themselves with this exercise, and practice themselves in this kind of hunting, and those who have slain the greatest number of them, having produced the horns in public, to serve as evidence, receive great praise. But not even when taken very young can they be rendered familiar to men and tamed. The size, shape, and appearance of their horns differ much from the horns of our oxen. These they anxiously seek after, and bind at the tips with silver, and use as cups at their most sumptuous entertainments.

6:29 Caesar, after he discovered through the Ubian scouts that the Suevi had retired into their woods, apprehending a scarcity of corn, because, as we have observed above, all the Germans pay very little attention to agriculture, resolved not to proceed any further; but, that he might not altogether relieve the

quo ex loco oriatur, acceperit: multaque in ea genera ferarum nasci constat, quae reliquis in locis visa non sint; ex quibus quae maxime differant ab ceteris et memoriae prodenda videantur haec sunt.

Est bos cervi figura, cuius a media fronte inter aures unum cornu exsistit excelsius magisque directum his, quae nobis nota sunt, cornibus: ab eius summo sicut palmae ramique late divunduntur. Eadem est feminae marisque natura, eadem forma magnitudoque cornuum.

Sunt item, quae appellantur alces. Harum est consimilis capris figura et varietas pellium, sed magnitudine paulo antecedunt mutilaeque sunt cornibus et crura sine nodis articulisque habent neque quietis causa procumbunt neque, si quo adflictae casu conciderunt, erigere sese aut sublevare possunt. His sunt arbores pro cubilibus: ad eas se applicant atque ita paulum modo reclinatae quietem capiunt. Quarum ex vestigiis cum est animadversum a venatoribus, quo se recipere consuerint, omnes eo loco aut ab radicibus subruunt aut accidunt arbores, tantum ut summa species earum stantium relinquatur. Huc cum se consuetudine reclinaverunt, infirmas arbores pondere adfligunt atque una ipsae concidunt.

Tertium est genus eorum, qui uri appellantur. Hi sunt magnitudine paulo infra elephantos, specie et colore et figura tauri. Magna vis eorum est et magna velocitas, neque homini neque ferae quam conspexerunt parcunt. Hos studiose foveis captos interficiunt. Hoc se labore durant adulescentes atque hoc genere venationis exercent, et qui plurimos ex his interfecerunt, relatis in publicum cornibus, quae sint testimonio, magnam ferunt laudem. Sed adsuescere ad homines et mansuefieri ne parvuli quidem excepti possunt. Amplitudo cornuum et figura et species multum a nostrorum boum cornibus differt. Haec studiose conquisita ab labris argento circumcludunt atque in amplissimis epulis pro poculis utuntur.

Caesar, postquam per Vbios exploratores comperit Suebos sese in silvas recepisse, inopiam frumenti veritus, quod, ut supra demonstravimus, minime omnes Germani agriculturae student, constituit non progredi longius; sed, ne omnino metum reditus sui

112

barbarians from the fear of his return, and that he might delay their succors, having led back his army, he breaks down, to the length of 200 feet, the further end of the bridge, which joined the banks of the Ubii, and at the extremity of the bridge raises towers of four stories, and stations a guard of twelve cohorts for the purpose of defending the bridge, and strengthens the place with considerable fortifications. Over that fort and guard he appointed C. Volcatius Tullus, a young man; he himself, when the corn began to ripen, having set forth for the war with Ambiorix (through the forest Arduenna, which is the largest of all Gaul, and reaches from the banks of the Rhine and the frontiers of the Treviri to those of the Nervii, and extends over more than 500 miles), he sends forward L. Minucius Basilus with all the cavalry, to try if he might gain any advantage by rapid marches and the advantage of time, he warns him to forbid fires being made in the camp, lest any indication of his approach be given at a distance: he tells him that he will follow immediately.

6:30 Basilus does as he was commanded; having performed his march rapidly, and even surpassed the expectations of all, he surprises in the fields many not expecting him; through their information he advances toward Ambiorix himself, to the place in which he was said to be with a few horse. Fortune accomplishes much, not only in other matters, but also in the art of war. For as it happened by a remarkable chance, that he fell upon [Ambiorix] himself unguarded and unprepared, and that his arrival was seen by the people before the report or information of his arrival was carried thither; so it was an incident of extraordinary fortune that, although every implement of war which he was accustomed to have about him was seized, and his chariots and horses surprised, yet he himself escaped death. But it was effected owing to this circumstance, that his house being surrounded by a wood (as are generally the dwellings of the Gauls, who, for the purpose of avoiding heat, mostly seek the neighborhood of woods and rivers), his attendants and friends in a narrow spot sustained for a short time the attack of our horse. While they were fighting, one of his followers mounted him on a horse; the woods sheltered him as he fled. Thus fortune tended much both toward his encountering and his escaping danger.

6:31 Whether Ambiorix did not collect his forces from cool deliberation, because he considered he ought not to engage in a battle, or [whether] he was debarred by time and prevented by the sudden arrival of our horse, when he supposed the rest of the army was closely following, is doubtful: but certainly, dispatching messengers through the country, he ordered every one to provide for himself; and a part of them fled into the forest

barbaris tolleret atque ut eorum auxilia tardaret, reducto exercitu partem ultimam pontis, quae ripas Vbiorum contingebat, in longitudinem pedum ducentorum rescindit atque in extremo ponte turrim tabulatorum quattuor constituit praesidiumque cohortium duodecim pontis tuendi causa ponit magnisque eum locum munitionibus firmat. Ei loco praesidioque Gaium Volcatium Tullum adulescentem praefecit. Ipse, cum maturescere frumenta inciperent, ad bellum Ambiorigis profectus per Arduennam silvam, quae est totius Galliae maxima atque ab ripis Rheni finibusque Treverorum ad Nervios pertinet milibusque amplius quingentis in longitudinem patet, Lucium Minucium Basilum cum omni equitatu praemittit, si quid celeritate itineris atque opportunitate temporis proficere possit; monet, ut ignes in castris fieri prohibeat, ne qua eius adventus procul significatio fiat: sese confestim subsequi dicit.

Basilus, ut imperatum est, facit. Celeriter contraque omnium opinionem confecto itinere multos in agris inopinantes deprehendit: eorum indicio ad ipsum Ambiorigem contendit, quo in loco cum paucis equitibus esse dicebatur. Multum cum in omnibus rebus tum in re militari potest fortuna. Nam sicut magno accidit casu ut in ipsum incautum etiam atque imparatum incideret, priusque eius adventus ab omnibus videretur, quam fama ac nuntius adferretur: sic magnae fuit fortunae omni militari instrumento, quod circum se habebat, erepto, raedis equisque comprehensis ipsum effugere mortem. Sed hoc quoque factum est, quod aedificio circumdato silva, ut sunt fere domicilia Gallorum, qui vitandi aestus causa plerumque silvarum atque fluminum petunt propinquitates, comites familiaresque eius angusto in loco paulisper equitum nostrorum vim sustinuerunt. His pugnantibus illum in equum quidam ex suis intulit: fugientem silvae texerunt. Sic et ad subeundum periculum et ad vitandum multum fortuna valuit.

Ambiorix copias suas iudicione non conduxerit, quod proelio dimicandum non existimarit, an tempore exclusus et repentino equitum adventu prohibitus, cum reliquum exercitum subsequi crederet, dubium est. Sed certe dimissis per agros nuntiis sibi quemque consulere iussit. Quorum pars in Arduennam silvam, pars in continentes paludes

Arduenna, a part into the extensive morasses; those who were nearest the ocean concealed themselves in the islands which the tides usually form; many, departing from their territories, committed themselves and all their possessions to perfect strangers. Cativolcus, king of one half of the Eburones, who had entered into the design together with Ambiorix, since, being now worn out by age, he was unable to endure the fatigue either of war or flight, having cursed Ambiorix with every imprecation, as the person who had been the contriver of that measure, destroyed himself with the juice of the yew-tree, of which there is a great abundance in Gaul and Germany.

6:32 The Segui and Condrusi, of the nation and number of the Germans, and who are between the Eburones and the Treviri, sent embassadors to Caesar to entreat that he would not regard them in the number of his enemies, nor consider that the cause of all the Germans on this side the Rhine was one and the same; that they had formed no plans of war, and had sent no auxiliaries to Ambiorix. Caesar, having ascertained this fact by an examination of his prisoners, commanded that if any of the Eburones in their flight had repaired to them, they should be sent back to him; he assures them that if they did that, he will not injure their territories. Then, having divided his forces into three parts, he sent the baggage of all the legions to Aduatuca. That is the name of a fort. This is nearly in the middle of the Eburones, where Titurius and Aurunculeius had been quartered for the purpose of wintering. This place he selected as well on other accounts as because the fortifications of the previous year remained, in order that he might relieve the labor of the soldiers. He left the fourteenth legion as a guard for the baggage, one of those three which he had lately raised in Italy and brought over. Over that legion and camp he places Q. Tullius Cicero and gives him 200 horse.

6:33 Having divided the army, he orders T. Labienus to proceed with three legions toward the ocean into those parts which border on the Menapii; he sends C. Trebonius with a like number of legions to lay waste that district which lies contiguous to the Aduatuci; he himself determines to go with the remaining three to the river Sambre, which flows into the Meuse, and to the most remote parts of Arduenna, whither he heard that Ambiorix had gone with a few horse. When departing, he promises that he will return before the end of the seventh day, on which day he was aware corn was due to that legion which was being left in garrison. He directs Labienus and Trebonius to return by the same day, if they can do so agreeably to the interests of the republic; so that their measures having been mutually imparted, and the plans of the enemy having been discovered, they might be able to commence a different line of operations.

profugit; qui proximi Oceano fuerunt, his insulis sese occultaverunt, quas aestus efficere consuerunt: multi ex suis finibus egressi se suaque omnia alienissimis crediderunt. Catuvolcus, rex dimidiae partis Eburonum, qui una cum Ambiorige consilium inierat, aetate iam confectus, cum laborem aut belli aut fugae ferre non posset, omnibus precibus detestatus Ambiorigem, qui eius consilii auctor fuisset, taxo, cuius magna in Gallia Germaniaque copia est, se exanimavit.

Segni Condrusique, ex gente et numero Germanorum, qui sunt inter Eburones Treverosque, legatos ad Caesarem miserunt oratum, ne se in hostium numero duceret neve omnium Germanorum, qui essent citra Rhenum, unam esse causam iudicaret: nihil se de bello cogitavisse, nulla Ambiorigi auxilia misisse. Caesar explorata re quaestione captivorum, si qui ad eos Eburones ex fuga convenissent, ad se ut reducerentur, imperavit; si ita fecissent, fines eorum se violaturum negavit. Tum copiis in tres partes distributis impedimenta omnium legionum Aduatucam contulit. Id castelli nomen est. Hoc fere est in mediis Eburonum finibus, ubi Titurius atque Aurunculeius hiemandi causa consederant. Hunc cum reliquis rebus locum probabat, tum quod superioris anni munitiones integrae manebant, ut militum laborem sublevaret. Praesidio impedimentis legionem quartamdecimam reliquit, unam ex eis tribus, quas proxime conscriptas ex Italia traduxerat. Ei legioni castrisque Quintum Tullium Ciceronem praeficit ducentosque equites attribuit.

Partito exercitu Titum Labienum cum legionibus tribus ad Oceanum versus in eas partes quae Menapios attingunt proficisci iubet; Gaium Trebonium cum pari legionum numero ad eam regionem quae ad Aduatucos adiacet depopulandam mittit; ipse cum reliquis tribus ad flumen Scaldem, quod influit in Mosam, extremasque Arduennae partis ire constituit, quo cum paucis equitibus profectum Ambiorigem audiebat. Discedens post diem septimum sese reversurum confirmat; quam ad diem ei legioni quae in praesidio relinquebatur deberi frumentum sciebat. Labienum Treboniumque hortatur, si rei publicae commodo facere possint, ad eum diem revertantur, ut rursus communicato consilio exploratisque hostium rationibus aliud initium

6:34 There was, as we have above observed, no regular army, nor a town, nor a garrison which could defend itself by arms; but the people were scattered in all directions. Where either a hidden valley, or a woody spot, or a difficult morass furnished any hope of protection or of security to any one, there he had fixed himself. These places were known to those who dwelt in the neighborhood, and the matter demanded great attention, not so much in protecting the main body of the army (for no peril could occur to them altogether from those alarmed and scattered troops), as in preserving individual soldiers; which in some measure tended to the safety of the army. For both the desire of booty was leading many too far, and the woods with their unknown and hidden routes would not allow them to go in large bodies. If he desired the business to be completed and the race of those infamous people to be cut off, more bodies of men must be sent in several directions and the soldiers must be detached on all sides; if he were disposed to keep the companies at their standards, as the established discipline and practice of the Roman army required, the situation itself was a safeguard to the barbarians, nor was there wanting to individuals the daring to lay secret ambuscades and beset scattered soldiers. But amid difficulties of this nature as far as precautions could be taken by vigilance, such precautions were taken; so that some opportunities of injuring the enemy were neglected, though the minds of all were burning to take revenge, rather than that injury should be effected with any loss to our soldiers. Caesar dispatches messengers to the neighboring states; by the hope of booty he invites all to him, for the purpose of plundering the Eburones, in order that the life of the Gauls might be hazarded in the woods rather than the legionary soldiers; at the same time, in order that a large force being drawn around them, the race and name of that state may be annihilated for such a crime. A large number from all quarters speedily assembles.

6:35 These things were going on in all parts of the territories of the Eburones, and the seventh day was drawing near, by which day Caesar had purposed to return to the baggage and the legion. Here it might be learned how much fortune achieves in war, and how great casualties she produces. The enemy having been scattered and alarmed, as we related above, there was no force which might produce even a slight occasion of fear. The report extends beyond the Rhine to the Germans that the Eburones are being pillaged, and that all were without distinction invited to the plunder. The Sigambri, who are nearest to the Rhine, by whom, we have mentioned above, the Tenchtheri and Usipetes were received after their retreat, collect 2,000 horse;

belli capere possint.

Erat, ut supra demonstravimus, manus certa nulla, non oppidum, non praesidium, quod se armis defenderet, sed in omnes partes dispersa multitudo. Vbi cuique aut valles abdita aut locus silvestris aut palus impedita spem praesidi aut salutis aliquam offerebat, consederat. Haec loca vicinitatibus erant nota, magnamque res diligentiam requirebat non in summa exercitus tuenda (nullum enim poterat universis ab perterritis ac dispersis periculum accidere), sed in singulis militibus conservandis; quae tamen ex parte res ad salutem exercitus pertinebat. Nam et praedae cupiditas multos longius evocabat, et silvae incertis occultisque itineribus confertos adire prohibebant. Si negotium confici stirpemque hominum sceleratorum interfici vellet, dimittendae plures manus diducendique erant milites; si continere ad signa manipulos vellet, ut instituta ratio et consuetudo exercitus Romani postulabat, locus ipse erat praesidio barbaris, neque ex occulto insidiandi et dispersos circumveniendi singulis deerat audacia. Vt in eiusmodi difficultatibus, quantum diligentia provideri poterat providebatur, ut potius in nocendo aliquid praetermitteretur, etsi omnium animi ad ulciscendum ardebant, quam cum aliquo militum detrimento noceretur. Dimittit ad finitimas civitates nuntios Caesar: omnes ad se vocat spe praedae ad diripiendos Eburones, ut potius in silvis Gallorum vita quam legionarius miles periclitetur, simul ut magna multitudine circumfusa pro tali facinore stirps ac nomen civitatis tollatur. Magnus undique numerus celeriter convenit.

Haec in omnibus Eburonum partibus gerebantur, diesque appetebat septimus, quem ad diem Caesar ad impedimenta legionemque reverti constituerat. Hic quantum in bello fortuna possit et quantos adferat casus cognosci potuit. Dissipatis ac perterritis hostibus, ut demonstravimus, manus erat nulla quae parvam modo causam timoris adferret. Trans Rhenum ad Germanos pervenit fama, diripi Eburones atque ultro omnes ad praedam evocari. Cogunt equitum duo milia Sugambri, qui sunt proximi Rheno, a quibus receptos ex fuga Tencteros atque Vsipetes supra docuimus. Transeunt Rhenum

they cross the Rhine in ships and barks thirty miles below that place where the bridge was entire and the garrison left by Caesar; they arrive at the frontiers of the Eburones, surprise many who were scattered in flight, and get possession of a large amount of cattle, of which barbarians are extremely covetous. Allured by booty, they advance further; neither morass nor forest obstructs these men, born amid war and depredations; they inquire of their prisoners in what part Caesar is; they find that he has advanced further, and learn that all the army has removed. Thereon one of the prisoners says, "Why do you pursue such wretched and trifling spoil; you, to whom it is granted to become even now most richly endowed by fortune? In three hours you can reach Aduatuca; there the Roman army has deposited all its fortunes; there is so little of a garrison that not even the wall can be manned, nor dare any one go beyond the fortifications." A hope having been presented them, the Germans leave in concealment the plunder they had acquired; they themselves hasten to Aduatuca, employing as their guide the same man by whose information they had become informed of these things.

6:36 Cicero, who during all the foregoing days had kept his soldiers in camp with the greatest exactness, and agreeable to the injunctions of Caesar, had not permitted even any of the camp-followers to go beyond the fortification, distrusting on the seventh day that Caesar would keep his promise as to the number of days, because he heard that he had proceeded further, and no report as to his return was brought to him, and being urged at the same time by the expressions of those who called his tolerance almost a siege, if, forsooth, it was not permitted them to go out of the camp, since he might expect no disaster, whereby he could be injured, within three miles of the camp, while nine legions and all the cavalry were under arms, and the enemy scattered and almost annihilated, sent five cohorts into the neighboring corn-lands, between which and the camp only one hill intervened, for the purpose of foraging. Many soldiers of the legions had been left invalided in the camp, of whom those who had recovered in this space of time, being about 300, are sent together under one standard; a large number of soldiers' attendants besides, with a great number of beasts of burden, which had remained in the camp, permission being granted, follow them.

6:37 At this very time, the German horse by chance came up, and immediately, with the same speed with which they had advanced, attempt to force the camp at the Decuman gate, nor were they seen, in consequence of woods lying in the way on that side, before they were just reaching the camp: so much so, that the sutlers who had their booths under the rampart had not

navibus ratibusque triginta milibus passuum infra eum locum, ubi pons erat perfectus praesidiumque ab Caesare relictum: primos Eburonum fines adeunt; multos ex fuga dispersos excipiunt, magno pecoris numero, cuius sunt cupidissimi barbari, potiuntur. Invitati praeda longius procedunt. Non hos palus in bello latrociniisque natos, non silvae morantur. Quibus in locis sit Caesar ex captivis quaerunt; profectum longius reperiunt omnemque exercitum discessisse cognoscunt. Atque unus ex captivis "Quid vos," inquit, "hanc miseram ac tenuem sectamini praedam, quibus licet iam esse fortunatissimos? Tribus horis Aduatucam venire potestis: huc omnes suas fortunas exercitus Romanorum contulit: praesidi tantum est, ut ne murus quidem cingi possit, neque quisquam egredi extra munitiones audeat." Oblata spe Germani quam nacti erant praedam in occulto relinquunt; ipsi Aduatucam contendunt usi eodem duce, cuius haec indicio cognoverant.

Cicero, qui omnes superiores dies praeceptis Caesaris cum summa diligentia milites in castris continuisset ac ne calonem quidem quemquam extra munitionem egredi passus esset, septimo die diffidens de numero dierum Caesarem fidem servaturum, quod longius progressum audiebat, neque ulla de reditu eius fama adferebatur, simul eorum permotus vocibus, qui illius patientiam paene obsessionem appellabant, siquidem ex castris egredi non liceret, nullum eiusmodi casum exspectans, quo novem oppositis legionibus maximoque equitatu dispersis ac paene deletis hostibus in milibus passuum tribus offendi posset, quinque cohortes frumentatum in proximas segetes mittit, quas inter et castra unus omnino collis intererat. Complures erant ex legionibus aegri relicti; ex quibus qui hoc spatio dierum convaluerant, circiter CCC, sub vexillo una mittuntur; magna praeterea multitudo calonum, magna vis iumentorum, quae in castris subsederant, facta potestate sequitur.

Hoc ipso tempore et casu Germani equites interveniunt protinusque eodem illo, quo venerant, cursu ab decumana porta in castra irrumpere conantur, nec prius sunt visi obiectis ab ea parte silvis, quam castris appropinquarent, usque eo ut qui sub vallo tenderent mercatores recipiendi sui

an opportunity of retreating within the camp. Our men, not anticipating it, are perplexed by the sudden affair, and the cohort on the outpost scarcely sustains the first attack. The enemy spread themselves on the other sides to ascertain if they could find any access. Our men with difficulty defend the gates; the very position of itself and the fortification secures the other accesses. There is a panic in the entire camp, and one inquires of another the cause of the confusion, nor do they readily determine whither the standards should be borne, nor into what quarter each should betake himself. One avows that the camp is already taken, another maintains that, the enemy having destroyed the army and commander-in-chief, are come hither as conquerors; most form strange superstitious fancies from the spot, and place before their eyes the catastrophe of Cotta and Titurius, who had fallen in the same fort. All being greatly disconcerted by this alarm, the belief of the barbarians is strengthened that there is no garrison within, as they had heard from their prisoner. They endeavor to force an entrance and encourage one another not to cast from their hands so valuable a prize.

6:38 P. Sextius Baculus, who had led a principal century under Caesar (of whom we have made mention in previous engagements), had been left an invalid in the garrison, and had now been five days without food. He, distrusting his own safety and that of all, goes forth from his tent unarmed; he sees that the enemy are close at hand and that the matter is in the utmost danger; he snatches arms from those nearest, and stations himself at the gate. The centurions of that cohort which was on guard follow him; for a short time they sustain the fight together. Sextius faints, after receiving many wounds; he is with difficulty saved, drawn away by the hands of the soldiers. This space having intervened, the others resume courage so far as to venture to take their place on the fortifications and present the aspect of defenders.

6:39 The foraging having in the mean time been completed, our soldiers distinctly hear the shout; the horse hasten on before and discover in what danger the affair is. But here there is no fortification to receive them, in their alarm: those last enlisted, and unskilled in military discipline turn their faces to the military tribune and the centurions; they wait to find what orders may be given by them. No one is so courageous as not to be disconcerted by the suddenness of the affair. The barbarians, espying our standard in the distance, desist from the attack; at first they suppose that the legions, which they had learned from their prisoners had removed further off, had returned; afterward, despising their small number, they make an attack on them at all sides.

facultatem non haberent. Inopinantes nostri re nova perturbantur, ac vix primum impetum cohors in statione sustinet. Circumfunduntur ex reliquis hostes partibus, si quem aditum reperire possent. Aegre portas nostri tuentur, reliquos aditus locus ipse per se munitioque defendit. Totis trepidatur castris, atque alius ex alio causam tumultus quaerit; neque quo signa ferantur neque quam in partem quisque conveniat provident. Alius iam castra capta pronuntiat, alius deleto exercitu atque imperatore victores barbaros venisse contendit; plerique novas sibi ex loco religiones fingunt Cottaeque et Tituri calamitatem, qui in eodem occiderint castello, ante oculos ponunt. Tali timore omnibus perterritis confirmatur opinio barbaris, ut ex captivo audierant, nullum esse intus praesidium. Perrumpere nituntur seque ipsi adhortantur, ne tantam fortunam ex manibus dimittant.

Erat aeger cum praesidio relictus Publius Sextius Baculus, qui primum pilum ad Caesarem duxerat, cuius mentionem superioribus proeliis fecimus, ac diem iam quintum cibo caruerat. Hic diffisus suae atque omnium saluti inermis ex tabernaculo prodit: videt imminere hostes atque in summo esse rem discrimine: capit arma a proximis atque in porta consistit. Consequuntur hunc centuriones eius cohortis quae in statione erat: paulisper una proelium sustinent. Relinquit animus Sextium gravibus acceptis vulneribus: aegre per manus tractus servatur. Hoc spatio interposito reliqui sese confirmant tantum, ut in munitionibus consistere audeant speciemque defensorum praebeant.

Interim confecta frumentatione milites nostri clamorem exaudiunt: praecurrunt equites; quanto res sit in periculo cognoscunt. Hic vero nulla munitio est quae perterritos recipiat: modo conscripti atque usus militaris imperiti ad tribunum militum centurionesque ora convertunt; quid ab his praecipiatur exspectant. Nemo est tam fortis quin rei novitate perturbetur. Barbari signa procul conspicati oppugnatione desistunt: redisse primo legiones credunt, quas longius discessisse ex captivis cognoverant; postea despecta paucitate ex omnibus partibus impetum faciunt.

6:40 The camp-followers run forward to the nearest rising ground; being speedily driven from this they throw themselves among the standards and companies: they thus so much the more alarm the soldiers already affrighted. Some propose that, forming a wedge, they suddenly break through, since the camp was so near; and if any part should be surrounded and slain, they fully trust that at least the rest may be saved; others, that they take their stand on an eminence, and all undergo the same destiny. The veteran soldiers whom we stated to have set out together [with the others] under a standard, do not approve of this. Therefore encouraging each other, under the conduct of Caius Trebonius, a Roman knight, who had been appointed over them, they break through the midst of the enemy, and arrive in the camp safe to a man. The camp attendants and the horse following close upon them with the same impetuosity, are saved by the courage of the soldiers. But those who had taken their stand upon the eminence having even now acquired no experience of military matters, neither could persevere in that resolution which they approved of, namely, to defend themselves from their higher position, nor imitate that vigor and speed which they had observed to have availed others; but, attempting to reach the camp, had descended into an unfavorable situation. The centurions, some of whom had been promoted for their valor from the lower ranks of other legions to higher ranks in this legion, in order that they might not forfeit their glory for military exploits previously acquired, fell together fighting most valiantly. The enemy having been dislodged by their valor, a part of the soldiers arrived safe in camp contrary to their expectations; a part perished, surrounded by the barbarians.

6:41 The Germans, despairing of taking the camp by storm, because they saw that our men had taken up their position on the fortifications, retreated beyond the Rhine with that plunder which they had deposited in the woods. And so great was the alarm, even after the departure of the enemy, that when C. Volusenus, who had been sent with the cavalry, arrived that night, he could not gain credence that Caesar was close at hand with his army safe. Fear had so pre-occupied the minds of all, that their reason being almost estranged, they said that all the other forces having been cut off, the cavalry alone had arrived there by flight, and asserted that, if the army were safe, the Germans would not have attacked the camp; which fear the arrival of Caesar removed.

6:42 He, on his return, being well aware of the casualties of war, complained of one thing [only], namely, that the cohorts had been sent away from the outposts and garrison [duty], and pointed out that room ought not to have been left for even the

Calones in proximum tumulum procurrunt. Hinc celeriter deiecti se in signa manipulosque coniciunt: eo magis timidos perterrent milites. Alii cuneo facto ut celeriter perrumpant censent, quoniam tam propinqua sint castra, et si pars aliqua circumventa ceciderit, at reliquos servari posse confidunt; alii, ut in iugo consistant atque eundem omnes ferant casum. Hoc veteres non probant milites, quos sub vexillo una profectos docuimus. Itaque inter se cohortati duce Gaio Trebonio, equite Romano, qui eis erat praepositus, per medios hostes perrumpunt incolumesque ad unum omnes in castra perveniunt. Hos subsecuti calones equitesque eodem impetu militum virtute servantur. At ei qui in iugo constiterant, nullo etiam nunc usu rei militaris percepto neque in eo quod probaverant consilio permanere, ut se loco superiore defenderent, neque eam quam prodesse aliis vim celeritatemque viderant imitari potuerunt, sed se in castra recipere conati iniquum in locum demiserunt. Centuriones, quorum nonnulli ex inferioribus ordinibus reliquarum legionum virtutis causa in superiores erant ordines huius legionis traducti, ne ante partam rei militaris laudem amitterent, fortissime pugnantes conciderunt. Militum pars horum virtute summotis hostibus praeter spem incolumis in castra pervenit, pars a barbaris circumventa periit.

Germani desperata expugnatione castrorum, quod nostros iam constitisse in munitionibus videbant, cum ea praeda quam in silvis deposuerant trans Rhenum sese receperunt. Ac tantus fuit etiam post discessum hostium terror ut ea nocte, cum Gaius Volusenus missus cum equitatu ad castra venisset, fidem non faceret adesse cum incolumi Caesarem exercitu. Sic omnino animos timor praeoccupaverat ut paene alienata mente deletis omnibus copiis equitatum se ex fuga recepisse dicerent neque incolumi exercitu Germanos castra oppugnaturos fuisse contenderent. Quem timorem Caesaris adventus sustulit.

Reversus ille eventus belli non ignorans unum, quod cohortes ex statione et praesidio essent emissae, questus ne minimo quidem casu locum relinqui debuisse, multum fortunam in repentino hostium

most trivial casualty; that fortune had exercised great influence in the sudden arrival of their enemy; much greater, in that she had turned the barbarians away from the very rampart and gates of the camp. Of all which events, it seemed the most surprising, that the Germans, who had crossed the Rhine with this object, that they might plunder the territories of Ambiorix, being led to the camp of the Romans, rendered Ambiorix a most acceptable service.

6:43 Caesar, having again marched to harass the enemy, after collecting a large number [of auxiliaries] from the neighboring states, dispatches them in all directions. All the villages and all the buildings, which each beheld, were on fire: spoil was being driven off from all parts; the corn not only was being consumed by so great numbers of cattle and men, but also had fallen to the earth, owing to the time of the year and the storms; so that if any had concealed themselves for the present, still, it appeared likely that they must perish through want of all things, when the army should be drawn off. And frequently it came to that point, as so large a body of cavalry had been sent abroad in all directions, that the prisoners declared Ambiorix had just then been seen by them in flight, and had not even passed out of sight, so that the hope of overtaking him being raised, and unbounded exertions having been resorted to, those who thought they should acquire the highest favor with Caesar, nearly overcame nature by their ardor, and continually, a little only seemed wanting to complete success; but he rescued himself by [means of] lurking-places and forests, and, concealed by the night made for other districts and quarters, with no greater guard than that of four horsemen, to whom along he ventured to confide his life.

6:44 Having devastated the country in such a manner, Caesar leads back his army with the loss of two cohorts to Durocortorum of the Remi, and, having summoned a council of Gaul to assemble at that place, he resolved to hold an investigation respecting the conspiracy of the Senones and Carnutes, and having pronounced a most severe sentence upon Acco, who had been the contriver of that plot, he punished him after the custom of our ancestors. Some fearing a trial, fled; when he had forbidden these fire and water, he stationed in winter quarters two legions at the frontiers of the Treviri, two among the Lingones, the remaining six at Agendicum, in the territories of the Senones; and, having provided corn for the army, he set out for Italy, as he had determined, to hold the assizes.

adventu potuisse iudicavit, multo etiam amplius, quod paene ab ipso vallo portisque castrorum barbaros avertisset. Quarum omnium rerum maxime admirandum videbatur, quod Germani, qui eo consilio Rhenum transierant, ut Ambiorigis fines depopularentur, ad castra Romanorum delati optatissimum Ambiorigi beneficium obtulerunt.

Caesar rursus ad vexandos hostes profectus magno coacto numero ex finitimis civitatibus in omnes partes dimittit. Omnes vici atque omnia aedificia quae quisque conspexerat incendebantur; praeda ex omnibus locis agebatur; frumenta non solum tanta multitudine iumentorum atque hominum consumebantur, sed etiam anni tempore atque imbribus procubuerant ut, si qui etiam in praesentia se occultassent, tamen his deducto exercitu rerum omnium inopia pereundum videretur. Ac saepe in eum locum ventum est tanto in omnes partes diviso equitatu, ut modo visum ab se Ambiorigem in fuga circumspicerent captivi nec plane etiam abisse ex conspectu contenderent, ut spe consequendi illata atque infinito labore suscepto, qui se summam ab Caesare gratiam inituros putarent, paene naturam studio vincerent, semperque paulum ad summam felicitatem defuisse videretur, atque ille latebris aut saltibus se eriperet et noctu occultatus alias regiones partesque peteret non maiore equitum praesidio quam quattuor, quibus solis vitam suam committere audebat.

Tali modo vastatis regionibus exercitum Caesar duarum cohortium damno Durocortorum Remorum reducit concilioque in eum locum Galliae indicto de coniuratione Senonum et Carnutum quaestionem habere instituit et de Accone, qui princeps eius consili fuerat, graviore sententia pronuntiata more maiorum supplicium sumpsit. Nonnulli iudicium veriti profugerunt. Quibus cum aqua atque igni interdixisset, duas legiones ad fines Treverorum, duas in Lingonibus, sex reliquas in Senonum finibus Agedinci in hibernis collocavit frumentoque exercitui proviso, ut instituerat, in Italiam ad conventus agendos profectus est.

Gallic Wars Book 7 (52 B.C.E.)

7:1 Gaul being tranquil, Caesar, as he had determined, sets out for Italy to hold the provincial assizes. There he receives intelligence of the death of Clodius; and, being informed of the decree of the senate, [to the effect] that all the youth of Italy should take the military oath, he determined to hold a levy throughout the entire province. Report of these events is rapidly borne into Transalpine Gaul. The Gauls themselves add to the report, and invent what the case seemed to require, [namely] that Caesar was detained by commotions in the city, and could not, amid so violent dissensions, come to his army. Animated by this opportunity, they who already, previously to this occurrence, were indignant that they were reduced beneath the dominion of Rome, begin to organize their plans for war more openly and daringly. The leading men of Gaul, having convened councils among themselves in the woods, and retired places, complain of the death of Acco: they point out that this fate may fall in turn on themselves: they bewail the unhappy fate of Gaul; and by every sort of promises and rewards, they earnestly solicit some to begin the war, and assert the freedom of Gaul at the hazard of their lives. They say that special care should be paid to this, that Caesar should be cut off from his army before their secret plans should be divulged. That this was easy, because neither would the legions, in the absence of their general, dare to leave their winter quarters, nor could the general reach his army without a guard: finally, that it was better to be slain in battle, than not to recover their ancient glory in war, and that freedom which they had received from their forefathers.

7:2 While these things are in agitation, the Carnutes declare "that they would decline no danger for the sake of the general safety, and promise" that they would be the first of all to begin the war; and since they can not at present take precautions, by giving and receiving hostages, that the affair shall not be divulged, they require that a solemn assurance be given them by oath and plighted honor, their military standards being brought together (in which manner their most sacred obligations are made binding), that they should not be deserted by the rest of the Gauls on commencing the war.

7:3 When the appointed day came, the Carnutes, under the command of Cotuatus and Conetodunus, desperate men, meet together at Genabum, and slay the Roman citizens who had settled there for the purpose of trading (among the rest, Caius Fusius Cita, a distinguished Roman knight, who by Caesar's

Quieta Gallia Caesar, ut constituerat, in Italiam ad conventus agendos proficiscitur. Ibi cognoscit de Clodii caede [de] senatusque consulto certior factus, ut omnes iuniores Italiae coniurarent, delectum tota provincia habere instituit. Eae res in Galliam Transalpinam celeriter perferuntur. Addunt ipsi et ad fingunt rumoribus Galli, quod res poscere videbatur, retineri urbano motu Caesarem neque in tantis dissensionibus ad exercitum venire posse. Hac impulsi occasione, qui iam ante se populi Romani imperio subiectos dolerent liberius atque audacius de bello consilia inire incipiunt. Indictis inter se principes Galliae conciliis silvestribus ac remotis locis queruntur de Acconis morte; posse hunc casum ad ipsos recidere demonstrant: miserantur communem Galliae fortunam: omnibus pollicitationibus ac praemius deposcunt qui belli initium faciant et sui capitis periculo Galliam in libertatem vindicent. In primis rationem esse habendam dicunt, priusquam eorum clandestina consilia efferantur, ut Caesar ab exercitu intercludatur. Id esse facile, quod neque legiones audeant absente imperatore ex hibernis egredi, neque imperator sine praesidio ad legiones pervenire possit. Postremo in acie praestare interfici quam non veterem belli gloriam libertatemque quam a maioribus acce perint recuperare.

His rebus agitatis profitentur Carnutes se nullum periculum communis salutis causa recusare principesque ex omnibus bellum facturos pollicentur et, quoniam in praesentia obsidibus cavere inter se non possint ne res efferatur, ut iureiurando ac fide sanciatur, petunt, collatis militaribus signis, quo more eorum gravissima caerimonia continetur, ne facto initio belli ab reliquis deserantur. Tum collaudatis Carnutibus, dato iureiurando ab omnibus qui aderant, tempore eius rei constituto ab concilio disceditur.

Vbi ea dies venit, Carnutes Cotuato et Conconnetodumno ducibus, desperatis hominibus, Cenabum signo dato concurrunt civesque Romanos, qui negotiandi causa ibi constiterant, in his Gaium Fufium Citam, honestum equitem Romanum, qui rei

orders had presided over the provision department), and plunder their property. The report is quickly spread among all the states of Gaul; for, whenever a more important and remarkable event takes place, they transmit the intelligence through their lands and districts by a shout; the others take it up in succession, and pass it to their neighbors, as happened on this occasion; for the things which were done at Genabum at sunrise, were heard in the territories of the Arverni before the end of the first watch, which is an extent of more than a hundred and sixty miles.

7:4 There in like manner, Vercingetorix the son of Celtillus the Arvernian, a young man of the highest power (whose father had held the supremacy of entire Gaul, and had been put to death by his fellow-citizens, for this reason, because he aimed at sovereign power), summoned together his dependents, and easily excited them. On his design being made known, they rush to arms: he is expelled from the town of Gergovia, by his uncle Gobanitio and the rest of the nobles, who were of opinion, that such an enterprise ought not to be hazarded: he did not however desist, but held in the country a levy of the needy and desperate. Having collected such a body of troops, he brings over to his sentiments such of his fellow-citizens as he has access to: he exhorts them to take up arms in behalf of the general freedom, and having assembled great forces he drives from the state his opponents, by whom he had been expelled a short time previously. He is saluted king by his partisans; he sends embassadors in every direction, he conjures them to adhere firmly to their promise. He quickly attaches to his interests the Senones, Parisii, Pictones, Cadurci, Turones, Aulerci, Lemovice, and all the others who border on the ocean; the supreme command is conferred on him by unanimous consent. On obtaining this authority, he demands hostages from all these states, he orders a fixed number of soldiers to be sent to him immediately; he determines what quantity of arms each state shall prepare at home, and before what time; he pays particular attention to the cavalry. To the utmost vigilance he adds the utmost rigor of authority; and by the severity of his punishments brings over the wavering: for on the commission of a greater crime he puts the perpetrators to death by fire and every sort of tortures; for a slighter cause, he sends home the offenders with their ears cut off, or one of their eyes put out, that they may be an example to the rest, and frighten others by the severity of their punishment.

7:5 Having quickly collected an army by their punishments, he sends Lucterius, one of the Cadurci, a man the utmost daring, with part of his forces, into the territory of the Ruteni; and marches in person into the country of the Bituriges. On his arrival, the Bituriges send embassadors to the Aedui, under

frumentariae iussu Caesaris praeerat, interficiunt bonaque eorum diripiunt. Celeriter ad omnes Galliae civitates fama perfertur. Nam ubicumque maior atque illustrior incidit res, clamore per agros regionesque significant; hunc alii deinceps excipiunt et proximis tradunt, ut tum accidit. Nam quae Cenabi oriente sole gesta essent, ante primam confectam vigiliam in finibus Arvernorum audita sunt, quod spatium est milium passuum circiter centum LX.

Simili ratione ibi Vercingetorix, Celtilli filius, Arvernus, summae potentiae adulescens, cuius pater principatum Galliae totius obtinuerat et ob eam causam, quod regnum appetebat, ab civitate erat interfectus, convocatis suis clientibus facile incendit. Cognito eius consilio ad arma concurritur. Prohibetur ab Gobannitione, patruo suo, reliquisque principibus, qui hanc temptandam fortunam non existimabant; expellitur ex oppido Gergovia; non destitit tamen atque in agris habet dilectum egentium ac perditorum. Hac coacta manu, quoscumque adit ex civitate ad suam sententiam perducit; hortatur ut communis libertatis causa arma capiant, magnisque coactis copiis adversarios suos a quibus paulo ante erat eiectus expellit ex civitate. Rex ab suis appellatur. Dimittit quoque versus legationes; obtestatur ut in fide maneant. Celeriter sibi Senones, Parisios, Pictones, Cadurcos, Turonos, Aulercos, Lemovices, Andos reliquosque omnes qui Oceanum attingunt adiungit: omnium consensu ad eum defertur imperium. Qua oblata potestate omnibus his civitatibus obsides imperat, certum numerum militum ad se celeriter adduci iubet, armorum quantum quaeque civitas domi quodque ante tempus efficiat constituit; in primis equitatui studet. Summae diligentiae summam imperi severitatem addit; magnitudine supplici dubitantes cogit. Nam maiore commisso delicto igni atque omnibus tormentis necat, leviore de causa auribus desectis aut singulis effossis oculis domum remittit, ut sint reliquis documento et magnitudine poenae perterreant alios.

His suppliciis celeriter coacto exercitu Lucterium Cadurcum, summae hominem audaciae, cum parte copiarum in Rutenos mittit; ipse in Bituriges proficiscitur. Eius adventu Bituriges ad Aeduos, quorum erant in fide, legatos mittunt subsidium

whose protection they were, to solicit aid in order that they might more easily resist the forces of the enemy. The Aedui, by the advice of the lieutenants whom Caesar had left with the army, send supplies of horse and foot to succor the Bituriges. When they came to the river Loire, which separates the Bituriges from the Aedui, they delayed a few days there, and, not daring to pass the river, return home, and send back word to the lieutenants that they had returned through fear of the treachery of the Bituriges, who, they ascertained, had formed this design, that if the Aedui should cross the river, the Bituriges on the one side, and the Arverni on the other, should surround them. Whether they did this for the reason which they alleged to the lieutenants, or influenced by treachery, we think that we ought not to state as certain, because we have no proof. On their departure, the Bituriges immediately unite themselves to the Arverni.

7:6 These affairs being announced to Caesar in Italy, at the time when he understood that matters in the city had been reduced to a more tranquil state by the energy of Cneius Pompey, he set out for Transalpine Gaul. After he had arrived there, he was greatly at a loss to know by what means he could reach his army. For if he should summon the legions into the province, he was aware that on their march they would have to fight in his absence; he foresaw too that if he himself should endeavor to reach the army, he would act injudiciously, in trusting his safety even to those who seemed to be tranquilized.

7:7 In the mean time Lucterius the Cadurcan, having been sent into the country of the Ruteni, gains over that state to the Arverni. Having advanced into the country of the Nitiobriges, and Gabali, he receives hostages from both nations, and, assembling a numerous force, marches to make a descent on the province in the direction of Narbo. Caesar, when this circumstance was announced to him, thought that the march to Narbo ought to take the precedence of all his other plans. When he arrived there, he encourages the timid and stations garrisons among the Ruteni, in the province of the Volcae Arecomici, and the country around Narbo which was in the vicinity of the enemy; he orders a portion of the forces from the province, and the recruits which he had brought from Italy, to rendezvous among the Helvii who border on the territories of the Arverni.

7:8 These matters being arranged, and Lucterius now checked and forced to retreat, because he thought it dangerous to enter the line of Roman garrisons, Caesar marches into the country of the Helvii; although mount Cevennes, which separates the Arverni from the Helvii, blocked up the way with very deep snow, as it was the severest season of the year; yet having cleared

rogatum, quo facilius hostium copias sustinere possint. Aedui de consilio legatorum, quos Caesar ad exercitum reliquerat, copias equitatus peditatusque subsidio Biturigibus mittunt. Qui cum ad flumen Ligerim venissent, quod Bituriges ab Aeduis dividit, paucos dies ibi morati neque flumen transire ausi domum revertuntur legatisque nostris renuntiant se Biturigum perfidiam veritos revertisse, quibus id consili fuisse cognoverint, ut, si flumen transissent, una ex parte ipsi, altera Arverni se circumsisterent. Id eane de causa, quam legatis pronuntiarunt, an perfidia adducti fecerint, quod nihil nobis constat, non videtur pro certo esse proponendum. Bituriges eorum discessu statim cum Arvernis iunguntur.

His rebus in Italiam Caesari nuntiatis, cum iam ille urbanas res virtute Cn. Pompei commodiorem in statum pervenisse intellegeret, in Transalpinam Galliam profectus est. Eo cum venisset, magna difficultate adficiebatur, qua ratione ad exercitum pervenire posset. Nam si legiones in provinciam arcesseret, se absente in itinere proelio dimicaturas intellegebat; si ipse ad exercitum contenderet, ne eis quidem eo tempore qui quieti viderentur suam salutem recte committi videbat.

Interim Lucterius Cadurcus in Rutenos missus eam civitatem Arvernis conciliat. Progressus in Nitiobriges et Gabalos ab utrisque obsides accipit et magna coacta manu in provinciam Narbonem versus eruptionem facere contendit. Qua re nuntiata Caesar omnibus consiliis antevertendum existimavit, ut Narbonem proficisceretur. Eo cum venisset, timentes confirmat, praesidia in Rutenis provincialibus, Volcis Arecomicis, Tolosatibus circumque Narbonem, quae loca hostibus erant finitima, constituit; partem copiarum ex provincia supplementumque, quod ex Italia adduxerat, in Helvios, qui fines Arvernorum contingunt, convenire iubet.

His rebus comparatis, represso iam Lucterio et remoto, quod intrare intra praesidia periculosum putabat, in Helvios proficiscitur. Etsi mons Cevenna, qui Arvernos ab Helviis discludit, durissimo tempore anni altissima nive iter impediebat, tamen discussa nive sex in altitudinem pedum atque ita viis patefactis

away the snow to the depth of six feet, and having opened the roads, he reaches the territories of the Arverni, with infinite labor to his soldiers. This people being surprised, because they considered themselves defended by the Cevennes as by a wall, and the paths at this season of the year had never before been passable even to individuals, he orders the cavalry to extend themselves as far as they could, and strike as great a panic as possible into the enemy. These proceedings are speedily announced to Vercingetorix by rumor and his messengers. Around him all the Arverni crowd in alarm, and solemnly entreat him to protect their property, and not to suffer them to be plundered by the enemy, especially as he saw that all the war was transferred into their country. Being prevailed upon by their entreaties he moves his camp from the country of the Bituriges in the direction of the Arverni.

7:9 Caesar, having delayed two days in that place, because he had anticipated that, in the natural course of events, such would be the conduct of Vercingetorix, leaves the army under pretense of raising recruits and cavalry: he places Brutus, a young man, in command of these forces; he gives him instructions that the cavalry should range as extensively as possible in all directions; that he would exert himself not to be absent from the camp longer than three days. Having arranged these matters, he marches to Vienna by as long journeys as he can, when his own soldiers did not expect him. Finding there a fresh body of cavalry, which he had sent on to that place several days before, marching incessantly night and day, he advanced rapidly through the territory of the Aedui into that of the Lingones, in which two legions were wintering, that, if any plan affecting his own safety should have been organized by the Aedui, he might defeat it by the rapidity of his movements. When he arrived there, he sends information to the rest of the legions, and gathers all his army into one place before intelligence of his arrival could be announced to the Arverni. Vercingetorix, on hearing this circumstance, leads back his army into the country of the Bituriges; and after marching from it to Gergovia, a town of the Boii, whom Caesar had settled there after defeating them in the Helvetian war, and had rendered tributary to the Aedui, he determined to attack it.

7:10 This action caused great perplexity to Caesar in the selection of his plans; [he feared] lest, if he should confine his legions in one place for the remaining portion of the winter, all Gaul should revolt when the tributaries of the Aedui were subdued, because it would appear that there was in him no protection for his friends; but if he should draw them too soon out of their winter quarters, he might be distressed by the want of provisions, in consequence of the difficulty of conveyance. It

summo militum sudore ad fines Arvernorum pervenit. Quibus oppressis inopinantibus, quod se Cevenna ut muro munitos existimabant, ac ne singulari quidem umquam homini eo tempore anni semitae patuerant, equitibus imperat, ut quam latissime possint vagentur et quam maximum hostibus terrorem inferant. Celeriter haec fama ac nuntiis ad Vercingetorigem perferuntur; quem perterriti omnes Arverni circumsistunt atque obsecrant, ut suis fortunis consulat, neve ab hostibus diripiautur, praesertim cum videat omne ad se bellum translatum. Quorum ille precibus per motus castra ex Biturigibus movet in Arveruos versus.

At Caesar biduum in his locis moratus, quod haec de Vercingetorige usu ventura opinione praeceperat, per causam supplementi equitatusque cogendi ab exercitu discedit; Brutum adulescentem his copiis praeficit; hunc monet, ut in omnes partes equites quam latissime pervagentur: daturum se operam, ne longius triduo ab castris absit. His constitutis rebus suis inopinantibus quam maximis potest itineribus Viennam pervenit. Ibi nactus recentem equitatum, quem multis ante diebus eo praemiserat, neque diurno neque nocturno itinere intermisso per fines Aeduorum in Lingones contendit, ubi duae legiones hiemabant, ut, si quid etiam de sua salute ab Aeduis iniretur consili, celeritate praecurreret. Eo cum pervenisset, ad reliquas legiones mittit priusque omnes in unum locum cogit quam de eius adventu Arvernis nuntiari posset. Hac re cognita Vercingetorix rursus in Bituriges exercitum reducit atque inde profectus Gorgobinam, Boiorum oppidum, quos ibi Helvetico proelio victos Caesar collocaverat Aeduisque attribuerat, oppugnare instituit.

Magnam haec res Caesari difficultatem ad consilium capiendum adferebat, si reliquam partem hiemis uno loco legiones contineret, ne stipendiariis Aeduorum expugnatis cuncta Gallia deficeret, quod nullum amicis in eo praesidium videretur positum esse; si maturius ex hibernis educeret, ne ab re frumentaria duris subvectionibus laboraret. Praestare visum est tamen omnis difficultates perpeti, quam tanta

seemed better, however, to endure every hardship than to alienate the affections of all his allies, by submitting to such an insult. Having, therefore, impressed on the Aedui the necessity of supplying him with provisions, he sends forward messengers to the Boii to inform them of his arrival, and encourage them to remain firm in their allegiance, and resist the attack of the enemy with great resolution. Having left two legions and the luggage of the entire army at Agendicum, he marches to the Boii.

7:11 On the second day, when he came to Vellaunodunum, a town of the Senones, he determined to attack it, in order that he might not leave an enemy in his rear, and might the more easily procure supplies of provisions, and draw a line of circumvallation around it in two days: on the third day, embassadors being sent from the town to treat of a capitulation, he orders their arms to be brought together, their cattle to be brought forth, and six hundred hostages to be given. He leaves Caius Trebonius his lieutenant, to complete these arrangements; he himself sets out with the intention of marching as soon as possible, to Genabum, a town of the Carnutes, who having then for the first time received information of the siege of Vellaunodunum, as they thought that it would be protracted to a longer time, were preparing a garrison to send to Genabum for the defense of that town. Caesar arrived here in two days; after pitching his camp before the town, being prevented by the time of the day, he defers the attack to the next day, and orders his soldiers to prepare whatever was necessary for that enterprise; and as a bridge over the Loire connected the town of Genabum with the opposite bank, fearing lest the inhabitants should escape by night from the town, he orders two legions to keep watch under arms. The people of Genabum came forth silently from the city before midnight, and began to cross the river. When this circumstance was announced by scouts, Caesar, having set fire to the gates, sends in the legions which he had ordered to be ready, and obtains possession of the town so completely, that very few of the whole number of the enemy escaped being taken alive, because the narrowness of the bridge and the roads prevented the multitude from escaping. He pillages and burns the town, gives the booty to the soldiers, then leads his army over the Loire, and marches into the territories of the Bituriges.

7:12 Vercingetorix, when he ascertained the arrival of Caesar, desisted from the siege [of Gergovia], and marched to meet Caesar. The latter had commenced to besiege Noviodunum; and when embassadors came from this town to beg that he would pardon them and spare their lives, in order that he might execute the rest of his designs with the rapidity by which he had accomplished most of them, he orders their arms to be

contumelia accepta omnium suorum voluntates alienare. Itaque cohortatus Aeduos de supportando commeatu praemittit ad Boios qui de suo adventu doceant hortenturque ut in fide maneant atque hostium impetum magno animo sustineant. Duabus Agedinci legionibus atque impedimentis totius exercitus relictis ad Boios proficiscitur.

Altero die cum ad oppidum Senonum Vellaunodunum venisset, ne quem post se hostem relinqueret, quo expeditiore re frumentaria uteretur, oppugnare instituit idque biduo circumvallavit; tertio die missis ex oppido legatis de deditione arma conferri, iumenta produci, sescentos obsides dari iubet. Ea qui conficeret, a. Trebonium legatum relinquit. Ipse, ut quam primum iter faceret, Cenabum Carnutum proficiscitur; qui tum primum allato nuntio de oppugnatione Vellaunoduni, cum longius eam rem ductum iri existimarent, praesidium Cenabi tuendi causa, quod eo mitterent, comparabant. Huc biduo pervenit. Castris ante oppidum positis diei tempore exclusus in posterum oppugnationem differt quaeque ad eam rem usui sint militibus imperat et, quod oppidum Cenabum pons fluminis Ligeris contingebat, veritus ne noctu ex oppido profugerent, duas legiones in armis excubare iubet. Cenabenses paulo ante mediam noctem silentio ex oppido egressi flumen transire coeperunt. Qua re per exploratores nuntiata Caesar legiones quas expeditas esse iusserat portis incensis intromittit atque oppido potitur, perpaucis ex hostium numero desideratis quin cuncti caperentur, quod pontis atque itinerum angustiae multitudinis fugam intercluserant. Oppidum diripit atque incendit, praedam militibus donat, exercitum Ligerem traducit atque in Biturigum fines pervenit.

Vercingetorix, ubi de Caesaris adventu cognovit, oppuguatione destitit atque obviam Caesari proficiscitur. Ille oppidum Biturigum positum in via Noviodunum oppugnare instituerat. Quo ex oppido cum legati ad eum venissent oratum ut sibi ignosceret suaeque vitae consuleret, ut celeritate reliquas res conficeret, qua pleraque erat

collected, their horses to be brought forth, and hostages to be given. A part of the hostages being now delivered up, when the rest of the terms were being performed, a few centurions and soldiers being sent into the town to collect the arms and horses, the enemy's cavalry which had outstripped the main body of Vercingetorix's army, was seen at a distance; as soon as the townsmen beheld them, and entertained hopes of assistance, raising a shout, they began to take up arms, shut the gates, and line the walls. When the centurions in the town understood from the signal-making of the Gauls that they were forming some new design, they drew their swords and seized the gates, and recovered all their men safe.

7:13 Caesar orders the horse to be drawn out of the camp, and commences a cavalry action. His men being now distressed, Caesar sends to their aid about four hundred German horse, which he had determined, at the beginning, to keep with himself. The Gauls could not withstand their attack, but were put to flight, and retreated to their main body, after losing a great number of men. When they were routed, the townsmen, again intimidated, arrested those persons by whose exertions they thought that the mob had been roused, and brought them to Caesar, and surrendered themselves to him. When these affairs were accomplished, Caesar marched to the Avaricum, which was the largest and best fortified town in the territories of the Bituriges, and situated in a most fertile tract of country; because he confidently expected that on taking that town, he would reduce beneath his dominion the state of the Bituriges.

7:14 Vercingetorix, after sustaining such a series of losses at Vellaunodunum, Genabum, and Noviodunum, summons his men to a council. He impresses on them "that the war must be prosecuted on a very different system from that which had been previously adopted; but they should by all means aim at this object, that the Romans should be prevented from foraging and procuring provisions; that this was easy, because they themselves were well supplied with cavalry, and were likewise assisted by the season of the year; that forage could not be cut; that the enemy must necessarily disperse, and look for it in the houses, that all these might be daily destroyed by the horse. Besides that the interests of private property must be neglected for the sake of the general safety; that the villages and houses ought to be fired, over such an extent of country in every direction from Boia, as the Romans appeared capable of scouring in their search for forage. That an abundance of these necessaries could be supplied to them, because they would be assisted by the resources of those in whose territories the war would be waged: that the Romans either would not bear the

consecutus, arma conferri, equos produci, obsides dari iubet. Parte iam obsidum tradita, cum reliqua administrarentur, centurionibus et paucis militibus intromissis, qui arma iumentaque conquirerent, equitatus hostium procul visus est, qui agmen Vercingetorigis antecesserat. Quem simul atque oppidani conspexerunt atque in spem auxili venerunt, clamore sublato arma capere, portas claudere, murum complere coeperunt. Centuriones in oppido, cum ex significatione Gallorum novi aliquid ab eis iniri consili intellexissent, gladiis destrictis portas occupaverunt suosque omnes incolumes receperunt.

Caesar ex castris equitatum educi iubet, proelium equestre committit: laborantibus iam suis Germanos equites circiter CCCC summittit, quos ab initio habere secum instituerat. Eorum impetum Galli sustinere non potuerunt atque in fugam coniecti multis amissis se ad agmen receperunt. Quibus profligatis rursus oppidani perterriti comprehensos eos, quorum opera plebem concitatam existimabant, ad Caesarem perduxerunt seseque ei dediderunt. Quibus rebus confectis, Caesar ad oppidum Avaricum, quod erat maximum munitissimumque in finibus Biturigum atque agri fertilissima regione, profectus est, quod eo oppido recepto civitatem Biturigum se in potestatem redacturum confidebat.

Vercingetorix tot continuis incommodis Vellaunoduni, Cenabi, Novioduni acceptis suos ad concilium convocat. Docet longe alia ratione esse bellum gerendum atque antea gestum sit. Omnibus modis huic rei studendum, ut pabulatione et commeatu Romani prohibeantur. Id esse facile, quod equitatu ipsi abundent et quod anni tempore subleventur. Pabulum secari non posse; necessario dispersos hostes ex aedificiis petere: hos omnes cotidie ab equitibus deligi posse. Praeterea salutis causa rei familiaris commoda neglegenda: vicos atque aedificia incendi oportere hoc spatio ab via quoque versus, quo pabulandi causa adire posse videantur. Harum ipsis rerum copiam suppetere, quod, quorum in finibus bellum geratur, eorum opibus subleventur: Romanos aut inopiam non laturos aut magno periculo longius ab castris processuros; neque interesse, ipsosne interficiant, impedimentisne exuant, quibus amissis bellum geri non possit.

privation, or else would advance to any distance from the camp with considerable danger; and that it made no difference whether they slew them or stripped them of their baggage, since, if it was lost, they could not carry on the war. Besides that, the towns ought to be burned which were not secured against every danger by their fortifications or natural advantages; that there should not be places of retreat for their own countrymen for declining military service, nor be exposed to the Romans as inducements to carry off abundance of provisions and plunder. If these sacrifices should appear heavy or galling, that they ought to consider it much more distressing that their wives and children should be dragged off to slavery, and themselves slain; the evils which must necessarily befall the conquered.

7:15 This opinion having been approved of by unanimous consent, more than twenty towns of the Bituriges are burned in one day. Conflagrations are beheld in every quarter; and although all bore this with great regret, yet they laid before themselves this consolation, that, as the victory was certain, they could quickly recover their losses. There is a debate concerning Avaricum in the general council, whether they should decide, that it should be burned or defended. The Bituriges threw themselves at the feet of all the Gauls, and entreat that they should not be compelled to set fire with their own hands to the fairest city of almost the whole of Gaul, which was both a protection and ornament to the state; they say that "they could easily defend it, owing to the nature of the ground, for, being inclosed almost on every side by a river and a marsh, it had only one entrance, and that very narrow." Permission being granted to them at their earnest request, Vercingetorix at first dissuades them from it, but afterward concedes the point, owing to their entreaties and the compassion of the soldiers. A proper garrison is selected for the town.

7:16 Vercingetorix follows closely upon Caesar by shorter marches, and selects for his camp a place defended by woods and marshes, at the distance of fifteen miles from Avaricum. There he received intelligence by trusty scouts, every hour in the day, of what was going on at Avaricum, and ordered whatever he wished to be done; he closely watched all our expeditions for corn and forage, and whenever they were compelled to go to a greater distance, he attacked them when dispersed, and inflicted severe loss upon them; although the evil was remedied by our men, as far as precautions could be taken, by going forth at irregular times' and by different ways.

7:17 Caesar pitching his camp at that side of the town which

Praeterea oppida incendi oportere, quae non munitione et loci natura ab omni sint periculo tuta, neu suis sint ad detractandam militiam receptacula neu Romanis proposita ad copiam commeatus praedamque tollendam. Haec si gravia aut acerba videautr, multo illa gravius aestimare, liberos, coniuges in servitutem abstrahi, ipsos interfici; quae sit necesse accidere victis.

Omnium consensu hac sententia probata uno die amplius XX urbes Biturigum iucenduntur. Hoc idem fit in reliquis civitatibus: in omnibus partibus incendia conspiciuntur; quae etsi magno cum dolore omnes ferebant, tamen hoc sibi solati proponebant, quod se prope explorata victoria celeriter amissa reciperaturos confidebant. Deliberatur de Avarico in communi concilio, incendi placeret an defendi. Procumbunt omnibus Gallis ad pedes Bituriges, ne pulcherrimam prope totius Galliae urbem, quae praesidio et ornamento sit civitati, suis manibus succendere cogerentur: facile se loci natura defensuros dicunt, quod prope ex omnibus partibus flumine et palude circumdata unum habeat et perangustum aditum. Datur petentibus venia dissuadente primo Vercingetorige, post concedente et precibus ipsorum et misericordia vulgi. Defensores oppido idonei deliguntur.

Vercingetorix minoribus Caesarem itineribus subsequitur et locum castris deligit paludibus silvisque munitum ab Avarico longe milia passuum XVI. Ibi per certos exploratores in singula diei tempora quae ad Avaricum agerentur cognoscebat et quid fieri vellet imperabat. Omnes nostras pabulationes frumentationesque observabat dispersosque, cum longius necessario procederent, adoriebatur magnoque incommodo adficiebat, etsi, quantum ratione provideri poterat, ab nostris occurrebatur, ut incertis temporibus diversisque itineribus iretur.

Castris ad eam partem oppidi positis Caesar, quae

was not defended by the river and marsh, and had a very narrow approach, as we have mentioned, began to raise the vineae and erect two towers: for the nature of the place prevented him from drawing a line of circumvallation. He never ceased to importune the Boii and Aedui for supplies of corn; of whom the one [the Aedui], because they were acting with no zeal, did not aid him much; the others [the Boii], as their resources were not great, quickly consumed what they had. Although the army was distressed by the greatest want of corn, through the poverty of the Boii, the apathy of the Aedui, and the burning of the houses, to such a degree, that for several days the soldiers were without corn, and satisfied their extreme hunger with cattle driven from the remote villages; yet no language was heard from them unworthy of the majesty of the Roman people and their former victories. Moreover, when Caesar addressed the legions, one by one, when at work, and said that he would raise the siege, if they felt the scarcity too severely, they unanimously begged him "not to do so; that they had served for several years under his command in such a manner that they never submitted to insult, and never abandoned an enterprise without accomplishing it; that they should consider it a disgrace if they abandoned the siege after commencing it; that it was better to endure every hardship than to not avenge the names of the Roman citizens who perished at Genabum by the perfidy of the Gauls." They intrusted the same declarations to the centurions and military tribunes, that through them they might be communicated to Caesar.

7:18 When the towers had now approached the walls, Caesar ascertained from the captives that Vercingetorix after destroying the forage, had pitched his camp nearer Avaricum, and that he himself with the cavalry and light-armed infantry, who generally fought among the horse, had gone to lay an ambuscade in that quarter, to which he thought that our troops would come the next day to forage. On learning these facts, he set out from the camp secretly at midnight, and reached the camp of the enemy early in the morning. They having quickly learned the arrival of Caesar by scouts, hid their cars and baggage in the thickest parts of the woods, and drew up all their forces in a lofty and open space: which circumstance being announced, Caesar immediately ordered the baggage to be piled, and the arms to be got ready.

7:19 There was a hill of a gentle ascent from the bottom; a dangerous and impassable marsh, not more than fifty feet broad, begirt it on almost every side. The Gauls, having broken down the bridges, posted themselves on this hill, in confidence of their position, and being drawn up in tribes according to their respective states, held all the fords and passages of that marsh

intermissa [a] flumine et a paludibus aditum, ut supra diximus, angustum habebat, aggerem apparare, vineas agere, turres duas constituere coepit: nam circumvallare loci natura prohibebat. De re frumentaria Boios atque Aeduos adhortari non destitit; quorum alteri, quod nullo studio agebant, non multum adiuvabant, alteri non magnis facultatibus, quod civitas erat exigua et infirma, celeriter quod habuerunt consumpserunt. Summa difficultate rei frumentariae adfecto exercitu tenuitate Boiorum, indiligentia Aeduorum, incendiis aedificiorum, usque eo ut complures dies frumento milites caruerint et pecore ex longinquioribus vicis adacto extremam famem sustentarent, nulla tamen vox est ab eis audita populi Romani maiestate et superioribus victoriis indigna. Quin etiam Caesar cum in opere singulas legiones appellaret et, si acerbius inopiam ferrent, se dimissurum oppugnationem diceret, universi ab eo, ne id faceret, petebant: sic se complures anuos illo imperante meruisse, ut nullam ignominiam acciperent, nusquam infecta re discederent: hoc se ignominiae laturos loco, si inceptam oppugnationem reliquissent: praestare omnes perferre acerbitates, quam non civibus Romanis, qui Cenabi perfidia Gallorum interissent, parentarent. Haec eadem centurionibus tribunisque militum mandabant, ut per eos ad Caesarem deferrentur.

Cum iam muro turres appropinquassent, ex captivis Caesar cognovit Vercingetorigem consumpto pabulo castra movisse propius Avaricum atque ipsum cum equitatu expeditisque, qui inter equites proeliari consuessent, insidiarum causa eo profectum, quo nostros postero die pabulatum venturos arbitraretur. Quibus rebus cognitis media nocte silentio profectus ad hostium castra mane pervenit. Illi celeriter per exploratores adventu Caesaris cognito carros impedimentaque sua in artiores silvas abdiderunt, copias omnes in loco edito atque aperto instruxerunt. Qua re nuntiata Caesar celeriter sarcinas conferri, arma expediri iussit.

Collis erat leniter ab infimo acclivis. Hunc ex omnibus fere partibus palus difficilis atque impedita cingebat non latior pedibus quinquaginta. Hoc se colle interruptis pontibus Galli fiducia loci continebant generatimque distributi in civitates omnia vada ac saltus eius paludis obtinebant sic animo parati, ut, si

with trusty guards, thus determined that if the Romans should attempt to force the marsh, they would overpower them from the higher ground while sticking in it, so that whoever saw the nearness of the position, would imagine that the two armies were prepared to fight on almost equal terms; but whoever should view accurately the disadvantage of position, would discover that they were showing off an empty affectation of courage. Caesar clearly points out to his soldiers, who were indignant that the enemy could bear the sight of them at the distance of so short a space, and were earnestly demanding the signal for action, "with how great loss and the death of how many gallant men the victory would necessarily be purchased: and when he saw them so determined to decline no danger for his renown, that he ought to be considered guilty of the utmost injustice if he did not hold their life dearer than his personal safety." Having thus consoled his soldiers, he leads them back on the same day to the camp, and determined to prepare the other things which were necessary for the siege of the town.

7:20 Vercingetorix, when he had returned to his men, was accused of treason, in that he had moved his camp nearer the Romans, in that he had gone away with all the cavalry, in that he had left so great forces without a commander, in that, on his departure, the Romans had come at such a favorable season, and with such dispatch; that all these circumstances could not have happened accidentally or without design; that he preferred holding the sovereignty of Gaul by the grant of Caesar to acquiring it by their favor. Being accused in such a manner, he made the following reply to these charges:--"That his moving his camp had been caused by want of forage, and had been done even by their advice; that his approaching near the Romans had been a measure dictated by the favorable nature of the ground, which would defend him by its natural strength; that the service of the cavalry could not have been requisite in marshy ground, and was useful in that place to which they had gone; that he, on his departure, had given the supreme command to no one intentionally, lest he should be induced by the eagerness of the multitude to hazard an engagement, to which he perceived that all were inclined, owing to their want of energy, because they were unable to endure fatigue any longer. That, if the Romans in the mean time came up by chance, they [the Gauls] should feel grateful to fortune; if invited by the information of some one they should feel grateful to him, because they were enabled to see distinctly from the higher ground the smallness of the number of their enemy, and despise the courage of those who, not daring to fight, retreated disgracefully into their camp. That he desired no power from Caesar by treachery, since he could have it by victory, which was now assured to himself and to all the Gauls;

eam paludem Romani perrumpere conarentur, haesitantes premerent ex loco superiore; ut qui propinquitatem loci videret paratos prope aequo Marte ad dimicandum existimaret, qui iniqui tatem condicionis perspiceret inani simulatione sese ostentare cognosceret. Indignantes milites Gaesar, quod conspectum suum hostes perferre possent tantulo spatio interiecto, et signum proeli ecentes edocet, quanto detrimento et quot virorum tortium morte necesse sit constare victoriam; quos cum sic animo paratos videat, ut nullum pro sua laude periculum recusent, summae se iniquitatis condemnari debere, nisi eorum vitam sua salute habeat cariorem. Sic milites consolatus eodem die reducit in castra reliquaque quae ad oppugnationem pertinebant oppidi administrare instituit.

Vercingetorix, cum ad suos redisset, proditionis insimulatus, quod castra propius Romanos movisset, quod cum omni equitatu discessisset, quod sine imperio tantas copias reliquisset, quod eius discessu Romani tanta opportunitate et celeritate venissent: non haec omnia fortuito aut sine consilio accidere potuisse; regnum illum Galliae malle Caesaris concessu quam ipsorum habere beneficio--tali modo accusatus ad haec respondit: Quod castra movisset, factum inopia pabuli etiam ipsis hortantibus; quod propius Romanos accessisset, persuasum loci opportunitate, qui se ipsum munitione defenderet: equitum vero operam neque in loco palustri desiderari debuisse et illic fuisse utilem, quo sint profecti. Summam imperi se consulto nulli discedentem tradidisse, ne is multitudinis studio ad dimicandum impelleretur; cui rei propter animi mollitiem studere omnes videret, quod diutius laborem ferre non possent. Romani si casu intervenerint, fortunae, si alicuius indicio vocati, huic habendam gratiam, quod et paucitatem eorum ex loco superiore cognoscere et virtutem despicere potuerint, qui dimicare non ausi turpiter se in castra receperint. Imperium se ab Caesare per proditionem nullum desiderare, quod habere victoria posset, quae iam esset sibi atque omnibus Gallis explorata: quin etiam ipsis remittere, si sibi magis honorem tribuere, quam ab se salutem accipere videantur. "Haec ut intellegatis," inquit, "a me sincere pronuntiari, audite

nay, that he would even give them back the command, if they thought that they conferred honor on him, rather than received safety from him. That you may be assured," said he, "that I speak these words with truth; -listen to these Roman soldiers!" He produces some camp-followers whom he had surprised on a foraging expedition some days before, and had tortured by famine and confinement. They being previously instructed in what answers they should make when examined, say, "That they were legionary soldiers, that, urged by famine and want, they had recently gone forth from the camp, [to see] if they could find any corn or cattle in the fields; that the whole army was distressed by a similar scarcity, nor had any one now sufficient strength, nor could bear the labor of the work; and therefore that the general was determined, if he made no progress in the siege, to draw off his army in three days." "These benefits," says Vercingetorix, "you receive from me, whom you accuse of treason-me, by whose exertions you see so powerful and victorious an army almost destroyed by famine, without shedding one drop of your blood; and I have taken precautions that no state shall admit within its territories this army in its ignominious flight from this place."

7:21 The whole multitude raise a shout and clash their arms, according to their custom, as they usually do in the case of him of whose speech they approve; [they exclaim] that Vercingetorix was a consummate general, and that they had no doubt of his honor; that the war could not be conducted with greater prudence. They determine that ten thousand men should be picked out of the entire army and sent into the town, and decide that the general safety should not be intrusted to the Bituriges alone, because they were aware that the glory of the victory must rest with the Bituriges, if they made good the defense of the town.

7:22 To the extraordinary valor of our soldiers, devices of every sort were opposed by the Gauls; since they are a nation of consummate ingenuity, and most skillful in imitating and making those things which are imparted by any one; for they turned aside the hooks with nooses, and when they had caught hold of them firmly, drew them on by means of engines, and undermined the mound the more skillfully on this account, because there are in their territories extensive iron mines, and consequently every description of mining operations is known and practiced by them. They had furnished, more over, the whole wall on every side with turrets, and had covered them with skins. Besides, in their frequent sallies by day and night, they attempted either to set fire to the mound, or attack our soldiers when engaged in the works; and, moreover, by splicing the upright timbers of their own towers, they equaled the height of

Romanos milites." Producit servos, quos in pabulatione paucis ante diebus exceperat et fame vinculisque excruciaverat. Hi iam ante edocti quae interrogati pronuntiarent, milites se esse legionarios dicunt; fame et inopia adductos clam ex castris exisse, si quid frumenti aut pecoris in agris reperire possent: simili omnem exercitum inopia premi, nec iam vires sufficere cuiusquam nec ferre operis laborem posse: itaque statuisse imperatorem, si nihil in oppugnatione oppidi profecissent, triduo exercitum deducere. "Haec," inquit, "a me," Vercingetorix, "beneficia habetis, quem proditionis insimulatis; cuius opera sine vestro sanguine tantum exercitum victorem fame consumptum videtis; quem turpiter se ex fuga recipientem ne qua civitas suis finibus recipiat a me provisum est."

Conclamat omnis multitudo et suo more armis concrepat, quod facere in eo consuerunt cuius orationem approbant: summum esse Vercingetorigem ducem, nec de eius fide dubitandum, nec maiore ratione bellum administrari posse. Statuunt, ut X milia hominum delecta ex omnibus copiis in oppidum mittantur, nec solis Biturigibus communem salutem committendam censent, quod paene in eo, si id oppidum retinuissent, summam victoriae constare intellegebant.

Singulari militum nostrorum virtuti consilia cuius que modi Gallorum occurrebant, ut est summae genus sollertiae atque ad omnia imitanda et efficienda, quae ab quoque traduntur, aptissimum. Nam et laqueis falces avertebant, quas, cum destinaverant, tormentis introrsus reducebant, et aggerem cuniculis subtrahebant, eo scientius quod apud eos magnae sunt ferrariae atque omne genus cuniculorum notum atque usitatum est. Totum autem murum ex omni parte turribus contabulaverant atque has coriis intexerant. Tum crebris diurnis nocturnisque eruptionibus aut aggeri ignem inferebant aut milites occupatos in opere adoriebantur, et nostrarum turrium altitudinem, quantum has cotidianus agger expresserat, commissis suarum turrium malis

ours, as fast as the mound had daily raised them, and countermined our mines, and impeded the working of them by stakes bent and sharpened at the ends, and boiling pitch and stones of very great weight, and prevented them from approaching the walls.

7:23 But this is usually the form of all the Gallic walls. Straight beams, connected lengthwise and two feet distant from each other at equal intervals, are placed together on the ground; these are mortised on the inside, and covered with plenty of earth. But the intervals which we have mentioned, are closed up in front by large stones. These being thus laid and cemented together, another row is added above, in such a manner, that the same interval may be observed, and that the beams may not touch one another, but equal spaces intervening, each row of beams is kept firmly in its place by a row of stones. In this manner the whole wall is consolidated, until the regular height of the wall be completed. This work, with respect to appearance and variety, is not unsightly, owing to the alternate rows of beams and stones, which preserve their order in right lines; and, besides, it possesses great advantages as regards utility and the defense of cities; for the stone protects it from fire, and the wood from the battering ram, since it [the wood] being mortised in the inside with rows of beams, generally forty feet each in length, can neither be broken through nor torn asunder.

7:24 The siege having been impeded by so many disadvantages, the soldiers, although they were retarded during the whole time by the mud, cold, and constant showers, yet by their incessant labor overcame all these obstacles, and in twenty-five days raised a mound three hundred and thirty feet broad and eighty feet high. When it almost touched the enemy's walls, and Caesar, according to his usual custom, kept watch at the work, and encouraged the soldiers not to discontinue the work for a moment: a little before the third watch they discovered that the mound was sinking, since the enemy had set it on fire by a mine; and at the same time a shout was raised along the entire wall, and a sally was made from two gates on each side of the turrets. Some at a distance were casting torches and dry wood from the wall on the mound, others were pouring on it pitch, and other materials, by which the flame might be excited, so that a plan could hardly be formed, as to where they should first run to the defense, or to what part aid should be brought. However, as two legions always kept guard before the camp by Caesar's orders, and several of them were at stated times at the work, measures were promptly taken, that some should oppose the sallying party, others draw back the towers and make a cut in the rampart; and moreover, that the whole army should hasten from the camp to extinguish the flames.

adaequabant, et apertos cuniculos praeusta et praeacuta materia et pice fervefacta et maximi ponderis saxis morabantur moenibusque appropinquare prohibebant.

Muri autem omnes Gallici hac fere forma sunt. Trabes derectae perpetuae in longitudinem paribus intervallis, distantes inter se binos pedes, in solo collocantur. Hae revinciuntur introrsus et multo aggere vestiuntur: ea autem, quae diximus, inter valla grandibus in fronte saxis effarciuntur. His collocatis et coagmentatis alius insuper ordo additur, ut idem illud intervallum servetur neque inter se contingant trabes, sed paribus intermissae spatiis singulae singulis saxis interiectis arte contineantur. Sic deinceps omne opus contexitur, dum iusta muri altitudo expleatur. Hoc cum in speciem varietatemque opus deforme non est alternis trabibus ac saxis, quae rectis lineis suos ordines servant, tum ad utilitatem et defensionem urbium summam habet opportunitatem, quod et ab incendio lapis et ab ariete materia defendit, quae perpetuis trabibus pedes quadragenos plerumque introrsus revincta neque perrumpi neque distrahi potest.

His tot rebus impedita oppugnatione milites, cum toto tempore frigore et assiduis imbribus tardarentur, tamen continenti labore omnia haec superaverunt et diebus XXV aggerem latum pedes CCCXXX, altum pedes LXXX exstruxerunt. Cum is murum hostium paene contingeret, et Caesar ad opus consuetudine excubaret milites que hortaretur, ne quod omnino tempus ab opere intermitteretur, paulo ante tertiam vigiliam est animadversum fumare aggerem, quem cuniculo hostes succenderant, eodemque tempore toto muro clamore sublato duabus portis ab utroque latere turrium eruptio fiebat, alii faces atque aridam materiem de muro in aggerem eminus iaciebant, picem reliquasque res, quibus ignis excitari potest, fundebant, ut quo primum curreretur aut cui rei ferretur auxilium vix ratio iniri posset. Tamen, quod instituto Caesaris semper duae legiones pro castris excubabant pluresque partitis temporibus erant in opere, celeriter factum est, ut alii eruptionibus resisterent, alii turres reducerent aggeremque inter scinderent, omnis vero ex castris multitudo ad restinguendum concurreret.

7:25 When the battle was going on in every direction, the rest of the night being now spent, and fresh hopes of victory always arose before the enemy: the more so on this account because they saw the coverings of our towers burnt away, and perceived, that we, being exposed, could not easily go to give assistance, and they themselves were always relieving the weary with fresh men, and considered that all the safety of Gaul rested on this crisis; there happened in my own view a circumstance which, having appeared to be worthy of record, we thought it ought not to be omitted. A certain Gaul before the gate of the town, who was casting into the fire opposite the turret balls of tallow and fire which were passed along to him, was pierced with a dart on the right side and fell dead. One of those next him stepped over him as he lay, and discharged the same office: when the second man was slain in the same manner by a wound from a crossbow, a third succeeded him, and a fourth succeeded the third: nor was this post left vacant by the besieged, until, the fire of the mound having been extinguished, and the enemy repulsed in every direction, an end was put to the fighting.

7:26 The Gauls having tried every expedient, as nothing had succeeded, adopted the design of fleeing from the town the next day, by the advice and order of Vercingetorix. They hoped that, by attempting it at the dead of night, they would effect it without any great loss of men, because the camp of Vercingetorix was not far distant from the town, and the extensive marsh which intervened, was likely to retard the Romans in the pursuit. And they were now preparing to execute this by night, when the matrons suddenly ran out-into the streets, and weeping cast themselves at the feet of their husbands, and requested of them, with every entreaty, that they should not abandon themselves and their common children to the enemy for punishment, because the weakness of their nature and physical powers prevented them from taking to flight. When they saw that they (as fear does not generally admit of mercy in extreme danger) persisted in their resolution, they began to shout aloud, and give intelligence of their flight to the Romans. The Gauls being intimidated by fear of this, lest the passes should be preoccupied by the Roman cavalry, desisted from their design.

7:27 The next day Caesar, the tower being advanced, and the works which he had determined to raise being arranged, a violent storm arising, thought this no bad time for executing his designs, because he observed the guards arranged on the walls a little too negligently, and therefore ordered his own men to engage in their work more remissly, and pointed out what he wished to be done. He drew up his soldiers in a secret position within the vineae, and exhorts them to reap, at least, the harvest of victory proportionate to their exertions. He proposed a reward

Cum in omnibus locis consumpta iam reliqua parte noctis pugnaretur, semperque hostibus spes victoriae redintegraretur, eo magis, quod deustos pluteos turrium videbant nec facile adire apertos ad auxiliandum animadvertebant, semperque ipsi recentes defessis succederent omnemque Galliae salutem in illo vestigio temporis positam arbitrarentur, accidit inspectantibus nobis quod dignum memoria visum praetereundum non existimavimus. Quidam ante portam oppidi Gallus per manus sebi ac picis traditas glebas in ignem e regione turris proiciebat: scorpione ab latere dextro traiectus exanimatusque concidit. Hunc ex proximis unus iacentem transgressus eodem illo munere fungebatur; eadem ratione ictu scorpionis exanimato alteri successit tertius et tertio quartus, nec prius ille est a propugnatoribus vacuus relictus locus quam restincto aggere atque omni ex parte summotis hostibus finis est pugnandi factus.

Omnia experti Galli, quod res nulla successerat, postero die consilium ceperunt ex oppido profugere hortante et iubente Vercingetorige. Id silentio noctis conati non magna iactura suorum sese effecturos sperabant, propterea quod neque longe ab oppido castra Vercingetorigis aberant, et palus, quae perpetua intercedebat, Romanos ad insequendum tardabat. Iamque hoc facere noctu apparabant, cum matres familiae repente in publicum procurrerunt flentesque proiectae ad pedes suorum omnibus precibus petierunt, ne se et communes liberos hostibus ad supplicium dederent, quos ad capiendam fugam naturae et virium infirmitas impediret. Vbi eos in sententia perstare viderunt, quod plerumque in summo periculo timor misericordiam non recipit, conclamare et significare de fuga Romanis coeperunt. Quo timore perterriti Galli, ne ab equitatu Romanorum viae praeoccuparentur, consilio destiterunt.

Postero die Caesar promota turri perfectisque operibus quae facere instituerat, magno coorto imbre non inutilem hanc ad capiendum consilium tempestatem arbitratus est, quod paulo incautius custodias in muro dispositas videbat, suosque languidius in opere versari iussit et quid fieri vellet ostendit. Legionibusque intra vineas in occulto expeditis, cohortatus ut aliquando pro tantis laboribus fructum victoriae perciperent, eis qui primi

for those who should first scale the walls, and gave the signal to the soldiers. They suddenly flew out from all quarters and quickly filled the walls.

7:28 The enemy being alarmed by the suddenness of the attack, were dislodged from the wall and towers, and drew up, in form of a wedge, in the market place and the open streets, with this intention that, if an attack should be made on any side, they should fight with their line drawn up to receive it. When they saw no one descending to the level ground, and the enemy extending themselves along the entire wall in every direction, fearing lest every hope of flight should be cut off, they cast away their arms, and sought, without stopping, the most remote parts of the town. A part was then slain by the infantry when they were crowding upon one another in the narrow passage of the gates; and a part having got without the gates, were cut to pieces by the cavalry: nor was there one who was anxious for the plunder. Thus, being excited by the massacre at Genabum and the fatigue of the siege, they spared neither those worn out with years, women, or children. Finally, out of all that number, which amounted to about forty thousand, scarcely eight hundred, who fled from the town when they heard the first alarm, reached Vercingetorix in safety: and he, the night being now far spent, received them in silence after their flight (fearing that any sedition should arise in the camp from their entrance in a body and the compassion of the soldiers), so that, having arranged his friends and the chiefs of the states at a distance on the road, he took precautions that they should be separated and conducted to their fellow countrymen, to whatever part of the camp had been assigned to each state from the beginning.

7:29 Vercingetorix having convened an assembly on the following day, consoled and encouraged his soldiers in the following words: "That they should not be too much depressed in spirit, nor alarmed at their loss; that the Romans did not conquer by valor nor in the field, but by a kind of art and skill in assault, with which they themselves were unacquainted; that whoever expected every event in the war to be favorable, erred; that it never was his opinion that Avaricum should be defended, of the truth of which statement he had themselves as witnesses, but that it was owing to the imprudence of the Bituriges, and the too ready compliance of the rest, that this loss was sustained; that, however, he would soon compensate it by superior advantages; for that he would, by his exertions, bring over those states which severed themselves from the rest of the Gauls, and would create a general unanimity throughout the whole of Gaul, the union of which not even the whole earth could withstand, and that he had it already almost effected; that in the mean time it was reasonable that he should prevail on them, for the sake of

murum ascendissent praemia proposuit militibusque signum dedit. Illi subito ex omnibus partibus evolaverunt murumque celeriter compleverunt.

Hostes re nova perterriti muro turribusque deiecti in foro ac locis patentioribus cuneatim constiterunt, hoc animo ut si qua ex parte obviam contra veniretur acie instructa depugnarent. Vbi neminem in aequum locum sese demittere, sed toto undique muro circumfundi viderunt, veriti ne omnino spes fugae tolleretur, abiectis armis ultimas oppidi partes continenti impetu petiverunt, parsque ibi, cum angusto exitu portarum se ipsi premerent, a militibus, pars iam egressa portis ab equitibus est interfecta; nec fuit quisquam, qui praedae studeret. Sic et Cenabi caede et labore operis incitati non aetate confectis, non mulieribus, non infantibus pepercerunt. Denique ex omni numero, qui fuit circiter milium XL, vix DCCC, qui primo clamore audito se ex oppido eiecerunt, incolumes ad Vercingetorigem pervenerunt. Quos ille multa iam nocte silentio ex fuga excepit, veritus ne qua in castris ex eorum concursu et misericordia vulgi seditio oreretur, ut procul in via dispositis familiaribus suis principibusque civitatum disparandos deducendosque ad suos curaret, quae cuique civitati pars castrorum ab initio obvenerat.

Postero die concilio convocato consolatus cohortatusque est ne se admodum animo demitterent, ne perturbarentur incommodo. Non virtute neque in acie vicisse Romanos, sed artificio quodam et scientia oppugnationis, cuius rei fuerint ipsi imperiti. Errare, si qui in bello omnes secundos rerum proventus exspectent. Sibi numquam placuisse Avaricum defendi, cuius rei testes ipsos haberet; sed factum imprudentia Biturigum et nimia obsequentia reliquorum uti hoc incommodum acciperetur. Id tamen se celeriter maioribus commodis sanaturum. Nam quae ab reliquis Gallis civitates dissentirent, has sua diligentia adiuncturum atque unum consilium totius Galliae effecturum, cuius consensui ne orbis quidem terrarum possit obsistere; idque se prope iam effectum habere. Interea aequum esse ab eis communis salutis causa impetrari ut castra munire instituerent, quo facilius

the general safety, to begin to fortify their camp, in order that they might the more easily sustain the sudden attacks of the enemy."

7:30 This speech was not disagreeable to the Gauls, principally, because he himself was not disheartened by receiving so severe a loss, and had not concealed himself, nor shunned the eyes of the people: and he was believed to possess greater foresight and sounder judgment than the rest, because, when the affair was undecided, he had at first been of opinion that Avaricum should be burnt, and afterward that it should be abandoned. Accordingly, as ill success weakens the authority of other generals, so, on the contrary, his dignity increased daily, although a loss was sustained: at the same time they began to entertain hopes, on his assertion, of uniting the rest of the states to themselves, and on this occasion, for the first time, the Gauls began to fortify their camps, and were so alarmed that although they were men unaccustomed to toil, yet they were of opinion that they ought to endure and suffer every thing which should be imposed upon them.

7:31 Nor did Vercingetorix use less efforts than he had promised, to gain over the other states, and [in consequence] endeavored to entice their leaders by gifts and promises. For this object he selected fitting emissaries, by whose subtle pleading or private friendship, each of the nobles could be most easily influenced. He takes care that those who fled to him on the storming of Avaricum should be provided with arms and clothes. At the same time that his diminished forces should be recruited, he levies a fixed quota of soldiers from each state, and defines the number and day before which he should wish them brought to the camp, and orders all the archers, of whom there was a very great number in Gaul, to be collected and sent to him. By these means, the troops which were lost at Avaricum are speedily replaced. In the mean time, Teutomarus, the son of Ollovicon, the king of the Nitiobriges, whose father had received the appellation of friend from our senate, came to him with a great number of his own horse and those whom he had hired from Aquitania.

7:32 Caesar, after delaying several days at Avaricum, and, finding there the greatest plenty of corn and other provisions, refreshed his army after their fatigue and privation. The winter being almost ended, when he was invited by the favorable season of the year to prosecute the war and march against the enemy, [and try] whether he could draw them from the marshes and woods, or else press them by a blockade; some noblemen of the Aedui came to him as embassadors to entreat "that in an extreme emergency he should succor their state; that their

repentinos hostium impetus sustinerent.

Fuit haec oratio non ingrata Gallis, et maxime, quod ipse animo non defecerat tanto accepto incommodo neque se in occultum abdiderat et conspectum multitudinis fugerat; plusque animo providere et praesentire existimabatur, quod re integra primo incendendum Avaricum, post deserendum censuerat. Itaque ut reliquorum imperatorum res adversae auctoritatem minuunt, sic huius ex contrario dignitas incommodo accepto in dies augebatur. Simul in spem veniebant eius adfirmatione de reliquis adiungendis civitatibus; primumque eo tempore Galli castra munire instituerunt et sic sunt animo confirmati, homines insueti laboris, ut omnia quae imperarentur sibi patienda existimarent.

Nec minus quam est pollicitus Vercingetorix animo laborabat ut reliquas civitates adiungeret, atque eas donis pollicitationibusque alliciebat. Huic rei idoneos homines deligebat, quorum quisque aut oratione subdola aut amicitia facillime capere posset. Qui Avarico expugnato refugerant, armandos vestiendosque curat; simul, ut deminutae copiae redintegrarentur, imperat certum numerum militum civitatibus, quem et quam ante diem in castra adduci velit, sagittariosque omnes, quorum erat permagnus numerus in Gallia, conquiri et ad se mitti iubet. His rebus celeriter id quod Avarici deperierat expletur. Interim Teutomatus, Olloviconis filius, rex Nitiobrigum, cuius pater ab senatu nostro amicus erat appellatus, cum magno equitum suorum numero et quos ex Aquitania conduxerat ad eum pervenit.

Caesar Avarici complures dies commoratus summamque ibi copiam frumenti et reliqui commeatus nactus exercitum ex labore atque inopia refecit. Iam prope hieme confecta cum ipso anni tempore ad gerendum bellum vocaretur et ad hostem proficisci constituisset, sive eum ex paludibus silvisque elicere sive obsidione premere posset, legati ad eum principes Aeduorum veniunt oratum ut maxime necessario tempore civitati subveniat:

affairs were in the utmost danger, because, whereas single magistrates had been usually appointed in ancient times and held the power of king for a single year, two persons now exercised this office, and each asserted that he was appointed according to their laws. That one of them was Convictolitanis, a powerful and illustrious youth; the other Cotus, sprung from a most ancient family, and personally a man of very great influence and extensive connections. His brother Valetiacus had borne the same office during the last year: that the whole state was up in arms; the senate divided, the people divided; that each of them had his own adherents; and that, if the animosity would be fomented any longer, the result would be that one part of the state would come to a collision with the other; that it rested with his activity and influence to prevent it."

7:33 Although Caesar considered it ruinous to leave the war and the enemy, yet, being well aware what great evils generally arise from internal dissensions, lest a state so powerful and so closely connected with the Roman people, which he himself had always fostered and honored in every respect, should have recourse to violence and arms, and that the party which had less confidence in its own power should summon aid from Vercingetorix, he determined to anticipate this movement; and because, by the laws of the Aedui, it was not permitted those who held the supreme authority to leave the country, he determined to go in person to the Aedui, lest he should appear to infringe upon their government and laws, and summoned all the senate, and those between whom the dispute was, to meet him at Decetia. When almost all the state had assembled there, and he was informed that one brother had been declared magistrate by the other, when only a few persons were privately summoned for the purpose, at a different time and place from what he ought, whereas the laws not only forbade two belonging to one family to be elected magistrates while each was alive, but even deterred them from being in the senate, he compelled Cotus to resign his office; he ordered Convictolitanis, who had been elected by the priests, according to the usage of the state, in the presence of the magistrates, to hold the supreme authority.

7:34 Having pronounced this decree between [the contending parties], he exhorted the Aedui to bury in oblivion their disputes and dissensions, and, laying aside all these things, devote themselves to the war, and expect from him, on the conquest of Gaul, those rewards which they should have earned, and send speedily to him all their cavalry and ten thousand infantry, which he might place in different garrisons to protect his convoys of provisions, and then divided his army into two parts: he gave Labienus four legions to lead into the country of the Senones

summo esse in periculo rem, quod, cum singuli magistratus antiquitus creari atque regiam potestatem annum obtinere consuessent, duo magistratum gerant et se uterque eorum legibus creatum esse dicat. Horum esse alterum Convictolitavem, florentem et illustrem adulescentem, alterum Cotum, antiquissima familia natum atque ipsum hominem summae potentiae et magnae cognationis, cuius frater Valetiacus proximo anno eundem magistratum gesserit. Civitatem esse omnem in armis; divisum senatum, divisum populum, suas cuiusque eorum clientelas. Quod si diutius alatur controversia, fore uti pars cum parte civitatis confligat. Id ne accidat, positum in eius diligentia atque auctoritate.

Caesar, etsi a bello atque hoste discedere detrimentosum esse existimabat, tamen non ignorans quanta ex dissensionibus incommoda oriri consuessent, ne tanta et tam coniuncta populo Romano civitas, quam ipse semper aluisset omnibusque rebus ornasset, ad vim atque arma descenderet, atque ea pars quae minus sibi confideret auxilia a Vercingetorige arcesseret, huic rei praevertendum existimavit et, quod legibus Aeduorum eis, qui summum magistra tum obtinerent, excedere ex finibus non liceret, ne quid de iure aut de legibus eorum deminuisse videretur, ipse in Aeduos proficisci statuit senatumque omnem et quos inter controversia esset ad se Decetiam evocavit. Cum prope omnis civitas eo convenisset, docereturque paucis clam convocatis alio loco, alio tempore atque oportuerit fratrem a fratre renuntiatum, cum leges duo ex una familia vivo utroque non solum magistratus creari vetarent, sed etiam in senatu esse prohiberent, Cotum imperium deponere coegit, Convictolitavem, qui per sacerdotes more civitatis intermissis magistratibus esset creatus, potestatem obtinere iussit.

Hoc decreto interposito cohortatus Aeduos, ut controversiarum ac dissensionis obliviscerentur atque omnibus omissis his rebus huic bello servirent eaque quae meruissent praemia ab se devicta Gallia exspectarent equitatumque omnem et peditum milia decem sibi celeriter mitterent, quae in praesidiis rei frumentariae causa disponeret, exercitum in duas partes divisit: quattuor legiones in Senones Parisiosque Labieno ducendas dedit, sex ipse in

134

and Parisii; and led in person six into the country of the Arverni, in the direction of the town of Gergovia, along the banks of the Allier. He gave part of the cavalry to Labienus and kept part to himself. Vercingetorix, on learning this circumstance, broke down all the bridges over the river and began to march on the other bank of the Allier.

7:35 When each army was in sight of the other, and was pitching their camp almost opposite that of the enemy, scouts being distributed in every quarter, lest the Romans should build a bridge and bring over their troops; it was to Caesar a matter attended with great difficulties, lest he should be hindered from passing the river during the greater part of the summer, as the Allier can not generally be forded before the autumn. Therefore, that this might not happen, having pitched his camp in a woody place opposite to one of those bridges which Vercingetorix had taken care should be broken down, the next day he stopped behind with two legions in a secret place; he sent on the rest of the forces as usual, with all the baggage, after having selected some cohorts, that the number of the legions might appear to be complete. Having ordered these to advance as far as they could, when now, from the time of day, he conjectured they had come to an encampment, he began to rebuild the bridge on the same piles, the lower part of which remained entire. Having quickly finished the work and led his legions across, he selected a fit place for a camp, and recalled the rest of his troops. Vercingetorix, on ascertaining this fact, went before him by forced marches, in order that he might not be compelled to come to an action against his will.

7:36 Caesar, in five days' march, went from that place to Gergovia, and after engaging in a slight cavalry skirmish that day, on viewing the situation of the city, which, being built on a very high mountain, was very difficult of access, he despaired of taking it by storm, and determined to take no measures with regard to besieging it before he should secure a supply of provisions. But Vercingetorix, having pitched his camp on the mountain near the town, placed the forces of each state separately and at small intervals around himself, and having occupied all the hills of that range as far as they commanded a view [of the Roman encampment], he presented a formidable appearance; he ordered the rulers of the states, whom he had selected as his council of war, to come to him daily at the dawn, whether any measure seemed to require deliberation or execution. Nor did he allow almost any day to pass without testing in a cavalry action, the archers being intermixed, what spirit and valor there was in each of his own men. There was a hill opposite the town, at the very foot of that mountain, strongly fortified and precipitous on every side (which if our men could

Arvernos ad oppidum Gergoviam secundum flumen Elaver duxit; equitatus partem illi attribuit, partem sibi reliquit. Qua re cognita Vercingetorix omnibus interruptis eius fluminis pontibus ab altera fluminis parte iter facere coepit.

Cum uterque utrimque exisset exercitus, in conspectu fereque e regione castris castra ponebant dispositis exploratoribus, necubi effecto ponte Romani copias traducerent. Erat in magnis Caesaris difficultatibus res, ne maiorem aestatis partem flumine impediretur, quod non fere ante autumnum Elaver vado transiri solet. Itaque, ne id accideret, silvestri loco castris positis e regione unius eorum pontium, quos Vercingetorix rescindendos curaverat, postero die cum duabus legionibus in occulto restitit; reliquas copias cum omnibus impedimentis, ut consueverat, misit, apertis quibusdam cohortibus, uti numerus legionum constare videretur. His quam longissime possent egredi iussis, cum iam ex diei tempore coniecturam ceperat in castra perventum, isdem sublicis, quarum pars inferior integra remanebat, pontem reficere coepit. Celeriter effecto opere legionibusque traductis et loco castris idoneo delecto reliquas copias revocavit. Vercingetorix re cognita, ne contra suam voluntatem dimicare cogeretur, magnis itineribus antecessit.

Caesar ex eo loco quintis castris Gergoviam pervenit equestrique eo die proelio levi facto perspecto urbis situ, quae posita in altissimo monte omnes aditus difficiles habebat, de expugnatione desperavit, de obsessione non prius agendum constituit, quam rem frumentariam expedisset. At Vercingetorix castris, prope oppidum positis, mediocribus circum se intervallis separatim singularum civitatium copias collocaverat atque omnibus eius iugi collibus occupatis, qua despici poterat, horribilem speciem praebebat; principesque earum civitatium, quos sibi ad consilium capiendum delegerat, prima luce cotidie ad se convenire iubebat, seu quid communicandum, seu quid administrandum videretur; neque ullum fere diem intermittebat quin equestri proelio interiectis sagittariis, quid in quoque esset animi ac virtutis suorum perspiceret. Erat e regione oppidi collis sub ipsis radicibus montis, egregie munitus atque ex omni parte circumcisus; quem si tenerent nostri, et

gain, they seemed likely to exclude the enemy from a great share of their supply of water, and from free foraging; but this place was occupied by them with a weak garrison): however, Caesar set out from the camp in the silence of night, and dislodging the garrison before succor could come from the town, he got possession of the place and posted two legions there, and drew from the greater camp to the less a double trench twelve feet broad, so that the soldiers could even singly pass secure from any sudden attack of the enemy.

7:37 While these affairs were going on at Gergovia, Convictolanis, the Aeduan, to whom we have observed the magistracy was adjudged by Caesar, being bribed by the Arverni, holds a conference with certain young men, the chief of whom were Litavicus and his brothers, who were born of a most noble family. He shares the bribe with them, and exhorts them to "remember that they were free and born for empire; that the state of the Aedui was the only one which retarded the most certain victory of the Gauls; that the rest were held in check by its authority; and, if it was brought over, the Romans would not have room to stand on in Gaul; that he had received some kindness from Caesar, only so far, however, as gaining a most just cause by his decision; but that he assigned more weight to the general freedom; for, why should the Aedui go to Caesar to decide concerning their rights and laws, rather than the Romans come to the Aedui?" The young men being easily won over by the speech of the magistrate and the bribe, when they declared that they would even be leaders in the plot, a plan for accomplishing it was considered, because they were confident their state could not be induced to undertake the war on slight grounds. It was resolved that Litavicus should have the command of the ten thousand, which were being sent to Caesar for the war, and should have charge of them on their march, and that his brothers should go before him to Caesar. They arrange the other measures, and the manner in which they should have them done.

7:38 Litavicus, having received the command of the army, suddenly convened the soldiers, when he was about thirty miles distant from Gergovia, and, weeping, said, "Soldiers, whither are we going? All our knights and all our nobles have perished. Eporedirix and Viridomarus, the principal men of the state, being accused of treason, have been slain by the Romans without any permission to plead their cause. Learn this intelligence from those who have escaped from the massacre; for I, since my brothers and all my relations have been slain, am prevented by grief from declaring what has taken place. Persons are brought forward whom he had instructed in what he would have them say, and make the same statements to the soldiery as Litavicus

aquae magna parte et pabulatione libera prohibituri hostes videbantur. Sed is locus praesidio ab his non nimis firmo tenebatur. Tamen silentio noctis Caesar ex castris egressus, priusquam subsidio ex oppido veniri posset, deiecto praesidio potitus loco duas ibi legiones collocavit fossamque duplicem duodenum pedum a maioribus castris ad minora perduxit, ut tuto ab repentino hostium incursu etiam singuli commeare possent.

Dum haec ad Gergoviam geruntur, Convictolitavis Aeduus, cui magistratum adiudicatum a Caesare demonstravimus, sollicitatus ab Arvernis pecunia cum quibusdam adulescentibus colloquitur; quorum erat princeps Litaviccus atque eius fratres, amplissima familia nati adulescentes. Cum his praemium communicat hortaturque, ut se liberos et imperio natos meminerint. Vnam esse Aeduorum civitatem, quae certissimam Galliae victoriam detineat; eius auctoritate reliquas contineri; qua traducta locum consistendi Romanis in Gallia non fore. Esse nonnullo se Caesaris beneficio adfectum, sic tamen, ut iustissimam apud eum causam obtinuerit; sed plus communi libertati tribuere. Cur enim potius Aedui de suo iure et de legibus ad Caesarem disceptatorem, quam Romani ad Aeduos veniant? Celeriter adulescentibus et oratione magistratus et praemio deductis, cum se vel principes eius consili fore profiterentur, ratio perficiendi quaerebatur, quod civitatem temere ad suscipiendum bellum adduci posse non confidebant. Placuit ut Litaviccus decem illis milibus, quae Caesari ad bellum mitterentur, praeficeretur atque ea ducenda curaret, fratresque eius ad Caesarem praecurrerent. Reliqua qua ratione agi placeat constituunt.

Litaviccus accepto exercitu, cum milia passuum circiter XXX ab Gergovia abesset, convocatis subito militibus lacrimans, "Quo proficiscimur," inquit, "milites? Omnis noster equitatus, omnis nobilitas interiit; principes civitatis, Eporedorix et Viridomarus, insimulati proditionis ab Romanis indicta causa interfecti sunt. Haec ab ipsis cognoscite, qui ex ipsa caede fugerunt: nam ego fratribus atque omnibus meis propinquis interfectis dolore prohibeor, quae gesta sunt, pronuntiare." Producuntur hi quos ille edocuerat quae dici vellet, atque eadem, quae Litaviccus pronuntiaverat, multitudini exponunt:

had made: that all the knights of the Aedui were slain because they were said to have held conferences with the Arverni; that they had concealed themselves among the multitude of soldiers, and had escaped from the midst of the slaughter. The Aedui shout aloud and conjure Litavicus to provide for their safety. As if, said he, it were a matter of deliberation, and not of necessity, for us to go to Gergovia and unite ourselves to the Arverni. Or have we any reasons to doubt that the Romans, after perpetrating the atrocious crime, are now hastening to slay us? Therefore, if there be any spirit in us, let us avenge the death of those who have perished in a most unworthy manner, and let us slay these robbers." He points to the Roman citizens, who had accompanied them, in reliance on his protection. He immediately seizes a great quantity of corn and provisions, cruelly tortures them, and then puts them to death, sends messengers throughout the entire state of the Aedui, and rouses them completely by the same falsehood concerning the slaughter of their knights and nobles; he earnestly advises them to avenge, in the same manner as he did, the wrongs, which they had received.

7:39 Eporedirix, the Aeduan, a young man born in the highest rank and possessing very great influence at home, and, along with Viridomarus, of equal age and influence, but of inferior birth, whom Caesar had raised from a humble position to the highest rank, on being recommended to him by Divitiacus, had come in the number of horse, being summoned by Caesar by name. These had a dispute with each other for precedence, and in the struggle between the magistrates they had contended with their utmost efforts, the one for Convictolitanis, the other for Cotus. Of these Eporedirix, on learning the design of Litavicus, lays the matter before Caesar almost at midnight; he entreats that Caesar should not suffer their state to swerve from the alliance with the Roman people, owing to the depraved counsels of a few young men which he foresaw would be the consequence if so many thousand men should unite themselves to the enemy, as their relations could not neglect their safety, nor the state regard it as a matter of slight importance.

7:40 Caesar felt great anxiety on this intelligence, because he had always especially indulged the state of the Aedui, and, without any hesitation, draws out from the camp four light-armed legions and all the cavalry: nor had he time, at such a crisis, to contract the camp, because the affair seemed to depend upon dispatch. He leaves Caius Fabius, his lieutenant, with two legions to guard the camp. When he ordered the brothers of Litavicus to be arrested, he discovers that they had fled a short time before to the camp of the enemy. He encouraged his soldiers "not to be disheartened by the labor of the journey on

multos equites Aeduorum interfectos, quod collocuti cum Arvernis dicerentur; ipsos se inter multitudinem militum occultasse atque ex media caede fugisse. Conclamant Aedui et Litaviccum obsecrant ut sibi consulat. "Quasi vero," inquit ille, "consili sit res, ac non necesse sit nobis Gergoviam contendere et cum Arvernis nosmet coniungere. An dubitamus quin nefario facinore admisso Romani iam ad nos interficiendos concurrant? Proinde, si quid in nobis animi est, persequamur eorum mortem qui indignissime interierunt, atque hos latrones interficiamus." Ostendit cives Romanos, qui eius praesidi fiducia una erant: magnum numerum frumenti commeatusque diripit, ipsos crudeliter excruciatos interfici. Nuntios tota civitate Aeduorum dimittit, eodem mendacio de caede equitum et principum permovet; hortatur ut simili ratione atque ipse fecerit suas iniurias persequantur.

Eporedorix Aeduus, summo loco natus adulescens et summae domi potentiae, et una Viridomarus, pari aetate et gratia, sed genere dispari, quem Caesar ab Diviciaeo sibi traditum ex humili loco ad summam dignitatem perduxerat, in equitum numero convenerant nominatim ab eo evocati. His erat inter se de principatu contentio, et in illa magistratuum controversia alter pro Convictolitavi, alter pro Coto summis opibus pugnaverant. Ex eis Eporedorix cognito Litavicci consilio media fere nocte rem ad Caesarem defert; orat ne patiatur civitatem pravis adulescentium consiliis ab amicitia populi Romani deficere; quod futurum provideat, si se tot hominum milia cum hostibus coniunxerint, quorum salutem neque propinqui neglegere, neque civitas levi momento aestimare posset.

Magna adfectus sollicitudine hoc nuntio Caesar, quod semper Aeduorum civitati praecipue indulserat, nulla interposita dubitatione legiones expeditas quattuor equitatumque omnem ex castris educit; nec fuit spatium tali tempore ad contrahenda castra, quod res posita in celeritate videbatur; Gaium Fabium legatum eum legionibus duabus castris praesidio relinquit. Fratres Litavicci eum comprehendi iussisset, paulo ante reperit ad hostes fugisse. Adhortatus milites, ne necessario tempore

such a necessary occasion," and, after advancing twenty-five miles, all being most eager, he came in sight of the army of the Aedui, and, by sending on his cavalry, retards and impedes their march; he then issues strict orders to all his soldiers to kill no one. He commands Eporedirix and Viridomarus, who they thought were killed, to move among the cavalry and address their friends. When they were recognized and the treachery of Litavicus discovered, the Aedui began to extend their hands to intimate submission, and, laying down their arms, to deprecate death. Litavicus, with his clansmen, who after the custom of the Gauls consider it a crime to desert their patrons, even in extreme misfortune, flees forth to Gergovia.

7:41 Caesar, after sending messengers to the state of the Aedui, to inform them that they whom he could have put to death by the right of war were spared through his kindness, and after giving three hours of the night to his army for his repose, directed his march to Gergovia. Almost in the middle of the journey, a party of horse that were sent by Fabius stated in how great danger matters were, they inform him that the camp was attacked by a very powerful army, while fresh men were frequently relieving the wearied, and exhausting our soldiers by the incessant toil, since on account of the size of the camp, they had constantly to remain on the rampart; that many had been wounded by the immense number of arrows and all kinds of missiles; that the engines were of great service in withstanding them; that Fabius, at their departure, leaving only two gates open, was blocking up the rest, and was adding breast-works to the ramparts, and was preparing himself for a similar casualty on the following day. Caesar, after receiving this information, reached the camp before sunrise owing to the very great zeal of his soldiers.

7:42 While these things are going on at Gergovia, the Aedui, on receiving the first announcements from Litavicus, leave themselves no time to ascertain the truth of those statements. Some are stimulated by avarice, others by revenge and credulity, which is an innate propensity in that race of men to such a degree that they consider a slight rumor as an ascertained fact. They plunder the property of the Roman citizens, and either massacre them or drag them away to slavery. Convictolitanis increases the evil state of affairs, and goads on the people to fury, that by the commission of some outrage they may be ashamed to return to propriety. They entice from the town of Cabillonus, by a promise of safety, Marcus Aristius, a military tribune, who was on his march to his legion; they compel those who had settled there for the purpose of trading to do the same. By constantly attacking them on their march they strip them of all their baggage; they besiege day and

itineris labore permoveantur, cupidissimis omnibus progressus milia passuum XXV agmen Aeduorum conspicatus immisso equitatu iter eorum moratur atque impedit interdicitque omnibus ne quemquam interficiant. Eporedorigem et Viridomarum, quos illi interfectos existimabant, inter equites versari suosque appellare iubet. His cognitis et Litavicci fraude perspecta Aedui manus tendere, deditionem significare et proiectis armis mortem deprecari incipiunt. Litaviccus cum suis clientibus, quibus more Gallorum nefas est etiam in extrema fortuna deserere patronos, Gergoviam profugit.

Caesar nuntiis ad civitatem Aeduorum missis, qui suo beneficio conservatos docerent quos iure belli interficere potuisset, tribusque horis noctis exercitui ad quietem datis castra ad Gergoviam movit. Medio fere itinere equites a Fabio missi, quanto res in periculo fuerit, exponunt. Summis copiis castra oppugnata demonstrant, cum crebro integri defessis succederent nostrosque assiduo labore defatigarent, quibus propter magnitudinem castrorum perpetuo esset isdem in vallo permanendum. Multitudine sagittarum atque omnis generis telorum multos vulneratos; ad haec sustinenda magno usui fuisse tormenta. Fabium discessu eorum duabus relictis portis obstruere ceteras pluteosque vallo addere et se in posterum diem similemque casum apparare. His rebus cognitis Caesar summo studio militum ante ortum solis in castra pervenit.

Dum haec ad Gergoviam geruntur, Aedui primis nuntiis ab Litavicco acceptis nullum sibi ad cognoscendum spatium relinquunt. Impellit alios avaritia, alios iracundia et temeritas, quae maxime illi hominum generi est innata, ut levem auditionem habeant pro re comperta. Bona civium Romanorum diripiunt, caedes faciunt, in servitutem abstrahunt. Adiuvat rem proclinatam Convictolitavis plebemque ad furorem impellit, ut facinore admisso ad sanitatem reverti pudeat. Marcum Aristium, tribunum militum, iter ad legionem facientem fide data ex oppido Cabillono educunt: idem facere cogunt eos, qui negotiandi causa ibi constiterant. Hos continuo (in) itinere adorti omnibus impedimentis exuunt; repugnantes diem noctemque obsident; multis utrimque interfectis maiorem multitudinem

138

night those that resisted; when many were slain on both sides, they excite a great number to arms.

7:43 In the mean time, when intelligence was brought that all their soldiers were in Caesar's power, they run in a body to Aristius; they assure him that nothing had been done by public authority; they order an inquiry to be made about the plundered property; they confiscate the property of Litavicus and his brothers; they send embassadors to Caesar for the purpose of clearing themselves. They do all this with a view to recover their soldiers; but being contaminated by guilt, and charmed by the gains arising from the plundered property, as that act was shared in by many, and being tempted by the fear of punishment, they began to form plans of war and stir up the other states by embassies. Although Caesar was aware of this proceeding, yet he addresses the embassadors with as much mildness as he can: "That he did not think worse of the state on account of the ignorance and fickleness of the mob, nor would diminish his regard for the Aedui." He himself, fearing a greater commotion in Gaul, in order to prevent his being surrounded by all the states, began to form plans as to the manner in which he should return from Gergovia and again concentrate his forces, lest a departure arising from the fear of a revolt should seem like a flight.

7:44 While he was considering these things an opportunity of acting successfully seemed to offer. For, when he had come into the smaller camp for the purpose of securing the works, he noticed that the hill in the possession of the enemy was stripped of men, although, on the former days, it could scarcely be seen on account of the numbers on it. Being astonished, he inquires the reason of it from the deserters, a great number of whom flocked to him daily. They all concurred in asserting, what Caesar himself had already ascertained by his scouts, that the back of that hill was almost level; but likewise woody and narrow, by which there was a pass to the other side of the town; that they had serious apprehensions for this place, and had no other idea, on the occupation of one hill by the Romans, than that, if they should lose the other, they would be almost surrounded, and cut off from all egress and foraging; that they were all summoned by Vercingetorix to fortify this place.

7:45 Caesar, on being informed of this circumstance, sends several troops of horse to the place immediately after midnight; he orders them to range in every quarter with more tumult than usual. At dawn he orders a large quantity of baggage to be drawn out of the camp, and the muleteers with helmets, in the appearance and guise of horsemen, to ride round the hills. To these he adds a few cavalry, with instructions to range more

armatorum concitant.

Interim nuntio allato omnes eorum milites in potestate Caesaris teneri, concurrunt ad Aristium, nihil publico factum consilio demonstrant; quaestionem de bonis direptis decernunt, Litavicci fratrumque bona publicant, legatos ad Caesarem sui purgandi gratia mittunt. Haec faciunt reciperandorum suorum causa; sed contaminati facinore et capti compendio ex direptis bonis, quod ea res ad multos pertinebat, timore poenae exterriti consilia clam de bello inire incipiunt civitatesque reliquas legationibus sollicitant. Quae tametsi Caesar intellegebat, tamen quam mitissime potest legatos appellat: nihil se propter inscientiam levitatemque vulgi gravius de civitate iudicare neque de sua in Aeduos benevolentia deminuere. Ipse maiorem Galliae motum exspectans, ne ab omnibus civitatibus circumsisteretur, consilia inibat quemadmodum ab Gergovia discederet ac rursus omnem exercitum contraheret, ne profectio nata ab timore defectionis similis fugae videretur.

Haec cogitanti accidere visa est facultas bene rei gerendae. Nam cum in minora castra operis perspiciendi causa venisset, animadvertit collem, qui ab hostibus tenebatur, nudatum hominibus, qui superioribus diebus vix prae multitudine cerni poterat. Admiratus quaerit ex perfugis causam, quorum magnus ad eum cotidie numerus confluebat. Constabat inter omnes, quod iam ipse Caesar per exploratores cognoverat, dorsum esse eius iugi prope aequum, sed hunc silvestrem et angustum, qua esset aditus ad alteram partem oppidi; huic loco vehementer illos timere nec iam aliter sentire, uno colle ab Romanis occupato, si alterum amisissent, quin paene circumvallati atque omni exitu et pabulatione interclusi viderentur: ad hunc muniendum omnes a Vercingetorige evocatos.

Hac re cognita Caesar mittit complures equitum turmas; eis de media nocte imperat, ut paulo tumultuosius omnibus locis vagarentur. Prima luce magnum numerum impedimentorum ex castris mulorumque produci deque his stramenta detrahi mulionesque cum cassidibus equitum specie ac simulatione collibus circumvehi iubet. His paucos

widely to make a show. He orders them all to seek the same quarter by a long circuit; these proceedings were seen at a distance from the town, as Gergovia commanded a view of the camp, nor could the Gauls ascertain at so great a distance, what certainty there was in the maneuver. He sends one legion to the same hill, and after it had marched a little, stations it in the lower ground, and congeals it in the woods. The suspicion of the Gauls are increased, and all their forces are marched to that place to defend it. Caesar, having perceived the camp of the enemy deserted, covers the military insignia of his men, conceals the standards, and transfers his soldiers in small bodies from the greater to the less camp, and points out to the lieutenants whom he had placed in command over the respective legions, what he should wish to be done; he particularly advises them to restrain their men from advancing too far, through their desire of fighting, or their hope of plunder, he sets before them what disadvantages the unfavorable nature of the ground carries with it; that they could be assisted by dispatch alone: that success depended on a surprise, and not on a battle. After stating these particulars, he gives the signal for action, and detaches the Aedui at the same time by another ascent on the right.

7:46 The town wall was 1200 paces distant from the plain and foot of the ascent, in a straight line, if no gap intervened; whatever circuit was added to this ascent, to make the hill easy, increased the length of the route. But almost in the middle of the hill, the Gauls had previously built a wall six feet high, made of large stones, and extending in length as far as the nature of the ground permitted, as a barrier to retard the advance of our men; and leaving all the lower space empty, they had filled the upper part of the hill, as far as the wall of the town, with their camps very close to one another. The soldiers, on the signal being given, quickly advance to this fortification, and passing over it, make themselves masters of the separate camps. And so great was their activity in taking the camps, that Teutomarus, the king of the Nitiobriges, being suddenly surprised in his tent, as he had gone to rest at noon, with difficulty escaped from the hands of the plunderers, with the upper part of his person naked, and his horse wounded.

7:47 Caesar, having accomplished the object which he had in view, ordered the signal to be sounded for a retreat; and the soldiers of the tenth legion, by which he was then accompanied, halted. But the soldiers of the other legions, not hearing the sound of the trumpet, because there was a very large valley between them, were however kept back by the tribunes of the soldiers and the lieutenants, according to Caesar's orders; but being animated by the prospect of speedy victory, and the flight

addit equites qui latius ostentationis causa vagarentur. Longo circuitu easdem omnes iubet petere regiones. Haec procul ex oppido videbantur, ut erat a Gergovia despectus in castra, neque tanto spatio certi quid esset explorari poterat. Legionem unam eodem iugo mittit et paulum progressam inferiore constituit loco silvisque occultat. Augetur Gallis suspicio, atque omnes illo ad munitionem copiae traducuntur. Vacua castra hostium Caesar conspicatus tectis insignibus suorum occultatisque signis militaribus raros milites, ne ex oppido animadverterentur, ex maioribus castris in minora traducit legatisque, quos singulis legionibus praefecerat, quid fieri velit ostendit: in primis monet ut contineant milites, ne studio pugnandi aut spe praedae longius progrediantur; quid iniquitas loci habeat incommodi proponit: hoc una celeritate posse mutari; occasionis esse rem, non proeli. His rebus eitis signum dat et ab dextra parte alio ascensu eodem tempore Aeduos mittit.

Oppidi murus ab planitie atque initio ascensus recta regione, si nullus anfractus intercederet, MCC passus aberat: quidquid huc circuitus ad molliendum clivum accesserat, id spatium itineris augebat. A medio fere colle in longitudinem, ut natura montis ferebat, ex grandibus saxis sex pedum murum qui nostrorum impetum tardaret praeduxerant Galli, atque inferiore omni spatio vacuo relicto superiorem partem collis usque ad murum oppidi densissimis castris compleverant. Milites dato signo celeriter ad munitionem perveniunt eamque transgressi trinis castris potiuntur; ac tanta fuit in castris capiendis celeritas, ut Teutomatus, rex Nitiobrigum, subito in tabernaculo oppressus, ut meridie conquieverat, superiore corporis parte nudata vulnerato equo vix se ex manibus praedantium militum eriperet.

Consecutus id quod animo proposuerat, Caesar receptui cani iussit legionique decimae, quacum erat, continuo signa constituit. Ac reliquarum legionum milites non exaudito sono tubae, quod satis magna valles intercedebat, tamen ab tribunis militum legatisque, ut erat a Caesare praeceptum, retinebantur. Sed elati spe celeris victoriae et hostium fuga et superiorum temporum secundis

of the enemy, and the favorable battles of former periods, they thought nothing so difficult that their bravery could not accomplish it; nor did they put an end to the pursuit, until they drew nigh to the wall of the town and the gates. But then, when a shout arose in every quarter of the city, those who were at a distance being alarmed by the sudden tumult, fled hastily from the town, since they thought that the enemy were within the gates. The matrons begin to cast their clothes and silver over the wall, and bending over as far as the lower part of the bosom, with outstretched hands beseech the Romans to spare them, and not to sacrifice to their resentment even women and children, as they had done at Avaricum. Some of them let themselves down from the walls by their hands, and surrendered to our soldiers. Lucius Fabius a centurion of the eighth legion, who, it was ascertained, had said that day among his fellow soldiers that he was excited by the plunder of Avaricum, and would not allow any one to mount the wall before him, finding three men of his own company, and being raised up by them, scaled the wall. He himself, in turn, taking hold of them one by one drew them up to the wall.

7:48 In the mean time those who had gone to the other part of the town to defend it, as we have mentioned above, at first, aroused by hearing the shouts, and, afterward, by frequent accounts, that the town was in possession of the Romans, sent forward their cavalry, and hastened in larger numbers to that quarter. As each first came he stood beneath the wall, and increased the number of his countrymen engaged in action. When a great multitude of them had assembled, the matrons, who a little before were stretching their hands from the walls to the Romans, began to beseech their countrymen, and after the Gallic fashion to show their disheveled hair, and bring their children into public view. Neither in position nor in numbers was the contest an equal one to the Romans; at the same time, being exhausted by running and the long continuation of the fight, they could not easily withstand fresh and vigorous troops.

7:49 Caesar, when he perceived that his soldiers were fighting on unfavorable ground, and that the enemy's forces were increasing, being alarmed for the safety of his troops, sent orders to Titus Sextius, one of his lieutenants, whom he had left to guard the smaller camp, to lead out his cohorts quickly from the camp, and post them at the foot of the hill, on the right wing of the enemy; that if he should see our men driven from the ground, he should deter the enemy from following too closely. He himself, advancing with the legion a little from that place where he had taken his post, awaited the issue of the battle.

7:50 While the fight was going on most vigorously, hand to

proeliis nihil adeo arduum sibi esse existimaverunt quod non virtute consequi possent, neque finem prius sequendi fecerunt quam muro oppidi portisque appropinquarunt. Tum vero ex omnibus urbis partibus orto clamore, qui longius aberant repentino tumultu perterriti, cum hostem intra portas esse existimarent, sese ex oppido eiecerunt. Matres familiae de muro vestem argentumque iactabant et pectore nudo prominentes passis manibus obtestabantur Romanos, ut sibi parcerent neu, sicut Avarici fecissent, ne a mulieribus quidem atque infantibus abstinerent: nonnullae de muris per manus demissae sese militibus tradebant. Lucius Fabius, centurio legionis VIII, quem inter suos eo die dixisse constabat excitari se Avaricensibus praemiis neque commissurum, ut prius quisquam murum ascenderet, tres suos nactus manipulares atque ab eis sublevatus murum ascendit: hos ipse rursus singulos exceptans in murum extulit.

Interim ei qui ad alteram partem oppidi, ut supra demonstravimus, munitionis causa convenerant, primo exaudito clamore, inde etiam crebris nuntiis incitati, oppidum a Romanis teneri, praemissis equitibus magno concursu eo contenderunt. Eorum ut quisque primus venerat, sub muro consistebat suorumque pugnantium numerum augebat. Quorum cum magna multitudo convenisset, matres familiae, quae paulo ante Romanis de muro manus tendebant, suos obtestari et more Gallico passum capillum ostentare liberosque in conspectum proferre coeperunt. Erat Romanis nec loco nec numero aequa contentio; simul et cursu et spatio pugnae defatigati non facile recentes atque integros sustinebant.

Caesar, cum iniquo loco pugnari hostiumque augeri copias videret, praemetuens suis ad Titum Sextium legatum, quem minoribus castris praesidio reliquerat, misit, ut cohortes ex castris celeriter educeret et sub infimo colle ab dextro latere hostium constitueret, ut, si nostros loco depulsos vidisset, quo minus libere hostes insequerentur terreret. Ipse paulum ex eo loco cum legione progressus, ubi constiterat, eventum pugnae exspectabat.

Cum acerrime comminus pugnaretur, hostes loco et

hand, and the enemy depended on their position and numbers, our men on their bravery, the Aedui suddenly appeared on our exposed flank, as Caesar had sent them by another ascent on the right, for the sake of creating a diversion. These, from the similarity of their arms, greatly terrified our men; and although they were discovered to have their right shoulders bare, which was usually the sign of those reduced to peace, yet the soldiers suspected that this very thing was done by the enemy to deceive them. At the same time Lucius Fabius the centurion, and those who had scaled the wall with him, being surrounded and slain, were cast from the wall. Marcus Petreius, a centurion of the same legion, after attempting to hew down the gates, was overpowered by numbers, and, despairing of his safety, having already received many wounds, said to the soldiers of his own company who followed him: "Since I can not save you as well as myself, I shall at least provide for your safety, since I, allured by the love of glory, led you into this danger, do you save yourselves when an opportunity is given." At the same time he rushed into the midst of the enemy, and slaying two of them, drove back the rest a little from the gate. When his men attempted to aid him, "In vain," he says, "you endeavor to procure me safety, since blood and strength are now failing me, therefore leave this, while you have the opportunity, and retreat to the legion." Thus he fell fighting a few moments after, and saved his men by his own death.

7:51 Our soldiers, being hard pressed on every side, were dislodged from their position, with the loss of forty-six centurions; but the tenth legion, which had been posted in reserve on ground a little more level, checked the Gauls in their eager pursuit. It was supported by the cohorts of the thirteenth legion, which, being led from the smaller camp, had, under the command of Titus Sextius, occupied the higher ground. The legions, as soon as they reached the plain, halted and faced the enemy. Vercingetorix led back his men from the part of the hill within the fortifications. On that day little less than seven hundred of the soldiers were missing.

7:52 On the next day, Caesar, having called a meeting, censured the rashness and avarice of his soldiers, "In that they had judged for themselves how far they ought to proceed, or what they ought to do, and could not be kept back by the tribunes of the soldiers and the lieutenants;" and stated, "what the disadvantage of the ground could effect, what opinion he himself had entertained at Avaricum, when having surprised the enemy without either general or cavalry, he had given up a certain victory, lest even a trifling loss should occur in the contest owing to the disadvantage of position. That as much as he admired the greatness of their courage, since neither the

numero, nostri virtute confiderent, subito sunt Aedui visi ab latere nostris aperto, quos Caesar ab dextra parte alio ascensu manus distinendae causa miserat. Hi similitudine armorum vehementer nostros perterruerunt, ac tametsi dextris humeris exsertis animadvertebantur, quod insigne +pacatum+ esse consuerat, tamen id ipsum sui fallendi causa milites ab hostibus factum existimabant. Eodem tempore Lucius Fabius centurio quique una murum ascenderant circumventi atque interfecti muro praecipitabantur. Marcus Petronius, eiusdem legionis centurio, cum portam excidere conatus esset, a multitudine oppressus ac sibi desperans multis iam vulneribus acceptis manipularibus suis, qui illum secuti erant, "Quoniam," inquit, "me una vobiscum servare non possum, vestrae quidem certe vitae prospiciam, quos cupiditate gloriae adductus in periculum deduxi. Vos data facultate vobis consulite." Simul in medios hostes irrupit duobusque interfectis reliquos a porta paulum summovit. Conantibus auxiliari suis "Frustra," inquit, "meae vitae subvenire conamini, quem iam sanguis viresque deficiunt. Proinde abite, dum est facultas, vosque ad legionem recipite." Ita puguans post paulum concidit ac suis saluti fuit.

Nostri, cum undique premerentur, XLVI centurionibus amissis deiecti sunt loco. Sed intolerantius Gallos insequentes legio decima tardavit, quae pro subsidio paulo aequiore loco constiterat. Hanc rursus XIII legionis cohortes exceperunt, quae ex castris minoribus eductae cum Tito Sextio legato ceperant locum superiorem. Legiones, ubi primum planitiem attigerunt, infestis contra hostes signis constiterunt. Vercingetorix ab radicibus collis suos intra munitiones reduxit. Eo die milites sunt paulo minus septingenti desiderati.

Postero die Caesar contione advocata temeritatem cupiditatemque militum reprehendit, quod sibi ipsi iudicavissent quo procedendum aut quid agendum videretur, neque signo recipiendi dato constitissent neque ab tribunis militum legatisque retineri potuissent. Euit quid iniquitas loci posset, quid ipse ad Avaricum sensisset, cum sine duce et sine equitatu deprehensis hostibus exploratam victoriam dimisisset, ne parvum modo detrimentum in contentione propter iniquitatem loci accideret. Quanto opere eorum animi magnitudinem

fortifications of the camp, nor the height of the mountain, nor the wall of the town could retard them; in the same degree he censured their licentiousness and arrogance, because they thought that they knew more than their general concerning victory, and the issue of actions: and that he required in his soldiers forbearance and self-command, not less than valor and magnanimity."

7:53 Having held this assembly, and having encouraged the soldiers at the conclusion of his speech, "That they should not be dispirited on this account, nor attribute to the valor of the enemy, what the disadvantage of position had caused;" entertaining the same views of his departure that he had previously had, he led forth the legions from the camp, and drew up his army in order of battle in a suitable place. When Vercingetorix, nevertheless, would not descend to the level ground, a slight cavalry action, and that a successful one, having taken place, he led back his army into the camp. When he had done this, the next day, thinking that he had done enough to lower the pride of the Gauls, and to encourage the minds of his soldiers, he moved his camp in the direction of the Aedui. The enemy not even then pursuing us, on the third day he repaired the bridge over the river Allier, and led over his whole army.

7:54 Having then held an interview with Viridomarus and Eporedirix the Aeduans, he learns that Litavicus had set out with all the cavalry to raise the Aedui; that it was necessary that they too should go before him to confirm the state in their allegiance. Although he now saw distinctly the treachery of the Aedui in many things, and was of opinion that the revolt of the entire state would be hastened by their departure; yet he thought that they should not be detained, lest he should appear either to offer an insult, or betray some suspicion of fear. He briefly states to them when departing his services toward the Aedui: in what a state and how humbled he had found them, driven into their towns, deprived of their lands, stripped of all their forces, a tribute imposed on them, and hostages wrested from them with the utmost insult; and to what condition and to what greatness he had raised them, [so much so] that they had not only recovered their former position, but seemed to surpass the dignity and influence of all the previous eras of their history. After giving these admonitions he dismissed them.

7:55 Noviodunum was a town of the Aedui, advantageously situated on the banks of the Loire. Caesar had conveyed hither all the hostages of Gaul, the corn, public money, a great part of his own baggage and that of his army; he had sent hither a great number of horses, which he had purchased in Italy and Spain on

admiraretur, quos non castrorum munitiones, non altitudo montis, non murus oppidi tardare potuisset, tanto opere licentiam arrogantiamque reprehendere, quod plus se quam imperatorem de victoria atque exitu rerum sentire existimarent; nec minus se ab milite modestiam et continentiam quam virtutem atque animi magnitudinem desiderare.

Hac habita contione et ad extremam orationem confirmatis militibus, ne ob hanc causam animo permoverentur neu quod iniquitas loci attulisset id virtuti hostium tribuerent, eadem de profectione cogitans quae ante senserat legiones ex castris eduxit aciemque idoneo loco constituit. Cum Vercingetorix nihil magis in aequum locum descenderet, levi facto equestri proelio atque secundo in castra exercitum reduxit. Cum hoc idem postero die fecisset, satis ad Gallicam ostentationem minuendam militumque animos confirmandos factum existimans in Aeduos movit castra. Ne tum quidem insecutis hostibus tertio die ad flumen Elaver venit; pontem refecit exercitumque traduxit.

Ibi a Viridomaro atque Eporedorige Aeduis appellatus discit cum omni equitatu Litaviccum ad sollicitandos Aeduos profectum: opus esse ipsos antecedere ad confirmandam civitatem. Etsi multis iam rebus perfidiam Aeduorum perspectam habebat atque horum discessu admaturari defectionem civitatis existimabat, tamen eos retinendos non constituit, ne aut inferre iniuriam videretur aut dare timoris aliquam suspicionem. Discedentibus his breviter sua in Aeduos merita euit, quos et quam humiles accepisset, compulsos in oppida, multatos agris omnibus ereptis copiis, imposito stipendio, obsidibus summa cum contumelia extortis, et quam in fortunam quamque in amplitudinem deduxisset, ut non solum in pristinum statum redissent, sed omnium temporum dignitatem et gratiam antecessisse viderentur. His datis mandatis eos ab se dimisit.

Noviodunum erat oppidum Aeduorum ad ripas Ligeris opportuno loco positum. Huc Caesar omnes obsides Galliae, frumentum, pecuniam publicam, suorum atque exercitus impedimentorum magnam partem contulerat; huc magnum numerum equorum

account of this war. When Eporedirix and Viridomarus came to this place, and received information of the disposition of the state, that Litavicus had been admitted by the Aedui into Bibracte, which is a town of the greatest importance among them, that Convictolitanis the chief magistrate and a great part of the senate had gone to meet him, that embassadors had been publicly sent to Vercingetorix to negotiate a peace and alliance; they thought that so great an opportunity ought not to be neglected. Therefore, having put to the sword the garrison of Noviodunum, and those who had assembled there for the purpose of trading or were on their march, they divided the money and horses among themselves; they took care that the hostages of the [different] states should be brought to Bibracte, to the chief magistrate; they burned the town to prevent its being of any service to the Romans, as they were of opinion that they could not hold it; they carried away in their vessels whatever corn they could in the hurry, they destroyed the remainder, by [throwing it] into the river or setting it on fire, they themselves began to collect forces from the neighboring country, to place guards and garrisons in different positions along the banks of the Loire, and to display the cavalry on all sides to strike terror into the Romans, [to try] if they could cut them off from a supply of provisions. In which expectation they were much aided, from the circumstance that the Loire had swollen to such a degree from the melting of the snows, that it did not seem capable of being forded at all.

7:56 Caesar on being informed of these movements was of opinion that he ought to make haste, even if he should run some risk in completing the bridges, in order that he might engage before greater forces of the enemy should be collected in that place. For no one even then considered it an absolutely necessary act, that changing his design he should direct his march into the Province, both because the infamy and disgrace of the thing, and the intervening mount Cevennes, and the difficulty of the roads prevented him; and especially because he had serious apprehensions for the safety of Labienus whom he had detached, and those legions whom he had sent with him. Therefore, having made very long marches by day and night, he came to the river Loire, contrary to the expectation of all; and having by means of the cavalry, found out a ford, suitable enough considering the emergency, of such depth that their arms and shoulders could be above water for supporting their accoutrements, he dispersed his cavalry in such a manner as to break the force of the current, and having confounded the enemy at the first sight, led his army across the river in safety; and finding corn and cattle in the fields, after refreshing his army with them, he determined to march into the country of the

huius belli causa in Italia atque Hispania coemptum miserat. Eo cum Eporedorix Viridomarusque venissent et de statu civitatis cognovissent, Litaviccum Bibracti ab Aeduis receptum, quod est oppidum apud eos maximae auctoritatis, Convictolitavim magistratum magnamque partem senatus ad eum convenisse, legatos ad Vercingetorigem de pace et amicitia concilianda publice missos, non praetermittendum tantum commodum existimaverunt. Itaque interfectis Novioduni custodibus quique eo negotiandi causa convenerant pecuniam atque equos inter se partiti sunt; obsides civitatum Bibracte ad magistratum deducendos curaverunt; oppidum, quod a se teneri non posse iudicabant, ne cui esset usui Romanis, incenderunt; frumenti quod subito potuerunt navibus avexerunt, reliquum flumine atque incendio corruperunt. Ipsi ex finitimis regionibus copias cogere, praesidia custodiasque ad ripas Ligeris disponere equitatumque omnibus locis iniciendi timoris causa ostentare coeperunt, si ab re frumentaria Romanos excludere aut adductos inopia in provinciam expellere possent. Quam ad spem multum eos adiuvabat, quod Liger ex nivibus creverat, ut omnino vado non posse transiri videretur.

Quibus rebus cognitis Caesar maturandum sibi censuit, si esset in perficiendis pontibus periclitandum, ut prius quam essent maiores eo coactae copiae dimicaret. Nam ut commutato consilio iter in provinciam converteret, id ne metu quidem necessario faciendum existimabat; cum infamia atque indignitas rei et oppositus mons Cevenna viarumque difficultas impediebat, tum maxime quod abiuncto Labieno atque eis legionibus quas una miserat vehementer timebat. Itaque admodum magnis diurnis nocturnisque itineribus confectis contra omnium opinionem ad Ligerem venit vadoque per equites invento pro rei necessitate opportuno, ut brachia modo atque humeri ad sustinenda arma liberi ab aqua esse possent, disposito equitatu qui vim fluminis refringeret, atque hostibus primo aspectu perturbatis, incolumem exercitum traduxit frumentumque in agris et pecoris copiam nactus repleto his rebus exercitu iter in Senones facere instituit.

Senones.

7:57 While these things are being done by Caesar, Labienus, leaving at Agendicum the recruits who had lately arrived from Italy, to guard the baggage, marches with four legions to Lutetia (which is a town of the Parisii, situated on an island on the river Seine), whose arrival being discovered by the enemy, numerous forces arrived from the neighboring states. The supreme command is intrusted to Camalugenus one of the Aulerci, who, although almost worn out with age, was called to that honor on account of his extraordinary knowledge of military tactics. He, when he observed that there was a large marsh which communicated with the Seine, and rendered all that country impassable, encamped there, and determined to prevent our troops from passing it.

7:58 Labienus at first attempted to raise Vineae, fill up the marsh with hurdles and clay, and secure a road. After he perceived that this was too difficult to accomplish, he issued in silence from his camp at the third watch, and reached Melodunum by the same route by which he came. This is a town of the Senones, situated on an island in the Seine, as we have just before observed of Lutetia. Having seized upon about fifty ships and quickly joined them together, and having placed soldiers in them, he intimidated by his unexpected arrival the inhabitants, of whom a great number had been called out to the war, and obtains possession of the town without a contest. Having repaired the bridge, which the enemy had broken down during the preceding days, he led over his army, and began to march along the banks of the river to Lutetia. The enemy, on learning the circumstance from those who had escaped from Melodunum, set fire to Lutetia, and order the bridges of that town to be broken down: they themselves set out from the marsh, and take their position on the banks of the Seine, over against Lutetia and opposite the camp of Labienus.

7:59 Caesar was now reported to have departed from Gergovia; intelligence was likewise brought to them concerning the revolt of the Aedui, and a successful rising in Gaul; and that Caesar, having been prevented from prosecuting his journey and crossing the Loire, and having been compelled by the want of corn, had marched hastily to the province. But the Bellovaci, who had been previously disaffected of themselves, on learning the revolt of the Aedui, began to assemble forces and openly to prepare for war. Then Labienus, as the change in affairs was so great, thought that he must adopt a very different system from what he had previously intended, and he did not now think of

Dum haec apud Caesarem geruntur, Labienus eo supplemento, quod nuper ex Italia venerat, relicto Agedinci, ut esset impedimentis praesidio, cum quattuor legionibus Lutetiam proficiscitur. Id est oppidum Parisiorum, quod positum est in insula fluminis Sequanae. Cuius adventu ab hostibus cognito magnae ex finitimis civitatibus copiae convenerunt. Summa imperi traditur Camulogeno Aulerco, qui prope confectus aetate tamen propter singularem scientiam rei militaris ad eum est honorem evocatus. Is cum animadvertisset perpetuam esse paludem, quae influeret in Sequanam atque illum omnem locum magnopere impediret, hic consedit nostrosque transitu prohibere instituit.

Labienus primo vineas agere, cratibus atque aggere paludem explere atque iter munire conabatur. Postquam id difficilius confieri animadvertit, silentio e castris tertia vigilia egressus eodem quo venerat itinere Metiosedum pervenit. Id est oppidum Senonum in insula Sequanae positum, ut paulo ante de Lutetia diximus. Deprensis navibus circiter quinquaginta celeriterque coniunctis atque eo militibus iniectis et rei novitate perterritis oppidanis, quorum magna pars erat ad bellum evocata, sine contentione oppido potitur. Refecto ponte, quem superioribus diebus hostes resciderant, exercitum traducit et secundo flumine ad Lutetiam iter facere coepit. Hostes re cognita ab eis, qui Metiosedo fugerant, Lutetiam incendi pontesque eius oppidi rescindi iubent; ipsi profecti a palude ad ripas Sequanae e regione Lutetiae contra Labieni castra considunt.

Iam Caesar a Gergovia discessisse audiebatur, iam de Aeduorum defectione et secundo Galliae motu rumores adferebantur, Gallique in colloquiis interclusum itinere et Ligeri Caesarem inopia frumenti coactum in provinciam contendisse confirmabant. Bellovaci autem defectione Aeduorum cognita, qui ante erant per se infideles, manus cogere atque aperte bellum parare coeperunt. Tum Labienus tanta rerum commutatione longe aliud sibi capiendum consilium atque antea senserat intellegebat, neque iam, ut aliquid adquireret

making any new acquisitions, or of provoking the enemy to an action; but that he might bring back his army safe to Agendicum. For, on one side, the Bellovaci, a state which held the highest reputation for prowess in Gaul, were pressing on him; and Camulogenus, with a disciplined and well-equipped army, held the other side; moreover, a very great river separated and cut off the legions from the garrison and baggage. He saw that, in consequence of such great difficulties being thrown in his way, he must seek aid from his own energy of disposition.

7:60 Having, therefore, called a council of war a little before evening, he exhorted his soldiers to execute with diligence and energy such commands as he should give; he assigns the ships which he had brought from Melodunum to Roman knights, one to each, and orders them to fall down the river silently for four miles, at the end of the fourth watch, and there wait for him. He leaves the five cohorts, which he considered to be the most steady in action, to guard the camp; he orders the five remaining cohorts of the same legion to proceed a little after midnight up the river with all their baggage, in a great tumult. He collects also some small boats; and sends them in the same direction, with orders to make a loud noise in rowing. He himself, a little after, marched out in silence, and, at the head of three legions, seeks that place to which he had ordered the ships to be brought.

7:61 When he had arrived there, the enemy's scouts, as they were stationed along every part of the river, not expecting an attack, because a great storm had suddenly arisen, were surprised by our soldiers: the infantry and cavalry are quickly transported, under the superintendence of the Roman knights, whom he had appointed to that office. Almost at the same time, a little before daylight, intelligence was given to the enemy that there was an unusual tumult in the camp of the Romans, and that a strong force was marching up the river, and that the sound of oars was distinctly heard in the same quarter, and that soldiers were being conveyed across in ships a little below. On hearing these things, because they were of opinion that the legions were passing in three different places, and that the entire army, being terrified by the revolt of the Aedui, were preparing for flight, they divided their forces also into three divisions. For leaving a guard opposite to the camp and sending a small body in the direction of Metiosedum, with orders to advance as far as the ships would proceed, they led the rest of their troops against Labienus.

7:62 By day-break all our soldiers were brought across, and the army of the enemy was in sight. Labienus, having encouraged his soldiers "to retain the memory of their ancient valor, and so

proelioque hostes lacesseret, sed ut incolumem exercitum Agedincum reduceret, cogitabat. Namque altera ex parte Bellovaci, quae civitas in Gallia maximam habet opinionem virtutis, instabant, alteram Camulogenus parato atque instructo exercitu tenebat; tum legiones a praesidio atque impedimentis interclusas maximum flumen distinebat. Tantis subito difficultatibus obiectis ab animi virtute auxilium petendum videbat.

Sub vesperum consilio convocato cohortatus ut ea quae imperasset diligenter industrieque administrarent, naves, quas Metiosedo deduxerat, singulas equitibus Romanis attribuit, et prima confecta vigilia quattuor milia passuum secundo flumine silentio progredi ibique se exspectari iubet. Quinque cohortes, quas minime firmas ad dimicandum esse existimabat, castris praesidio relinquit; quinque eiusdem legionis reliquas de media nocte cum omnibus impedimentis adverso flumine magno tumultu proficisci imperat. Conquirit etiam lintres: has magno sonitu remorum incitatus in eandem partem mittit. Ipse post paulo silentio egressus cum tribus legionibus eum locum petit quo naves appelli iusserat.

Eo cum esset ventum, exploratores hostium, ut omni fluminis parte erant dispositi, inopinantes, quod magna subito erat coorta tempestas, ab nostris opprimumtur; exercitus equitatusque equitibus Romanis administrantibus, quos ei negotio praefecerat, celeriter transmittitur. Vno fere tempore sub lucem hostibus nuntiatur in castris Romanorum praeter consuetudinem tumultuari et magnum ire agmen adverso flumine sonitumque remorum in eadem parte exaudiri et paulo infra milites navibus transportari. Quibus rebus auditis, quod existimabant tribus locis transire legiones atque omnes perturbatos defectione Aeduorum fugam parare, suas quoque copias in tres partes distribuerunt. Nam praesidio e regione castrorum relicto et parva manu Metiosedum versus missa, quae tantum progrediatur, quantum naves processissent, reliquas copias contra Labienum duxerunt.

Prima luce et nostri omnes erant transportati, et hostium acies cernebatur. Labienus milites cohortatus ut suae pristinae virtutis et

many most successful actions, and imagine Caesar himself, under whose command they had so often routed the enemy, to be present," gives the signal for action. At the first onset the enemy are beaten and put to flight in the right wing, where the seventh legion stood: on the left wing, which position the twelfth legion held, although the first ranks fell transfixed by the javelins of the Romans, yet the rest resisted most bravely; nor did any one of them show the slightest intention of flying. Camulogenus, the general of the enemy, was present and encouraged his troops. But when the issue of the victory was still uncertain, and the circumstances which were taking place on the left wing were announced to the tribunes of the seventh legion, they faced about their legion to the enemy's rear and attacked it: not even then did any one retreat, but all were surrounded and slain. Camulogenus met the same fate. But those who were left as a guard opposite the camp of Labienus, when they heard that the battle was commenced, marched to aid their countrymen and take possession of a hill, but were unable to withstand the attack of the victorious soldiers. In this manner, mixed with their own fugitives, such as the woods and mountains did not shelter were cut to pieces by our cavalry. When this battle was finished, Labienus returns to Agendicum, where the baggage of the whole army had been left: from it he marched with all his forces to Caesar.

7:63 The revolt of the Aedui being known, the war grows more dangerous. Embassies are sent by them in all directions: as far as they can prevail by influence, authority, or money, they strive to excite the state [to revolt]. Having got possession of the hostages whom Caesar had deposited with them, they terrify the hesitating by putting them to death. The Aedui request Vercingetorix to come to them and communicate his plans of conducting the war. On obtaining this request they insist that the chief command should be assigned to them; and when the affair became a disputed question, a council of all Gaul is summoned to Bibracte. They came together in great numbers and from every quarter to the same place. The decision is left to the votes of the mass; all to a man approve of Vercingetorix as their general. The Remi, Lingones, and Treviri were absent from this meeting; the two former because they attached themselves to the alliance of Rome; the Treviri because they were very remote and were hard pressed by the Germans; which was also the reason of their being absent during the whole war, and their sending auxiliaries to neither party. The Aedui are highly indignant at being deprived of the chief command; they lament the change of fortune, and miss Caesar's indulgence toward

secundissimorum proeliorum retinerent memoriam atque ipsum Caesarem, cuius ductu saepe numero hostes superassent, praesentem adesse existimarent, dat signum proeli. Primo concursu ab dextro cornu, ubi septima legio constiterat, hostes pelluntur atque in fugam coniciuntur; ab sinistro, quem locum duodecima legio tenebat, cum primi ordines hostium transfixi telis concidissent, tamen acerrime reliqui resistebant, nec dabat suspicionem fugae quisquam. Ipse dux hostium Camulogenus suis aderat atque eos cohortabatur. Incerto nunc etiam exitu victoriae, cum septimae legionis tribunis esset nuntiatum quae in sinistro cornu gererentur, post tergum hostium legionem ostenderunt signaque intulerunt. Ne eo quidem tempore quisquam loco cessit, sed circumventi omnes interfectique sunt. Eandem fortunam tulit Camulogenus. At ei qui praesidio contra castra Labieni erant relicti, cum proelium commissum audissent, subsidio suis ierunt collemque ceperunt, neque nostrorum militum victorum impetum sustinere potuerunt. Sic cum suis fugientibus permixti, quos non silvae montesque texerunt, ab equitatu sunt interfecti. Hoc negotio confecto Labienus revertitur Agedincum, ubi impedimenta totius exercitus relicta erant: inde cum omnibus copiis ad Caesarem pervenit.

Defectione Aeduorum cognita bellum augetur. Legationes in omnes partes circummittuntur: quantum gratia, auctoritate, pecunia valent, ad sollicitandas civitates nituntur; nacti obsides, quos Caesar apud eos deposuerat, horum supplicio dubitantes territant. Petunt a Vercingetorige Aedui ut ad se veniat rationesque belli gerendi communicet. Re impetrata contendunt ut ipsis summa imperi tradatur, et re in controversiam deducta totius Galliae concilium Bibracte indicitur. Eodem conveniunt undique frequentes. Multitudinis suffragiis res permittitur: ad unum omnes Vercingetorigem probant imperatorem. Ab hoc concilio Remi, Lingones, Treveri afuerunt: illi, quod amicitiam Romanorum sequebantur; Treveri, quod aberant longius et ab Germanis premebantur, quae fuit causa quare toto abessent bello et neutris auxilia mitterent. Magno dolore Aedui ferunt se deiectos principatu, queruntur fortunae commutationem et Caesaris indulgentiam in se requirunt, neque tamen suscepto bello suum consilium ab reliquis separare audent. Inviti summae

them; however, after engaging in the war, they do not dare to pursue their own measures apart from the rest. Eporedirix and Viridomarus, youths of the greatest promise, submit reluctantly to Vercingetorix.

7:64 The latter demands hostages from the remaining states; nay, more, appointed a day for this proceeding; he orders all the cavalry, fifteen thousand in number, to quickly assemble here; he says that he will be content with the infantry which he had before, and would not tempt fortune nor come to a regular engagement; but since he had abundance of cavalry, it would be very easy for him to prevent the Romans from obtaining forage or corn, provided that they themselves should resolutely destroy their corn and set fire to their houses; by which sacrifice of private property they would evidently obtain perpetual dominion and freedom. After arranging these matters, he levies ten thousand infantry on the Aedui and Segusiani, who border on our province: to these he adds eight hundred horse. He sets over them the brother of Eporedirix, and orders him to wage war against the Allobroges. On the other side he sends the Gabali and the nearest cantons of the Arverni against the Helvii; he likewise sends the Ruteni and Cadurci to lay waste the territories of the Volcae Arecomici. Besides, by secret messages and embassies, he tampers with the Allobroges, whose minds, he hopes, had not yet settled down after the excitement of the late war. To their nobles he promises money, and to their state the dominion of the whole province.

7:65 The only guards provided against all these contingencies were twenty-two cohorts, which were collected from the entire province by Lucius Caesar, the lieutenant, and opposed to the enemy in every quarter. The Helvii, voluntarily engaging in battle with their neighbors, are defeated, and Caius Valerius Donotaurus, the son of Caburus, the principal man of the state, and several others, being slain, they are forced to retire within their towns and fortifications. The Allobroges, placing guards along the course of the Rhine, defend their frontiers with great vigilance and energy. Caesar, as he perceived that the enemy were superior in cavalry, and he himself could receive no aid from the Province or Italy, while all communication was cut off, sends across the Rhine into Germany to those states which he had subdued in the preceding campaigns, and summons from them cavalry and the light-armed infantry, who were accustomed to engage among them. On their arrival, as they were mounted on unserviceable horses, he takes horses from the military tribunes and the rest, nay, even from the Roman knights and veterans, and distributes them among the Germans.

7:66 In the mean time, whilst these things are going on, the

spei adulescentes Eporedorix et Viridomarus Vercingetorigi parent.

Ipse imperat reliquis civitatibus obsides diemque ei rei constituit. Omnes equites, quindecim milia numero, celeriter convenire iubet; peditatu quem antea habuerit se fore contentum dicit, neque fortunam temptaturum aut in acie dimicaturum, sed, quoniam abundet equitatu, perfacile esse factu frumentationibus pabulationibusque Romanos prohibere, aequo modo animo sua ipsi frumenta corrumpant aedificiaque incendant, qua rei familiaris iactura perpetuum imperium libertatemque se consequi videant. His constitutis rebus Aeduis Segusiavisque, qui sunt finitimi provinciae, decem milia peditum imperat; huc addit equites octingentos. His praeficit fratrem Eporedorigis bellumque inferri Allobrogibus iubet. Altera ex parte Gabalos proximosque pagos Arvernorum in Helvios, item Rutenos Cadurcosque ad fines Volcarum Arecomicorum depopulandos mittit. Nihilo minus clandestinis nuntiis legationibusque Allobrogas sollicitat, quorum mentes nondum ab superiore bello resedisse sperabat. Horum principibus pecunias, civitati autem imperium totius provinciae pollicetur.

Ad hos omnes casus provisa erant praesidia cohortium duarum et viginti, quae ex ipsa provincia ab Lucio Caesare legato ad omnes partes opponebantur. Helvii sua sponte cum finitimis proelio congressi pelluntur et Gaio Valerio Donnotauro, Caburi filio, principe civitatis, compluribusque aliis interfectis intra oppida ac muros compelluntur. Allobroges crebris ad Rhodanum dispositis praesidiis magna cum cura et diligentia suos fines tuentur. Caesar, quod hostes equitatu superiores esse intellegebat et interclusis omnibus itineribus nulla re ex provincia atque Italia sublevari poterat, trans Rhenum in Germaniam mittit ad eas civitates quas superioribus annis pacaverat, equitesque ab his arcessit et levis armaturae pedites, qui inter eos proeliari consuerant. Eorum adventu, quod minus idoneis equis utebantur, a tribunis militum reliquisque equitibus Romanis atque evocatis equos sumit Germanisque distribuit.

Interea, dum haec geruntur, hostium copiae ex

forces of the enemy from the Arverni, and the cavalry which had been demanded from all Gaul, meet together. A great number of these having been collected, when Caesar was marching into the country of the Sequani, through the confines of the Lingones, in order that he might the more easily render aid to the province, Vercingetorix encamped in three camps, about ten miles from the Romans: and having summoned the commanders of the cavalry to a council, he shows that the time of victory was come; that the Romans were fleeing into the Province and leaving Gaul; that this was sufficient for obtaining immediate freedom; but was of little moment in acquiring peace and tranquillity for the future; for the Romans would return after assembling greater forces and would not put an end to the war. Therefore they should attack them on their march, when encumbered. If the infantry should [be obliged to] relieve their cavalry, and be retarded by doing so, the march could not be accomplished: if, abandoning their baggage they should provide for their safety (a result which, he trusted, was more like to ensue), they would lose both property and character. For as to the enemy's horse, they ought not to entertain a doubt that none of them would dare to advance beyond the main body. In order that they [the Gauls] may do so with greater spirit, he would marshal all their forces before the camp, and intimidate the enemy. The cavalry unanimously shout out, "That they ought to bind themselves by a most sacred oath, that he should not be received under a roof, nor have access to his children, parents, or wife, who shall not twice have ridden through the enemy's army."

7:67 This proposal receiving general approbation, and all being forced to take the oath, on the next day the cavalry were divided into three parts, and two of these divisions made a demonstration on our two flanks; while one in front began to obstruct our march. On this circumstance being announced, Caesar orders his cavalry also to form three divisions and charge the enemy. Then the action commences simultaneously in every part: the main body halts; the baggage is received within the ranks of the legions. If our men seemed to be distressed, or hard pressed in any quarter, Caesar usually ordered the troops to advance, and the army to wheel round in that quarter; which conduct retarded the enemy in the pursuit, and encouraged our men by the hope of support. At length the Germans, on the right wing, having gained the top of the hill, dislodge the enemy from their position and pursue them even as far as the river at which Vercingetorix with the infantry was stationed, and slay several of them. The rest, on observing this action, fearing lest they should be surrounded, betake themselves to flight. A slaughter ensues in every direction, and

Arvernis equitesque qui toti Galliae erant imperati conveniunt. Magno horum coacto numero, cum Caesar in Sequanos per extremos Lingonum fines iter faceret, quo facilius subsidium provinciae ferri posset, circiter milia passuum decem ab Romanis trinis castris Vercingetorix consedit convocatisque ad concilium praefectis equitum venisse tempus victoriae demonstrat. Fugere in provinciam Romanos Galliaque excedere. Id sibi ad praesentem obtinendam libertatem satis esse; ad reliqui temporis pacem atque otium parum profici: maioribus enim coactis copiis reversuros neque finem bellandi facturos. Proinde agmine impeditos adorirantur. Si pedites suis auxilium ferant atque in eo morentur, iter facere non posse; si, id quod magis futurum confidat, relictis impedimentis suae saluti consulant, et usu rerum necessariarum et dignitate spoliatum iri. Nam de equitibus hostium, quin nemo eorum progredi modo extra agmen audeat, et ipsos quidem non debere dubitare, et quo maiore faciant animo, copias se omnes pro castris habiturum et terrori hostibus futurum. Conclamant equites sanctissimo iureiurando confirmari oportere, ne tecto recipiatur, ne ad liberos, ne ad parentes, ad uxorem aditum habeat, qui non bis per agmen hostium perequitasset.

Probata re atque omnibus iureiurando adactis postero die in tres partes distributo equitatu duae se acies ab duobus lateribus ostendunt, una primo agmine iter impedire coepit. Qua re nuntiata Caesar suum quoque equitatum tripertito divisum contra hostem ire iubet. Pugnatur una omnibus in partibus. Consistit agmen; impedimenta intra legiones recipiuntur. Si qua in parte nostri laborare aut gravius premi videbantur, eo signa inferri Caesar aciemque constitui iubebat; quae res et hostes ad insequendum tardabat et nostros spe auxili confirmabat. Tandem Germani ab dextro latere summum iugum nacti hostes loco depellunt; fugientes usque ad flumen, ubi Vercingetorix cum pedestribus copiis consederat, persequuntur compluresque interficiunt. Qua re animadversa reliqui ne circumirentur veriti se fugae mandant. Omnibus locis fit caedes. Tres nobilissimi Aedui capti ad Caesarem perducuntur: Cotus, praefectus

three of the noblest of the Aedui are taken and brought to Caesar: Cotus, the commander of the cavalry, who had been engaged in the contest with Convictolitanis the last election, Cavarillus, who had held the command of the infantry after the revolt of Litavicus, and Eporedirix, under whose command the Aedui had engaged in war against the Sequani, before the arrival of Caesar.

7:68 All his cavalry being routed, Vercingetorix led back his troops in the same order as he had arranged them before the camp, and immediately began to march to Alesia, which is a town of the Mandubii, and ordered the baggage to be speedily brought forth from the camp, and follow him closely. Caesar, having conveyed his baggage to the nearest hill, and having left two legions to guard it, pursued as far as the time of day would permit, and after slaying about three thousand of the rear of the enemy, encamped at Alesia on the next day. On reconnoitering the situation of the city, finding that the enemy were panic-stricken, because the cavalry in which they placed their chief reliance, were beaten, he encouraged his men to endure the toil, and began to draw a line of circumvallation round Alesia.

7:69 The town itself was situated on the top of a hill, in a very lofty position, so that it did not appear likely to be taken, except by a regular siege. Two rivers, on two different sides, washed the foot of the hill. Before the town lay a plain of about three miles in length; on every other side hills at a moderate distance, and of an equal degree of height, surrounded the town. The army of the Gauls had filled all the space under the wall, comprising a part of the hill which looked to the rising sun, and had drawn in front a trench and a stone wall six feet high. The circuit of that fortification, which was commenced by the Romans, comprised eleven miles. The camp was pitched in a strong position, and twenty-three redoubts were raised in it, in which sentinels were placed by day, lest any sally should be made suddenly; and by night the same were occupied by watches and strong guards.

7:70 The work having been begun, a cavalry action ensues in that plain, which we have already described as broken by hills, and extending three miles in length. The contest is maintained on both sides with the utmost vigor; Caesar sends the Germans to aid our troops when distressed, and draws up the legions in front of the camp, lest any sally should be suddenly made by the enemy's infantry. The courage of our men is increased by the additional support of the legions; the enemy being put to flight, hinder one another by their numbers, and as only the narrower gates were left open, are crowded together in them; then the

equitum, qui controversiam cum Convictolitavi proximis comitiis habuerat, et Cavarillus, qui post defectionem Litavicci pedestribus copiis praefuerat, et Eporedorix, quo duce ante adventum Caesaris Aedui cum Sequanis bello contenderant.

Fugato omni equitatu Vercingetorix copias, ut pro castris collocaverat, reduxit protinusque Alesiam, quod est oppidum Mandubiorum, iter facere coepit celeriterque impedimenta ex castris educi et se subsequi iussit. Caesar impedimentis in proximum collem deductis, duabus legionibus praesidio relictis, secutus quantum diei tempus est passum, circiter tribus milibus hostium ex novissimo agmine interfectis altero die ad Alesiam castra fecit. Perspecto urbis situ perterritisque hostibus, quod equitatu, qua maxime parte exercitus confidebant, erant pulsi, adhortatus ad laborem milites circumvallare instituit.

Ipsum erat oppidum Alesia in colle summo admodum edito loco, ut nisi obsidione expugnari non posse videretur; cuius collis radices duo duabus ex partibus flumina subluebant. Ante id oppidum planities circiter milia passuum tria in longitudinem patebat: reliquis ex omnibus partibus colles mediocri interiecto spatio pari altitudinis fastigio oppidum cingebant. Sub muro, quae pars collis ad orientem solem spectabat, hunc omnem locum copiae Gallorum compleverant fossamque et maceriam sex in altitudinem pedum praeduxerant. Eius munitionis quae ab Romanis instituebatur circuitus XI milia passuum tenebat. Castra opportunis locis erant posita ibique castella viginti tria facta, quibus in castellis interdiu stationes ponebantur, ne qua subito eruptio fieret: haec eadem noctu excubitoribus ac firmis praesidiis tenebantur.

Opere instituto fit equestre proelium in ea planitie, quam intermissam collibus tria milia passuum in longitudinem patere supra demonstravimus. Summa vi ab utrisque contenditur. Laborantibus nostris Caesar Germanos summittit legionesque pro castris constituit, ne qua subito irruptio ab hostium peditatu fiat. Praesidio legionum addito nostris animus augetur: hostes in fugam coniecti se ipsi multitudine impediunt atque angustioribus portis relictis coacervantur. Germani acrius usque ad munitiones

Germans pursue them with vigor even to the fortifications. A great slaughter ensues; some leave their horses, and endeavor to cross the ditch and climb the wall. Caesar orders the legions which he had drawn up in front of the rampart to advance a little. The Gauls, who were within the fortifications, were no less panic-stricken, thinking that the enemy were coming that moment against them, and unanimously shout "to arms;" some in their alarm rush into the town; Vercingetorix orders the gates to be shut, lest the camp should be left undefended. The Germans retreat, after slaying many and taking several horses.

7:71 Vercingetorix adopts the design of sending away all his cavalry by night, before the fortifications should be completed by the Romans. He charges them when departing "that each of them should go to his respective state, and press for the war all who were old enough to bear arms; he states his own merits, and conjures them to consider his safety, and not surrender him who had deserved so well of the general freedom, to the enemy for torture; he points out to them that, if they should be remiss, eighty thousand chosen men would perish with him; that upon making a calculation, he had barely corn for thirty days, but could hold out a little longer by economy." After giving these instructions he silently dismisses the cavalry in the second watch, [on that side] where our works were not completed; he orders all the corn to be brought to himself; he ordains capital punishment to such as should not obey; he distributes among them, man by man, the cattle, great quantities of which had been driven there by the Mandubii; he began to measure out the corn sparingly, and by little and little; he receives into the town all the forces which he had posted in front of it. In this manner he prepares to await the succors from Gaul, and carry on the war.

7:72 Caesar, on learning these proceedings from the deserters and captives, adopted the following system of fortification; he dug a trench twenty feet deep, with perpendicular sides, in such a manner that the base of this trench should extend so far as the edges were apart at the top. He raised all his other works at a distance of four hundred feet from that ditch; [he did] that with this intention, lest (since he necessarily embraced so extensive an area, and the whole works could not be easily surrounded by a line of soldiers) a large number of the enemy should suddenly, or by night, sally against the fortifications; or lest they should by day cast weapons against our men while occupied with the works. Having left this interval, he drew two trenches fifteen feet broad, and of the same depth; the innermost of them, being in low and level ground, he filled with water conveyed from the river. Behind these he raised a rampart and wall twelve feet high; to this he added a parapet and battlements, with large

sequuntur. Fit magna caedes: nonnulli relictis equis fossam transire et maceriam transcendere conantur. Paulum legiones Caesar quas pro vallo constituerat promoveri iubet. Non minus qui intra munitiones erant perturbantur Galli: veniri ad se confestim existimantes ad arma conclamant; nonnulli perterriti in oppidum irrumpunt. Vercingetorix iubet portas claudi, ne castra nudentur. Multis interfectis, compluribus equis captis Germani sese recipiunt.

Vercingetorix, priusquam munitiones ab Romanis perficiantur, consilium capit omnem ab se equitatum noctu dimittere. Discedentibus mandat ut suam quisque eorum civitatem adeat omnesque qui per aetatem arma ferre possint ad bellum cogant. Sua in illos merita proponit obtestaturque ut suae salutis rationem habeant neu se optime de communi libertate meritum in cruciatum hostibus dedant. Quod si indiligentiores fuerint, milia hominum delecta octoginta una secum interitura demonstrat. Ratione inita se exigue dierum triginta habere frumentum, sed paulo etiam longius tolerari posse parcendo. His datis mandatis, qua opus erat intermissum, secunda vigilia silentio equitatum mittit. Frumentum omne ad se referri iubet; capitis poenam eis qui non paruerint constituit: pecus, cuius magna erat copia ab Mandubiis compulsa, viritim distribuit; frumentum parce et paulatim metiri instituit; copias omnes quas pro oppido collocaverat in oppidum recepit. His rationibus auxilia Galliae exspectare et bellum parat administrare.

Quibus rebus cognitis ex perfugis et captivis, Caesar haec genera munitionis instituit. Fossam pedum viginti directis lateribus duxit, ut eius fossae solum tantundem pateret quantum summae fossae labra distarent. Reliquas omnes munitiones ab ea fossa pedes quadringentos reduxit, [id] hoc consilio, quoniam tantum esset necessario spatium complexus, nec facile totum corpus corona militum cingeretur, ne de improviso aut noctu ad munitiones hostium multitudo advolaret aut interdiu tela in nostros operi destinatos conicere possent. Hoc intermisso spatio duas fossas quindecim pedes latas, eadem altitudine perduxit, quarum interiorem campestribus ac demissis locis aqua ex flumine derivata complevit. Post eas aggerem ac vallum duodecim pedum exstruxit. Huic loricam pinnasque

stakes cut like stags' horns, projecting from the junction of the parapet and battlements, to prevent the enemy from scaling it, and surrounded the entire work with turrets, which were eighty feet distant from one another.

7:73 It was necessary, at one and the same time, to procure timber [for the rampart], lay in supplies of corn, and raise also extensive fortifications, and the available troops were in consequence of this reduced in number, since they used to advance to some distance from the camp, and sometimes the Gauls endeavored to attack our works, and to make a sally from the town by several gates and in great force. Caesar thought that further additions should be made to these works, in order that the fortifications might be defensible by a small number of soldiers. Having, therefore, cut down the trunks of trees or very thick branches, and having stripped their tops of the bark, and sharpened them into a point, he drew a continued trench every where five feet deep. These stakes being sunk into this trench, and fastened firmly at the bottom, to prevent the possibility of their being torn up, had their branches only projecting from the ground. There were five rows in connection with, and intersecting each other; and whoever entered within them were likely to impale themselves on very sharp stakes. The soldiers called these "cippi." Before these, which were arranged in oblique rows in the form of a quincunx, pits three feet deep were dug, which gradually diminished in depth to the bottom. In these pits tapering stakes, of the thickness of a man's thigh; sharpened at the top and hardened in the fire, were sunk in such a manner as to project from the ground not more than four inches; at the same time for the purpose of giving them strength and stability, they were each filled with trampled clay to the height of one foot from the bottom: the rest of the pit was covered over with osiers and twigs, to conceal the deceit. Eight rows of this kind were dug, and were three feet distant from each other. They called this a lily from its resemblance to that flower. Stakes a foot long, with iron hooks attached to them, were entirely sunk in the ground before these, and were planted in every place at small intervals; these they called spurs.

7:74 After completing these works, saving selected as level ground as he could, considering the nature of the country, and having inclosed an area of fourteen miles, he constructed, against an external enemy, fortifications of the same kind in every respect, and separate from these, so that the guards of the fortifications could not be surrounded even by immense numbers, if such a circumstance should take place owing to the departure of the enemy's cavalry; and in order that the Roman soldiers might not be compelled to go out of the camp with great risk, ho orders all to provide forage and corn for thirty days.

adiecit grandibus cervis eminentibus ad commissuras pluteorum atque aggeris, qui ascensum hostium tardarent, et turres toto opere circumdedit, quae pedes LXXX inter se distarent.

Erat eodem tempore et materiari et frumentari et tantas munitiones fieri necesse deminutis nostris copiis quae longius ab castris progrediebantur: ac non numquam opera nostra Galli temptare atque eruptionem ex oppido pluribus portis summa vi facere conabantur. Quare ad haec rursus opera addendum Caesar putavit, quo minore numero militum munitiones defendi possent. Itaque truncis arborum aut admodum firmis ramis abscisis atque horum delibratis ac praeacutis cacuminibus perpetuae fossae quinos pedes altae ducebantur. Huc illi stipites demissi et ab infimo revincti, ne revelli possent, ab ramis eminebant. Quini erant ordines coniuncti inter se atque implicati; quo qui intraverant, se ipsi acutissimis vallis induebant. Hos cippos appellabant. Ante quos obliquis ordinibus in quincuncem dispositis scrobes tres in altitudinem pedes fodiebantur paulatim angustiore ad infimum fastigio. Huc teretes stipites feminis crassitudine ab summo praeacuti et praeusti demittebantur, ita ut non amplius digitis quattuor ex terra eminerent; simul confirmandi et stabiliendi causa singuli ab infimo solo pedes terra exculcabantur, reliqua pars scrobis ad occultandas insidias viminibus ac virgultis integebatur. Huius generis octoni ordines ducti ternos inter se pedes distabant. Id ex similitudine floris lilium appellabant. Ante haec taleae pedem longae ferreis hamis infixis totae in terram infodiebantur mediocribusque intermissis spatiis omnibus locis disserebantur; quos stimulos nominabant.

His rebus perfectis regiones secutus quam potuit aequissimas pro loci natura quattuordecim milia passuum complexus pares eiusdem generis munitiones, diversas ab his, contra exteriorem hostem perfecit, ut ne magna quidem multitudine, si ita accidat, munitionum praesidia circumfundi possent; ac ne cum periculo ex castris egredi cogatur, dierum triginta pabulum frumentumque habere omnes convectum iubet.

7:75 While those things are carried on at Alesia, the Gauls, having convened a council of their chief nobility, determine that all who could bear arms should not be called out, which was the opinion of Vercingetorix, but that a fixed number should be levied from each state; lest, when so great a multitude assembled together, they could neither govern nor distinguish their men, nor have the means of supplying them with corn. They demand thirty-five thousand men from the Aedui and their dependents, the Segusiani, Ambivareti, and Aulerci Brannovices; an equal number from the Arverni in conjunction with the Eleuteti Cadurci, Gabali, and Velauni, who were accustomed to be under the command of the Arverni; twelve thousand each from the Senones, Sequani, Bituriges, Sentones, Ruteni, and Carnutes; ten thousand from the Bellovaci; the same number from the Lemovici; eight thousand each from the Pictones, and Turoni, and Parisii, and Helvii; five thousand each from the Suessiones, Ambiani, Mediomatrici, Petrocorii, Nervii, Morini, and Nitiobriges; the same number from the Aulerci Cenomani; four thousand from the Atrebates; three thousand each from the Bellocassi, Lexovii, and Aulerci Eburovices; thirty thousand from the Rauraci, and Boii; six thousand from all the states together, which border on the Atlantic, and which in their dialect are called Armoricae (in which number are comprehended the Curisolites, Rhedones, Ambibari, Caltes, Osismii, Lemovices, Veneti, and Unelli). Of these the Bellovaci did not contribute their number, as they said that they would wage war against the Romans on their own account, and at their own discretion, and would not obey the order of any one: however, at the request of Commius, they sent two thousand, in consideration of a tie of hospitality which subsisted between him and them.

7:76 Caesar had, as we have previously narrated, availed himself of the faithful and valuable services of this Commius, in Britain, in former years: in consideration of which merits he had exempted from taxes his [Commius's] state, and had conferred on Commius himself the country of the Morini. Yet such was the unanimity of the Gauls in asserting their freedom, and recovering their ancient renown in war, that they were influenced neither by favors, nor by the recollection of private friendship; and all earnestly directed their energies and resources to that war, and collected eight thousand cavalry, and about two hundred and forty thousand infantry. These were reviewed in the country of the Aedui, and a calculation was made of their numbers: commanders were appointed: the supreme command is intrusted to Commius the Atrebatian, Viridomarus and Eporedirix the Aeduans, and Vergasillaunus the Arvernan, the cousin-german of Vercingetorix. To them are assigned men

Dum haec apud Alesiam geruntur, Galli concilio principum indicto non omnes eos qui arma ferre possent, ut censuit Vercingetorix, convocandos statuunt, sed certum numerum cuique ex civitate imperandum, ne tanta multitudine confusa nec moderari nec discernere suos nec frumentandi rationem habere possent. Imperant Aeduis atque eorum clientibus, Segusiavis, Ambivaretis, Aulercis Brannovicibus, Blannoviis, milia XXXV; parem numerum Arvernis adiunctis Eleutetis, Cadurcis, Gabalis, Vellaviis, qui sub imperio Arvernorum esse consuerunt; Sequanis, Senonibus, Biturigibus, Santonis, Rutenis, Carnutibus duodena milia; Bellovacis X; totidem Lemovicibus; octona Pictonibus et Turonis et Parisiis et Helvetiis; [Suessionibus,] Ambianis, Mediomatricis, Petrocoriis, Nerviis, Morinis, Nitiobrigibus quina milia; Aulercis Cenomanis totidem; Atrebatibus [IIII milibus]; Veliocassis, Lexoviis et Aulercis Eburovicibus terna; Rauracis et Boiis bina; [XXX milia] universis civitatibus, quae Oceanum attingunt quaeque eorum consuetudine Armoricae appellantur, quo sunt in numero Curiosolites, Redones, Ambibarii, Caletes, Osismi, Veneti, Lemovices, Venelli. Ex his Bellovaci suum numerum non compleverunt, quod se suo nomine atque arbitrio cum Romanis bellum gesturos dicebant neque cuiusquam imperio obtemperaturos; rogati tamen ab Commio pro eius hospitio duo milia una miserunt.

Huius opera Commi, ut antea demonstravimus, fideli atque utili superioribus annis erat usus in Britannia Caesar; quibus ille pro meritis civitatem eius immunem esse iusserat, iura legesque reddiderat atque ipsi Morinos attribuerat. Tamen tanta universae Galliae consensio fuit libertatis vindicandae et pristinae belli laudis recuperandae, ut neque beneficiis neque amicitiae memoria moverentur, omnesque et animo et opibus in id bellum incumberent. Coactis equitum VIII milibus et peditum circiter CCL haec in Aeduorum finibus recensebantur, numerusque inibatur, praefecti constituebantur. Commio Atrebati, Viridomaro et Eporedorigi Aeduis, Vercassivellauno Arverno, consobrino Vercingetorigis, summa imperi traditur. His delecti ex civitatibus attribuuntur, quorum consilio

selected from each state, by whose advice the war should be conducted. All march to Alesia, sanguine and full of confidence: nor was there a single individual who imagined that the Romans could withstand the sight of such an immense host: especially in an action carried on both in front and rear, when [on the inside] the besieged would sally from the town and attack the enemy, and on the outside so great forces of cavalry and infantry would be seen.

7:77 But those who were blockaded at Alesia, the day being past, on which they had expected auxiliaries from their countrymen, and all their corn being consumed ignorant of what was going on among the Aedui, convened an assembly and deliberated on the exigency of their situation. After various opinions had been expressed among them, some of which proposed a surrender, others a sally, while their strength would support it, the speech of Critognatus ought not to be omitted for its singular and detestable cruelty. He sprung from the noblest family among the Arverni, and possessing great influence, says, "I shall pay no attention to the opinion of those who call a most disgraceful surrender by the name of a capitulation; nor do I think that they ought to be considered as citizens, or summoned to the council. My business is with those who approve of a sally: in whose advice the memory of our ancient prowess seems to dwell in the opinion of you all. To be unable to bear privation for a short time is disgraceful cowardice, not pukka valor. Those who voluntarily offer themselves to death are more easily found than those who would calmly endure distress. And I would approve of this opinion (for honor is a powerful motive with me), could I foresee no other loss, save that of life; but let us, in adopting our design, look back on all Gaul, which we have stirred up to our aid. What courage do you think would our relatives and friends have, if eighty thousand men were butchered in one spot, supposing that they should be forced to come to an action almost over our corpses? Do not utterly deprive them of your aid, for they have spurned all thoughts of personal danger on account of your safety; nor by your folly, rashness, and cowardice, crush all Gaul and doom it to an eternal slavery. Do you doubt their fidelity and firmness because they have not come at the appointed day? What then? Do you suppose that the Romans are employed every day in the outer fortifications for mere amusement? If you can not be assured by their dispatches, since every avenue is blocked up, take the Romans as evidence that there approach is drawing near; since they, intimidated by alarm at this, labor night and day at their works. What, therefore, is my design? To do as our ancestors did in the war against the Cimbri and Teutones, which was by no means equally momentous who, when driven into their towns,

bellum administraretur. Omnes alacres et fiduciae pleni ad Alesiam proficiscuntur, neque erat omnium quisquam qui aspectum modo tantae multitudinis sustineri posse arbitraretur, praesertim ancipiti proelio, cum ex oppido eruptione pugnaretur, foris tantae copiae equitatus peditatusque cernerentur.

At ei, qui Alesiae obsidebantur praeterita die, qua auxilia suorum exspectaverant, consumpto omni frumento, inscii quid in Aeduis gereretur, concilio coacto de exitu suarum fortunarum consultabant. Ac variis dictis sententiis, quarum pars deditionem, pars, dum vires suppeterent, eruptionem censebat, non praetereunda oratio Critognati videtur propter eius singularem et nefariam crudelitatem. Hic summo in Arvernis ortus loco et magnae habitus auctoritatis, "Nihil," inquit, "de eorum sententia dicturus sum, qui turpissimam servitutem deditionis nomine appellant, neque hos habendos civium loco neque ad concilium adhibendos censeo. Cum his mihi res sit, qui eruptionem probant; quorum in consilio omnium vestrum consensu pristinae residere virtutis memoria videtur. Animi est ista mollitia, non virtus, paulisper inopiam ferre non posse. Qui se ultro morti offerant facilius reperiuntur quam qui dolorem patienter ferant. Atque ego hanc sententiam probarem (tantum apud me dignitas potest), si nullam praeterquam vitae nostrae iacturam fieri viderem: sed in consilio capiendo omnem Galliam respiciamus, quam ad nostrum auxilium concitavimus. Quid hominum milibus LXXX uno loco interfectis propinquis consanguineisque nostris animi fore existimatis, si paene in ipsis cadaveribus proelio decertare cogentur? Nolite hos vestro auxilio exspoliare, qui vestrae salutis causa suum periculum neglexerunt, nec stultitia ac temeritate vestra aut animi imbecillitate omnem Galliam prosternere et perpetuae servituti subicere. An, quod ad diem non venerunt, de eorum fide constantiaque dubitatis? Quid ergo? Romanos in illis ulterioribus munitionibus animine causa cotidie exerceri putatis? Si illorum nuntiis confirmari non potestis omni aditu praesaepto, his utimini testibus appropinquare eorum adventum; cuius rei timore exterriti diem noctemque in opere versantur. Quid ergo mei consili est? Facere, quod nostri maiores nequaquam pari bello

and oppressed by similar privations, supported life by the corpses of those who appeared useless for war on account of their age, and did not surrender to the enemy: and even if we had not a precedent for such cruel conduct, still I should consider it most glorious that one should be established, and delivered to posterity. For in what was that war like this? The Cimbri, after laying Gaul waste, and inflicting great calamities, at length departed from our country, and sought other lands; they left us our rights, laws, lands, and liberty. But what other motive or wish have the Romans, than, induced by envy, to settle in the lands and states of those whom they have learned by fame to be noble and powerful in war, and impose on them perpetual slavery? For they never have carried on wars on any other terms. But if you know not these things which are going on in distant countries, look to the neighboring Gaul, which being reduced to the form of a province, stripped of its rights and laws, and subjected to Roman despotism, is oppressed by perpetual slavery."

7:78 When different opinions were expressed, they determined that those who, owing to age or ill health, were unserviceable for war, should depart from the town, and that themselves should try every expedient before they had recourse to the advice of Critognatus: however, that they would rather adopt that design, if circumstances should compel them and their allies should delay, than accept any terms of a surrender or peace. The Mandubii, who had admitted them into the town, are compelled to go forth with their wives and children. When these came to the Roman fortifications, weeping, they begged of the soldiers by every entreaty to receive them as slaves and relieve them with food. But Caesar, placing guards on the rampart, forbade them to be admitted.

7:79 In the mean time, Commius and the rest of the leaders, to whom the supreme command had been intrusted, came with all their forces to Alesia, and having occupied the entire hill, encamped not more than a mile from our fortifications. The following day, having led forth their cavalry from the camp, they fill all that plain, which, we have related, extended three miles in length, and drew out their infantry a little from that place, and post them on the higher ground. The town Alesia commanded a view of the whole plain. The besieged run together when these auxiliaries were seen; mutual congratulations ensue, and the minds of all are elated with joy. Accordingly, drawing out their troops, they encamp before the town, and cover the nearest trench with hurdles and fill it up with earth, and make ready for a sally and every casualty.

Cimbrorum Teutonumque fecerunt; qui in oppida compulsi ac simili inopia subacti eorum corporibus qui aetate ad bellum inutiles videbantur vitam toleraverunt neque se hostibus tradiderunt. Cuius rei si exemplum non haberemus, tamen libertatis causa institui et posteris prodi pulcherrimum iudicarem. Nam quid illi simile bello fuit? Depopulata Gallia Cimbri magnaque illata calamitate finibus quidem nostris aliquando excesserunt atque alias terras petierunt; iura, leges, agros, libertatem nobis reliquerunt. Romani vero quid petunt aliud aut quid volunt, nisi invidia adducti, quos fama nobiles potentesque bello cognoverunt, horum in agris civitatibusque considere atque his aeternam iniungere servitutem? Neque enim ulla alia condicione bella gesserunt. Quod si ea quae in longinquis nationibus geruntur ignoratis, respicite finitimam Galliam, quae in provinciam redacta iure et legibus commutatis securibus subiecta perpetua premitur servitute."

Sententiis dictis constituunt ut ei qui valetudine aut aetate inutiles sunt bello oppido excedant, atque omnia prius experiantur, quam ad Critognati sententiam descendant: illo tamen potius utendum consilio, si res cogat atque auxilia morentur, quam aut deditionis aut pacis subeundam condicionem. Mandubii, qui eos oppido receperant, cum liberis atque uxoribus exire coguntur. Hi, cum ad munitiones Romanorum accessissent, flentes omnibus precibus orabant, ut se in servitutem receptos cibo iuvarent. At Caesar dispositis in vallo custodibus recipi prohibebat.

Interea Commius reliquique duces quibus summa imperi permissa erat cum omnibus copiis ad Alesiam perveniunt et colle exteriore occupato non longius mille passibus ab nostris munitionibus considunt. Postero die equitatu ex castris educto omnem eam planitiem, quam in longitudinem tria milia passuum patere demonstravimus, complent pedestresque copias paulum ab eo loco abditas in locis superioribus constituunt. Erat ex oppido Alesia despectus in campum. Concurrunt his auxiliis visis; fit gratulatio inter eos, atque omnium animi ad laetitiam excitantur. Itaque productis copiis ante oppidum considunt et proximam fossam cratibus integunt atque aggere explent seque ad eruptionem

7:80 Caesar, having stationed his army on both sides of the fortifications, in order that, if occasion should arise, each should hold and know his own post, orders the cavalry to issue forth from the camp and commence action. There was a commanding view from the entire camp, which occupied a ridge of hills; and the minds of all the soldiers anxiously awaited the issue of the battle. The Gauls had scattered archers and light-armed infantry here and there, among their cavalry, to give relief to their retreating troops, and sustain the impetuosity of our cavalry. Several of our soldiers were unexpectedly wounded by these, and left the battle. When the Gauls were confident that their countrymen were the conquerors in the action, and beheld our men hard pressed by numbers, both those who were hemmed in by the line of circumvallation and those who had come to aid them, supported the spirits of their men by shouts and yells from every quarter. As the action was carried on in sight of all, neither a brave nor cowardly act could be concealed; both the desire of praise and the fear of ignominy, urged on each party to valor. After fighting from noon almost to sunset, without victory inclining in favor of either, the Germans, on one side, made a charge against the enemy in a compact body, and drove them back; and, when they were put to flight, the archers were surrounded and cut to pieces. In other parts, likewise, our men pursued to the camp the retreating enemy, and did not give them an opportunity of rallying. But those who had come forth from Alesia returned into the town dejected and almost despairing of success.

7:81 The Gauls, after the interval of a day and after making, during that time, an immense number of hurdles, scaling-ladders, and iron hooks, silently went forth from the camp at midnight and approached the fortifications in the plain. Raising a shout suddenly, that by this intimation those who were besieged in the town might learn their arrival, they began to cast down hurdles and dislodge our men from the rampart by slings, arrows, and stones, and executed the other movements which are requisite in storming. At the same time, Vercingetorix, having heard the shout, gives the signal to his troops by a trumpet, and leads them forth from the town. Our troops, as each man's post had been assigned him some days before, man the fortifications; they intimidate the Gauls by slings, large stones, stakes which they had placed along the works, and bullets. All view being prevented by the darkness, many wounds are received on both sides; several missiles, are thrown from the engines. But Marcus Antonius, and Caius Trebonius, the lieutenants, to whom the defense of these parts had been

atque omnes casus comparant.

Caesar omni exercitu ad utramque partem munitionum disposito, ut, si usus veniat, suum quisque locum teneat et noverit, equitatum ex castris educi et proelium committi iubet. Erat ex omnibus castris, quae summum undique iugum tenebant, despectus, atque omnes milites intenti pugnae proventum exspectabant. Galli inter equites raros sagittarios expeditosque levis armaturae interiecerant, qui suis cedentibus auxilio succurrerent et nostrorum equitum impetus sustinerent. Ab his complures de improviso vulnerati proelio excedebant. Cum suos pugna superiores esse Galli confiderent et nostros multitudine premi viderent, ex omnibus partibus et ei qui munitionibus continebantur et hi qui ad auxilium convenerant clamore et ululatu suorum animos confirmabant. Quod in conspectu omnium res gerebatur neque recte ac turpiter factum celari poterat, utrosque et laudis cupiditas et timor ignominiae ad virtutem excitabant. Cum a meridie prope ad solis occasum dubia victoria pugnaretur, Germani una in parte confertis turmis in hostes impetum fecerunt eosque propulerunt; quibus in fugam coniectis sagittarii circumventi interfectique sunt. Item ex reliquis partibus nostri cedentes usque ad castra insecuti sui colligendi facultatem non dederunt. At ei qui ab Alesia processerant maesti prope victoria desperata se in oppidum receperunt.

Vno die intermisso Galli atque hoc spatio magno cratium, scalarum, harpagonum numero effecto media nocte silentio ex castris egressi ad campestres munitiones accedunt. Subito clamore sublato, qua significatione qui in oppido obsidebantur de suo adventu cognoscere possent, crates proicere, fundis, sagittis, lapidibus nostros de vallo proturbare reliquaque quae ad oppugnationem pertinent parant administrare. Eodem tempore clamore exaudito dat tuba signum suis Vercingetorix atque ex oppido educit. Nostri, ut superioribus diebus, ut cuique erat locus attributus, ad munitiones accedunt; fundis librilibus sudibusque quas in opere disposuerant ac glandibus Gallos proterrent. Prospectu tenebris adempto multa utrimque vulnera accipiuntur. Complura tormentis tela coniciuntur. At Marcus Antonius et Gaius Trebonius legati, quibus hae partes ad defendendum obvenerant, qua ex parte

allotted, draughted troops from the redoubts which were more remote, and sent them to aid our troops, in whatever direction they understood that they were hard pressed.

7:82 While the Gauls were at a distance from the fortification, they did more execution, owing to the immense number of their weapons: after they came nearer, they either unawares empaled themselves on the spurs, or were pierced by the mural darts from the ramparts and towers, and thus perished. After receiving many wounds on all sides, and having forced no part of the works, when day drew nigh, fearing lest they should be surrounded by a sally made from the higher camp on the exposed flank, they retreated to their countrymen. But those within, while they bring forward those things which had been prepared by Vercingetorix for a sally, fill up the nearest trenches; having delayed a long time in executing these movements, they learned the retreat of their countrymen before they drew nigh to the fortifications. Thus they returned to the town without accomplishing their object.

7:83 The Gauls, having been twice repulsed with great loss, consult what they should do; they avail themselves of the information of those who were well acquainted with the country; from them they ascertain the position and fortification of the upper camp. There was, on the north side, a hill, which our men could not include in their works, on account of the extent of the circuit, and had necessarily made their camp in ground almost disadvantageous, and pretty steep. Caius Antistius Reginus, and Caius Caninius Rebilus, two of the lieutenants, with two legions, were in possession of this camp. The leaders of the enemy, having reconnoitered the country by their scouts, select from the entire army sixty thousand men, belonging to those states, which bear the highest character for courage; they privately arrange among themselves what they wished to be done, and in what manner; they decide that the attack should take place when it should seem to be noon. They appoint over their forces Vergasillaunus, the Arvernian, one of the four generals, and a near relative of Vercingetorix. He, having issued from the camp at the first watch, and having almost completed his march a little before the dawn, hid himself behind the mountain, and ordered his soldiers to refresh themselves after their labor during the night. When noon now seemed to draw nigh, he marched hastily against that camp which we have mentioned before; and, at the same time, the cavalry began to approach the fortifications in the plain, and the rest of the forces to make a demonstration in front of the camp.

7:84 Vercingetorix, having beheld his countrymen from the citadel of Alesia, issues forth from the town; he brings forth from

nostros premi intellexerant, his auxilio ex ulterioribus castellis deductos summittebant.

Dum longius ab munitione aberant Galli, plus multitudine telorum proficiebant; posteaquam propius successerunt, aut se stimulis inopinantes induebant aut in scrobes delati transfodiebantur aut ex vallo ac turribus traiecti pilis muralibus interibant. Multis undique vulneribus acceptis nulla munitione perrupta, cum lux appeteret, veriti ne ab latere aperto ex superioribus castris eruptione circumvenirentur, se ad suos receperunt. At interiores, dum ea quae a Vercingetorige ad eruptionem praeparata erant proferunt, priores fossas explent, diutius in his rebus administrandis morati prius suos discessisse cognoverunt, quam munitionibus appropinquarent. Ita re infecta in oppidum reverterunt.

Bis magno cum detrimento repulsi Galli quid agant consulunt; locorum peritos adhibent: ex his superiorum castrorum situs munitionesque cognoscunt. Erat a septentrionibus collis, quem propter magnitudinem circuitus opere circumplecti non potuerant nostri: necessario paene iniquo loco et leniter declivi castra fecerunt. Haec Gaius Antistius Reginus et Gaius Caninius Rebilus legati cum duabus legionibus obtinebant. Cognitis per exploratores regionibus duces hostium LX milia ex omni numero deligunt earum civitatum quae maximam virtutis opinionem habebant; quid quoque pacto agi placeat occulte inter se constituunt; adeundi tempus definiunt, cum meridies esse videatur. His copiis Vercassivellaunum Arvernum, unum ex quattuor ducibus, propinquum Vercingetorigis, praeficiunt. Ille ex castris prima vigilia egressus prope confecto sub lucem itinere post montem se occultavit militesque ex nocturno labore sese reficere iussit. Cum iam meridies appropinquare videretur, ad ea castra quae supra demonstravimus contendit; eodemque tempore equitatus ad campestres munitiones accedere et reliquae copiae pro castris sese ostendere coeperunt.

Vercingetorix ex arce Alesiae suos conspicatus ex oppido egreditur; crates, longurios, musculos, falces

the camp long hooks, movable pent-houses, mural hooks, and other things, which he had prepared for the purpose of making a sally. They engage on all sides at once and every expedient is adopted. They flocked to whatever part of the works seemed weakest. The army of the Romans is distributed along their extensive lines, and with difficulty meets the enemy in every quarter. The shouts which were raised by the combatants in their rear, had a great tendency to intimidate our men, because they perceived that their danger rested on the valor of others: for generally all evils which are distant most powerfully alarm men's minds.

7:85 Caesar, having selected a commanding situation, sees distinctly whatever is going on in every quarter, and sends assistance to his troops when hard pressed. The idea uppermost in the minds of both parties is, that the present is the time in which they would have the fairest opportunity of making a struggle; the Gauls despairing of all safety, unless they should succeed in forcing the lines: the Romans expecting an end to all their labors if they should gain the day. The principal struggle is at the upper lines, to which as we have said Vergasillaunus was sent. The least elevation of ground, added to a declivity, exercises a momentous influence. Some are casting missiles, others, forming a testudo, advance to the attack; fresh men by turns relieve the wearied. The earth, heaped up by all against the fortifications, gives the means of ascent to the Gauls, and covers those works which the Romans had concealed in the ground. Our men have no longer arms or strength.

7:86 Caesar, on observing these movements, sends Labienus with six cohorts to relieve his distressed soldiers: he orders him, if he should be unable to withstand them, to draw off the cohorts and make a sally; but not to do this except through necessity. He himself goes to the rest, and exhorts them not to succumb to the toil; he shows them that the fruits of all former engagements depend on that day and hour. The Gauls within, despairing of forcing the fortifications in the plains on account of the greatness of the works, attempt the places precipitous in ascent: hither they bring the engines which they had prepared; by the immense number of their missiles they dislodge the defenders from the turrets: they fill the ditches with clay and hurdles, then clear the way; they tear down the rampart and breast-work with hooks.

7:87 Caesar sends at first young Brutus, with six cohorts, and afterward Caius Fabius, his lieutenant, with seven others: finally, as they fought more obstinately, he leads up fresh men to the assistance of his soldiers. After renewing the action, and repulsing the enemy, he marches in the direction in which he

reliquaque quae eruptionis causa paraverat profert. Pugnatur uno tempore omnibus locis, atque omnia temptantur: quae minime visa pars firma est, huc concurritur. Romanorum manus tantis munitionibus distinetur nec facile pluribus locis occurrit. Multum ad terrendos nostros valet clamor, qui post tergum pugnantibus exstitit, quod suum periculum in aliena vident salute constare: omnia enim plerumque quae absunt vehementius hominum mentes perturbant.

Caesar idoneum locum nactus quid quaque ex parte geratur cognoscit; laborantibus summittit. Vtrisque ad animum occurrit unum esse illud tempus, quo maxime contendi conveniat: Galli, nisi perfregerint munitiones, de omni salute desperant; Romani, si rem obtinuerint, finem laborum omnium exspectant. Maxime ad superiores munitiones laboratur, quo Vercassivellaunum missum demonstravimus. Iniquum loci ad declivitatem fastigium magnum habet momentum. Alii tela coniciunt, alii testudine facta subeunt; defatigatis in vicem integri succedunt. Agger ab universis in munitionem coniectus et ascensum dat Gallis et ea quae in terra occultaverant Romani contegit; nec iam arma nostris nec vires suppetunt.

His rebus cognitis Caesar Labienum cum cohortibus sex subsidio laborantibus mittit: imperat, si sustinere non posset, deductis cohortibus eruptione pugnaret; id nisi necessario ne faciat. Ipse adit reliquos, cohortatur ne labori succumbant; omnium superiorum dimicationum fructum in eo die atque hora docet consistere. Interiores desperatis campestribus locis propter magnitudinem munitionum loca praerupta ex ascensu temptant: huc ea quae paraverant conferunt. Multitudine telorum ex turribus propugnantes deturbant, aggere et cratibus fossas explent, falcibus vallum ac loricam rescindunt.

Mittit primo Brutum adulescentem cum cohortibus Caesar, post cum aliis Gaium Fabium legatum; postremo ipse, cum vehementius pugnaretur, integros subsidio adducit. Restituto proelio ac repulsis hostibus eo quo Labienum miserat

had sent Labienus, drafts four cohorts from the nearest redoubt, and orders part of the cavalry to follow him, and part to make the circuit of the external fortifications and attack the enemy in the rear. Labienus, when neither the ramparts or ditches could check the onset of the enemy, informs Caesar by messengers of what he intended to do. Caesar hastens to share in the action.

7:88 His arrival being known from the color of his robe, and the troops of cavalry, and the cohorts which he had ordered to follow him being seen, as these low and sloping grounds were plainly visible from the eminences, the enemy join battle. A shout being raised by both sides, it was succeeded by a general shout along the ramparts and whole line of fortifications. Our troops, laying aside their javelins, carry on the engagement with their swords. The cavalry is suddenly seen in the rear of the Gauls; the other cohorts advance rapidly; the enemy turn their backs; the cavalry intercept them in their flight, and a great slaughter ensues. Sedulius the general and chief of the Lemovices is slain; Vergasillaunus the Arvernian, is taken alive in the flight, seventy-four military standards are brought to Caesar, and few out of so great a number return safe to their camp. The besieged, beholding from the town the slaughter and flight of their countrymen, despairing of safety, lead back their troops from the fortifications. A flight of the Gauls from their camp immediately ensues on hearing of this disaster, and had not the soldiers been wearied by sending frequent reinforcements, and the labor of the entire day, all the enemy's forces could have been destroyed. Immediately after midnight, the cavalry are sent out and overtake the rear, a great number are taken or cut to pieces, the rest by flight escape in different directions to their respective states.

7:89 Vercingetorix, having convened a council the following day, declares, "That he had undertaken that war, not on account of his own exigences, but on account of the general freedom; and since he must yield to fortune, he offered himself to them for either purpose, whether they should wish to atone to the Romans by his death, or surrender him alive. Embassadors are sent to Caesar on this subject. He orders their arms to be surrendered, and their chieftains delivered up. He seated himself at the head of the lines in front of the camp, the Gallic chieftains are brought before him. They surrender Vercingetorix, and lay down their arms. Reserving the Aedui and Arverni, [to try] if he could gain over, through their influence, their respective states, he distributes one of the remaining captives to each soldier, throughout the entire army, as plunder.

contendit; cohortes quattuor ex proximo castello deducit, equitum partem sequi, partem circumire exteriores munitiones et ab tergo hostes adoriri iubet. Labienus, postquam neque aggeres neque fossae vim hostium sustinere poterant, coactis una XL cohortibus, quas ex proximis praesidus deductas fors obtulit, Caesarem per nuntios facit certiorem quid faciendum existimet. Accelerat Caesar, ut proelio intersit.

Eius adventu ex colore vestitus cognito, quo insigni in proeliis uti consuerat, turmisque equitum et cohortibus visis quas se sequi iusserat, ut de locis superioribus haec declivia et devexa cernebantur, hostes proelium committunt. Vtrimque clamore sublato excipit rursus ex vallo atque omnibus munitionibus clamor. Nostri omissis pilis gladiis rem gerunt. Repente post tergum equitatus cernitur; cohortes aliae appropinquant. Hostes terga vertunt; fugientibus equites occurrunt. Fit magna caedes. Sedulius, dux et princeps Lemovicum, occiditur; Vercassivellaunus Arvernus vivus in fuga comprehenditur; signa militaria septuaginta quattuor ad Caesarem referuntur: pauci ex tanto numero se incolumes in castra recipiunt. Conspicati ex oppido caedem et fugam suorum desperata salute copias a munitionibus reducunt. Fit protinus hac re audita ex castris Gallorum fuga. Quod nisi crebris subsidiis ac totius diei labore milites essent defessi, omnes hostium copiae deleri potuissent. De media nocte missus equitatus novissimum agmen consequitur: magnus numerus capitur atque interficitur; reliqui ex fuga in civitates discedunt.

Postero die Vercingetorix concilio convocato id bellum se suscepisse non suarum necessitatium, sed communis libertatis causa demonstrat, et quoniam sit fortunae cedendum, ad utramque rem se illis offerre, seu morte sua Romanis satisfacere seu vivum tradere velint. Mittuntur de his rebus ad Caesarem legati. Iubet arma tradi, principes produci. Ipse in munitione pro castris consedit: eo duces producuntur; Vercingetorix deditur, arma proiciuntur. Reservatis Aeduis atque Arvernis, si per eos civitates reciperare posset, ex reliquis captivis toto exercitui capita singula praedae nomine distribuit.

7:90 After making these arrangements, he marches into the [country of the] Aedui, and recovers that state. To this place embassadors are sent by the Arveni, who promise that they will execute his commands. He demands a great number of hostages. He sends the legions to winter-quarters; he restores about twenty thousand captives to the Aedui and Arverni; he orders Titus Labienus to march into the [country of the] Sequani with two legions and the cavalry, and to him he attaches Marcus Sempronius Rutilus; he places Caius Fabius, and Lucius Minucius Basilus, with two legions in the country of the Remi, lest they should sustain any loss from the Bellovaci in their neighborhood. He sends Caius Antistius Reginus into the [country of the] Ambivareti, Titus Sextius into the territories of the Bituriges, and Caius Caninius Rebilus into those of the Ruteni, with one legion each. He stations Quintus Tullius Cicero, and Publius Sulpicius among the Aedui at Cabillo and Matisco on the Saone, to procure supplies of corn. He himself determines to winter at Bibracte. A supplication of twenty-days is decreed by the senate at Rome, on learning these successes from Caesar's dispatches.

His rebus confectis in Aeduos proficiscitur; civitatem recipit. Eo legati ab Arvernis missi quae imperaret se facturos pollicentur. Imperat magnum numerum obsidum. Legiones in hiberna mittit. Captivorum circiter viginti milia Aeduis Arvernisque reddit. Titum Labienum duabus cum legionibus et equitatu in Sequanos proficisci iubet: huic Marcum Sempronium Rutilum attribuit. Gaium Fabium legatum et Lucium Minucium Basilum cum legionibus duabus in Remis collocat, ne quam ab finitimis Bellovacis calamitatem accipiant. Gaium Antistium Reginum in Ambivaretos, Titum Sextium in Bituriges, Gaium Caninium Rebilum in Rutenos cum singulis legionibus mittit. Quintum Tullium Ciceronem et Publium Sulpicium Cabilloni et Matiscone in Aeduis ad Ararim rei frumentariae causa collocat. Ipse Bibracte hiemare constituit. His litteris cognitis Romae dierum viginti supplicatio redditur.

Gallic Wars Book 8 (51-50 B.C.E.)

8:0 Prevailed on by your continued solicitations, Balbus, I have engaged in a most difficult task, as my daily refusals appear to plead not my inability, but indolence, as an excuse. I have compiled a continuation of the Commentaries of our Caesar's Wars in Gaul, not indeed to be compared to his writings, which either precede or follow them; and recently, I have completed what he left imperfect after the transactions in Alexandria, to the end, not indeed of the civil broils, to which we see no issue, but of Caesar's life. I wish that those who may read them could know how unwillingly I undertook to write them, as then I might the more readily escape the imputation of folly and arrogance, in presuming to intrude among Caesar's writings. For it is agreed on all hands, that no composition was ever executed with so great care, that it is not exceeded in elegance by these Commentaries, which were published for the use of historians, that they might not want memoirs of such achievements; and they stand so high in the esteem of all men, that historians seem rather deprived of, than furnished with material. At which we have more reason to be surprised than other men; for they can only appreciate the elegance and correctness with which he finished them, while we know with what ease and expedition. Caesar possessed not only an uncommon flow of language and elegance of style, but also a thorough knowledge of the method of conveying his ideas. But I had not even the good fortune to share in the Alexandrian or African war; and though these were partly communicated to me by Caesar himself, in conversation, yet we listen with a different degree of attention to those things which strike us with admiration by their novelty, and those which we design to attest to posterity. But, in truth, while I urge every apology, that I may not be compared to Caesar, I incur the charge of vanity, by thinking it possible that I can in the judgment of any one be put in competition with him. Farewell.

8:1 Gaul being entirely reduced, when Caesar having waged war incessantly during the former summer, wished to recruit his soldiers after so much fatigue, by repose in winter quarters, news was brought him that several states were simultaneously renewing their hostile intention, and forming combinations. For which a probable reason was assigned; namely, that the Gauls were convinced that they were not able to resist the Romans, with any force they could collect in one place; and hoped that if several states made war in different places at the same time, the Roman army would neither have aid, nor time, nor forces, to

Coactus assiduis tuis vocibus, Balbe, cum cotidiana mea recusatio non difficultatis excusationem, sed inertiae videretur deprecationem habere, rem difficillimam suscepi. Caesaris nostri commentarios rerum gestarum Galliae, non comparantibus superioribus atque insequentibus eius scriptis, contexui novissimumque imperfectum ab rebus gestis Alexandriae confeci usque ad exitum non quidem civilis dissensionis, cuius finem nullum videmus, sed vitae Caesaris. Quos utinam qui legent scire possint quam invitus susceperim scribendos, qua facilius caream stultitiae atque arrogantiae crimine, qui me mediis interposuerim Caesaris scriptis. Constat enim inter omnes nihil tam operose ab aliis esse perfectum, quod non horum elegantia commentariorum superetur: qui sunt editi, ne scientia tantarum rerum scriptoribus deesset, adeoque probantur omnium iudicio ut praerepta, non praebita, facultas scriptoribus videatur. Cuius tamen rei maior nostra quam reliquorum est admiratio: ceteri enim, quam bene atque emendate, nos etiam, quam facile atque celeriter eos perfecerit scimus. Erat autem in Caesare cum facultas atque elegantia summa scribendi, tum verissima scientia suorum consiliorum explicandorum. Mihi ne illud quidem accidit, ut Alexandrino atque Africano bello interessem; quae bella quamquam ex parte nobis Caesaris sermone sunt nota, tamen aliter audimus ea, quae rerum novitate aut admiratione nos capiunt, aliter, quae pro testimonio sumus dicturi. Sed ego nimirum, dum omnes excusationis causas colligo ne cum Caesare conferar, hoc ipsum crimen arrogantiae subeo, quod me iudicio cuiusquam existimem posse cum Caesare comparari. Vale.

Omni Gallia devicta Caesar cum a superiore aestate nullum bellandi tempus intermisisset militesque hibernorum quiete reficere a tantis laboribus vellet, complures eodem tempore civitates renovare belli consilia nuntiabantur coniurationesque facere. Cuius rei verisimilis causa adferebatur, quod Gallis omnibus cogrutum esset neque ulla multitudine in unum locum coacta resisti posse Romanis, nec, si diversa bella complures eodem tempore intulissent civitates, satis auxili aut spati aut copiarum

prosecute them all: nor ought any single state to decline any inconveniences that might befall them, provided that by such delay, the rest should be enabled to assert their liberty.

8:2 That this notion might not be confirmed among the Gauls, Caesar left Marcus Antonius, his questor, in charge of his quarters, and set out himself with a guard of horse, the day before the kalends of January, from the town Bibracte, to the thirteenth legion, which he had stationed in the country of the Bituriges, not far from the territories of the Aedui, and joined to it the eleventh legion which was next it. Leaving two cohorts to guard the baggage, he leads the rest of his army into the most plentiful part of the country of the Bituriges; who, possessing an extensive territory and several towns, were not to be deterred, by a single legion quartered among them, from making warlike preparation, and forming combinations.

8:3 By Caesar's sudden arrival, it happened, as it necessarily must, to an unprovided and dispersed people, that they were surprised by our horse, while cultivating the fields without any apprehensions, before they had time to fly to their towns. For the usual sign of an enemy's invasion, which is generally intimated by the burning of their towns, was forbidden by Caesar's orders; lest if he advanced far, forage and corn should become scarce, or the enemy be warned by the fires to make their escape. Many thousands being taken, as many of the Bituriges as were able to escape the first coming of the Romans, fled to the neighboring states, relying either on private friendship, or public alliance. In vain; for Caesar, by hasty marches, anticipated them in every place, nor did he allow any state leisure to consider the safety of others, in preference to their own. By this activity, he both retained his friends in their loyalty, and by fear, obliged the wavering to accept offers of peace. Such offers being made to the Bituriges, when they perceived that through Caesar's clemency, an avenue was open to his friendship, and that the neighboring states had given hostages, without incurring any punishment, and had been received under his protection, they did the same.

8:4 Caesar promises his soldiers, as a reward for their labor and patience, in cheerfully submitting to hardships from the severity of the winter, the difficulty of the roads, and the intolerable cold, two hundred sestertii each, and to every centurian two thousand, to be given instead of plunder: and sending his legions back to quarters, he himself returned on the fortieth day to Bibracte. While he was dispensing justice there, the Bituriges send embassadors to him, to entreat his aid against the Carnutes, who they complained had made war against them.

habiturum exercitum populi Romani ad omnia persequenda; non esse autem alicui civitati sortem incommodi recusandam, si tali mora reliquae possent se vindicare in libertatem.

Quae ne opinio Gallorum confirmaretur, Caesar Marcum Antonium quaestorem suis praefecit hibernis; ipse equitum praesidio pridie Kal. Ianuarias ab oppido Bibracte proficiscitur ad legionem XIII, quam non longe a finibus Aeduorum collocaverat in finibus Biturigum, eique adiungit legionem XI, quae proxima fuerat. Binis cohortibus ad impedimenta tuenda relictis reliquum exercitum in copiosissimos agros Biturigum inducit, qui, cum latos fines et complura oppida haberent, unius legionis hibernis non potuerint contineri quin bellum pararent coniurationesque facerent.

Repentino adventu Caesaris accidit, quod imparatis disiectisque accidere fuit necesse, ut sine timore ullo rura colentes prius ab equitatu opprimerentur quam confugere in oppida possent. Namque etiam illud vulgare incursionis hostium signum, quod incendiis aedificiorum intellegi consuevit, Caesaris erat interdicto sublatum, ne aut copia pabuli frumentique, si longius progredi vellet, deficeretur, aut hostes incendius terrerentur. Multis hominum milibus captis perterriti Bituriges; qui primum adventum potuerant effugere Romanorum, in finitimas civitates aut privatis hospitiis confisi aut societate consiliorum confugerant. Frustra: nam Caesar magni sitineribus omnibus locis occurrit nec dat ulli civitati spatium de aliena potius quam de domestica salute cogitandi; qua celeritate et fideles amicos retinebat et dubitantes terrore ad condiciones pacis adducebat. Tali condicione proposita Bituriges, cum sibi viderent clementia Caesaris reditum patere in eius amicitiam finitimasque civitates sine ulla poena dedisse obsides atque in fidem receptas esse, idem fecerunt.

Caesar militibus pro tanto labore ac patientia, qui brumalibus diebus itineribus difficillimis, frigoribus intolerandis studiosissime permanserant in labore, ducenos sestertios, centurionibus tot milia nummum praedae nomine condonanda pollicetur legionibusque in hiberna remissis ipse se recipit die XXXX Bibracte. Ibi cum ius diceret, Bituriges ad eum legatos mittunt auxilium petitum contra Carnutes, quos intulisse bellum sibi querebantur. Qua re

Upon this intelligence, though he had not remained more than eighteen days in winter quarters, he draws the fourteenth and sixth legion out of quarters on the Saone, where he had posted them as mentioned in a former Commentary, to procure supplies of corn. With these two legions he marches in pursuit of the Carnutes.

8:5 When the news of the approach of our army reached the enemy, the Carnutes, terrified by the suffering of other states, deserted their villages and towns (which were small buildings, raised in a hurry, to meet the immediate necessity, in which they lived to shelter themselves against the winter, for, being lately conquered, they had lost several towns), and dispersed and fled. Caesar, unwilling to expose his soldiers to the violent storms that break out, especially at that season, took up his quarters at Genabum, a town of the Carnutes; and lodged his men in houses, partly belonging to the Gauls, and partly built to shelter the tents, and hastily covered with thatch. But the horse and auxiliaries he sends to all parts to which he was told the enemy had marched; and not without effect, as our men generally returned loaded with booty. The Carnutes, overpowered by the severity of the winter, and the fear of danger, and not daring to continue long in any place, as they were driven from their houses, and not finding sufficient protection in the woods, from the violence of the storms, after losing a considerable number of their men, disperse, and take refuge among the neighboring states.

8:6 Caesar, being contented, at so severe a season, to disperse the gathering foes, and prevent any new war from breaking out, and being convinced, as far as reason could foresee, that no war of consequence could be set on foot in the summer campaign, stationed Caius Trebonius, with the two legions which he had with him, in quarters at Genabum: and being informed by frequent embassies from the Remi, that the Bellovaci (who exceed all the Gauls and Belgae in military prowess), and the neighboring states, headed by Correus, one of the Bellovaci, and Comius, the Atrebatian, were raising an army, and assembling at a general rendezvous, designing with their united forces to invade the territories of the Suessiones, who were put under the patronage of the Remi: and moreover, considering that not only his honor, but his interest was concerned, that such of his allies, as deserved well of the republic, should suffer no calamity; he again draws the eleventh legion out of quarters, and writes besides to Caius Fabius, to march with his two legions to the country of the Suessiones; and he sends to Trebonius for one of his two legions. Thus, as far as the convenience of the quarters, and the management of the war admitted, he laid the burden of the expedition on the legions

cognita, cum dies non amplius decem et octo in hibernis esset moratus, legiones XIIII et VI ex hibernis ab Arare educit, quas ibi collocatas explicandae rei frumentariae causa superiore commentario demonstratum est: ita cum duabus legionibus ad persequendos Carnutes proficiscitur.

Cum fama exercitus ad hostes esset perlata, calamitate ceterorum ducti Carnutes desertis vicis oppidisque, quae tolerandae hiemis causa constitutis repente exiguis ad necessitatem aedificiis incolebant (nuper enim devicti complura oppida dimiserant), dispersi profugiunt. Caesar erumpentes eo maxime tempore acerrimas tempestates cum subire milites nollet, in oppido Carnutum Cenabo castra ponit atque in tecta partim Gallorum, partim quae coniectis celeriter stramentis tentoriorum integendorum gratia erant inaedificata, milites compegit. Equites tamen et auxiliarios pedites in omnes partes mittit quascumque petisse dicebantur hostes; nec frustra: nam plerumque magna praeda potiti nostri revertuntur. Oppressi Carnutes hiemis difficultate, terrore periculi, cum tectis expulsi nullo loco diutius consistere auderent nec silvarum praesidio tempestatibus durissimis tegi possent, dispersi magna parte amissa suorum dissipantur in finitimas civitates.

Caesar tempore anni difficillimo, cum satis haberet convenientes manus dissipare, ne quod initium belli nasceretur, quantumque in ratione esset, exploratum haberet sub tempus aestivorum nullum summum bellum posse conflari, Gaium Trebonium cum duabus legionibus, quas secum habebat, in hibernis Cenabi collocavit; ipse, cum crebris legationibus Remorum certior fieret Bellovacos, qui belli gloria Gallos omnes Belgasque praestabant, finitimasque his civitates duce Correo Bellovaco et Commio Atrebate exercitus comparare atque in unum locum cogere, ut omni multitudine in fines Suessionum, qui Remis erant attributi, facerent impressionem, pertinere autem non tantum ad dignitatem sed etiam ad salutem suam iudicaret nullam calamitatem socios optime de re publica meritos accipere, legionem ex hibernis evocat rursus undecimam; litteras autem ad Gaium Fabium mittit, ut in fines Suessionum legiones duas quas habebat adduceret, alteramque ex duabus ab Labieno arcessit. Ita, quantum hibernorum opportunitas bellique ratio

by turns, without any intermission to his own toils.

8:7 As soon as his troops were collected, he marched against the Bellovaci: and pitching his camp in their territories, detached troops of horse all round the country, to take prisoners, from whom he might learn the enemy's plan. The horse, having executed his orders bring him back word, that but few were found in the houses: and that even these had not stayed at home to cultivate their lands (for the emigration was general from all parts) but had been sent back to watch our motions. Upon Caesar's inquiring from them, where the main body of the Bellovaci were posted, and what was their design: they made answer, "that all the Bellovaci, fit for carrying arms, had assembled in one place, and along with them the Ambiani, Aulerci, Caletes, Velocasses, and Atrebates, and that they had chosen for their camp, an elevated position, surrounded by a dangerous morass: that they had conveyed all their baggage into the most remote woods: that several noblemen were united in the management of the war; but that the people were most inclined to be governed by Correus, because they knew that he had the strongest aversion to the name of the Roman people: that a few days before Comius had left the camp to engage the Germans to their aid whose nation bordered on theirs, and whose numbers were countless: that the Bellovaci had come to a resolution, with the consent of all the generals and the earnest desire of the people, if Caesar should come with only three legions, as was reported, to give him battle, that they might not be obliged to encounter his whole army on a future occasion, when they should be in a more wretched and distressed condition; but if he brought a stronger force, they intended to remain in the position they had chosen, and by ambuscade to prevent the Romans from getting forage (which at that season was both scarce and much scattered), corn, and other necessaries.

8:8 When Caesar was convinced of the truth of this account from the concurring testimony of several persons, and perceived that the plans which were proposed were full of prudence, and very unlike the rash resolves of a barbarous people, he considered it incumbent on him to use every exertion, in order that the enemy might despise his small force and come to an action. For he had three veteran legions of distinguished valor, the seventh, eighth and ninth. The eleventh consisted of chosen youth of great hopes, who had served eight campaigns, but who, compared with the others, had not yet acquired any great reputation for experience and valor. Calling therefore a council, and laying before it the intelligence which he had received, he encouraged his soldiers. In order if possible to entice the enemy

postulabat, perpetuo suo labore in vicem legionibus expeditionum onus iniungebat.

His copiis coactis ad Bellovacos proficiscitur castrisque in eorum finibus positis equitum turmas dimittit in omnes partes ad aliquos excipiendos ex quibus hostium consilia cognosceret. Equites officio functi renuntiant paucos in aedificiis esse inventos, atque hos, non qui agrorum colendorum causa remansissent (namque esse undique diligenter demigratum), sed qui speculandi causa essent remissi. A quibus cum quaereret Caesar quo loco multitudo esset Bellovacorum quodve esset consilium eorum, inveniebat Bellovacos omnes qui arma ferre possent in unum locum convenisse, itemque Ambianos, Aulercos, Caletos, Veliocasses, Atrebatas; locum castris excelsum in silva circumdata palude delegisse, impedimenta omnia in ulteriores silvas contulisse. Complures esse principes belli auctores, sed multitudinem maxime Correo obtemperare, quod ei summo esse odio nomen populi Romani intellexissent. Paucis ante diebus ex his castris Atrebatem Commium discessisse ad auxilia Germanorum adducenda; quorum et vicinitas propinqua et multitudo esset infinita. Constituisse autem Bellovacos omnium principum consensu, summa plebis cupiditate, si, ut diceretur, Caesar cum tribus legionibus veniret, offerre se ad dimicandum, ne miseriore ac duriore postea condicione cum toto exercitu decertare cogerentur; si maiores copias adduceret, in eo loco permanere quem delegissent, pabulatione autem, quae propter anni tempus cum exigua tum disiecta esset, et frumentatione et reliquo commeatu ex insidiis prohibere Romanos.

Quae Caesar consentientibus pluribus cum cognosset atque ea quae proponerentur consilia plena prudentiae longeque a temeritate barbarorum remota esse iudicaret, omnibus rebus inserviendum statuit, quo celerius hostis contempta sua paucitate prodiret in aciem. Singularis enim virtutis veterrimas legiones VII, VIII, VIIII habebat, summae spei delectaeque iuventutis XI, quae octavo iam stipendio tamen in collatione reliquarum nondum eandem vetustatis ac virtutis ceperat opinionem. Itaque consilio advocato, rebus eis quae ad se essent delatae omnibus eitis animos multitudinis confirmat. Si forte hostes trium legionum numero posset elicere

to an engagement by the appearance of only three legions, he ranged his army in the following manner, that the seventh, eighth, and ninth legions should march before all the baggage; that then the eleventh should bring up the rear of the whole train of baggage (which however was but small, as is usual on such expeditions), so that the enemy could not get a sight of a greater number than they themselves were willing to encounter. By this disposition he formed his army almost into a square, and brought them within sight of the enemy sooner than was anticipated.

8:9 When the Gauls, whose bold resolutions had been reported to Caesar, saw the legions advance with a regular motion, drawn up in battle array; either from the danger of an engagement, or our sudden approach, or with the design of watching our movements, they drew up their forces before the camp, and did not quit the rising ground. Though Caesar wished to bring them to battle, yet being surprised to see so vast a host of the enemy, he encamped opposite to them, with a valley between them, deep rather than extensive. He ordered his camp to be fortified with a rampart twelve feet high, with breastworks built on it proportioned to its height and two trenches, each fifteen feet broad, with perpendicular sides to be sunk: likewise several turrets, three stories high, to be raised, with a communication to each other by galleries laid across and covered over; which should be guarded in front by small parapets of osiers; that the enemy might be repulsed by two rows of soldiers. The one of whom, being more secure from danger by their height might throw their darts with more daring and to a greater distance; the other which was nearer the enemy, being stationed on the rampart, would be protected by their galleries from darts falling on their heads. At the entrance he erected gates and turrets of a considerable height.

8:10 Caesar had a double design in this fortification; for he both hoped that the strength of his works, and his [apparent] fears would raise confidence in the barbarians; and when there should be occasion to make a distant excursion to get forage or corn, he saw that his camp would be secured by the works with a very small force. In the mean time there were frequent skirmishes across the marsh, a few on both sides sallying out between the two camps. Sometimes, however, our Gallic or German auxiliaries crossed the marsh, and furiously pursued the enemy; or on the other hand the enemy passed it and beat back our men. Moreover there happened in the course of our daily foraging, what must of necessity happen, when corn is to be collected by a few scattered men out of private houses, that our foragers dispersing in an intricate country were surrounded by the enemy; by which, though we suffered but an inconsiderable

ad dimicandum, agminis ordinem ita constituit, ut legio septima, octava, nona ante omnia irent impedimenta, deinde omnium impedimentorum agmen, quod tamen erat mediocre, ut in expeditionibus esse consuevit, cogeret undecima, ne maioris multitudinis species accidere hostibus posset quam ipsi depoposcissent. Hac ratione paene quadrato agmine instructo in conspectum hostium celérius opinione eorum exercitum adducit.

Cum repente instructas velut in acie certo gradu legiones accedere Galli viderent, quorum erant ad Caesarem plena fiduciae consilia perlata, sive certamiuis periculo sive subito adventu sive exspectatione nostri consili copias instruunt pro castris nec loco superiore decedunt. Caesar, etsi dimicare optaverat, tamen admiratus tantam multitudinem hostium valle intermissa magis in altitudinem depressa quam late patente castra castris hostium confert. Haec imperat vallo pedum XII muniri, loriculam pro [hac] ratione eius altitudinis inaedificari; fossam duplicem pedum denum quinum lateribus deprimi directis; turres excitari crebras in altitudinem trium tabulatorum, pontibus traiectis constratisque coniungi, quorum frontes viminea loricula munirentur; ut ab hostibus duplici fossa, duplici propugnatorum ordine defenderentur, quorum alter ex pontibus, quo tutior altitudine esset, hoc audacius longiusque permitteret tela, alter, qui propior hostem in ipso vallo collocatus esset, ponte ab incidentibus telis tegeretur. Portis fores altioresque turres imposuit.

Huius munitionis duplex erat consilium. Namque et operum magnitudinem et timorem suum sperabat fiduciam barbaris allaturum, et cum pabulatum frumentatumque longius esset proficiscendum, parvis copiis castra munitione ipsa videbat posse defendi. Interim crebro paucis utrimque procurrentibus inter bina castra palude interiecta contendebatur; quam tamen paludem nonnumquam aut nostra auxilia Gallorum Germanorumque transibant acriusque hostes insequebantur, aut vicissim hostes eadem transgressi nostros longius summovebant. Accidebat autem cotidianis pabulationibus (id quod accidere erat necesse, cum raris disiectisque ex aedificius pabulum conquireretur), ut impeditis locis dispersi pabulatores

loss of cattle and servants, yet it raised foolish hopes in the barbarians; but more especially, because Comius, who I said had gone to get aid from the Germans, returned with some cavalry, and though the Germans were only 500, yet the barbarians were elated by their arrival.

8:11 Caesar, observing that the enemy kept for several days within their camp, which was well secured by a morass and its natural situation, and that it could not be assaulted without a dangerous engagement, nor the place inclosed with lines without an addition to his army, wrote to Trebonius to send with all dispatch for the thirteenth legion which was in winter quarters among the Bituriges under Titus Sextius, one of his lieutenants; and then to come to him by forced marches with the three legions. He himself sent the cavalry of the Remi, and Lingones, and other states, from whom he had required a vast number, to guard his foraging parties, and to support them in case of any sudden attack of the enemy.

8:12 As this continued for several days, and their vigilance was relaxed by custom (an effect which is generally produced by time), the Bellovaci, having made themselves acquainted with the daily stations of our horse, lie in ambush with a select body of foot in a place covered with woods; to it they sent their horse the next day, who were first to decoy our men into the ambuscade, and then when they were surrounded, to attack them. It was the lot of the Remi to fall into this snare, to whom that day had been allotted to perform this duty; for, having suddenly got sight of the enemy's cavalry, and despising their weakness, in consequence of their superior numbers, they pursued them too eagerly, and were surrounded on every side by the foot. Being, by this means thrown into disorder they returned with more precipitation than is usual in cavalry actions, with the loss of Vertiscus the governor of their state, and the general of their horse, who, though scarcely able to sit on horseback through years, neither, in accordance with the custom of the Gauls, pleaded his age in excuse for not accepting the command, nor would he suffer them to fight without him. The spirits of the barbarians were puffed up, and inflated at the success of this battle, in killing the prince, and general of the Remi; and our men were taught by this loss, to examine the country, and post their guards with more caution, and to be more moderate in pursuing a retreating enemy.

8:13 In the mean time daily skirmishes take place continually in view of both camps; these were fought at the ford and pass of

circumvenirentur; quae res, etsi mediocre detrimentum iumentorum ac servorum nostris adferebat, tamen stultas cogitationes incitabat barbarorum, atque eo magis, quod Commius, quem profectum ad auxilia Germanorum arcessenda docui, cum equitibus venerat; qui, tametsi numero non amplius erant quingenti, tamen Germanorum adventu barbari nitebantur.

Caesar, cum animadverteret hostem complures dies castris palude et loci natura munitis se tenere neque oppugnari castra eorum sine dimicatione perniciosa nec locum munitionibus claudi nisi a maiore exercitu posse, litteras ad Trebonium mittit, ut quam celerrime posset legionem XIII, quae cum T. Sextio legato in Biturigibus hiemabat, arcesseret atque ita cum tribus legionibus magnis itineribus ad se veniret; ipse equites in vicem Remorum ac Lingonum reliquarumque civitatum, quorum magnum numerum evocaverat, praesidio pabulationibus mittit, qui subitas hostium incursiones sustinerent.

Quod cum cotidie fieret ac iam consuetudine diligentia minueretur, quod plerumque accidit diu turnitate, Bellovaci delecta manu peditum cognitis stationibus cotidianis equitum nostrorum silvestribus locis insidias disponunt eodemque equites postero die mittunt, qui primum elicerent nostros, deinde circumventos aggrederentur. Cuius mali sors incidit Remis, quibus ille dies fungendi muneris obvenerat. Namque hi, cum repente hostium equites animad vertissent ac numero superiores paucitatem contempsissent, cupidius insecuti peditibus undique sunt circumdati. Quo facto perturbati celerius quam consuetudo fert equestris proeli se receperunt amisso Vertisco, principe civitatis, praefecto equitum; qui cum vix equo propter aetatem posset uti, tamen consuetudine Gallorum neque aetatis excusatione in suscipienda praefectura usus erat neque dimicari sine se voluerat. Inflantur atque incitantur hostium animi secundo proelio, principe et praefecto Remorum interfecto, nostrique detrimento admonentur diligentius exploratis locis stationes disponere ac mode ratius cedentem insequi hostem.

Non intermittunt interim cotidiana proelia in conspectu utrorumque castrorum, quae ad vada

the morass. In one of these contests the Germans, whom Caesar had brought over the Rhine, to fight, intermixed with the horse, having resolutely crossed the marsh, and slain the few who made resistance, and boldly pursued the rest, so terrified them, that not only those who were attacked hand to hand, or wounded at a distance, but even those who were stationed at a greater distance to support them, fled disgracefully; and being often beaten from the rising grounds, did not stop till they had retired into their camp, or some, impelled by fear, had fled further. Their danger threw their whole army into such confusion, that it was difficult to judge whether they were more insolent after a slight advantage or more dejected by a trifling calamity.

8:14 After spending several days in the same camp, the guards of the Bellovaci, learning that Caius Trebonius was advancing nearer with his legions, and fearing a siege like that of Alesia, send off by night all who were disabled by age or infirmity, or unarmed, and along with them their whole baggage. While they are preparing their disorderly and confused troop for march (for the Gauls are always attended by a vast multitude of wagons, even when they have very light baggage), being overtaken by day-light, they drew their forces out before their camp, to prevent the Romans attempting a pursuit before the line of their baggage had advanced to a considerable distance. But Caesar did not think it prudent to attack them when standing on their defense, with such a steep hill in their favor, nor keep his legions at such a distance that they could quit their post without danger: but, perceiving that his camp was divided from the enemy's by a deep morass, so difficult to cross that he could not pursue with expedition, and that the hill beyond the morass, which extended almost to the enemy's camp, was separated from it only by a small valley, he laid a bridge over the morass and led his army across, and soon reached the plain on the top of the hill, which was fortified on either side by a steep ascent. Having there drawn up his army in order of battle, he marched to the furthest hill, from which he could, with his engines, shower darts upon the thickest of the enemy.

8:15 The Gauls, confiding in the natural strength of their position, though they would not decline an engagement if the Romans attempted to ascend the hill, yet dared not divide their forces into small parties, lest they should be thrown into disorder by being dispersed, and therefore remained in order of battle.

transitus que fiebant paludis. Qua contentione Germani, quos propterea Caesar traduxerat Rhenum ut equitibus interpositi proeliarentur, cum constantius universi paludem transissent paucisque resistentibus interfectis pertinacius reliquam multitudinem essent insecuti, perterriti non solum ei qui aut comminus opprimebantur aut eminus vulnerabantur, sed etiam qui longius subsidiari consuerant, turpiter refugerunt, nec prius finem fugae fecerunt saepe amissis superioribus locis quam se aut in castra suorum reciperent, aut nonnulli pudore coacti longius profugerent. Quorum periculo sic omnes copiae sunt perturbatae ut vix iudicari posset, utrum secundis minimisque rebus insolentiores an adverso mediocri casu timidiores essent.

Compluribus diebus isdem in castris consumptis, cum propius accessisse legiones et Gaium Trebonium legatum cognossent, duces Bellovacorum veriti similem obsessionem Alesiae noctu dimittunt eos quos aut aetate aut viribus inferiores aut inermes habebant, unaque reliqua impedimenta. Quorum perturbatum et confusum dum explicant agmen (magna enim multitudo carrorum etiam expeditos sequi Gallos consuevit), oppressi luce copias armatorum pro suis instruunt castris, ne prius Romani persequi se inciperent quam longius agmen impedimentorum suorum processisset. At Caesar neque resistentes adgrediendos tanto collis ascensu iudicabat, neque non usque eo legiones admovendas ut discedere ex eo loco sine periculo barbari militibus instantibus non possent. Ita, cum palude impedita a castris castra dividi videret, quae trans eundi difficultas celeritatem insequendi tardare posset, adque id iugum quod trans paludem paene ad hostium castra pertineret mediocri valle a castris eorum intercisum animum adverteret, pontibus palude constrata legiones traducit celeriterque in summam planitiem iugi pervenit, quae declivi fastigio duobus ab lateribus muniebatur. Ibi legionibus instructis ad ultimum iugum pervenit aciemque eo loco constituit unde tormento missa tela in llostium cuneos conici possent.

Barbari confisi loci natura, cum dimicare non recusarent, si forte Romani subire collem conarentur, paulatim copias distributas dimittere non possent, ne dispersi perturbarentur, in acie permanserunt. Quorum pertinacia cogruta Caesar XX cohortibus

Caesar, perceiving that they persisted in their resolution, kept twenty cohorts in battle array, and, measuring out ground there for a camp, ordered it to be fortified. Having completed his works, he drew up his legions before the rampart and stationed the cavalry in certain positions, with their horses bridled. When the Bellovaci saw the Romans prepared to pursue them, and that they could not wait the whole night, or continue longer in the same place without provisions, they formed the following plan to secure a retreat. They handed to one another the bundles of straw and sticks on which they sat (for it is the custom of the Gauls to sit when drawn up in order of battle, as has been asserted in former commentaries), of which they had great plenty in their camp, and piled them in the front of their line; and at the close of the day, on a certain signal, set them all on fire at one and the same time. The continued blaze soon screened all their forces from the sight of the Romans, which no sooner happened than the barbarians fled with the greatest precipitation.

8:16 Though Caesar could not perceive the retreat of the enemy for the intervention of the fire, yet, suspecting that they had adopted that method to favor their escape, he made his legions advance, and sent a party of horse to pursue them; but, apprehensive of an ambuscade, and that the enemy might remain in the same place and endeavor to draw our men into a disadvantageous situation, he advances himself but slowly. The horse, being afraid to venture into the smoke and dense line of flame, and those who were bold enough to attempt it being scarcely able to see their horse's heads, gave the enemy free liberty to retreat, through fear of an ambuscade. Thus by a flight, full at once of cowardice and address, they advanced without any loss about ten miles, and encamped in a very strong position. From which, laying numerous ambuscades, both of horse and foot, they did considerable damage to the Roman foragers.

8:17 After this had happened several times, Caesar discovered from a certain prisoner, that Correus, the general of the Bellovaci, had selected six thousand of his bravest foot and a thousand horse, with which he designed to lie in ambush in a place to which he suspected the Romans would send to look for forage, on account of the abundance of corn and grass. Upon receiving information of their design Caesar drew out more legions than he usually did, and sent forward his cavalry as usual, to protect the foragers. With these he intermixed a guard of light infantry, and himself advanced with the legions as fast as he could.

8:18 The Gauls, placed in ambush, had chosen for the seat of

instructis castrisque eo loco metatis muniri iubet castra. Absolutis operibus pro vallo legiones instructas collocat, equites frenatis equis in statione disponit. Bellovaci, cum Romanos ad insequendum paratos viderent neque pernoctare aut diutius permanere sine periculo eodem loco possent, tale consilium sui recipiendi ceperunt. Fasces, ubi consederant (namque in acie sedere Gallos consuesse superioribus commentariis Caesaris declaratum est), per manus stramentorum ac virgultorum, quorum summa erat in castris copia, inter se traditos ante aciem collocarunt extremoque tempore diei signo pronuntiato uno tempore incenderunt. Ita continens flamma copias omnes repente a conspectu texit Romanorum. Quod ubi accidit, barbari vehementissimo cursu refugerunt.

Caesar, etsi discessum hostium animadvertere non poterat incendiis oppositis, tamen id consilium cum fugae causa initum suspicaretur, legiones promovet, turmas mittit ad insequendum; ipse veritus insidias, ne forte in eodem loco subsistere hostis atque elicere nostros in locum conaretur iniquum, tardius procedit. Equites cum intrare fumum et flammam densissimam timerent ac, si qui cupidius intraverant, vix suorum ipsi priores partes animadverterent equorum, insidias veriti liberam facultatem sui recipiendi Bellovacis dederunt. Ita fuga timoris simul calliditatisque plena sine ullo detrimento milia non amplius decem progressi hostes loco munitissimo castra posuerunt. Inde cum saepe in insidiis equites peditesque disponerent, magna detrimenta Romanis in pabulationibus inferebant.

Quod cum crebrius accideret, ex captivo quodam comperit Caesar Correum, Bellovacorum ducem, fortissimorum milia sex peditum delegisse equitesque ex omni numero mille, quos in insidiis eo loco collocaret, quem in locum propter copiam frumenti ac pabuli Romanos missuros suspicaretur. Quo cognito consilio legiones plures quam solebat educit equitatumque, qua consuetudine pabulatoribus mittere praesidio consuerat, praemittit: huic interponit auxilia levis armaturae; ipse cum legionibus quam potest maxime appropinquat.

Hostes in insidus dispositi, cum sibi delegissent

action a level piece of ground, not more than a mile in extent, inclosed on every side by a thick wood or a very deep river, as by a toil, and this they surrounded. Our men, apprised of the enemy's design, marched in good order to the ground, ready both in heart and hand to give battle, and willing to hazard any engagement when the legions were at their back. On their approach, as Correus supposed that he had got an opportunity of effecting his purpose, he at first shows himself with a small party and attacks the foremost troops. Our men resolutely stood the charge, and did not crowd together in one place, as commonly happens from surprise in engagements between the horse, whose numbers prove injurious to themselves.

8:19 When by the judicious arrangement of our forces only a few of our men fought by turns, and did not suffer themselves to be surrounded, the rest of the enemy broke out from the woods while Correus was engaged. The battle was maintained in different parts with great vigor, and continued for a long time undecided, till at length a body of foot gradually advanced from the woods in order of battle and forced our horse to give ground: the light infantry, which were sent before the legions to the assistance of the cavalry, soon came up, and, mixing with the horse, fought with great courage. The battle was for some time doubtful, but, as usually happens, our men, who stood the enemy's first charge, became superior from this very circumstance that, though suddenly attacked from an ambuscade, they had sustained no loss. In the mean time the legions were approaching, and several messengers arrived with notice to our men and the enemy that the [Roman] general was near at hand, with his forces in battle array. Upon this intelligence, our men, confiding in the support of the cohorts, fought most resolutely, fearing, lest if they should be slow in their operations they should let the legions participate in the glory of the conquest. The enemy lose courage and attempt to escape by different ways. In vain; for they were themselves entangled in that labyrinth in which they thought to entrap the Romans. Being defeated and put to the rout, and having lost the greater part of their men, they fled in consternation whithersoever chance carried them; some sought the woods, others the river, but were vigorously pursued by our men and put to the sword. Yet, in the mean time, Correus, unconquered by calamity, could not be prevailed on to quit the field and take refuge in the woods, or accept our offers of quarter, but, fighting courageously and wounding several, provoked our men, elated with victory, to discharge their weapons against him.

campum ad rem gerendam non amplius patentem in omnes partes passibus mille, silvis undique aut impeditissimo flumine munitum, velut indagine hunc insidiis circumdederunt. Explorato hostium consilio nostri ad proeliandum animo atque armis parati, cum subsequentibus legionibus nullam dimicationem recusarent, turmatim in eum locum devenerunt. Quorum adventu cum sibi Correus oblatam occasionem rei gerendae existimaret, primum cum paucis se ostendit atque in proximas turmas impetum fecit. Nostri constanter incursum sustinent insidiatorum neque plures in unum locum conveniunt; quod plerumque equestribus proeliis cum propter aliquem timorem accidit, tum multitudine ipsorum detrimentum accipitur.

Cum dispositis turmis in vicem rari proeliarentur neque ab lateribus circumveniri suos paterentur, erumpunt ceteri Correo proeliante ex silvis. Fit magna contentione diversum proelium. Quod cum diutius pari Marte iniretur, paulatim ex silvis instructa multitudo procedit peditum, quae nostros coegit cedere equites. Quibus celeriter subveniunt levis armaturae pedites, quos ante legiones missos docui, turmisque nostrorum interpositi constanter proeliantur. Pugnatur aliquamdiu pari contentione; deinde, ut ratio postulabat proeli, qui sustinuerant primos impetus insidiarum hoc ipso fiunt superiores, quod nullum ab insidiantibus imprudentes acceperant detrimentum. Accedunt propius interim legiones, crebrique eodem tempore et nostris et hostibus nuntii adferuntur, imperatorem instructis copiis adesse. Qua re cognita praesidio cohortium confisi nostri acerrime proeliantur, ne, si tardius rem gessissent, victoriae gloriam communicasse cum legionibus viderentur; hostes concidunt animis atque itineribus diversis fugam quaerunt. Nequiquam: nam quibus difficultatibus locorum Romanos claudere voluerant, eis ipsi tenebantur. Victi tamen perculsique maiore parte amissa consternati profugiunt partim silvis petitis, partim flumine (qui tamen in fuga a nostris acriter insequentibus conficiuntur), eum interim nulla calamitate victus Correus excedere proelio silvasque petere aut invitantibus nostris ad deditionem potuit adduci, quin fortissime proeliando compluresque vulnerando cogeret elatos iracundia victores in se tela conicere.

8:20 After this transaction, Caesar, having come up immediately after the battle, and imagining that the enemy, upon receiving the news of so great a defeat, would be so depressed that they would abandon their camp, which was not above eight miles distant from the scene of action, though he saw his passage obstructed by the river, yet he marched his army over and advanced. But the Bellovaci and the other states, being informed of the loss they had sustained by a few wounded men who having escaped by the shelter of the woods, had returned to them after the defeat, and learning that every thing had turned out unfavorable, that Correus was slain, and the horse and most valiant of their foot cut off, imagined that the Romans were marching against them, and calling a council in haste by sound of trumpet, unanimously cry out to send embassadors and hostages to Caesar.

8:21 This proposal having met with general approbation, Comius the Atrebatian fled to those Germans from whom he had borrowed auxiliaries for that war. The rest instantly send embassadors to Caesar; and requested that he would be contented with that punishment of his enemy, which if he had possessed the power to inflict on them before the engagement, when they were yet uninjured, they were persuaded from his usual clemency and mercy, he never would have inflicted; that the power of the Bellovaci was crushed by the cavalry action; that many thousand of their choicest foot had fallen, that scarce a man had escaped to bring the fatal news. That, however, the Bellovaci had derived from the battle one advantage, of some importance, considering their loss; that Correus, the author of the rebellion, and agitator of the people, was slain: for that while he lived the senate had never equal influence in the state with the giddy populace.

8:22 Caesar reminded the embassadors who made these supplications, that the Bellovaci had at the same season the year before, in conjunction with other states of Gaul, undertaken a war, and that they had persevered the most obstinately of all in their purpose, and were not brought to a proper way of thinking by the submission of the rest: that he knew and was aware that the guilt of a crime was easily transferred to the dead; but that no one person could have such influence, as to be able by the feeble support of the multitude to raise a war and carry it on without the consent of the nobles, in opposition to the senate, and in despite of every virtuous man; however he was satisfied with the punishment, which they had drawn upon themselves.

8:23 The night following the embassadors bring back his answer to their countrymen and prepare the hostages. Embassadors

Tali modo re gesta recentibus proeli vestigiis ingressus Caesar, cum victos tanta calamitate existimaret hostes nuntio accepto locum castrorum relicturos, quae non longius ab ea caede abesse plus minus octo milibus dicebantur, tametsi flumine impeditum transitum videbat, tamen exercitu traducto progreditur. At Bellovaci reliquaeque civitates repente ex fuga paucis atque his vulneratis receptis, qui silvarum benefieio casum evitaverant, omnibus adversis, cognita calamitate, interfecto Correo, amisso equitatu et fortissimis pcditibus, cum adventare Romanos existimarent, concilio repente cantu tubarum convocato conclamant, legati obsidesque ad Caesarem mittantur.

Hoc omnibus probato consilio Commius Atrebas ad eos confugit Germanos, a quibus ad id bellum auxilia mutuatus erat. Ceteri e vestigio mittunt ad Caesarem legatos petuntque, ut ea poena sit contentus hostium, quam si sine dimicatione inferre integris posset, pro sua clementia atque humanitate numquam profecto esset illaturus. Adflictas opes equestri proelio Bellovacorum esse; delectorum peditum multa milia interisse, vix refugisse nuntios caedis. Tamen magnum ut in tanta calamitate Bellovacos eo proelio commodum esse consecutos, quod Correus, auctor belli, concitator multitudinis, esset interfectus. Numquam enim senatum tantum in civitate illo vivo quantum imperitam plebem potuisse.

Haec orantibus legatis commemorat Caesar: Eodem tempore superiore anno Bellovacos ceterasque Galliae civitates suscepisse bellum: pertinacissime hos ex omnibus in sententia permansisse neque ad sanitatem reliquorum deditione esse perductos. Scire atque intellegere se causam peccati facillime mortuis delegari. Neminem vero tantum pollere, ut invitis principibus, resistente senatu, omnibus bonis repugnantibus infirma manu plebis bellum concitare et gerere posset. Sed tamen se contentum fore ea poena quam sibi ipsi contraxissent.

Nocte insequenti legati responsa ad suos referunt, obsides conficiunt. Concurrunt reliquarum civitatium

flock in from the other states, which were waiting for the issue of the [war with the] Bellovaci: they give hostages, and receive his orders; all except Comius, whose fears restrained him from intrusting his safety to any person's honor. For the year before, while Caesar was holding the assizes in Hither Gaul, Titus Labienus, having discovered that Comius was tampering with the state, and raising a conspiracy against Caesar, thought he might punish his infidelity without perfidy; but judging that he would not come to his camp at his invitation, and unwilling to put him on his guard by the attempt, he sent Caius Volusenus Quadratus, with orders to have him put to death under pretense of conference. To effect his purpose, he sent with him some chosen centurions. When they came to the conference, and Volusenus, as had been agreed on, had taken hold of Comius by the hand, and one of the centurions, as if surprised at so uncommon an incident, attempted to kill him, he was prevented by the friends of Comius, but wounded him severely in the head by the first blow. Swords were drawn on both sides, not so much with a design to fight as to effect an escape, our men believing that Comius had received a mortal stroke; and the Gauls, from the treachery which they had seen, dreading that a deeper design lay concealed. Upon this transaction, it was said that Comius made a resolution never to come within sight of any Roman.

8:24 When Caesar, having completely conquered the most warlike nations, perceived that there was now no state which could make preparations for war to oppose him, but that some were removing and fleeing from their country to avoid present subjection, he resolved to detach his army into different parts of the country. He kept with himself Marcus Antonius the quaestor, with the eleventh legion; Caius Fabius was detached with twenty-five cohorts into the remotest part of Gaul, because it was rumored that some states had risen in arms, and he did not think that Caius Caninius Rebilus, who had the charge of that country, was strong enough to protect it with two legions. He ordered Titus Labienus to attend himself, and sent the twelfth legion which had been under him in winter quarters, to Hither Gaul, to protect the Roman colonies, and prevent any loss by the inroads of barbarians similar to that which had happened the year before to the Tergestines, who were cut off by a sudden depredation and attack. He himself marched to depopulate the country of Ambiorix, whom he had terrified and forced to fly, but despaired of being able to reduce under his power; but he thought it most consistent with his honor to waste his country both of inhabitants, cattle, and buildings, so that from the abhorrence of his countrymen, if fortune suffered any to survive,

legati, quae Bellovacorum speculabantur eventum; obsides dant, imperata faciunt excepto Commio, quem timor prohibebat cuiusquam fidei suam committere salutem. Nam superiore anno Titus Labienus, Caesare in Gallia citeriore ius dicente, cum Commium comperisset sollicitare civitates et coniurationem contra Caesarem facere, infidelitatem eius sine ulla perfidia iudicavit comprimi posse. Quem quia non arbitrabatur vocatum in castra venturum, ne temptando cautiorem faceret, Gaium Volusenum Quadratum misit, qui eum per simulationem colloqui curaret interficiendum. Ad eam rem delectos idoneos ei tradit centuriones. Cum in colloquium ventum esset, et, ut convenerat, manum Commi Volusenus arripuisset, centurio vel insueta re permotus vel celeriter a familiaribus prohibitus Commi conficere hominem non potuit; graviter tamen primo ictu gladio caput percussit. Cum utrimque gladii destricti essent, non tam pugnandi quam diffugiendi fuit utrorumque consilium: nostrorum, quod mortifero vulnere Commium credebant adfectum; Gallorum, quod insidiis cognitis plura quam videbant extimescebant. Quo facto statuisse Commius dicebatur numquam in conspectum cuiusquam Romani venire.

Bellicosissimis gentibus devictis Caesar, cum videret nullam iam esse civitatem quae bellum pararet quo sibi resisteret, sed nonnullos ex oppidis demigrare, ex agris diffugere ad praesens imperium evitandum, plures in partes exercitum dimittere constituit. M. Antonium quaestorem cum legione duodecima sibi coniungit. C. Fabium legatum cum cohortibus XXV mittit in diversissimam partem Galliae, quod ibi quasdam civitates in armis esse audiebat neque C. Caninium Rebilum legatum, qui in illis regionibus erat, satis firmas duas legiones habere existimabat. Titum Labienum ad se evocat; legionem autem XV, quae cum eo fuerat in hibernis, in togatam Galliam mittit ad colonias civium Romanorum tuendas, ne quod simile incommodum accideret decursione barbarorum ac superiore aestate Tergestinis acciderat, qui repentino latrocinio atque impetu illorum erant oppressi. Ipse ad vastandos depopulandosque fines Ambiorigis proficiscitur; quem perterritum ac fugientem cum redigi posse in suam potestatem desperasset, proximum suae dignitatis esse ducebat, adeo fines eius vastare

he might be excluded from a return to his state for the calamities which he had brought on it.

8:25 After he had sent either his legions or auxiliaries through every part of Ambiorix's dominions, and wasted the whole country by sword, fire, and rapine, and had killed or taken prodigious numbers, he sent Labienus with two legions against the Treviri, whose state, from its vicinity to Germany, being engaged in constant war, differed but little from the Germans, in civilization and savage barbarity; and never continued in its allegiance, except when awed by the presence of his army.

8:26 In the mean time Caius Caninius, a lieutenant, having received information by letters and messages from Duracius, who had always continued in friendship to the Roman people, though a part of his state had revolted, that a great multitude of the enemy were in arms in the country of the Pictones, marched to the town Limonum. When he was approaching it, he was informed by some prisoners, that Duracius was shut up by several thousand men, under the command of Dumnacus, general of the Andes, and that Limonum was besieged, but not daring to face the enemy with his weak legions, he encamped in a strong position: Dumnacus, having notice of Caninius's approach, turned his whole force against the legions, and prepared to assault the Roman camp. But after spending several days in the attempt, and losing a considerable number of men, without being able to make a breach in any part of the works, he returned again to the siege of Limonum.

8:27 At the same time, Caius Fabius, a lieutenant, brings back many states to their allegiance, and confirms their submission by taking hostages; he was then informed by letters from Caninius, of the proceedings among the Pictones. Upon which he set off to bring assistance to Duracius. But Dumnacus, hearing of the approach of Fabius, and despairing of safety, if at the same time he should be forced to withstand the Roman army without, and observe, and be under apprehension from the town's people, made a precipitate retreat from that place with all his forces. Nor did he think that he should be sufficiently secure from danger, unless he led his army across the Loire, which was too deep a river to pass except by a bridge. Though Fabius had not yet come within sight of the enemy, nor joined Caninius; yet being informed of the nature of the country, by persons acquainted with it, he judged it most likely that the enemy would take that way, which he found they did take. He therefore marched to that bridge with his army, and ordered his cavalry to

civibus, aedificiis, pecore, ut odio suorum Ambiorix, si quos fortuna reliquos fecisset, nullum reditum propter tantas calamitates haberet in civitatem.

Cum in omnes partes finium Ambiorigis aut legiones aut auxilia dimisisset atque omnia caedibus, incendius, rapinis vastasset, magno numero hominum interfecto aut capto Labienum cum duabus legionibus in Treveros mittit, quorum civitas propter Germaniae vicinitatem cotidianis exercitata bellis cultu et feritate non multum a Germanis differebat neque imperata umquam nisi exercitu coacta faciebat.

Interim Gaius Caninius legatus, cum magnam multitudinem convenisse hostium in fines Pictonum litteris nuntiisque Durati cognosceret, qui perpetuo in amicitia manserat Romanorum, cum pars quaedam civitatis eius defecisset, ad oppidum Lemonum contendit. Quo cum adventaret atque ex captivis certius cognosceret multis hominum milibus a Dumnaco, duce Andium, Duratium clausum Lemoni oppugnari neque infirmas legiones hostibus committere auderet, castra posuit loco munito. Dumnacus, cum appropinquare Caninium cognosset, copiis omnibus ad legiones conversis castra Romanorum oppugnare instituit. Cum complures dies in oppugnatione consumpsisset et magno suorum detrimento nullam partem munitionum convellere potuisset, rursus ad obsidendum Lemonum redit.

Eodem tempore C. Fabius legatus complures civitates in fidem recipit, obsidibus firmat litterisque Gai Canini Rebili fit certior quae in Pictonibus gerantur. Quibus rebus cognitis proficiscitur ad auxilium Duratio ferendum. At Dumnacus adventu Fabi cognito desperata salute, si tempore eodem coactus esset et Romanum externum sustinere hostem et respicere ac timere oppidanos, repente ex eo loco cum copiis recedit nec se satis tutum fore arbitratur, nisi flumine Ligeri, quod erat ponte propter magnitudinem transeundum, copias traduxisset. Fabius, etsi nondum in conspectum venerat hostibus neque se Caninio coniunxerat, tamen doctus ab eis qui locorum noverant naturam potissimum credidit hostes perterritos eum locum, quem petebant, petituros. Itaque cum copiis ad eundem pontem contendit equitatumque tantum procedere ante

advance no farther before the legions than that they could return to the same camp at night, without fatiguing their horses. Our horse pursued according to orders, and fell upon Dumnacus's rear and attacking them on their march, while fleeing, dismayed, and laden with baggage, they slew a great number, and took a rich booty. Having executed the affair so successfully, they retired to the camp.

8:28 The night following, Fabius sent his horse before him, with orders to engage the enemy, and delay their march till he himself should come up. That his orders might be faithfully performed, Quintus Atius Varus, general of the horse, a man of uncommon spirit and skill, encouraged his men, and pursuing the enemy, disposed some of his troops in convenient places, and with the rest gave battle to the enemy. The enemy's cavalry made a bold stand, the foot relieving each other, and making a general halt, to assist their horse against ours. The battle was warmly contested. For our men, despising the enemy whom they had conquered the day before, and knowing that the legions were following them, animated both by the disgrace of retreating, and a desire of concluding the battle expeditiously by their own courage, fought most valiantly against the foot: and the enemy, imagining that no more forces would come against them, as they had experienced the day before, thought they had got a favorable opportunity of destroying our whole cavalry.

8:29 After the conflict had continued for some time with great violence, Dumnacus drew out his army in such a manner, that the foot should by turns assist the horse. Then the legions, marching in close order, came suddenly in sight of the enemy. At this sight, the barbarian horse were so astonished, and the foot so terrified, that breaking through the line of baggage, they betook themselves to flight with a loud shout, and in great disorder. But our horse, who a little before had vigorously engaged them, while they made resistance, being elated with joy at their victory, raising a shout on every side, poured round them as they ran, and as long as their horses had strength to pursue, or their arms to give a blow, so long did they continue the slaughter of the enemy in that battle, and having killed above twelve thousand men in arms, or such as threw away their arms through fear, they took their whole train of baggage.

8:30 After this defeat, when it was ascertained that Drapes, a Senonian (who in the beginning of the revolt of Gaul had collected from all quarters men of desperate fortunes, invited the slaves to liberty, called in the exiles of the whole kingdom, given an asylum to robbers, and intercepted the Roman baggage and provisions), was marching to the province with five thousand men, being all he could collect after the defeat, and that Luterius

agmen imperat legionum, quantum cum processisset, sine defatigatione equorum in eadem se reciperet castra. Consecuntur equites nostri, ut erat praeceptum, invaduntque Dumnaci agmen et fugientes perterritosque sub sarcinis in itinere adgressi magna praeda multis interfectis potiuntur. Ita re bene gesta se recipiunt in castra.

Insequenti nocte Fabius equites praemittit sic paratos ut confligerent atque omne agmen morarentur, dum consequeretur ipse. Cuius praeceptis ut res gereretur, Quintus Atius Varus, praefectus equitum, singularis et animi et prudentiae vir, suos hortatur agmenque hostium consecutus turmas partim idoneis locis disponit, parte equitum proelium committit. Confligit audacius equitatus hostium succedentibus sibi peditibus, qui toto agmine subsistentes equitibus suis contra nostros ferunt auxilium. Fit proelium acri certamine. Namque nostri contemptis pridie superatis hostibus, cum subsequi legiones meminissent, et pudore cedendi et cupiditate per se conficiendi proeli fortissime contra pedites proeliantur, hostesque nihil amplius copiarum accessurum credentes, ut pridie cognoverant, delendi equitatus nostri nacti occasionem videbantur.

Cum aliquamdiu summa contentione dimicaretur, Dumnacus instruit aciem quae suis esset equitibus in vicem praesidio, cum repente confertae legiones in conspectum hostium veniunt. Quibus visis perculsae barbarorum turmae ac perterritae acies hostium, perturbato impedimentorum agmine, magno clamore discursuque passim fugae se mandant. At nostri equites, qui paulo ante cum resistentibus fortissime conflixerant, laetitia victoriae elati magno undique clamore sublato cedentibus circumfusi, quantum equorum vires ad persequendum dextraeque ad caedendum valent, tantum eo proelio interficiunt. Itaque amplius milibus XII aut armatorum aut eorum qui eo timore arma proiecerant interfectis omnis multitudo capitur impedimentorum.

Qua ex fuga cum constaret Drappetem Senonem, qui, ut primum defecerat Gallia, collectis undique perditis hominibus, servis ad libertatem vocatis, exulibus omnium civitatum adscitis, receptis latronibus impedimenta et commeatus Romanorum interceperat, non amplius hominum duobus milibus ex fuga collectis provinciam petere unaque consilium

a Cadurcian who, as it has been observed in a former commentary, had designed to make an attack on the Province in the first revolt of Gaul, had formed a junction with him, Caius Caninius went in pursuit of them with two legions, lest great disgrace might be incurred from the fears or injuries done to the Province by the depredations of a band of desperate men.

8:31 Caius Fabius set off with the rest of the army to the Carnutes and those other states, whose force he was informed, had served as auxiliaries in that battle, which he fought against Dumnacus. For he had no doubt that they would be more submissive after their recent sufferings, but if respite and time were given them, they might be easily excited by the earnest solicitations of the same Dumnacus. On this occasion Fabius was extremely fortunate and expeditious in recovering the states. For the Carnutes, who, though often harassed had never mentioned peace, submitted and gave hostages: and the other states, which lie in the remotest parts of Gaul, adjoining the ocean, and which are called Armoricae, influenced by the example of the Carnutes, as soon as Fabius arrived with his legions, without delay comply with his command. Dumnacus, expelled from his own territories, wandering and skulking about, was forced to seek refuge by himself in the most remote parts of Gaul.

8:32 But Drapes in conjunction with Luterius, knowing that Caninius was at hand with the legions, and that they themselves could not without certain destruction enter the boundaries of the province, while an army was in pursuit of them, and being no longer at liberty to roam up and down and pillage, halt in the country of the Cadurci, as Luterius had once in his prosperity possessed a powerful influence over the inhabitants, who were his countrymen, and being always the author of new projects, had considerable authority among the barbarians; with his own and Drapes' troops he seized Uxellodunum, a town formerly in vassalage to him, and strongly fortified by its natural situation; and prevailed on the inhabitants to join him.

8:33 After Caninius had rapidly marched to this place, and perceived that all parts of the town were secured by very craggy rocks, which it would be difficult for men in arms to climb even if they met with no resistance; and moreover, observing that the town's people were possessed of effects, to a considerable amount, and that if they attempted to convey them away in a clandestine manner, they could not escape our horse, or even our legions; he divided his forces into three parts, and pitched three camps on very high ground, with the intention of drawing lines round the town by degrees, as his forces could bear the

cum eo Lucterium Cadurcum cepisse, quem superiore commentario prima defectione Galliae facere in provinciam voluisse impetum cognitum est, Caninius legatus cum legionibus duabus ad eos persequendos contendit, ne detrimento aut timore provinciae magna infamia perditorum hominum latrociniis caperetur.

Gaius Fabius cum reliquo exercitu in Carnutes ceterasque proficiscitur civitates, quarum eo proelio, quod cum Dumnaco fecerat, copias esse accisas sciebat. Non enim dubitabat quin recenti calamitate summissiores essent futurae, dato vero spatio ac tempore eodem instigante Dumnaco possent concitari. Qua in re summa felicitas celeritasque in recipiendis civitatibus Fabium consequitur. Nam Carnutes, qui saepe vexati numquam pacis fecerant mentionem, datis obsidibus veniunt in deditionem, ceteraeque civitates positae in ultimis Galliae finibus Oceano coniunctae, quae Armoricae appellantur, auctoritate adductae Carnutum adventu Fabi legio numque imperata sine mora faciunt. Dumnacus suis finibus expulsus errans latitansque solus extremas Galliae regiones petere est coactus.

At Drappes unaque Lucterius, cum legiones Caniniumque adesse cognoscerent nec se sine certa pernicie persequente exercitu putarent provinciae fines intrare posse nec iam libere vagandi latrociniorumque faciendorum facultatem haberent, in finibus consistunt Cadurcorum. Ibi cum Lucterius apud suos cives quondam integris rebus multum potuisset, semperque auctor novorum consiliorum magnam apud barbaros auctoritatem haberet, oppidum Vxellodunum, quod in clientela fuerat eius, egregie natura loci munitum, occupat suis et Drappetis copiis oppidanosque sibi coniungit.

Quo cum confestim Gaius Caninius venisset animadverteretque omnes oppidi partes praeruptissimis saxis esse munitas, quo defendente nullo tamen armatis ascendere esset difficile, magna autem impedimenta oppidanorum videret, quae si clandestina fuga subtrahere conarentur, effugere non modo equitatum, sed ne legiones quidem possent, tripertito cohortibus divisis trina excelsissimo loco castra fecit; a quibus paulatim, quantum copiae patiebantur, vallum in oppidi circuitum ducere

fatigue.

8:34 When the townsmen perceived his design, being terrified by the recollection of the distress at Alesia, they began to dread similar consequences from a siege; and above all Luterius, who had experienced that fatal event, cautioned them to make provisions of corn; they therefore resolve by general consent to leave part of their troops behind, and set out with their light troops to bring in corn. The scheme having met with approbation, the following night Drapes and Luterius leaving two thousand men in the garrison, marched out of the town with the rest. After a few days' stay in the country of the Cadurci (some of whom were disposed to assist them with corn, and others were unable to prevent their taking it) they collected a great store. Sometimes also attacks were made on our little forts by sallies at night. For this reason Caninius deferred drawing his works round the whole town, lest he should be unable to protect them when completed, or by disposing his garrisons in several places, should make them too weak.

8:35 Drapes and Luterius, having laid in a large supply of corn, occupying a position at about ten miles distance from the town, intending from it to convey the corn into the town by degrees. They chose each his respective department. Drapes stayed behind in the camp with part of the army to protect it; Luterius conveys the train with provisions into the town. Accordingly, having disposed guards here and there along the road, about the tenth hour of the night, he set out by narrow paths through the woods, to fetch the corn into the town. But their noise being heard by the sentinels of our camp, and the scouts which we had sent out, having brought an account of what was going on, Caninius instantly with the ready-armed cohorts from the nearest turrets made an attack on the convoy at the break of day. They, alarmed at so unexpected an evil, fled by different ways to their guard: which as soon as our men perceived, they fell with great fury on the escort, and did not allow a single man to be taken alive. Luterius escaped thence with a few followers, but did not return to the camp.

8:36 After this success, Caninius learned from some prisoners, that a part of the forces was encamped with Drapes, not more than ten miles off: which being confirmed by several, supposing that after the defeat of one general, the rest would be terrified, and might be easily conquered, he thought it a most fortunate event that none of the enemy had fled back from the slaughter to the camp, to give Drapes notice of the calamity which had befallen him. And as he could see no danger in making the attempt, he sent forward all his cavalry and the German foot,

instituit.

Quod cum animadverterent oppidani miserrimaque Alesiae memoria solliciti similem casum obsessionis vererentur, maximeque ex omnibus Lucterius, qui fortunae illius periculum fecerat, moneret frumenti rationem esse habendam, constituunt omnium consensu parte ibi relicta copiarum ipsi cum expeditis ad importandum frumentum proficisci. Eo consilio probato proxima nocte duobus milibus armatorum relictis reliquos ex oppido Drappes et Lucterius educunt. Hi paucos dies morati ex finibus Cadurcorum, qui partim re frumentaria sublevare eos cupiebant, partim prohibere quo minus sumerent non poterant, magnum numerum frumenti comparant, nonnumquam autem expeditionibus nocturnis castella nostrorum adoriuntur. Quam ob causam Gaius Caninius toto oppido munitiones circumdare moratur, ne aut opus effectum tueri non possit aut plurimis in locis infirma disponat praesidia.

Magna copia frumenti comparata considunt Drappes et Lucterius non longius ab oppido X milibus, unde paulatim frumentum in oppidum supportarent. Ipsi inter se provincias partiuntur: Drappes castris praesidio cum parte copiarum restitit; Lucterius agmen iumentorum ad oppidum ducit. Dispositis ibi praesidiis hora noctis circiter decima silvestribus angustisque itineribus frumentum importare in oppidum instituit. Quorum strepitum vigiles castrorum cum sensissent, exploratoresque missi quae gererentur renuntiassent, Caninius celeriter cum cohortibus armatis ex proximis castellis in frumentarios sub ipsam lucem impetum fecit. Ei repentino malo perterriti diffugiunt ad sua praesidia; quae nostri ut viderunt, acrius contra armatos incitati neminem ex eo numero vivum capi patiuntur. Profugit inde cum paucis Lucterius nec se recipit in castra.

Re bene gesta Caninius ex captivis comperit partem copiarum cum Drappete esse in castris a milibus longe non amplius XII. Qua re ex compluribus cognita, cum intellegeret fugato duce altero perterritos reliquos facile opprimi posse, magnae felicitatis esse arbitrabatur neminem ex caede refugisse in castra qui de accepta calamitate nuntium Drappeti perferret. Sed in experiendo cum periculum nullum videret, equitatum omnem Germanosque

men of great activity, to the enemy's camp. He divides one legion among the three camps, and takes the other without baggage along with him. When he had advanced near the enemy, he was informed by scouts, which he had sent before him, that the enemy's camp, as is the custom of barbarians, was pitched low, near the banks of a river, and that the higher grounds were unoccupied: but that the German horse had made a sudden attack on them, and had begun the battle. Upon this intelligence, he marched up with his legion, armed and in order of battle. Then, on a signal being suddenly given on every side, our men took possession of the higher grounds. Upon this the German horse observing the Roman colors, fought with great vigor. Immediately all the cohorts attack them on every side; and having either killed or made prisoners of them all, gained great booty. In that battle, Drapes himself was taken prisoner.

8:37 Caninius, having accomplished the business so successfully, without having scarcely a man wounded, returned to besiege the town; and, having destroyed the enemy without, for fear of whom he had been prevented from strengthening his redoubts, and surrounding the enemy with his lines, he orders the work to be completed on every side. The next day, Caius Fabius came to join him with his forces, and took upon him the siege of one side.

8:38 In the mean time, Caesar left Caius Antonius in the country of the Bellovaci, with fifteen cohorts, that the Belgae might have no opportunity of forming new plans in future. He himself visits the other states, demands a great number of hostages, and by his encouraging language allays the apprehensions of all. When he came to the Carnutes, in whose state he has in a former commentary mentioned that the war first broke out; observing, that from a consciousness of their guilt, they seemed to be in the greatest terror: to relieve the state the sooner from its fear, he demanded that Guturvatus, the promoter of that treason, and the instigator of that rebellion, should be delivered up to punishment. And though the latter did not dare to trust his life even to his own countrymen, yet such diligent search was made by them all, that he was soon brought to our camp. Caesar was forced to punish him, by the clamors of the soldiers, contrary to his natural humanity, for they alleged that all the dangers and losses incurred in that war, ought to be imputed to Guturvatus. Accordingly, he was whipped to death, and his head cut off.

8:39 Here Caesar was informed by numerous letters from Caninius of what had happened to Drapes and Luterius, and in what conduct the town's people persisted: and though he despised the smallness of their numbers, yet he thought their

pedites, summae velocitatis homines, ad castra hostium praemittit; ipse legionem unam in trina castra distribuit, alteram secum expeditam ducit. Cum propius hostes accessisset, ab exploratoribus quos praemiserat cognoscit castra eorum, ut barbarorum fere consuetudo est, relictis locis superioribus ad ripas fluminis esse demissa; at Germanos equitesque imprudentibus omnibus de improviso advolasse proeliumque commisisse. Qua re cognita legionem armatam instructamque adducit. Ita repente omnibus ex partibus signo dato loca superiora capiuntur. Quod ubi accidit, Germani equitesque signis legionis visis vehementissime proeliantur. Confestim cohortes undique impetum faciunt omnibusque aut interfectis aut captis magna praeda potiuntur. Capitur ipse eo proelio Drappes.

Caninius felicissime re gesta sine ullo paene militis vulnere ad obsidendos oppidanos revertitur externoque hoste deleto, cuius timore antea dividere praesidia et munitione oppidanos circumdare prohibitus erat, opera undique imperat administrari. Venit eodem cum suis copiis postero die Gaius Fabius partemque oppidi sumit ad obsidendum.

Caesar interim M. Antonium quaestorem cum cohortibus XV in Bellovacis relinquit, ne qua rursus novorum consiliorum capiendorum Belgis facultas daretur. Ipse reliquas civitates adit, obsides plures imperat, timentes omnium animos consolatione sanat. Cum in Carnutes venisset, quorum in civitate superiore commentario Caesar euit initium belli esse ortum, quod praecipue eos propter conscientiam facti timere animadvertebat, quo celerius civitatem timore liberaret, principem sceleris illius et concitatorem belli, Gutruatum, ad supplicium deposcit. Qui etsi ne civibus quidem suis se committebat, tamen celeriter omnium cura quaesitus in castra perducitur. Cogitur in eius supplicium Caesar contra suam naturam concursu maximo militum, qui ei omnia pericula et detrimenta belli accepta referebant, adeo ut verberibus exanimatum corpus securi feriretur.

Ibi crebris litteris Canini fit certior quae de Drappete et Lucterio gesta essent, quoque in consilio permanerent oppidani. Quorum etsi paucitatem contemnebat, tamen pertinaciam magna poena esse

obstinacy deserving a severe punishment, lest Gaul in general should adopt an idea that she did not want strength but perseverance to oppose the Romans; and lest the other states, relying on the advantage of situation, should follow their example and assert their liberty; especially as he knew that all the Gauls understood that his command was to continue but one summer longer, and if they could hold out for that time, that they would have no further danger to apprehend. He therefore left Quintus Calenus, one of his lieutenants, behind him, with two legions, and instructions to follow him by regular marches. He hastened as much as he could with all the cavalry to Caninius.

8:40 Having arrived at Uxellodunum, contrary to the general expectation, and perceiving that the town was surrounded by the works, and that the enemy had no possible means of retiring from the assault, and being likewise informed by the deserters that the townsmen had abundance of corn, he endeavoured to prevent their getting water. A river divided the valley below, which almost surrounded the steep craggy mountain on which Uxellodunum was built. The nature of the ground prevented his turning the current: for it ran so low down at the foot of the mountain, that no drains could be sunk deep enough to draw it off in any direction. But the descent to it was so difficult, that if we made opposition, the besieged could neither come to the river nor retire up the precipice without hazard of their lives. Caesar perceiving the difficulty, disposed archers and slingers, and in some places, opposite to the easiest descents, placed engines, and attempted to hinder the townsmen from getting water at the river, which obliged them afterward to go all to one place to procure water.

8:41 Close under the walls of the town, a copious spring gushed out on that part, which for the space of nearly three hundred feet, was not surrounded by the river. While every other person wished that the besieged could be debarred from this spring, Caesar alone saw that it could be effected, though not without great danger. Opposite to it he began to advance the vineae toward the mountain, and to throw up a mound, with great labor and continual skirmishing. For the townsmen ran down from the high ground, and fought without any risk, and wounded several of our men, yet they obstinately pushed on and were not deterred from moving forward the vineae, and from surmounting by their assiduity the difficulties of situation. At the same time they work mines, and move the crates and vineae to the source of the fountain. This was the only work which they could do without danger or suspicion. A mound sixty feet high was raised; on it was erected a turret of ten stories, not with the intention that it should be on a level with the wall (for that could not be

adficiendam iudicabat, ne universa Gallia non sibi vires defuisse ad resistendum Romanis, sed constantiam putaret, neve hoc exemplo ceterae civitates locorum opportunitate fretae se vindicarent in libertatem, cum omnibus Gallis notum esse sciret reliquam esse unam aestatem suae provinciae, quam si sustinere potuissent, nullum ultra periculum vererentur. Itaque Q. Calenum legatum cum legionibus reliquit qui iustis itineribus subsequeretur; ipse cum omni equitatu quam potest celerrime ad Caninium contendit.

Cum contra exspectationem omnium Caesar Vxellodunum venisset oppidumque operibus clausum animadverteret neque ab oppugnatione recedi videret ulla condicione posse, magna autem copia frumenti abundare oppidanos ex perfugis cognosset, aqua prohibere hostem temptare coepit. Flumen infimam vallem dividebat, quae totum paene montem cingebat, in quo positum erat praeruptum undique oppidum Vxellodunum. Hoc avertere loci natura prohibebat: in infimis enim sic radicibus montis ferebatur, ut nullam in partem depressis fossis derivari posset. Erat autem oppidanis difficilis et praeruptus eo descensus, ut prohibentibus nostris sine vulneribus ac periculo vitae neque adire flumen neque arduo se recipere possent ascensu. Qua difficultate eorum cogmta Caesar sagittariis funditoribusque dispositis, tormentis etiam quibusdam locis contra facillimos descensus collocatis aqua fluminis prohibebat oppidanos.

Quorum omnis postea multitudo aquatorum unum in locum conveniebat sub ipsius oppidi murum, ubi magnus fons aquae prorumpebat ab ea parte, quae fere pedum CCC intervallo fluminis circuitu vacabat. Hoc fonte prohiberi posse oppidanos cum optarent reliqui, Caesar unus videret, e regione eius vineas agere adversus montem et aggerem instruere coepit magno cum labore et continua dimicatione. Oppidani enim loco superiore decurrunt et eminus sine periculo proeliantur multosque pertinaciter succedentes vulnerant; non deterrentur tamen milites nostri vineas proferre et labore atque operibus locorum vincere difficultates. Eodem tempore cuniculos tectos ab vineis agunt ad caput fontis; quod genus operis sine ullo periculo, sine suspicione hostium facere licebat. Exstruitur agger in altitudinem pedum sexaginta, collocatur in eo turris decem

effected by any works), but to rise above the top of the spring. When our engines began to play from it upon the paths that led to the fountain, and the townsmen could not go for water without danger, not only the cattle designed for food and the working cattle, but a great number of men also died of thirst.

8:42 Alarmed at this calamity, the townsmen fill barrels with tallow, pitch, and dried wood: these they set on fire, and roll down on our works. At the same time, they fight most furiously, to deter the Romans, by the engagement and danger, from extinguishing the flames. Instantly a great blaze arose in the works. For whatever they threw down the precipice, striking against the vineae and agger, communicated the fire to whatever was in the way. Our soldiers on the other hand, though they were engaged in a perilous sort of encounter, and laboring under the disadvantages of position, yet supported all with very great presence of mind. For the action happened in an elevated situation, and in sight of our army; and a great shout was raised on both sides; therefore every man faced the weapons of the enemy and the flames in as conspicuous a manner as he could, that his valor might be the better known and attested.

8:43 Caesar, observing that several of his men were wounded, ordered the cohorts to ascend the mountain on all sides, and, under pretense of assailing the walls, to raise a shout: at which the besieged being frightened, and not knowing what was going on in other places, call off their armed troops from attacking our works, and dispose them on the walls. Thus our men without hazarding a battle, gained time partly to extinguish the works which had caught fire, and partly to cut off the communication. As the townsmen still continued to make an obstinate resistance, and even, after losing the greatest part of their forces by drought, persevered in their resolution: at last the veins of the spring were cut across by our mines, and turned from their course. By this their constant spring was suddenly dried up, which reduced them to such despair that they imagined that it was not done by the art of man, but the will of the gods; forced, therefore, by necessity, they at length submitted.

8:44 Caesar, being convinced that his lenity was known to all men, and being under no fears of being thought to act severely from a natural cruelty, and perceiving that there would be no end to his troubles if several states should attempt to rebel in like manner and in different places, resolved to deter others by inflicting an exemplary punishment on these. Accordingly he cut off the hands of those who had borne arms against him. Their

tabulatorum, non quidem quae moenibus aequaret (id enim nullis operibus effici poterat), sed quae superare fontis fastigium posset. Ex ea cum tela tormentis iacerentur ad fontis aditum, nec sine periculo possent aquari oppidani, non tantum pecora atque iumenta, sed etiam magna hostium multitudo siti consumebatur.

Quo malo perterriti oppidani cupas sebo, pice, scandulis complent; eas ardentes in opera provolvunt eodemque tempore acerrime proeliantur, ut ab incendio restinguendo dimicationis periculo deterreant Romanos. Magna repente in ipsis operibus flamma exstitit. Quaecumque enim per locum praecipitem missa erant, ea vineis et aggere suppressa comprehendebant id ipsum quod morabatur. Milites contra nostri, quamquam periculoso genere proeli locoque iniquo premebantur, tamen omnia fortissimo sustinebant animo. Res enim gerebatur et excelso loco et in conspectu exercitus nostri, magnusque utrimque clamor oriebatur. Ita quam quisque poterat maxime insignis, quo notior testatiorque virtus esset eius, telis hostium flammaeque se offerebat.

Caesar cum complures suos vulnerari videret, ex omnibus oppidi partibus cohortes montem ascendere et simulatione moenium occupandorum clamorem undique iubet tollere. Quo facto perterriti oppidani, cum quid ageretur in locis reliquis essent suspensi, revocant ab impugnandis operibus armatos murisque disponunt. Ita nostri fine proeli facto celeriter opera flamma comprehensa partim restinguunt, partim interscindunt. Cum pertinaciter resisterent oppidani, magna etiam parte amissa siti suorum in sententia permanerent, ad postremum cuniculis venae fontis intercisae sunt atque aversac. Quo facto repente perennis exaruit fons tantamque attulit oppidanis salutis desperationem, ut id non hominum consilio, sed deorum voluntate factum putarent. Itaque se necessitate coacti tradiderunt.

Caesar, cum suam lenitatem cognnitam omnibus sciret neque vereretur ne quid crudelitate naturae videretur asperius fecisse, neque exitum consiliorum suorum animadverteret, si tali ratione diversis in locis plures consilia inissent, exemplo supplici deterrendos reliquos existimavit. Itaque omnibus qui arma tulerant manus praecidit vitamque concessit, quo

lives he spared, that the punishment of their rebellion might be the more conspicuous. Drapes, who I have said was taken by Caninius, either through indignation and grief arising from his captivity, or through fear of severer punishments, abstained from food for several days, and thus perished. At the same time, Luterius, who, I have related, had escaped from the battle, having fallen into the hands of Epasnactus, an Arvernian (for he frequently changed his quarters, and threw himself on the honor of several persons, as he saw that he dare not remain long in one place, and was conscious how great an enemy he deserved to have in Caesar), was by this Epasnactus, the Arvernian, a sincere friend of the Roman people, delivered without any hesitation, a prisoner to Caesar.

8:45 In the mean time, Labienus engages in a successful cavalry action among the Treviri; and, having killed several of them and of the Germans, who never refused their aid to any person against the Romans, he got their chiefs alive into his power, and, among them, Surus, an Aeduan, who was highly renowned both for his valor and birth, and was the only Aeduan that had continued in arms till that time.

8:46 Caesar, being informed of this, and perceiving that he had met with good success in all parts of Gaul, and reflecting that, in former campaigns [Celtic] Gaul had been conquered and subdued; but that he had never gone in person to Aquitania, but had made a conquest of it, in some degree, by Marcus Crassus, set out for it with two legions, designing to spend the latter part of the summer there. This affair he executed with his usual dispatch and good fortune. For all the states of Aquitania sent embassadors to him and delivered hostages. These affairs being concluded, he marched with a guard of cavalry toward Narbo, and drew off his army into winter quarters by his lieutenants. He posted four legions in the country of the Belgae, under Marcus Antonius, Caius Trebonius, Publius Vatinius, and Quintus Tullius, his lieutenants. Two he detached to the Aedui, knowing them to have a very powerful influence throughout all Gaul. Two he placed among the Turoni, near the confines of the Carnutes, to keep in awe the entire tract of country bordering on the ocean; the other two he placed in the territories of the Lemovices, at a small distance from the Arverni, that no part of Gaul might be without an army. Having spent a few days in the province, he quickly ran through all the business of the assizes, settled all public disputes, and distributed rewards to the most deserving; for he had a good opportunity of learning how every person was disposed toward the republic during the general revolt of Gaul, which he had withstood by the fidelity and assistance of the Province.

testatior esset poena improborum. Drappes, quem captum esse a Caninio docui, sive indignitate et dolore vinculorum sive timore gravioris supplici paucis diebus cibo se abstinuit atque ita interiit. Eodem tempore Lacterius, quem profugisse ex proelio scripsi, cum in potestatem venisset Epasnacti Arverni (crebro enim mutandis locis multorum fidei se committebat, quod nusquam diutius sine periculo commoraturus videbatur, cum sibi conscius esset, quam inimicum deberet Caesarem habere), hunc Epasnactus Arvernus, amicissimus populi Romani, sine dubitatione ulla vinctum ad Caesarem deduxit.

Labienus interim in Treveris equestre proelium facit secundum compluribusque Treveris interfectis et Germanis, qui nullis adversus Romanos auxilia denegabant, principes eorum vivos redigit in suam potestatem atque in his Surum Aedmlm, qui et virtutis et generis summam nobilitatem habebat solusque ex Aeduis ad id tempus permanserat in armis.

Ea re cognita Caesar, cum in omnibus partibus Galliae bene res geri videret iudicaretque superioribus aestivis Galliam devictam subactamque esse, Aquitaniam numquam adisset, per Publium Crassum quadam ex parte devicisset, cum duabus legionibus in eam partem Galliae est profectus, ut ibi extremum tempus consumeret aestivorum. Quam rem sicuti cetera celeriter feliciterque confecit. Namque omnes Aquitaniae civitates legatos ad Caesarem miserunt obsidesque ei dederunt. Quibus rebus gestis ipse equitum praesidio Narbonem profecto est, exercitum per legatos in hiberna deduxit: quattuor legiones in Belgio collocavit cum M. Antonio et C. Trebonio et P. Vatinio legatis, duas legiones in Aeduos deduxit, quorum in omni Gallia summam esse auctoritatem sciebat, duas in Turonis ad fines Carnutum posuit, quae omnem illam regionem coniunctam Oceano continerent, duas reliquas in Lemovicum finibus non longe ab Arvernis, ne qua pars Galliae vacua ab exercitu esset. Paucos dies ipse in provincia moratus, cum celeriter omnes conventus percucurrisset, publicas controversias cognosset, bene meritis praemia tribuisset (cognoscendi enim maximam facultatem habebat, quali quisque fuisset animo in totius Galliae defectione, quam sustinuerat fidelitate atque auxiliis

8:47 Having finished these affairs, he returned to his legions among the Belgae and wintered at Nemetocenna: there he got intelligence that Comius, the Atrebatian had had an engagement with his cavalry. For when Antonius had gone into winter quarters, and the state of the Atrebates continued in their allegiance, Comius, who, after that wound which I before mentioned, was always ready to join his countrymen upon every commotion, that they might not want a person to advise and head them in the management of the war, when his state submitted to the Romans, supported himself and his adherents on plunder by means of his cavalry, infested the roads, and intercepted several convoys which were bringing provisions to the Roman quarters.

8:48 Caius Volusenus Quadratus was appointed commander of the horse under Antonius, to winter with him: Antonius sent him in pursuit of the enemy's cavalry; now Volusenus added to that valor which was pre-eminent in him, a great aversion to Comius, on which account he executed the more willingly the orders which he received. Having, therefore, laid ambuscades, he had several encounters with his cavalry and came off successful. At last, when a violent contest ensued, and Volusenus, through eagerness to intercept Comius, had obstinately pursued him with a small party; and Comius had, by the rapidity of his flight, drawn Volusenus to a considerable distance from his troops, he, on a sudden, appealed to the honor of all about him for assistance not to suffer the wound, which he had perfidiously received, to go without vengeance; and, wheeling his horse about, rode unguardedly before the rest up to the commander. All his horse following his example, made a few of our men turn their backs and pursued them. Comius, clapping spurs to his horse, rode up to Volusenus, and, pointing his lance, pierced him in the thigh with great force. When their commander was wounded, our men no longer hesitated to make resistance, and, facing about, beat back the enemy. When this occurred, several of the enemy, repulsed by the great impetuosity of our men, were wounded, and some were trampled to death in striving to escape, and some were made prisoners. Their general escaped this misfortune by the swiftness of his horse. Our commander, being severely wounded, so much so that he appeared to run the risk of losing his life, was carried back to the camp. But Comius, having either gratified his resentment, or, because he had lost the greatest part of his followers, sent embassadors to Antonius, and assured him that he would give hostages as a security that he would go wherever Antonius should prescribe, and would comply with his orders, and only entreated that this

provinciae illius), his confectis rebus ad legiones in Belgium se recipit hibernatque Nemetocennae.

Ibi cognoscit Commium Atrebatem proelio cum equitatu suo contendisse. Nam cum Antonius in hiberna venisset, civitasque Atrebatum in officio esset, Commius, qui post illam vulnerationem, quam supra commemoravi, semper ad omnes motus paratus suis civibus esse consuesset, ne consilia belli quaerentibus auctor armorum duxque deesset, parente Romanis civitate cum suis equitibus latrociniis se suos que alebat infestisque itineribus commeatus complures, qui comportabantur in hiberna Romanorum, intercipiebat.

Erat attributus Antonio praefectus equitum C. Volusenus Quadratus qui cum eo hibernaret. Hunc Antonius ad persequendum equitatum hostium mittit. Volusenus ad eam virtutem, quae singularis erat in eo, magnum odium Commi adiungebat, quo libentius id faceret quod imperabatur. Itaque dispositis insidiis saepius equites eius adgressus secunda proelia faciebat. Novissime, cum vehementius contenderetur, ac Volusenus ipsius intercipiendi Commi cupiditate pertinacius eum cum paucis insecutus esset, ille autem fuga vehementi Volusenum produxisset longius, inimicus homini suorum invocat fidem atque auxilium, ne sua vulnera per fidem imposita paterentur impunita, conversoque equo se a ceteris incautius permittit in praefectum. Faciunt hoc idem omnes eius equites paucosque nostros convertunt atque insequuntur. Commius incensum calcaribus equum coniungit equo Quadrati lanceaque infesta magnis viribus medium femur traicit Voluseni. Praefecto vulnerato non dubitant nostri resistere et conversis equis hostem pellere. Quod ubi accidit, complures hostium magno nostrorum impetu perculsi vulnerantur ac partim in fuga proteruntur, partim intercipiuntur; quod malum dux equi velocitate evitavit: graviter adeo vulneratus praefectus, ut vitae periculum aditurus videretur, refertur in castra. Commius autem sive expiato suo dolore sive magna parte amissa suorum legatos ad Antonium mittit seque et ibi futurum, ubi praescripserit, et ea facturum, quae imperarit, obsidibus firmat; unum illud orat, ut timori suo concedatur, ne in conspectum veniat cuiusquam

concession should be made to his fears, that he should not be obliged to go into the presence of any Roman. As Antonius judged that his request originated in a just apprehension, he indulged him in it and accepted his hostages. Caesar, I know, has made a separate commentary of each year's transactions, which I have not thought it necessary for me to do, because the following year, in which Lucius Paulus and Caius Marcellus were consuls, produced no remarkable occurrences in Gaul. But that no person may be left in ignorance of the place where Caesar and his army were at that time, have thought proper to write a few words in addition to this commentary.

8:49 Caesar, while in winter quarters in the country of the Belgae, made it his only business to keep the states in amity with him, and to give none either hopes of, or pretext for a revolt. For nothing was further from his wishes than to be under the necessity of engaging in another war at his departure; lest, when he was drawing his army out of the country, any war should be left unfinished, which the Gauls would cheerfully undertake, when there was no immediate danger. Therefore, by treating the states with respect, making rich presents to the leading men, imposing no new burdens, and making the terms of their subjection lighter, he easily kept Gaul (already exhausted by so many unsuccessful battles) in obedience.

8:50 When the winter quarters were broken up he himself, contrary to his usual practice, proceeded to Italy, by the longest possible stages, in order to visit the free towns and colonies, that he might recommend to them the petition of Marcus Antonius, his treasurer, for the priesthood. For he exerted his interest both cheerfully in favor of a man strongly attached to him, whom he had sent home before him to attend the election, and zealously to oppose the faction and power of a few men, who, by rejecting Marcus Antonius, wished to undermine Caesar's influence when going out of office. Though Caesar heard on the road, before he reached Italy that he was created augur, yet he thought himself in honor bound to visit the free towns and colonies, to return them thanks for rendering such service to Antonius by their presence in such great numbers [at the election], and at the same time to recommend to them himself, and his honor in his suit for the consulate the ensuing year. For his adversaries arrogantly boasted that Lucius Lentulus and Caius Marcellus had been appointed consuls, who would strip Caesar of all honor and dignity: and that the consulate had been injuriously taken from Sergius Galba, though he had been much superior in votes and interest, because he was united to Caesar, both by friendship, and by serving as lieutenant under him.

Romani. Cuius postulationem Antonius cum iudicaret ab iusto nasci timore, veniam petenti dedit, obsides accepit. Scio Caesarem singulorum annorum singulos commentarios confecisse; quod ego non existimavi mihi esse faciendum, propterea quod insequens annus, L. Paulo C. Marcello consulibus, nullas habet magnopere Galliae res gestas. Ne quis tamen ignoraret, quibus in locis Caesar exercitusque eo tempore fuissent, pauca esse scribenda coniungendaque huic commentario statui.

Caesar in Belgio cum hiemaret, unum illud propositum habebat, continere in amicitia civitates, nulli spem aut causam dare armorum. Nihil enim minus volebat quam sub decessu suo necessitatem sibi aliquam imponi belli gerendi, ne, cum exercitum deducturus esset, bellum aliquod relinqueretur quod omnis Gallia libenter sine praesenti periculo susciperet. Itaque honorifice civitates appellando, principes maximis praemiis adficiendo, nulla onera iniungendo defessam tot adversis proeliis Galliam condicione parendi meliore facile in pace continuit.

Ipse hibernis peractis contra consuetudinem in Italiam quam maximis itineribus est profectus, ut municipia et colonias appellaret, quibus M. Antoni quaestoris sui, commendaverat sacerdoti petitionem. Contendebat enim gratia cum libenter pro homine sibi coniunctissimo, quem paulo ante praemiserat ad petitionem, tum acriter contra factionem et potentiam paucorum, qui M. Antoni repulsa Caesaris decedentis gratiam convellere cupiebant. Hunc etsi augurem prius faetum quam Italiam attingeret in itinere audierat, tamen non minus iustam sibi causam municipia et colonias adeundi existimavit, ut eis gratias ageret, quod frequentiam atque officium suum Antonio praestitissent, simulque se et honorem suum sequentis anni commendaret, propterea quod insolenter adversarii sui gloriarentur L. Lentulum et C. Marcellum consules creatos qui omnem honorem et dignitatem Caesaris spoliarent, ereptum Ser. Galbae consulatum, cum is multo plus gratia suffragiisque valuisset, quod sibi coniunctus et familiaritate et consuetudine legationis esset.

8:51 Caesar, on his arrival, was received by the principal towns and colonies with incredible respect and affection; for this was the first time he came since the war against united Gaul. Nothing was omitted which could be thought of for the ornament of the gates, roads, and every place through which Caesar was to pass. All the people with their children went out to meet him. Sacrifices were offered up in every quarter. The market places and temples were laid out with entertainments, as if anticipating the joy of a most splendid triumph. So great was the magnificence of the richer and zeal of the poorer ranks of the people.

8:52 When Caesar had gone through all the states of Cisalpine Gaul, he returned with the greatest haste to the army at Nemetocenna; and having ordered all his legions to march from winter quarters to the territories of the Treviri, he went thither and reviewed them. He made Titus Labienus governor of Cisalpine Gaul, that he might be the more inclined to support him in his suit for the consulate. He himself made such journeys as he thought would conduce to the health of his men by change of air; and though he was frequently told that Labienus was solicited by his enemies, and was assured that a scheme was in agitation by the contrivance of a few, that the senate should interpose their authority to deprive him of a part of his army; yet he neither gave credit to any story concerning Labienus, nor could be prevailed upon to do any thing in opposition to the authority of the senate; for he thought that his cause would be easily gained by the free voice of the senators. For Caius Curio, one of the tribunes of the people, having undertaken to defend Caesar's cause and dignity, had often proposed to the senate, "that if the dread of Caesar's arms rendered any apprehensive, as Pompey's authority and arms were no less formidable to the forum, both should resign their command, and disband their armies. That then the city would be free, and enjoy its due rights." And he not only proposed this, but of himself called upon the senate to divide on the question. But the consuls and Pompey's friends interposed to prevent it; and regulating matters as they desired, they broke up the meeting.

8:53 This testimony of the unanimous voice of the senate was very great, and consistent with their former conduct; for the preceding year, when Marcellus attacked Caesar's dignity, he proposed to the senate, contrary to the law of Pompey and Crassus, to dispose of Caesar's province, before the expiration of his command, and when the votes were called for, and Marcellus, who endeavored to advance his own dignity, by raising envy against Caesar, wanted a division, the full senate went over to the opposite side. The spirit of Caesar's foes was

Exceptus est Caesaris adventus ab omnibus municipiis et coloniis incredibili honore atque amore. Tum primum enim veniebat ab illo universae Galliae bello. Nihil relinquebatur quod ad ornatum portarum, itinerum, locorum omnium qua Caesar iturus erat excogitari poterat. Cum liberis omnis multitudo obviam procedebat, hostiae omnibus locis immolabantur, tricliniis stratis fora templaque occupabantur, ut vel exspectatissimi triumphi laetitia praecipi posset. Tanta erat magnificentia apud opulentiores, cupiditas apud humiliores.

Cum omnes regiones Galliae togatae Caesar percucurrisset, summa celeritate ad exercitum Nemetocennam rediit legionibusque ex omnibus hibernis ad fines Treverorum evocatis eo profectus est ibique exercitum lustravit. T. Labienum Galliae togatae praefecit, quo maiore commendatione conciliaretur ad consulatus petitionem. Ipse tantum itinerum faciebat, quantum satis esse ad mutationem locorum propter salubritatem existimabat. Ibi quamquam crebro audiebat Labienum ab inimicis suis sollicitari certiorque fiebat id agi paucorum consiliis, ut interposita senatus auctoritate aliqua parte exercitus spoliaretur, tamen neque de Labieno credidit quidquam neque contra senatus auctoritatem ut aliquid faceret potuit adduci. Iudicabat enim liberis sententiis patrum conscriptorum causam suam facile obtineri. Nam C. Curio, tribunus plebis, cum Caesaris causam dignitatemque defendendam suscepisset, saepe erat senatui pollicitus, si quem timor armorum Caesaris laederet, et quoniam Pompei dominatio atque arma non minimum terrorem foro inferrent, discederet uterque ab armis exercitusque dimitteret: fore eo facto liberam et sui iuris civitatem. Neque hoc tantum pollicitus est, sed etiam sc. per discessionem facere coepit; quod ne fieret consules amicique Pompei iusserunt atque ita rem morando discusserunt.

Magnum hoc testimonium senatus erat universi conveniensque superiori facto. Nam Marcellus proximo anno, cum impugnaret Caesaris dignitatem, contra legem Pompei et Crassi rettulerat ante tempus ad senatum de Caesaris provinciis, sententiisque dictis discessionem faciente Marcello, qui sibi omnem dignitatem ex Caesaris invidia quaerebat, senatus frequens in alia omnia transiit. Quibus non frangebantur animi inimicorum Caesaris,

not broken by this, but it taught them, that they ought to strengthen their interest by enlarging their connections, so as to force the senate to comply with whatever they had resolved on.

8:54 After this a decree was passed by the senate, that one legion should be sent by Pompey, and another by Caesar, to the Parthian war. But these two legions were evidently drawn from Caesar alone. For the first legion which Pompey sent to Caesar, he gave Caesar, as if it belonged to himself, though it was levied in Caesar's province. Caesar, however, though no one could doubt the design of his enemies, sent the legion back to Cneius Pompey, and in compliance with the decree of the senate, ordered the fifteenth, belonging to himself, and which was quartered in Cisalpine Gaul, to be delivered up. In its room he sent the thirteenth into Italy, to protect the garrisons from which he had drafted the fifteenth. He disposed his army in winter quarters, placed Caius Trebonius, with four legions among the Belgae, and detached Caius Fabius, with four more, to the Aedui; for he thought that Gaul would be most secure, if the Belgae, a people of the greatest valor, and the Aedui, who possessed the most powerful influence, were kept in awe by his armies.

8:55 He himself set out for Italy; where he was informed on his arrival, that the two legions sent home by him, and which by the senate's decree, should have been sent to the Parthian war, had been delivered over to Pompey, by Caius Marcellus the consul, and were retained in Italy. Although from this transaction it was evident to every one that war was designed against Caesar, yet he resolved to submit to any thing, as long as there were hopes left of deciding the dispute in an equitable manner, rather than to have recourse to arms.

sed admonebantur quo maiores pararent necessitates, quibus cogi posset senatus id probare, quod ipsi constituissent.

Fit deinde senatus consultum, ut ad bellum Parthi cum legio una a Cn. Pompeio, altera a C. Caesare mitteretur; neque obscure duae legiones uni detrahuntur. Nam Cn. Pompeius legionem primam, quam ad Caesarem miserat, confectam ex delectu provinciae Caesaris, eam tamquam ex suo numero dedit. Caesar tamen, cum de voluntate minime dubium esset adversariorum suorum, Pompeio legionem remisit et suo nomine quintam decimam, quam in Gallia citeriore habuerat, ex senatus consulto iubet tradi. In eius locum tertiam decimam legionem in Italiam mittit quae praesidia tueretur, ex quibus praesidiis quinta decima deducebatur. Ipse exercitui distribuit hiberna: C. Trebonium cum legionibus quattuor in Belgio collocat, C. Fabium cum totidem in Aeduos deducit. Sic enim existimabat tutissimam fore Galliam, si Belgae, quorum maxima virtus, Aedui, quorum auctoritas summa esset, exercitibus continerentur. Ipse in Italiam profectus est.

Quo cum venisset, cognoscit per C. Marcellum consulem legiones duas ab se remissas, quae ex senatus consulto deberent ad Parthicum bellum duci, Cn. Pompeio traditas atque in Italia retentas esse. Hoc facto quamquam nulli erat dubium, quidnam contra Caesarem pararetur, tamen Caesar omnia patienda esse statuit, quoad sibi spes aliqua relinqueretur iure potius disceptandi quam belligerandi.

GAUL
CAESAR'S CAMPAIGN IN GAUL
The Campaign Against The Helvetii, 58 B.C.

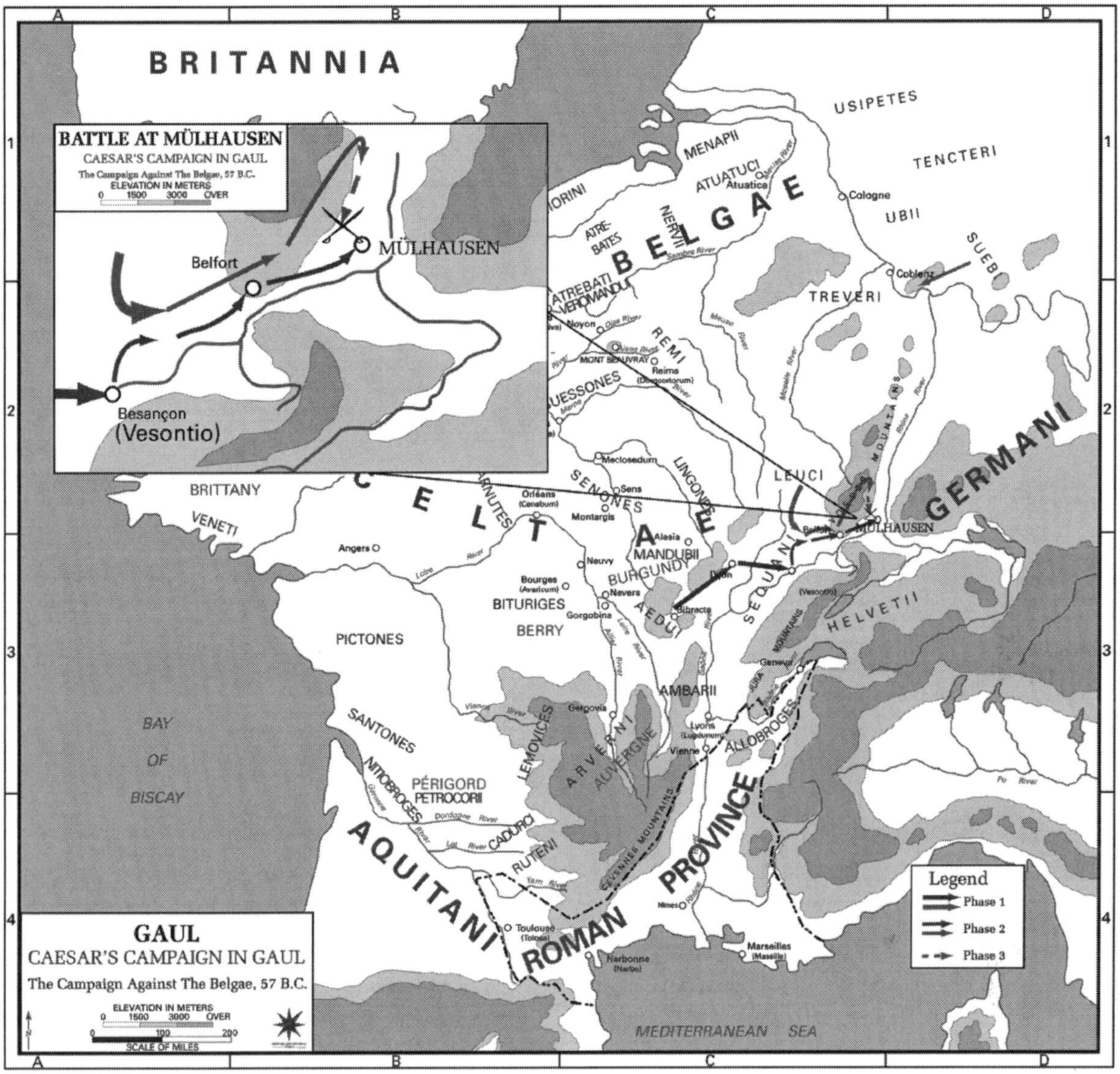
BRITANNIA
BATTLE AT MÜLHAUSEN
CAESAR'S CAMPAIGN IN GAUL
The Campaign Against The Belgae, 57 B.C.
ELEVATION IN METERS
0 1500 3000 OVER
Belfort
MÜLHAUSEN
Besançon
(Vesontio)
USIPETES
MENAPII
TENCTERI
ATUATUCI
Atuatica
MORINI
BELGAE
Cologne
UBII
ATREBATES
NERVII
SUEBI
Coblenz
TREVERI
ATREBATI
VEROMANDUI
Noyon
REMI
MONT BEAUVRAY
Reims
SUESSONES
MOUNTAINS
GERMANI
Metlosedum
LINGONES
LEUCI
BRITTANY
CELTAE
Sens
SENONES
VENETI
Orléans
Montargis
Belfort
MÜLHAUSEN
Angers
Alesia
MANDUBII
Neuvy
BURGUNDY
Bourges
Nevers
Bibracte
AEDUI
SEQUANI
HELVETII
BITURIGES
Gorgobina
BERRY
PICTONES
Geneva
AMBARII
BAY
OF
BISCAY
SANTONES
Gergovia
Lyons
ARVERNI
AUVERGNE
LEMOVICES
Vienne
ALLOBROGES
NITIOBROGES
PÉRIGORD
PETROCORII
CADURCI
RUTENI
CEVENNES MOUNTAINS
AQUITANI
PROVINCE
ROMAN
Nimes
Toulouse
Narbonne
Marseilles
Legend
Phase 1
Phase 2
Phase 3
MEDITERRANEAN SEA
GAUL
CAESAR'S CAMPAIGN IN GAUL
The Campaign Against The Belgae, 57 B.C.
ELEVATION IN METERS
0 1500 3000 OVER
0 100 200
SCALE OF MILES

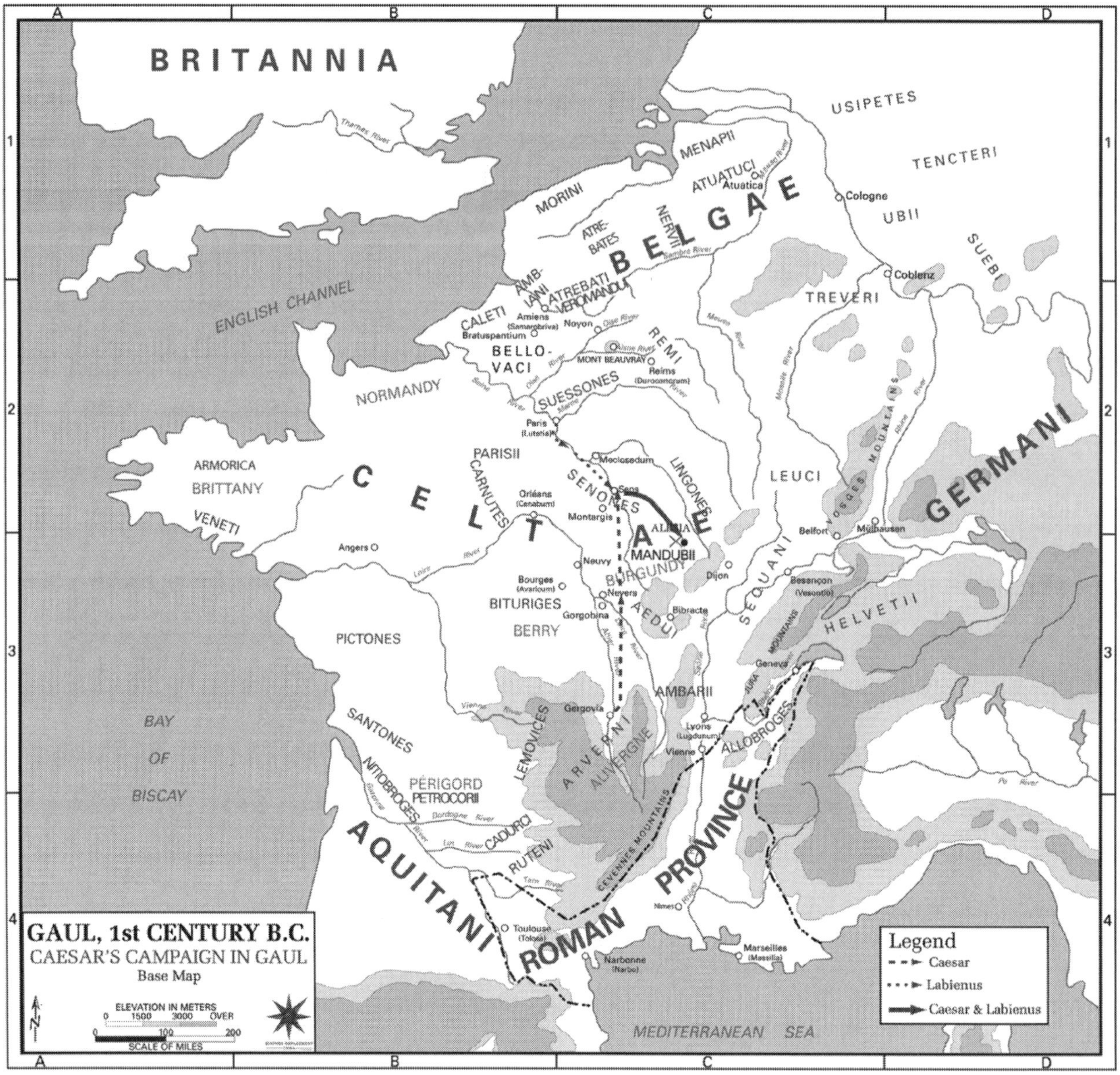
GAUL, 1st CENTURY B.C.
CAESAR'S CAMPAIGN IN GAUL
Base Map
ELEVATION IN METERS
0 1500 3000 OVER
SCALE OF MILES
0 100 200
Legend
Caesar
Labienus
Caesar & Labienus
BRITANNIA
ENGLISH CHANNEL
BAY OF BISCAY
MEDITERRANEAN SEA
BELGAE
CELTAE
AQUITANI
ROMAN PROVINCE
GERMANI
USIPETES
TENCTERI
MENAPII
ATUATUCI
Atuatica
Cologne
UBII
SUEBI
Coblenz
MORINI
ATREBATES
NERVII
AMBIANI
ATREBATI
VEROMANDUI
TREVERI
CALETI
Amiens (Samarobriva)
Bratuspantium
Noyon
REMI
BELLOVACI
MONT BEAUVRAY
Reims (Durocortorum)
NORMANDY
SUESSONES
Paris (Lutetia)
ARMORICA
BRITTANY
VENETI
PARISII
CARNUTES
Orléans (Cenabum)
Montargis
SENONES
Sens
Melodunum
LINGONES
LEUCI
VOSGES MOUNTAINS
ALESIA
MANDUBII
Angers
Neuvy
Bourges (Avaricum)
BITURIGES
BERRY
Nevers
Gorgobina
BURGUNDY
AEDUI
Bibracte
Dijon
SEQUANI
Belfort
Mülhausen
Besançon (Vesontio)
HELVETII
JURA MOUNTAINS
Geneva
PICTONES
SANTONES
AMBARRI
Gergovia
LEMOVICES
ARVERNI
AUVERGNE
Lyons (Lugdunum)
Vienne
ALLOBROGES
NITIOBROGES
PÉRIGORD
PETROCORII
CADURCI
RUTENI
CEVENNES MOUNTAINS
Nimes
Toulouse (Tolosa)
Narbonne (Narbo)
Marseilles (Massilia)
Thames River
Meuse River
Sambre River
Oise River
Aisne River
Marne River
Seine River
Moselle River
Rhine River
Loire River
Vienne River
Dordogne River
Lot River
Tarn River
Allier River
Rhone River
Po River

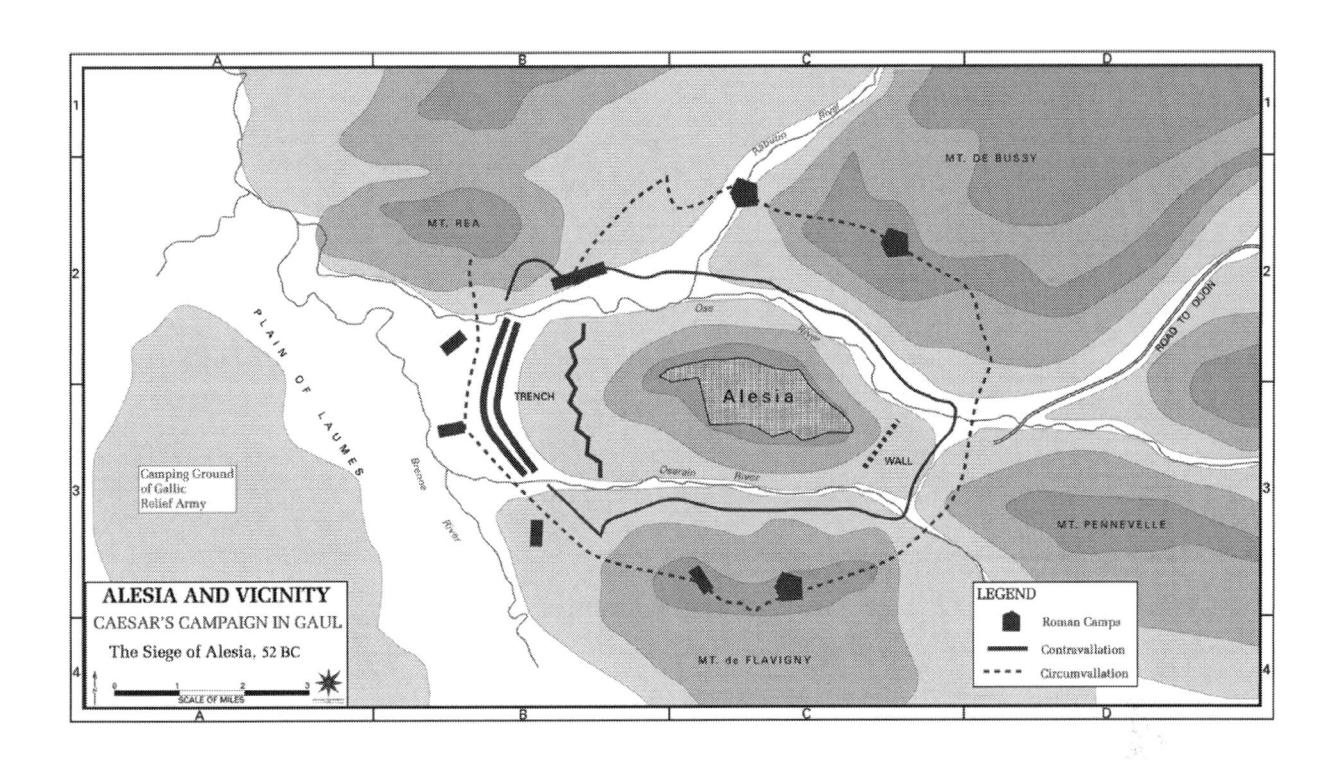

ALESIA AND VICINITY
CAESAR'S CAMPAIGN IN GAUL
The Siege of Alesia, 52 BC

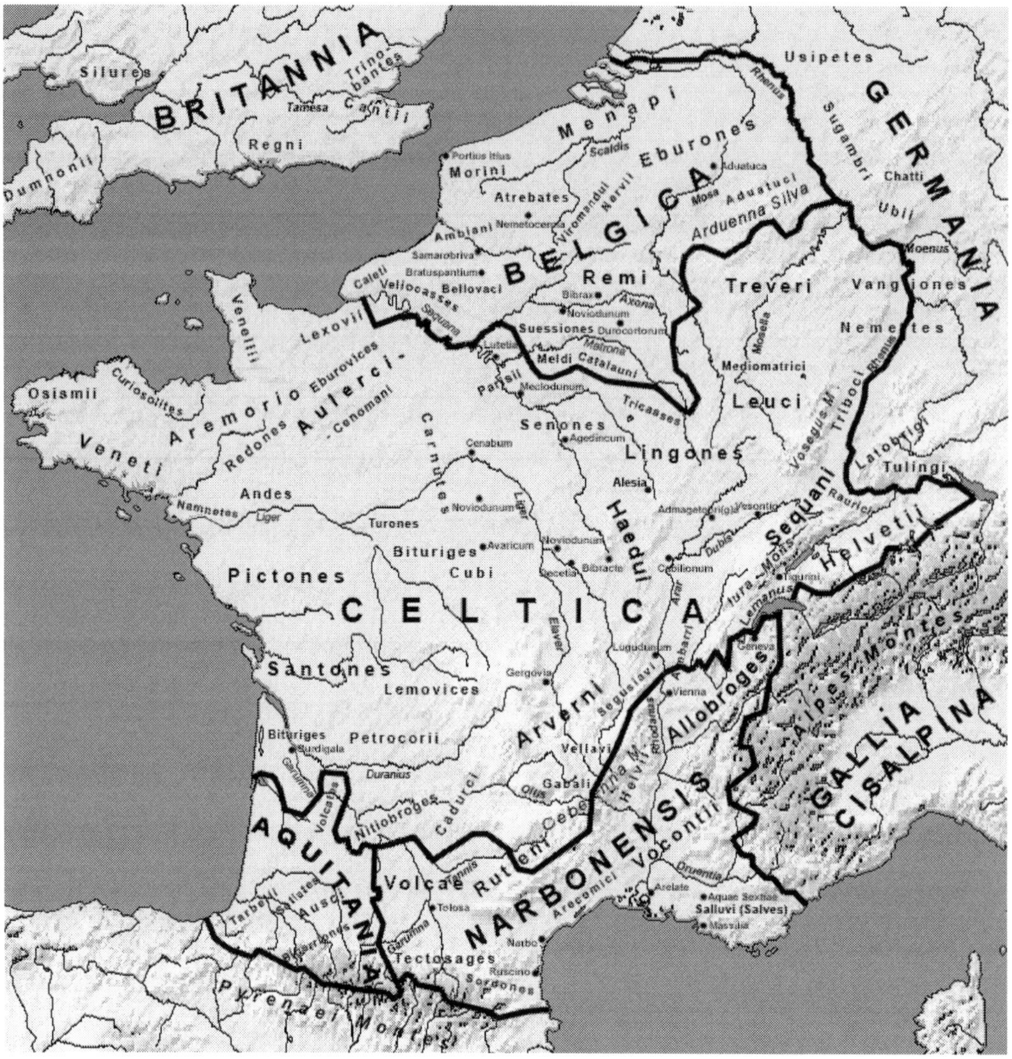
BRITANNIA
Silures
Trinobantes
Tamesa
Cantii
Regni
Dumnonii
Menapi
Morini
Portius Itius
Atrebates
Ambiani
Nemetocenna
Samarobriva
Bratuspantium
Caleti
Veliocasses
Bellovaci
BELGICA
Remi
Eburones
Aduatuca
Aduatuci
Arduenna Silva
Mosa
Nervii
Viromandui
Scaldis
Usipetes
Rhenus
Sugambri
GERMANIA
Chatti
Ubii
Moenus
Treveri
Vangiones
Nemetes
Mediomatrici
Mosella
Leuci
Triboci
Vosegus M.
Latobrigi
Tulingi
Rauraci
Sequani
Helvetii
Vesontio
Lingones
Tricasses
Senones
Agedincum
Alesia
Haedui
Bibracte
Cabillonum
Arar
Lugudunum
Vienna
Allobroges
Geneva
Lemanus
Iura Mons
Dubis
Tigurini
Alpes Montes
GALLIA CISALPINA
Segusiavi
Arverni
Gergovia
Vellavi
Gabali
Helvii
Cebenna M.
Vocontii
NARBONENSIS
Druentia
Arelate
Aquae Sextiae
Salluvi (Salyes)
Massalia
Arecomici
Ruteni
Cadurci
Nitiobroges
Volcae
Tectosages
Tolosa
Garumna
Narbo
Ruscino
Sordones
Pyrenaei Montes
AQUITANIA
Tarbelli
Ausci
Bigerriones
Vocates
Bituriges
Burdigala
Petrocorii
Duranius
Olis
Santones
Lemovices
Pictones
CELTICA
Bituriges
Cubi
Avaricum
Noviodunum
Decetia
Elaver
Turones
Andes
Namnetes
Liger
Carnutes
Cenabum
Redones
Veneti
Osismii
Curiosolites
Aremorici
Aulerci
Eburovices
Cenomani
Lexovii
Venelli
Sequana
Parisii
Lutetia
Meldi
Catalauni
Matrona
Suessiones
Durocortorum
Bibrax
Axona
Metlodunum

www.arepo.biz

Pericla Navarchi Magonis
Mysterium Arcae Boule
Puer Zingiberi Panis et Fabulae Alterae
Fabulae Faciles
Insula Thesauraria
De Expugnatione Terrae Sanctae per Saladinum Libellus
Historia Apollonii Regis Tyrii
Historia Regni Henrici Septimi Regis Angliae
Iter Subterraneum
Liber Kalilae et Dimnae
Rebilii Crusonis Annalium
Gesta Romanorum
Fabulae Divales vel Fairy Tales in Latin

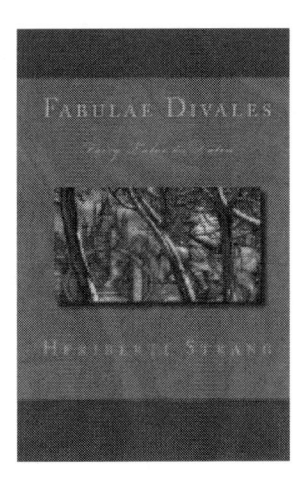

www.arepo.biz

Envocation to Priapus
The Life of Apollonius of Tyana
The Pneumatics of Heron of Alexandria
The Religion of Numa
Chinese Sketches
The Broken Road
The Drum
Romance of Lust
Queen Sheba's Ring
The Summons
Nada the Lily

www.arepo.biz